# Home Networking For Dummies®, 3rd [Edition]

## Networking Jargon at a Glance

Tear out this handy list of frequently used networking terms and stick it to a wall, the dog, or anything else that doesn't move much. If you encounter terms that don't appear in this list (or if you're just looking for something to do until dinner's ready), turn to the Glossary at the back of this book for more networking lingo.

**administrator:** The person in charge of maintaining the network — probably you.

**backup:** A copy of the files on your computer that can be used to restore data in the event that a computer in your network meets with disaster.

**bus:** Frequently used to refer to a slot on the motherboard, a bus is actually the data transmission path from the card in the slot to the processor.

**Cat5 cable (Category 5):** Ethernet network cable. Also called *twisted pair cable*.

**client:** A computer that uses hardware and services on another computer (called the *server*).

**client/server network:** A network model in which one computer (the *server*) provides services for the other computers (the *clients*).

**concentrator:** The home base of an Ethernet network to which all lengths of cable from the network computers are attached. The concentrator can be a hub or a switch.

**dial-up networking:** A feature in Windows that enables your modem to connect to the Internet through an Internet Service Provider.

**driver:** Software that enables the operating system to communicate with the hardware in your computer.

**IP address:** A number that identifies a computer's location on the Internet.

**IRQ (Interrupt Request):** A communication channel assigned to a device so that it can communicate with the PC's processor.

**ISP (Internet service provider):** A company that provides Internet access to individuals and businesses.

**LAN (Local Area Network):** Multiple computers connected by cable.

**Mbps:** Millions of bits per second (mega*bits per second*). A measurement of the speed at which data can be transmitted.

**NetBIOS (Network Basic Input/Output System):** A communication system in networks that enables the various applications running on computers in the network to communicate with other computers on a network.

**network:** Two or more computers connected to each other with network interface cards, cable, and networking software to communicate and exchange data.

**NIC (network interface card):** A hardware device that enables networking by providing the features necessary for cable (or wireless) communication.

**peer-to-peer network:** A network model in which each computer has the same capabilities as the others, and each computer can communicate with all the other computers.

**protocol:** A set of rules (sometimes referred to as a *language*) that computers use to communicate with each other across networks.

**RJ-45:** The connector at the end of Ethernet cable. Looks like the connector at the end of telephone cable.

**router:** A hardware device that lets network computers connect to a single DSL/cable modem.

**server:** A computer that provides services for other computers (called *workstations* or *clients*) on a network. Also called a *host*.

**shared Internet connection:** A system that permits all the computers on a network to be connected to the Internet at the same time.

**shared resources:** Resources such as files, folders, printers, and other peripherals that are attached to one computer and configured for access by users on other network computers.

**TCP/IP (Transmission Control Protocol/Internet Protocol):** The basic suite of communication languages (*protocols*) of the Internet. TCP/IP can also be used as the primary protocol for home networks.

**workstation:** A network computer that uses the resources of one or more servers. Also called a *client*.

# Home Networking For Dummies®, 3rd Edition

Cheat Sheet

## Stuff I Need to Know about My Network Computers

A time may come when one of the computers on your home network goes down and you have to reconnect the network settings. Rebuilding your network settings is a lot easier if you don't have to start from scratch — you shouldn't waste time trying to find the original documentation if you don't have to. You can find the essential information you need to get in, set up the connection, and get out again by double-clicking the Network icon in the Control Panel. Then select each item and click Properties to see that item's settings. Write down the specifications and keep them in a safe place — just in case Murphy's Law comes a-calling.

### Computer 1

Computer name: ______________________

NIC brand: ______________________

Network components installed: ______________________

______________________

### Computer 2

Computer name: ______________________

NIC brand: ______________________

Network components installed: ______________________

______________________

### Computer 3

Computer name: ______________________

NIC brand: ______________________

Network components installed: ______________________

______________________

## Stuff I Need to Know about My Network Printers

Every day, you have a list of important things you need to remember. (You remember that you need to fill the car up with gas, but you can't remember where you left your car keys, where you left the car, and you sure as heck don't remember why there's a list of networking terms pinned to the dog.) Simplify your life — write down the important stuff once (and only once), leave the list in a handy place (don't forget where you put it!), and go on with your life until you really need to know about toner and shared resources.

### Printer 1

Printer manufacturer and model: ______________________

______________________

Ink or toner cartridge part number: ______________________

Attached to Computer #: ______________________

Shared as (share name): ______________________

### Printer 2

Printer manufacturer and model: ______________________

______________________

Ink or toner cartridge part number: ______________________

Attached to Computer #: ______________________

Shared as (share name): ______________________

**by Kathy Ivens**

Wiley Publishing, Inc.

**Home Networking For Dummies®, 3rd Edition**

Published by
**Wiley Publishing, Inc.**
111 River Street
Hoboken, NJ 07030-5774



Published by Wiley Publishing, Inc., Indianapolis, Indiana

Published simultaneously in Canada



For general information on our other products and services, please contact our Customer Care Department within the U.S. at 800-762-2974, outside the U.S. at 317-572-3993, or fax 317-572-4002.

For technical support, please visit `www.wiley.com/techsupport`.

Wiley also publishes its books in a variety of electronic formats. Some content that appears in print may not be available in electronic books.

Library of Congress Control Number: 2005923223

ISBN-13: 978-0-7645-8849-5

ISBN-10: 0-7645-8849-4

Manufactured in the United States of America

10 9 8 7 6 5 4 3 2 1

3B/RR/QU/QV/IN

# About the Author

**Kathy Ivens** has written more than 50 books about computers and has spent many years installing corporate networks. She's a Senior Contributing Editor for *Windows & .NET Magazine* and has several syndicated columns for home computer users. She runs multiple computer networks in her own home.

# Dedication

This book is dedicated to Sarah, Amy, and Leah, with love from Grandma.

# Acknowledgments

A great many very talented people worked hard to make sure this book provided information in a way that makes it easy for you to perform all the technical tasks involved in setting up a home network. Some of them really have to be acknowledged specifically, because they were so much a part of my daily work as I wrote this book.

It's always a great pleasure to work with Acquisitions Editor Melody Layne, who is exceptionally personable, and thoroughly professional. Colleen Totz, the Project Editor, was resourceful and proficient as she moved this book through the complicated processes that change a manuscript into a book. Copy Editor Jean Rogers made sure you don't learn how little I really know about spelling and punctuation, and covered for me when my writing rambled or went in circles. Technical Editor Tom Riegsecker brought the expertise that makes it possible for me to say "the stuff in here is technically correct" with confidence. I owe thanks and kudos to these wonderful folks, and to all the people at Wiley Publishing who contributed their talents to this effort.

## Publisher's Acknowledgments

We're proud of this book; please send us your comments through our online registration form located at www.dummies.com/register/.

Some of the people who helped bring this book to market include the following:

***Acquisitions, Editorial, and Media Development***

**Project Editor:** Colleen Totz

*(Previous Edition: Christine Berman)*

**Acquisitions Editor:** Melody Layne

**Copy Editor:** Jean Rogers

**Technical Editor:** Tom Riegsecker

**Editorial Manager:** Carol Sheehan

**Media Development Supervisor:** Richard Graves

**Editorial Assistant:** Amanda Foxworth

**Cartoons:** Rich Tennant, www.the5thwave.com

***Composition Services***

**Project Coordinator:** Adrienne L. Martinez

**Layout and Graphics:** Carl Byers, Andrea Dahl, Joyce Haughey, Barry Offringa, Lynsey Osborn, Heather Ryan

**Proofreaders:** Leeann Harney, Jessica Kramer, Joe Niesen, Carl William Pierce, Sossity R. Smith

**Indexer:** Ty Koontz

***Special Help***

Mark Enochs

---

**Publishing and Editorial for Technology Dummies**

**Richard Swadley,** Vice President and Executive Group Publisher

**Andy Cummings,** Vice President and Publisher

**Mary Bednarek,** Executive Acquisitions Director

**Mary C. Corder,** Editorial Director

**Publishing for Consumer Dummies**

**Diane Graves Steele,** Vice President and Publisher

**Joyce Pepple,** Acquisitions Director

**Composition Services**

**Gerry Fahey,** Vice President of Production Services

**Debbie Stailey,** Director of Composition Services

# Contents at a Glance

# Table of Contents

# Introduction

If you have more than one computer in your home, you should have a network. I used to consider that statement an opinion, but it's so logical that I now think of it as a fact of nature. Nobody has ever presented a convincing (to me) argument that supports keeping multiple computers isolated from each other.

Using and managing multiple computers is easier if you create a network. You don't have to remember which computer you were using when you started that letter to Uncle Harry because you can just reach across the network to finish it, using any computer in the house. A home network allows you to do the work you have to do better and more efficiently.

One of the best reasons to set up a home network is that when you install it, you become the *network administrator,* the person who controls which files your spouse and children can access, as well as which printers they can use. Talk about power! And the wonderful thing about being a network administrator is that the title makes it sound like you do a lot of hard work (but you don't — you'll be amazed at how easy all of this is).

## About This Book

This book isn't a novel or a mystery, so you don't have to start at page one and read every chapter in order — you can't spoil the ending. This book is meant to be digested on a subject-by-subject, not a chapter-by-chapter, basis. Each chapter is self-contained, covering a specific subject.

However, because the process of creating the network requires that tasks be performed in a certain order, I recommend that you check out the chapters in either Part I or Part II before you go to any of the other chapters.

After you get up to speed on the basics, you can decide which chapters you want to look at next and figure out which network features you want to add to your home network.

# Conventions Used in This Book

Keeping things consistent makes them easier to understand. In this book, those consistent elements are *conventions.* Notice how the word *conventions* is in italics? In this book, I put new terms in italics and then define them so that you know what they mean.

Here are some other conventions I use in this book:

- When you have to type something in a text box, I put it in **bold** type so that it is easy to see.
- When I cite URLs (Web addresses) within a paragraph, they appear in monofont: `www.symantec.com`. Similarly, all text formatted as *code* (commands you have to type) also appears in monofont.

# What You Don't Need to Read

I've learned that some people are really curious about why some computer functions work the way they do. Other people don't care why; they just want to find out *how* to perform those functions.

I put technical explanations that you don't need to read, but may be of interest to the little computer geek in your head, in sidebars or passages of text marked with a Technical Stuff icon. You can safely skip this information if you don't care about those details. (I'll never know.)

# Foolish Assumptions

I am making several assumptions.

- You use PCs that run either Windows 98 Second Edition, Windows Me, Windows 2000 Professional, or Windows XP.
- You want to share computers on a network, whether they're desktop computers or laptops.
- You have more people in the household than computers, so more than one person may use any single computer.

Regarding the differences between the various versions of Windows, I discuss the operating systems separately when a difference exists in the way they work. Otherwise, I just use the term *Windows.*

# How This Book Is Organized

This book is divided into five parts to make it easier to find what you need. Each part has a number of chapters (some have more than others).

## Part I: Network Basics

Part I helps you plan and install your home network. You have some decisions to make and some hardware to buy. You also have to play architect as you design the placement of computers around the house. This part shows you how to put it all together.

- Planning your network and buying the hardware (Chapter 1)
- Installing the network hardware in your computers (Chapter 2)
- Cabling your house to connect the computers (Chapter 3)
- Using wires that already exist in your home: telephone lines and electric lines (Chapter 4)
- Connecting computers without wires (Chapter 5)

The information you find here may seem geeky and complicated, but it really isn't as complex as it sounds. If you perform each step in the right order, building a network is no harder than assembling a complicated toy for your kids. To make things as easy as possible, I take you through each task one step at a time.

## Part II: Configuring Computers for Networking

After you've installed all the network hardware, you have to perform some software tasks, including the following:

- Installing the files that Windows needs for networking (Chapter 6)
- Sharing an Internet connection with everybody on the network (Chapter 7)
- Setting up each computer to share stuff — and keep other stuff private (Chapter 8)
- Setting up users and learning about logins (Chapter 9)

This part tells you how to fine-tune your network — getting the computers to talk to each other and setting up users so everyone can maintain his or her own, personalized computer-configuration options.

## Part III: Communicating Across the Network

This part introduces you to the meat of networking. Here's where you get to put all your setup work into action.

- Setting up network printing (Chapter 10)
- Accessing the other computers on the network (Chapter 11)
- Using files from other computers while you're working in software (Chapter 12)

The fun of networking is actually doing stuff across the network. Time to test it all out. Sit in front of any computer on the network and get stuff from any other computer. Ahhh, the power!

## Part IV: Network Security and Maintenance

If you're going to create a network, any network, whether in the office or at home, that makes you the network administrator. After all the work you do creating this network, you'll want to make sure the network is safe and happy. The chapters in Part IV cover the following:

- Protecting the computers against harm from viruses and Internet intruders (Chapter 13)
- Preparing for disaster by making sure you don't lose your data when a computer dies (Chapter 14)
- Keeping computers healthy with the aid of some nifty tools (Chapter 15)

## Part V: The Part of Tens

In true *For Dummies* style, this book includes a Part of Tens. These chapters introduce lists of ten items about a variety of informative topics. Here you find additional resources, hints, and tips, plus other gold nuggets of knowledge. The Part of Tens is a resource you can turn to again and again.

# Icons Used in This Book

To make your experience with this book easier, I use various icons in the margins of the book to indicate particular points of interest.

This icon points out technical stuff that computer nerds or highly curious people may find interesting. You can accomplish all the important tasks in this book without reading any of the material next to these icons.

This icon means "Read this or suffer the consequences." You find it wherever problems may arise if you don't pay attention.

Pay attention to the text this icon flags if you want to make setting up and using your network easier (and who wouldn't want that?). Think of this cute little target as a gift from one network administrator (me) to another (you).

This icon is a friendly reminder or a marker for something that you want to make sure that you cache in your memory for later use.

# Where to Go from Here

Go ahead — check out the Table of Contents to see which neat networking feature you want to install first. But I do suggest that you check out Parts I and II for some networking basics.

It's quite possible that members of your family have opinions about the order in which you should install networking features — especially the kids, who seem to be born with an advanced knowledge of computing. Have a family meeting and listen to everyone's opinions — make sure the person who has the strongest views about which features should be implemented "volunteers" to help you install and maintain your network. (In my family, when one of my children is urging the family to do something, I listen carefully and then say, "Great idea, honey, you do it, and don't forget to let us know how you're doing.")

Creating a home network is satisfying, fun, and incredibly useful. Have a good time. You're on the cutting edge of computer technology. By reading this book, you prove that you're a networking nerd — and as far as I'm concerned, that's a compliment.

# Part I
# Network Basics

## In this part . . .

Part I of this book covers all the planning and hardware purchases required for building a network. You can't jump into this project willy-nilly; you have to design your network before you actually build it. The stuff you need to know isn't complicated, and the hardware installation is very easy — anyone can do it.

Lots of different types of hardware are available, so you need to decide what hardware to use in your network; Chapter 1 helps you through that process. After you make your hardware decisions, you have to install the hardware, which you find out how to do in the other chapters in this part.

You're starting a great adventure, and when you cross the finish line, you'll be a network expert. You'll even be able to throw technical jargon into your conversations, words like *NIC, Ethernet,* and *switch* (don't worry; before you finish Chapter 1, you'll know what those words mean). Then all of your non-expert friends, who have no idea how easy this stuff is, will be amazed by your geekiness.

# Chapter 1

# Planning the Lay of the LAN

### In This Chapter

- Deciding to create a home network
- Honing in on the right operating system
- Understanding how networks work
- Figuring out what hardware you need
- Purchasing kits or individual components

A *network* is a system of two or more computers that are connected in some manner (you have lots of choices about the "manner"). Each computer on the network has access to the files and peripheral equipment (such as printers or modems) on all the other computers on the network. You create those connections with the following elements:

- Hardware in each computer that permits the computer to communicate.
- A cable or a wireless technology that sends data between the computers (using the hardware you installed).
- Software (called a *driver*) that operates the hardware. (Drivers are covered in Chapter 6.)

Believe it or not, installing the hardware and software you need on each computer is not complicated at all. Start with the first computer, and go through the process one step at a time. After you finish setting up that first computer, you'll see how logical and simple the tasks are.

In fact, anyone who knows how to turn on a computer and use the keyboard and mouse can create a network in an amazingly short amount of time. Many people who installed their own home networks found it so easy and satisfying that they helped neighbors, friends, and relatives. Some have gone on to neighborhood fame and fortune as part-time consultants to other households who want home networks. They never give away the secret that all of this is extremely easy to do.

In this chapter, I explain some reasons for setting up a network in your home, explain your software and hardware alternatives, and tell you more about how different networks *work.* I also discuss some of the technology that's available for your network.

The particulars and the installation steps for all the different types of networking hardware and software are found throughout this book — look for the appropriate chapter titles or check the index to find the particular pages you need.

# Why Would I Want a Home Network?

I believe that anyone who has more than one computer in the house should definitely have a network. That belief has its roots in the fact that I'm generally lazy and miserly, and I believe everyone should do everything in the easiest and cheapest manner. Here's a list of just some of the ways a home network can benefit your whole household:

- **You can work anywhere, even in bed if you want to.** Suppose that you have an important presentation for your boss, and it's due tomorrow morning. But it's Sunday morning, and you're having your second cup of coffee in your bedroom. It would be so cozy and comfy to use your laptop, in bed, to finish the presentation. Then you realize that when you were working on the presentation *yesterday,* you were sitting at the kitchen computer, slaving away at the presentation while eating a turkey sandwich. You don't have to leave your cozy bed and stumble downstairs to find the most recently saved version of the document — you can open the file that's on the kitchen computer right on the laptop in your bedroom.
- **Your kids won't argue as much.** Sally doesn't have to stop using the computer in the den because Bobby needs to retrieve his homework assignment from it. Bobby can go to the computer in the basement and open the file that's on the computer in the den right on the computer in the basement. There's no need to copy the file to a floppy disk; it's as available and handy as it would be on the basement computer.
- **You can put an end to the demands for the computer with the Internet connection.** Because you can set up your network so that everyone in the household can be on the Internet at the same time, those arguments about whose turn it is to surf the Net are a thing of the past.
- **You can buy yourself an expensive piece of jewelry with the money you save on peripherals.** Okay, not quite, but you will save money because you won't have to buy a printer and modem every time you buy a computer because everyone shares those tools across the network. Even better, the sharing is simultaneous, so you can avoid "It's my turn!" arguments.

- **You can become a god (or goddess).** Another benefit of setting up a home network is that when you install it, you become the *network administrator* (that's what the people who installed the network at your office are called). You may even get to invent user names and passwords. You'll be in charge of decisions about whether Mom can see Bobby's files, or Bobby can see Mom's files. All of this knowledge and power make you a computer geek. Because I think that being called a computer geek is a compliment, I offer my congratulations to you.

# Network Operating Systems (Nothing to Do with Surgery)

You don't have to start creating your network with computers that already contain the hardware and software required for networking because you can easily install that stuff yourself (with the help of this book). However, you must have computers that already run on an operating system that can participate in a network environment.

You can use any of the following versions of Windows for your network:

- Windows XP
- Windows 2000
- Windows NT
- Windows Me
- Windows 98SE (Second Edition)
- Windows 98
- Windows 95

In this book, I assume that at least one computer in your home is running Windows 98SE or a later version of Windows. Windows 95 and Windows 98 are really obsolete, and I doubt that many people still have computers running those versions of Windows. As a result, you won't see specific instructions for performing tasks on those versions. However, if you happen to have a computer running Windows 95 or Windows 98, most of the instructions I give for Windows 98SE should work for you.

Check out the Introduction of this book for other assumptions I've so flippantly made about you.

## Which Windows versions have Internet Connection Sharing?

One of the most compelling reasons to set up a home network is to share an Internet connection. Everybody in the household can be on the Internet at the same time (well, everyone who's in front of a computer — few households have as many computers as family members). You have two ways to set up a shared Internet connection: You can use the features built into Windows, or you can use a hardware device called a *router.*

Starting with Windows 98SE, all versions of Windows include the Internet Connection Sharing feature (usually called ICS). ICS is a separate Windows software component that comes with these versions of Windows, and all you have to do is click your mouse a couple of times to install the component.

If you're running Windows 98, you can't tell at a glance whether it's Windows 98 or Windows 98 Second Edition. When you click the Start button, the menu that opens just says Windows 98 (sideways, along the left side of the menu). To see whether your computer is running plain old Windows 98, or Windows 98 Second Edition, right-click the My Computer icon on the desktop and click Properties. In the System Properties dialog box that appears, look in the General tab for the text "Second Edition" under the text "Windows 98."

You can use the built-in functions of the Windows Internet Connection Sharing feature to perform the following tasks:

- **Set up a host computer.** The *host computer* has the modem and the version of Windows that enables you to share an Internet connection with the other computers in your network.
- **Set up all the client computers.** The *client computers* are the other computers that share the host's Internet connection. The client computers don't need to run a version of Windows that has Internet Connection Sharing built in because these computers get the Internet Connection Sharing feature from the host computer, which is running one of the Windows versions that supports ICS. That's why you need only one computer in the house that's running Windows 98 Second Edition or later.

## What can I do if I don't have the right version for Internet Connection Sharing?

If you don't have one computer running a version of Windows that has Internet Connection Sharing built in and you use a telephone modem to get to the Internet, you can still create a shared Internet connection using software that's available from stores and on the Internet.

### DSL and cable modem users don't have to care about Windows versions

If you have a DSL or cable modem, you don't have to worry about software. You can use a hardware device called a *router* to share your high-speed connection with all the computers on your network. In fact, you can use the router to connect an Ethernet network instead of buying a concentrator (a hub or a switch).

Chapter 7 contains all the instructions for setting up Internet Connection Sharing.

## Network Types — Just Like Personality Types

You can configure networks to operate in any of several *modes,* or configuration types. Like personality types, some network configuration types are interested in controlling computer users; other network types are more relaxed about controls. You can choose a mode for your current needs and then easily change your network to another mode if the circumstances warrant. The basic hardware and configuration stuff that goes into creating a network (and that I cover in this book) doesn't change much among the network types, so your choices mostly depend on how you want to communicate among computers.

### Client/server networks for control freaks

Networking schemes that operate in *client/server* mode are common in businesses. These schemes include a main computer (a *server*) that controls users and holds files and peripherals shared by all the other computers (*clients* or *workstations*).

One of the most important reasons to install a client/server network is user authentication, which is a security feature. The server on a client/server network checks to see if a Suzie Q. user is who she says she is and controls whether she can join the network. If she's eligible, the server continues to control her network tasks, determining what she can do. For example, perhaps she can read files but not delete them. The good news is that if you set up the network, you can control *everything.* (Heh, heh, heh.)

All the client computers are connected in a way that gives them physical access to the server. Everyone who works at a client computer can use files and peripherals that are on his or her individual computer (the local computer) or on the server. Look at Figure 1-1 to see the communication between computers in a client/server environment.

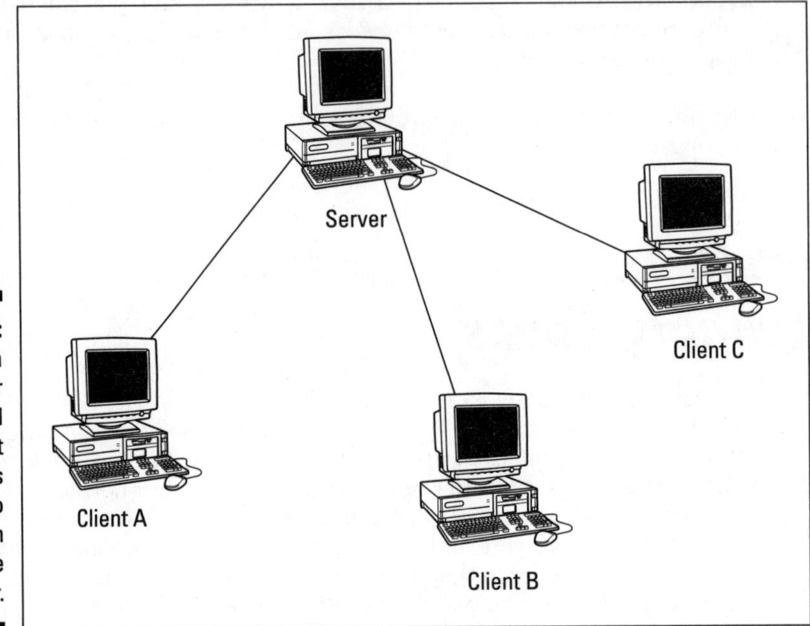


**Figure 1-1:** In a client/server network, all the client computers have to check in with the server.

Even though all the computers are connected to each other, each client usually communicates with the server. However, you can configure the network so that the users on client computers can also access the other client computers on the network.

Large client/server networks (usually found in the workplace) frequently have multiple servers, and each server has a specific job. For example, one server is used for authenticating users, one manages everyone's e-mail, one contains the accounting software, and yet another has the word processing software. The common network operating systems used for servers on client/server networks are Windows NT, Windows 2000, Novell NetWare, and UNIX/Linux. These kinds of networks may be a *little* more than you need — unless you're thinking of running an enormous enterprise-like business out of your home.

## Peer-to-peer networks are more relaxed about controls

*Peer-to-peer networks* permit all the computers on a network to communicate with each other. In Figure 1-2, you can see a typical peer-to-peer network communication structure.

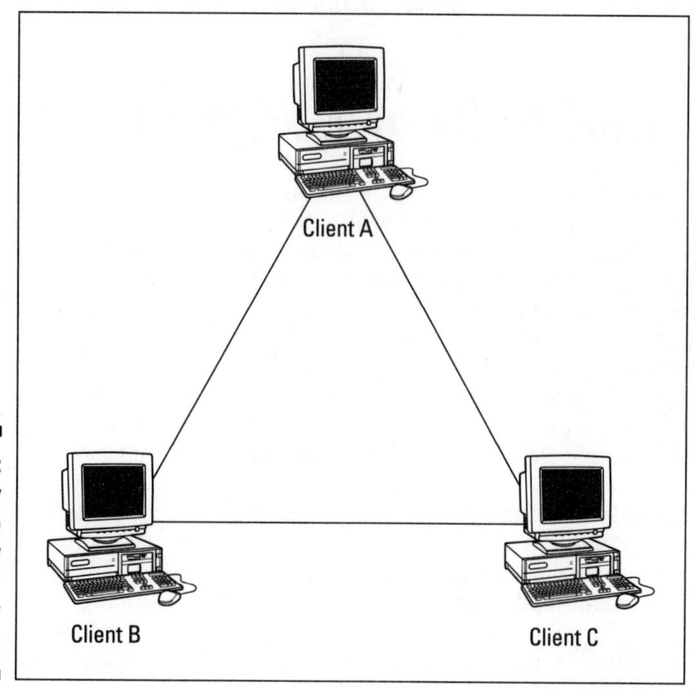


**Figure 1-2:** Everybody talks to everybody in a peer-to-peer network.

If you have computers running Windows (95/98/Me/XP), you can have a peer-to-peer network because the support for this type of network is built into the operating system.

In fact, this book is about creating a peer-to-peer network in your home, so I assume that you have one of those Windows operating systems on every PC in your house.

With a peer-to-peer network, you can impose security on some resources, such as files, but most of the security features don't come close to the security of a client/server network. The exception is the security available in Windows XP, which is modeled on Microsoft's corporate versions of Windows.

### Mixed networks fit all types

Just so that you don't think that the computer world is rigid, I'll point out that some networks are both client/server and peer-to-peer at the same time. Users log on to the network server and then use it to access software and store the documents that they create. Because the peer-to-peer network is built into the operating system, users can also transfer files from other clients and access printers connected to other clients. A mixed network is the best-of-all-worlds scenario for many businesses.

## The Nuts and Bolts of Hardware

To create a network, the primary hardware device that you need is a network adapter, also called a *network interface card* (NIC). A NIC must be installed in each computer on the network. It's actually the NICs (not the computer boxes) that are connected to create a network. NICs are traditionally connected via cable. I say *traditionally* because wireless solutions are also available for small networks, and you may prefer to take that route. Also, even though the term NIC is still commonly used, not all network interface devices are cards anymore. Today, you can connect a network interface adapter device to a Universal Serial Bus (USB). However, because of the widespread use of the jargon NIC, I'll use that term generically.

The only rule for creating a network is that you must install a NIC in each computer. Beyond that, you have enough choices to make your head spin. I'll try to slow the spin rate by explaining the options before I drag you into the actual installation process (which you can find in Chapter 2).

NICs come in lots of flavors, and when you buy NICs, you must match them to two important elements:

- The type of network interface device that your computer accepts.
- The type of network cabling that you want to use. (See the section, "Connections: Cables, wires, and thin air," later in this chapter.)

### Your NIC has to get on the right bus

Forget public transportation — bus means something else in computer jargon. A *bus* is a slot on your computer's motherboard into which you insert cards. Technically, the name of the slot is *expansion slot,* and the bus is the data path along which information flows to the card. However, the common term in computerese is *bus.*

Each card (sometimes called a *controller card*) that you insert into a bus has a specific use. Your computers may have video cards, sound cards, hard drive controller cards, or other assorted cards.

Instead of using cards, some computers have one or more of the previously mentioned devices built right into a chip on the motherboard. These built-in devices are called *embedded cards* or *embedded controllers.*

The NIC you purchase must go into an empty bus, and you must make sure that the NIC is manufactured for the bus type that's available on your motherboard. The common bus types are

- **ISA (Industry Standard Architecture):** ISA is a standard bus that's been used for a number of years. It's a 16-bit card, which means that it sends 16 bits of data at a time between the motherboard and the card (and any device attached to the card).
- **PCI (Peripheral Component Interconnect):** The PCI bus is built for speed. Most new computers contain a PCI bus, which comes in two configurations: 32-bit and 64-bit. Its technology is far more advanced (and complicated) than the technology of the ISA bus.

You can read the documentation that comes with your computer to find out what kind of cards you must buy. However, if you have mixed bus types on the motherboard (most of today's computers contain both PCI and ISA slots), the documentation doesn't tell you which slots are already occupied. You have to open your computer to find out what type of NIC you need to buy.

You can tell at a glance what type of bus is available if you know what to look for. An ISA bus is usually black, with metal pins or teeth in the center and a small crossbar about two-thirds of the way down the slot. Check out an ISA bus in Figure 1-3.

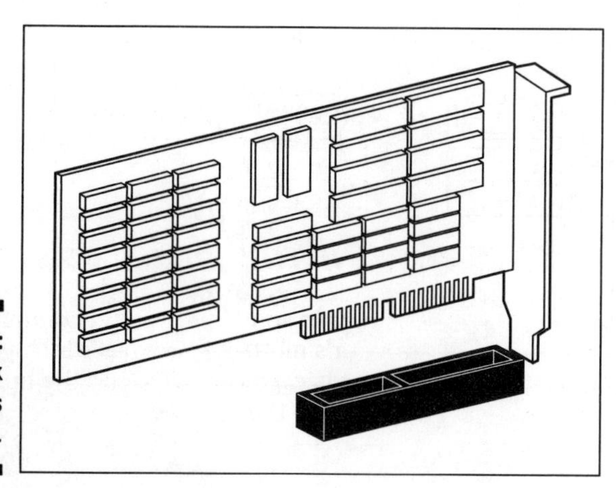

**Figure 1-3:** If it's black and long, it's an ISA bus.

A PCI bus is usually white, and it's shorter than an ISA bus, as shown in Figure 1-4. A PCI bus has a crossbar about three-quarters of the way along its length.

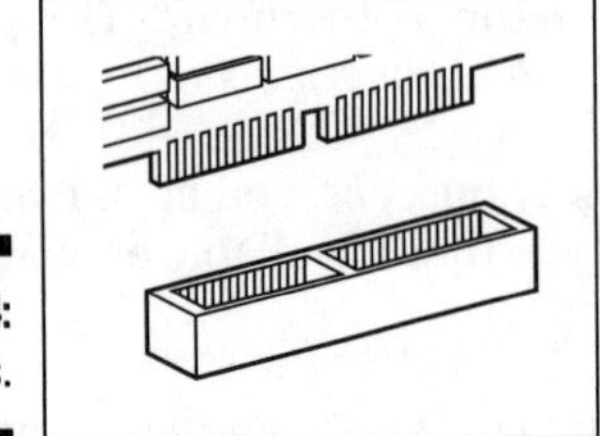

**Figure 1-4:** A PCI bus.

## Some NICs don't take the bus

Although motherboard NICs are the most common type of network connections, you have several other options available.

### USB connectors

Most of today's computers come with a USB port (in fact, most come with two or more), and you can buy NICs that plug into a USB port. The best part of a USB connection is that you don't even have to open your computer because USB ports are external. Look for port connectors that look like those shown in Figure 1-5.

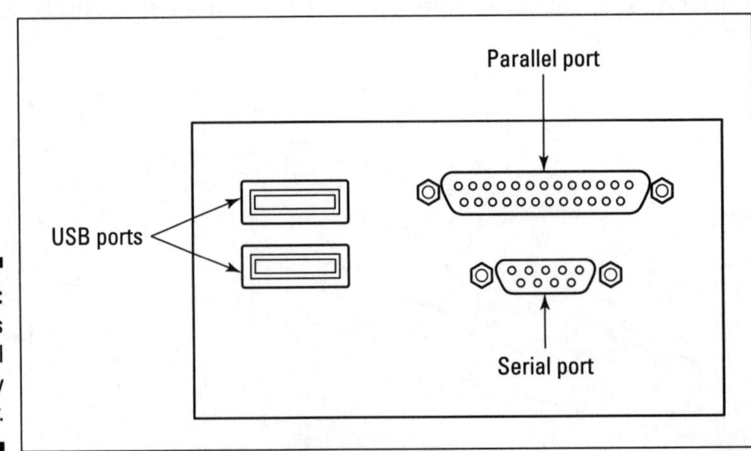


**Figure 1-5:** USB ports are identical in every computer.

USB connectors are available for all types of network cabling and wireless connections.

### PC cards for laptops

Most laptops have one or two USB ports, but you can also insert a NIC in the laptop's PC card slot (also called a PCMCIA slot). In fact, you can purchase a PC card that functions as both a NIC and a modem.

## Connections: Cables, wires, and thin air

You have one more decision to make before you go shopping for your hardware — you have to choose a cabling system. Your decision affects not only the type of cable you buy, but also the type of NICs you buy. The NIC has a device that accepts the cable connector, so the NIC must be built specifically for the cable you choose.

You have several choices for cabling your computers into a network:

- Ethernet cable
- Telephone wires already in your house
- Electrical wires already in your house
- None (wireless connections)
- Mixed (using more than one type)

During the following discussions, I'm going to be mentioning the speed with which cable types transfer data among computers. Network speeds are rated in megabits per second (Mbps). A *megabit* is a million binary pulses, and the best way to put that into perspective is to think about a modem. The fastest telephone modems are rated to transmit data at the rate of 56,000 bits per second (56 kilobits per second, or 56 Kbps).

Don't pooh-pooh the notion of speed; it is important. Everyone who uses computers changes his or her definition of the word *fast.* If you started using computers years ago, think about how fast the computer seemed at first, and then how impatient you became whenever you had to wait for a task to complete. Soon after, you bought a faster computer. Then you got over the feeling that this was the fastest machine you'd ever seen, and impatience set in again. Waiting a long time for a file to open in a software application, or for a file to be copied from one machine to another, can drive you nuts.

### Ethernet cable

Ethernet cable is the connection type of choice. It's fast, accurate, pretty much trouble-free, and simply the best. Ethernet can transfer data across the network at up to 1000 Mbps, depending on the rated speed of the NICs and the hub or switch. Some older NICs and hubs can send data at only 10 Mbps, but today's Ethernet equipment can determine the speed of individual devices on the network and automatically drop or raise the speed to match the device's capabilities.

Ethernet is the cable that you find in business networks. Today, Ethernet cable is purchased in the form of *twisted-pair cable* or *Category 5 UTP cable* (nicknamed *CAT-5*). Although Ethernet cable looks like telephone wire, it's not the same thing. Ethernet cable is designed to transmit data rather than voice. Using Ethernet cable requires the purchase of a *concentrator,* which is sometimes called a *hub.* All the network computers are connected to the concentrator, which distributes the data among the connected computers, as shown in Figure 1-6.

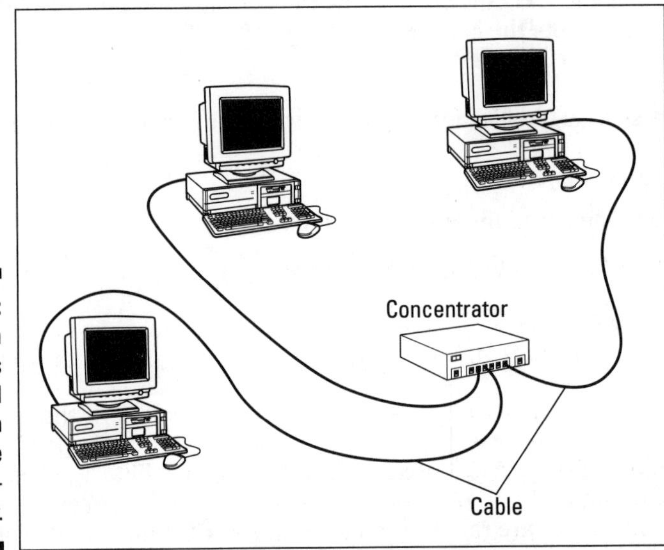


**Figure 1-6:** Each computer is connected to its own port in the concentrator.

The connector at the end of the cable looks like the connector at the end of your telephone cable, but it's actually slightly fatter. The 10Base-T cable connectors are *RJ-45 connectors* (telephone connectors are *RJ-11 connectors*).

### Telephone line cable

Telephone line cable is another option you can choose for wiring your home network. It transmits data at the rate of about 10 Mbps, which isn't nearly as fast as the speed of Ethernet cable. Telephone line networking is increasing in popularity, especially because most of the computer and device manufacturers have developed and accepted standards. Having standardized technology makes it easier to buy equipment; you know it all works together. You can find out more about the technology at `www.homepna.org`.

To use telephone cable for home networks, you just connect a regular telephone cable between the telephone-cable NIC you install in your computer and the telephone wall jack. Telephone cable is inexpensive and available everywhere, including your local supermarket. The networking processes use a part of your telephone line that voice communication doesn't use, so your telephone lines are still available for normal household telephone use (and for modem use).

You can use your wall jack for both a telephone and a network connection at the same time. You just have to adapt the wall jack so that it can do two things at once. Luckily, this is easy to do. You need to buy a *splitter* (the techy term is *modular duplex jack*), which is a little doohickey that you can purchase for a couple of bucks just about anywhere — at an office supply store, one of those megastores, or even the supermarket. The splitter, as shown in Figure 1-7, plugs into the wall jack to give you two places to plug in phone cables instead of just one. You plug the network cable into one connector and your telephone cable into the other connector. It doesn't matter which cable goes into which socket.

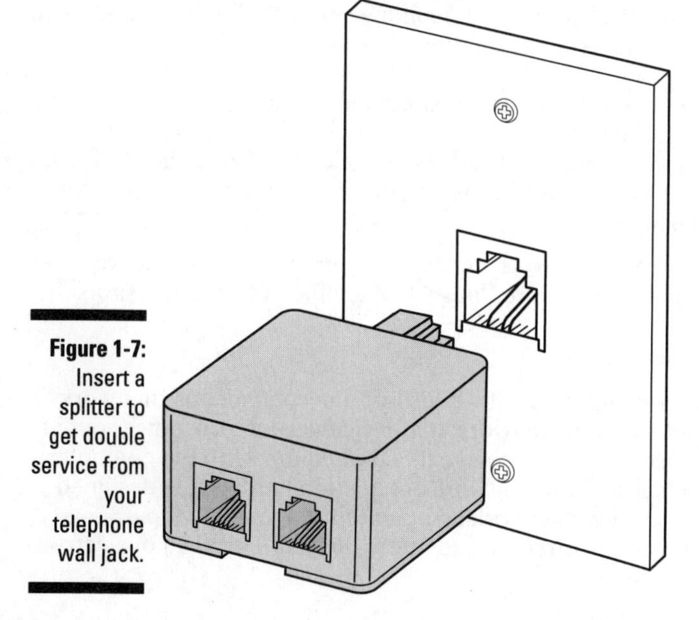

**Figure 1-7:** Insert a splitter to get double service from your telephone wall jack.

However, to avoid confusion, put some nail polish, a little sticky star, or some other add-on near the connector of your network connection cable so that you know which is which if you want to move the telephone.

For shared Internet access, only one computer needs to have a modem. If that computer has an external modem, follow these steps:

1. **Plug the modem, not the telephone, into the second side of the splitter.**
2. **Plug the telephone into the appropriate connector on the modem.**

   Now you have three devices on your telephone jack: a network connection, a modem, and a telephone.

If the computer that's hosting the shared Internet access has an internal modem, you need a *Y-connector,* which is an adapter that looks like the capital letter *Y*. The bottom of the connector, where the two sides of the Y meet, plugs into the wall jack (to join the network). The two ends of the Y plug into the modem and the NIC (it doesn't matter which connector goes into which device).

If you have multiple telephone lines in your house, all the computers on your network must be connected through the same telephone line (telephone number). Computers can't communicate across different telephone lines. (Your regular telephone service can't do this either. For example, if someone is talking on line 1, you can't pick up a telephone connected to line 2 and eavesdrop, er, I mean, join the conversation.)

Here are a couple of drawbacks to using telephone wiring:

- Every computer must be near a telephone jack. Very few households have a telephone jack in every room, so this may limit your choices for computer placement.
- The maximum distance between any two computers is about 1,000 feet, but unless you live in the White House, that shouldn't be a major problem.

### Electrical wires

You can network your computers with electrical line connections that work by plugging the manufacturer's network adapter device into the power outlet on the wall. The device has an attached cable that connects to the computer. Today, most of the electrical-wire network-connection hardware is designed for a USB port. Electrical-wire networking operates at about 10 Mbps. Some network equipment manufacturers use the term *powerline* instead of electrical wire.

I'm not kidding when I say *wall outlet device.* Plugging the network adapter into a power strip doesn't work.

- **Um, where do you plug it in?** If your house is like most houses, only one wall outlet is near the computer, and you're already using both plugs: one for the computer and one for the monitor. Most manufacturers of electrical line networking hardware supply a special power strip into which you can plug your computer and monitor. You can plug that power strip into the plug that the network device isn't using.
- **How friendly do you want to be with your neighbor?** I could get into all the gory details about hubs and transformers and radio waves, but I'll cut to the bottom line: If your neighbor has a home network that's connected through electrical wires, your neighbor may be able to access your network because you probably share the same transformer. That's either terribly convenient or terribly scary, depending on your relationship with your neighbor. But, to resolve this problem, the network equipment manufacturers provide software to help guard your system against unauthorized users. That software requires a separate installation and configuration process, which must be repeated whenever you add a computer to your network. Be sure to use it!

## Wireless connections for the cable-phobic

Generally, people choose wireless connections because they're willing to give up the speed and reliability of Ethernet (or phoneline or powerline) to avoid dealing with cable. This attitude comes from one of two motivations (or, in some cases, both of two motivations): They don't want to go through the effort of pulling cable through the house, or they hate the sight of the cable because it doesn't match their decorating scheme. When installing home networks, it's been my experience that the man of the house would love the "fun" of pulling cable through the house, and the woman of the house says "ugh, ugly."

If you're interested in wireless networking, the best advice I can give you is to make sure all your computers are running Windows XP. No other version of Windows support wireless networks as well as Windows XP, especially with Service Pack 2 installed.

If you opt for wireless technology, you'll be working with radio frequency (RF) communication technology. Some manufacturers offer infrared (IR) network communication technology devices, but I don't recommend them. In fact, except for the next section that explains why I don't recommend them, I won't mention IR again in this book.

### Infrared wireless connections

Infrared (IR) technology works by creating a direct signal, via a light beam, between computers. Your TV remote control device (the frequently used technical jargon for that device is *clicker*) uses IR technology; you have a little red square on the remote control device and a red square on the television set or cable box. You point one little red square at the other square to use the device. This means you can't select a channel using the remote control device if you're holding it while you're in the kitchen and the television set is in the living room.

Computer IR networking works the same way. The infrared connectors must "see" each other, which limits IR networks to those that have all the computers in the same room. Also, one computer can't make a straight-line connection with two other computers at the same time, so if your network has more than two computers, you have to buy additional IR hardware devices that collect and bounce the IR signals around the room.

One problem I've encountered during my tests of IR connections is that bright sunlight interferes with the signal. You need opaque window coverings if you want to go with IR connections, unless you only plan to use your computers at night. On top of all of those inconveniences, IR connections are slow.

'Nuff said.

### *Radio frequency wireless connections*

Radio frequency (RF) technology isn't new; it's been around for a long time. I used it when I was a child (many eons ago) for walkie-talkie conversations with friends in the neighborhood. You probably use it today to open and close your garage door or to connect windows on upper floors to your household security system. I used to use it to unlock my car door, but I learned to hate the beeps, and I set off my car alarm system so often that I had the whole system disabled. (Even if your car doesn't beep and blink its lights at you in a parking lot as you push your little RF device to unlock it, I'm sure you're familiar with the technology.)

Here are some things to consider about RF network connections:

- They require a network adapter that's specific to RF technology, which means the adapter has to be equipped with the devices necessary to transmit and receive RF signals. Today, all network device manufacturers are making RF devices, and the NICs are available for motherboards (both PCI and ISA bus types), USB ports, and PC cards for laptops.
- The RF signals can usually travel about 150 feet, passing through walls, ceilings, and floors. This distance should be sufficient for most home network schemes, but the actual distance that you can achieve may vary from manufacturer to manufacturer. If you need greater distance, you can often extend the signal by placing a special box called an Access Point in a central location.

- The only things that can stop the RF signal dead in its tracks are metal and large bodies of water. Although you may think that only means you can't use RF technology in your castle with an iron drawbridge and moat, think again. Putting the computer (with its RF technology device attached) under a metal desk can interfere with transmission. A wall that has a lot of metal plumbing pipes can also keep computers from communicating. The only problem with large bodies of water I can think of are those that crop up if you've installed a pond or swimming pool in your den, or if you're trying to communicate between two submarines or from an underwater office in a Sea World type of amusement park.

  When I was testing RF technology, several manufacturers assured me that the 150-foot limit applies only indoors and that most RF devices can achieve far greater distances with no walls or floors in their way. Uh huh, thanks. I'll appreciate that in the summer when I move all my computers onto my lawn, or take them to a park.

- You may experience interference from cell phones, pagers, home alarm systems, microwave ovens, and other wireless devices frequently found in your neighborhood. If those RF devices are properly shielded, however, you shouldn't have any problems. The newer RF devices, based on newer RF technical standards, eliminate a lot of the annoyances of interference.

- Technically, anyone with a computer equipped with RF technology can "join" your network without your knowledge. A neighbor or stranger could come within 150 feet of your house with a laptop, find the right frequency, and copy any files he finds. For security, some manufacturers of RF networking kits have built in a clever design feature that slows malevolent outsiders who are trying to grab your frequency and get into your system — the frequency changes periodically.

  The RF signal that's sent and received across the network moves up and down within a given range (the technology is called *frequency hopping*), and this happens often enough to make it difficult to latch on to the current frequency — as soon as someone gets a bead on it, it moves. By the way, the idea of frequency hopping for security comes from an invention, and a patent, that is credited to a movie star named Hedy Lamarr. (Is anyone besides me old enough to remember her?)

Frequency hopping also acts as a performance enhancer. The speed is improved because you're effectively transmitting across a wider spectrum.

# Saving Time, Trouble, and Money When You Buy Hardware

A slew of manufacturers make the equipment that you need to build your network, and you should make your purchasing decisions with an eye on both reliability and price.

I'm going to mention some places to go for general research as you do your homework and also some places to buy equipment that I think provide good prices and service. None of these outlets know that I'm telling you about this, so they aren't paying me any commission or giving me special treatment in exchange for telling you about them. I'm just one of those people who can't resist giving specific advice (which, as all parents know, doesn't work well with children, but I don't expect readers to respond with "Oh, Motherrrrr," and leave the room). You may discover resources that I don't mention here, and my omission isn't significant. It just means that I didn't know about (or knew about but didn't remember) that resource.

## Doing your homework: Just like being in school

Making decisions about hardware, cable types, and other networking gizmos without first doing some homework is foolish. You're going to live with your decisions for a long time. In fact, everybody in the household will have to live with your decisions, so to avoid listening to gripes later, get everyone to help in the decision-making process. Home networking is a hot topic, and computer experts have been testing technologies and reporting their findings. Use their expertise to gain knowledge, and then discuss your findings with the rest of the family. You can find reviews of the pros and cons of networking schemes in the following places:

- **Start with any friends, relatives, or neighbors who are computer geeks.** All computer geeks are used to this treatment; people ask us for free advice at dinner parties, while we're in line at the movie theater, and almost anywhere else. Do what most people do — call the geek and pretend it's a social call. Then, after you ask, "How are you?" and before the geek has a chance to answer that question, ask your technical questions. (This is how most people interact with their computer-savvy friends.)
- **Paw through newsstands, especially those in bookstores.** You can find an enormous array of computer magazines on the shelves. Look for magazines that fit your situation. For example, a computer magazine named *Programming Tricks for C++* is probably less suitable than *Home PC Magazine*. Look for *PC World, PC Magazine, FamilyPC,* and other similar publications. If the current issue doesn't have an article on home networking, check the masthead (the page where all the editors are listed) to see where you can call or write to ask for specific issues.
- **Search the Internet for articles and advice.** Type **home networking** into any search box, and you'll probably find that the number of results is overwhelming. If that approach seems onerous, try some of these popular sites that surely have the information you're seeking: `www.pcworld.com`, `www.zdnet.com`, or `www.cnet.com`. These sites all have search features, so you can find information easily. They also have reviews, technical advice, and "best buy" lists.

## Plunking down the money: Tips for buying

After you make your decision about the type of hardware and cabling you want to use for your home network, you need to buy the stuff. You can buy kits or individual components, and many people buy both. Your cost should be less than $60 per computer to create your network.

Most manufacturers offer kits, which is a way to buy everything you need at once. Here are some things to keep in mind before you buy a kit:

- **Most kits are designed for a two-computer network.** If you have a third computer, just buy the additional components individually. Some manufacturers make four-computer and five-computer kits.
- **Kits work only if every computer on your network needs the same hardware.** For example, if you've decided to install an Ethernet network, the kit has two NICs, two pieces of Ethernet cable, and one concentrator. However, both NICs are going to be the same bus type. If one of your computers has only an empty ISA bus, and the other computer has an empty PCI bus, you can't buy a kit.
- **Kits aren't necessary if one of your computers has a built-in network adapter.** Many computer manufacturers sell computers that are already set up with network hardware (usually with an Ethernet NIC).

In Table 1-1, I list some reliable manufacturers of products for networking.

**Table 1-1 Network Connection Manufacturers**

| *Manufacturer* | *Web Site* |
|---|---|
| 3Com | www.3com.com |
| Belkin | www.belkin.com |
| D-Link | www.dlink.com |
| Intel | www.intel.com |
| Intellon | www.intellon.com |
| Linksys | www.linksys.com |
| Netgear | www.netgear.com |

Even if you buy a kit, you may also have to buy individual components. Perhaps you have three computers, or maybe one of the Ethernet cables in the kit isn't long enough to reach the computer on the second floor. After you measure the distances, figure out where the available ports are, and do all the rest of your research, you may find that buying individual components is the only approach you can take. A plan that doesn't match a kit isn't uncommon, and kits are really a convenience, not a money-saver. Most people find that buying individual components costs about the same as buying kits.

Every retail computer store sells hardware components for all types of network connections, and your city or town probably has many small independent computer stores, in addition to major chains such as CompUSA. Most appliance retailers also carry computer networking equipment (Circuit City, Best Buy, and others). The office-supply stores also carry these products (Staples, Office Max, and others). Even some of the warehouse outlets carry networking equipment. On the Internet, visit `www.cdw.com` and `www.buy.com`.

Be sure you know an online merchant's return policy before you purchase. And, be sure that the Web site is secure before you give out your credit card number. When you're on a secure Web site, the address bar displays `https://` instead of `http://` (the *s* is for secure). Furthermore, at the bottom of your browser window, you should see an icon that looks like a closed lock.

## Chapter 2

# Installing Network Adapters

### In This Chapter

- Putting NICs on the bus
- Hooking up external network adapters
- Installing adapters to laptops

After you decide what type of connection to use (I'm rooting for Ethernet; I don't see any reason to compromise on speed and performance), you need to install the hardware that enables the network connection. This task must be performed on every computer on the network.

Depending on the connection types available on your computers, or the type of kit or components you decided to buy, you may have to open the computer to install the network interface card (NIC). If the NIC is for a Universal Serial Bus (USB) port, you'll be able to install the hardware without taking your computer apart.

In this chapter, I discuss the installation of these technical doodads. But don't worry, I don't leave you high and dry. If you don't know your computer's chassis from the chassis of a 1967 T-bird (my all-time favorite car, and I'm old enough to remember riding in one), I walk you through the steps.

If your computer came with a network adapter, you don't have to install one as long as you're using the connection type that adapter is built for. For example, if your computer has an Ethernet adapter, but you want to have a wireless network, you have to bypass (ignore) the built-in adapter and install a wireless adapter.

## It's Okay to Mix and Match NICs

Every computer on your network doesn't have to have the same type of NIC connection. Although you must use an Ethernet NIC for all the computers that are being connected with Ethernet cable, you can use a USB NIC on one computer and an internal NIC in another computer. To understand this, you have to understand the difference between network connection type and network device connection types:

- The *network connection type* is the network wiring type, as in Ethernet, phone line, wireless, and so on.
- The *network device connection type* is the way the NIC connects to the computer. Your choices are internal (bus), USB, and PC card (for laptops).

# Before You Start

If you have to open a computer to install an internal NIC, you need to make sure you have the right equipment to do the job. Lucky for you, the necessities are pretty low-tech. You need

- A work table (the kitchen table will do fine).
- A medium-size Phillips screwdriver.
- A small-size Phillips screwdriver.
- Sticky tape (duct tape, cellophane tape, Band-Aids, whatever — this is for pasting labels on ports and cables).
- A very long pair of tweezers (if you have one). If not, don't worry; I just like to use them for fishing out screws that I drop into the chassis — something I invariably do.
- A felt-tip pen.
- Small self-stick labels or small pieces of paper.

You're almost ready to install the necessary hardware for your home network, but before you open your computer, make sure that you follow these safety tips:

- **Don't use a magnetic screwdriver.** Magnets and disk drives do not peacefully coexist — magnetic attraction can delete data.
- **Discharge any static electricity in your body before you touch anything inside the computer.** You can get rid of static electricity by touching a metal object.
- **Make sure that the computer is turned off and unplugged.** Either pull the plug from the wall or pull the plug from the back of the computer.
- **Remove any metal jewelry, especially rings.** Gold in particular conducts electricity, including static electricity.

# Putting a NIC on the Bus

If you opt to use a standard network interface card (NIC), you must open your computer to install it. This type of adapter is the hardware that enables PCs in your home network to recognize each other. Putting the NIC in a bus (a special motherboard slot) requires several separate steps, but they're all easy. Work on one computer at a time instead of putting all the computers on your worktable. That way, you won't mix up parts, and you'll have plenty of workspace. (For more on NICs and buses, peruse Chapter 1.)

## Disassembling your computer: Open sesame

Because the NIC needs to be installed internally, you have to do a bit of disassembly work on the computers in your network. To properly disassemble a computer, follow these steps:

1. **Unplug the computer.**

   You'll find the process much easier if you yank (ahem, I mean *gently pull*) the plug from the back of the computer instead of pulling out the plug from the wall outlet.

2. **Disconnect the cables that are attached to the ports at the back of the computer.**

   Disconnect your keyboard, mouse, modem, printer, camera, and any other peripheral devices that are connected to your computer with cables.

3. **As you disconnect each cable, write the name of its peripheral device on a small piece of paper and stick the paper on the end of the cable.**

   Use the felt-tip pen to mark the ports — for example, write *M* for mouse and *K* for keyboard — because you may have a hard time telling the ports apart. Do the same for the serial port (write *modem* or *camera*) and the parallel port (label it *printer*).

4. **Move the computer chassis to a worktable.**

   *Chassis* is just a fancy name for the box that holds all of your PC's gooey innards. You can use this opportunity to vacuum or sweep the area where your computer sat. I'm guessing it's probably very dusty. Don't feel guilty; computers attract dust.

   In addition, invest in either a can of compressed air or a computer vacuum so that you can clean out the ports from which you just disconnected cables.

5. **Remove the exterior case of the chassis.**

   Use the medium-size Phillips screwdriver to remove the screws that attach the exterior case to the computer chassis. If your computer uses some sort of snap-up or pop-up closing device instead of screws, removing the case is even easier.

## Removing the backplate

You have to get the bus ready to accept your NIC, which means removing the metal backplate at the end of the bus slot (at the back of the computer). Check out what one looks like in Figure 2-1. The backplate is attached to the edge of the computer with a small machine screw — use your small Phillips screwdriver to remove it. You can throw away the metal plate, unless you think that you may want to remove the NIC and close that slot again. Some computers have a solid metal slug, which you need to push out and throw away. Remove with care, because the edges are sharp.

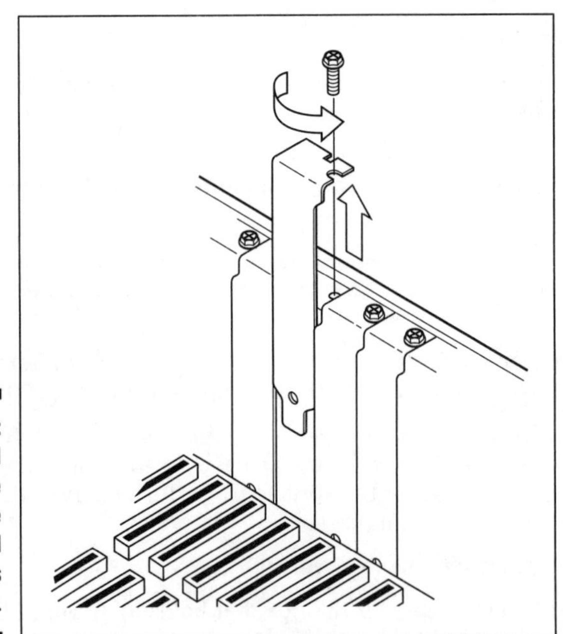

**Figure 2-1:** You need to remove the piece of metal that covers the slot.

A *machine screw* has a relatively flat tip, unlike a wood screw, which is pointy so that it can be easily drilled into the wood.

Remove the screw and place it on a piece of sticky tape. Placing the screw on the tape prevents it from rolling off the table and onto the floor, where you can't possibly find it — these are very small screws — or you'll hear that little clinky noise the next time you vacuum. If you don't have a rug, the screw will bounce on your wooden or tile floor and land far from the table. Finding the screw takes a long time. Want to guess how I know these things?

## Inserting the NIC

Now you can insert the NIC. Open the static-free bag and remove the NIC from it. Touch something metal (the computer case you removed should be handy) to discharge any static electricity in your body. Follow these steps to insert the NIC in the bus. (You won't be confused about which way it fits into the bus because the back edge of the NIC replaces the metal plate you removed from the back of the computer, as shown in Figure 2-2.)

1. **Position the metal edge of the NIC in the open slot at the back of the computer.**

   You may have to tilt and wield the adapter a bit to line it up properly.

2. **Position the teeth on the bottom of the NIC in the bus, and then push down on the NIC.**

   You may have to apply a bit of pressure, which is okay — don't worry about it. You can tell the NIC is inserted properly when you feel the metal edge fit neatly into the slot at the back of the computer.

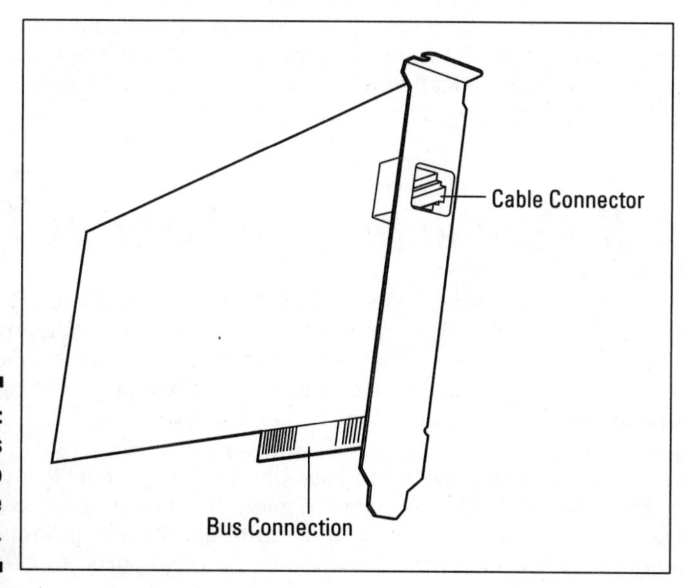


**Figure 2-2:** The NIC is shaped to match the bus and slot.

3. **Replace the screw that you removed when you took out the metal plate.**

   Make sure the overhanging *flange* (or rim) at the top edge of the NIC nestles against the top edge of the computer frame. In fact, if everything's lined up right, you should see the screw hole because the flange has an opening for the screw.

4. **Put the cover back on the computer and replace the screws that you removed when you opened it.**

If you drop a screw into the computer and you can't get to it, try any of the following:

- Grab the screw with a long pair of tweezers.
- Dangle a long piece of sticky tape to nudge the screw to a place where you can reach it.
- Turn the computer upside down over the table and let the screw drop, but beware of another possible problem — the screw landing on the floor and rolling out of sight.

You're finished! Wasn't that easy? Now, close the computer, reconnect all the cables that you disconnected (easy if you marked everything as I suggested), and repeat these steps for every computer in your network.

When you restart your computer, Windows notices that you've installed new hardware and displays a message offering to complete the software side of the installation of your network adapter. That means special driver files that control your use of the device are transferred to your computer. Consult the documentation that came with your network adapter and walk through the wizard to install the files. If you're using Windows XP, you may not even see the wizard — instead you'll just see a message telling you that the software has been installed automatically. Windows XP is almost magical in its ability to install hardware devices.

# Adding USB Connectors — Easy as Pie

If you purchased a kit or an individual connector that is designed to work with a Universal Serial Bus (USB) port, installation is a snap. You don't even have to open your computer. In fact, you don't even have to turn off the computer. Just push the USB end of the cable into your USB port (see Figure 2-3). (You can find out more about USB ports in Chapter 1.)

You may decide to add a USB hub to your USB port, especially if you attach (or intend to attach) several peripheral devices to a computer. *USB hubs* are hardware devices that enable you to add additional USB peripherals when you run out of USB ports. Most PCs have only two USB ports, so after you have installed two USB peripherals (for example, a camera and a scanner), attaching a hub to one of your USB ports enables you to expand your USB device use. The hub holds additional USB ports, and you can even use a special method of connecting a second hub (called *daisy chaining*) just in case you keep purchasing USB devices. One end of the hub looks like the regular USB connector, and this end goes into the USB port on your computer. The other end of the hub is a set of USB connectors that are the same as the connectors on the back of your computer.

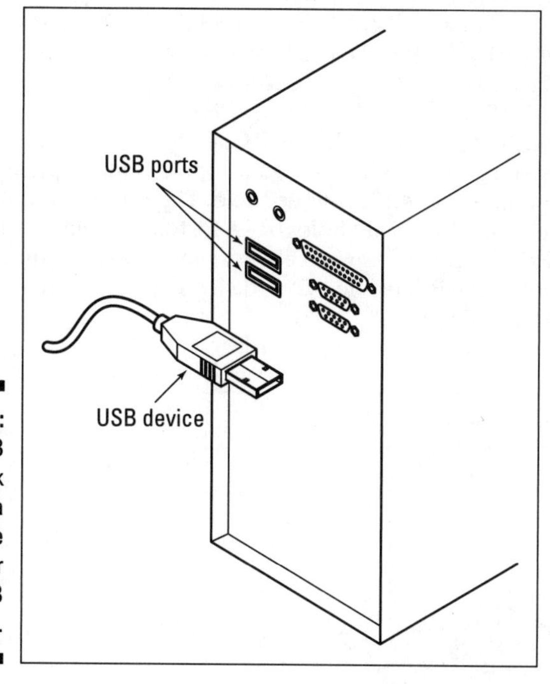


**Figure 2-3:** Your USB network device has a cable connector for the USB port.

If your computer is running when you connect the cable to the USB port, the operating system notices what you did and immediately displays a message offering to complete the software side of the installation of your network device. That means special driver files that control your use of the device are transferred to your computer. Consult the documentation that came with your USB adapter and walk through the wizard to install the files. If you're using Windows XP, you may not even see the wizard — instead you'll just see a message telling you that the software has been installed automatically.

# Installing Laptop Adapters

Why should desktop computers have all the fun? Laptop network adapters enable you to add your laptop computer to your home network. Most laptops have USB ports, so if that's the method you want to use to connect your laptop to your network, follow the instructions in the previous section to attach the USB network adapter.

If your laptop doesn't have USB ports, or you're already using the USB ports for other things, you can use a PC card network adapter, which is sometimes called a PCMCIA network adapter. (*PCMCIA* stands for Personal Computer Memory Card Interface Adapter.)

The PC card is about the size of a credit card. One end of the card is the *external* side. That side has a device that provides a connection for the network, in the form of an RJ-45 connector for Ethernet cable. The other end of the card, the *internal* side, has a row of 68 tiny holes. By a fortunate coincidence, the back of the PC card slot in the laptop has 68 tiny pins. An arrow on the card indicates which way to plug it into the PC card slot so that the holes meet the pins inside the slot (see Figure 2-4).

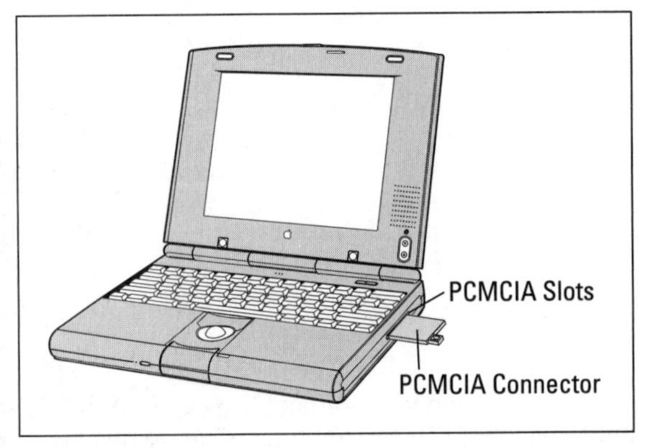


**Figure 2-4:** PC cards are clearly marked so that you know how to insert them.

Push the card into the slot firmly. When the card is fully engaged, a little button next to the slot pops out — you press the button when you want to eject the card (the same way a floppy drive works). Your laptop probably has two PC card slots, one on top of the other. The slots are usually on the side of the computer, hidden behind a flip-down cover that protects both slots.

Unless the documentation for your laptop has instructions to the contrary, it doesn't matter which slot you use for your adapter.

If you turned off your computer before you inserted the PC card, when you restart the computer, Windows notices the new hardware device. Use the documentation that came with your network adapter as a reference and walk through the wizard that installs the driver for your PC card. If you didn't turn off the computer, follow the directions in the documentation to install the drivers.

# Troubleshooting Network Adapters

Sometimes adapters don't work properly (or at all). In this section, I go over the common adapter problems and their solutions. Some of these problems may not show up until after you've completed the configuration of your adapter (covered in Chapter 6). The problems and possible solutions presented here are for trouble that's specific to adapters, not general network communications problems. For example, a failure to communicate may be the result of incorrect network settings, not the result of a problem with the physical adapter.

## No adapter icon on the taskbar

For computers running Windows 2000 or Windows XP, you can display an icon for your network adapter on the taskbar. The icon is handy because you can click it to open the adapter's Properties dialog box (instead of using all the steps required to get to it through Control Panel). In addition, the taskbar icon displays error messages when a problem arises.

If you don't have an icon for your adapter on the right side of your taskbar, open the adapter's Properties dialog box and select the option to display one (the language differs depending on the version of Windows).

## Two adapter icons?

I get a great many calls from people who say they have two adapters listed in Control Panel (and two icons on their taskbars).

If you're using Internet Connection Sharing to share a DSL or cable modem that's attached to a computer (instead of using a router), the computer that has the modem is supposed to have two adapters. One adapter is connected to the modem with Ethernet cable, and the other adapter is connected to the network with the type of wiring you've chosen for your network.

If you're not using ICS, you don't need two adapters. If your computer has a built-in adapter (usually Ethernet), and you installed an adapter for another type of wiring, you can remove the Ethernet adapter (in Windows 98SE/Me) or disable it (in Windows 2000/XP):

- To remove an adapter in Windows 98SE or Windows Me, open Control Panel and double-click Network. Select the adapter you're not using and click Remove.
- To disable an adapter in Windows 2000 or Windows XP, open Control Panel and open Network and Dialup Connections. Right-click the listing for the adapter you're not using and choose Disable.

If you use a PC card on a laptop that's displaying two adapters, and you're absolutely sure there is no built-in adapter, the problem is that you don't use the same PC card slot every time you insert your adapter.

Windows treats each PC card slot as a unique device, with its own hardware identification, and it retains information on inserted devices even when they're no longer inserted. If you open Device Manager and examine the hardware Properties of both adapters, you'll find that one adapter is displaying an error indicating that it's not connected (for a wired network), or indicating no signal can be found (for a wireless network).

It's perfectly safe to ignore the duplicate connections, because the PC card that's inserted will work properly. If the situation bothers you, just remember to use the same PC card slot every time you insert the adapter. Then disable or remove the other connection, using the directions earlier in this section.

## Cable Unplugged error

In Windows 2000 and Windows XP, an adapter icon may display an error indicating a network cable is unplugged. The error may be in a balloon over the taskbar icon (which is probably displaying a red X on top of the icon), as shown in Figure 2-5, or in the status message that's displayed when you select the adapter in Control Panel.

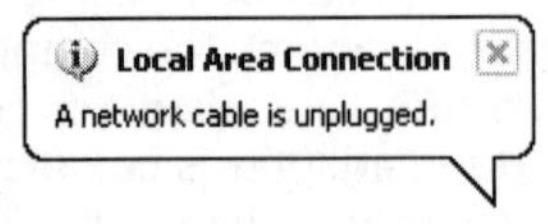


**Figure 2-5:** An unplugged cable means a problem.

Of course, the first thing to do is check the cable connection on the adapter. Even if the cable appears to be connected, give it a push to make sure it's plugged in properly. If the connection is good, check the connection at the concentrator (hub, switch, or router).

If the connections seem to be okay, move the connector to another port on the concentrator. Unplug a cable you know is working (because the computer it's connected to isn't displaying an error message), and plug the cable from the errant computer into that port. If that works, the port is bad on the concentrator. A bad port almost always means the concentrator is having a problem that will soon spread to the other ports (which translates to "you need a new concentrator").

If changing the port doesn't work, change the cable. Run another cable between the computer and the concentrator. If that works, toss the old cable in the trash can.

If neither of those steps cures the problem, the adapter is probably bad and needs to be replaced. If your warranty is still in effect, contact the manufacturer for a replacement.

## No Signal Can Be Found error

For a wireless adapter, the error No Signal Can Be Found is the equivalent of the Ethernet "Cable Unplugged" error. It means the adapter can't find the network.

Start by checking around the computer (and its adapter) for interference. Is the computer near metal (such as a file cabinet) or a cordless phone base unit? If so, move the computer (always move closer to the Access Point) to see if the adapter can find the signal.

The problem may be distance, or interference you can't easily see (such as metal in the walls). To determine if this is your difficulty, try moving the computer into the same room as the Access Point. If the signal is restored, move back towards your original computer location in small increments. When you lose the signal, you know you're past the point of connectivity and you must relocate the computer.

If you can't get a signal anywhere, and you know the adapter's settings and your network configuration are correct, your adapter is probably bad. If it's under warranty, arrange for a replacement.

# Chapter 3

# Installing Ethernet Cable

***In This Chapter***

- Planning the cable runs
- Deciding on the location of the concentrator
- Running cable around the house

Installing Ethernet network interface cards (NICs) provides only half of the connections needed for computer-to-computer communication. Now you need to let the NICs communicate with each other. You accomplish this connection via Ethernet cable. In this chapter, I tell you everything you need to know to connect NICs using Ethernet cable. When you're finished, you have the fastest, most reliable network connectivity available.

## Ready, Set, Run

The way cable is strung through a building is called a *run,* and your plan for running the cable depends on how easily you can string the cable between the computers and the concentrator. Your run is actually a series of runs because each computer must be individually attached to the concentrator. (The concentrator is the device that holds all the connections and provides the conversation pit for your computers; it can be a hub, a switch, or a router.)

### Ethernet cable has many aliases

Ethernet cable comes in many forms, but today's standard cable (and the only form that I cover in this book) is called CAT-5. CAT-5 is a nickname, and it's short for Category 5 twisted-pair cable. (Categories run from CAT-1 through CAT-6.)

CAT-5 cable is also called *twisted-pair cable* because it's descriptive — the cable's wires are twisted along the length of the cable (see Figure 3-1).

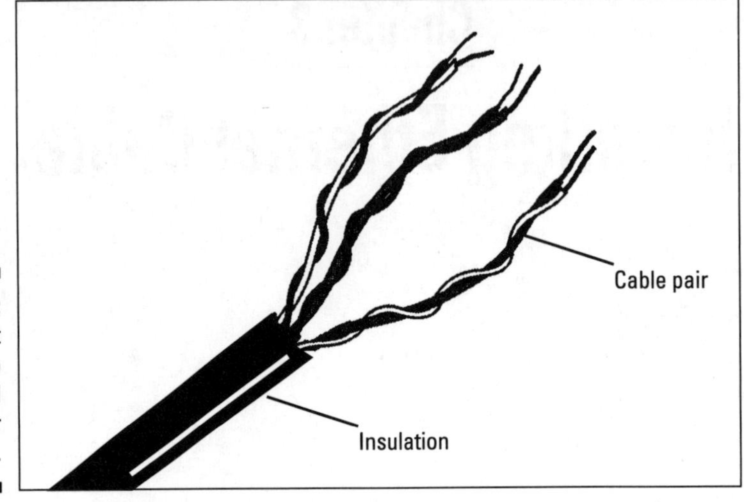


**Figure 3-1:** Ethernet cable is also called twisted-pair cable.

The names 10Base-T and 100Base-T are acronyms that are derived as follows:

- **10 or 100:** This part of the acronym represents the speed of data transmission in megabits (a megabit is a million bits). Until a few years ago, 10Base-T was the standard, but today 100Base-T is the standard, and 1000 Mbps is also available. The Ethernet hardware devices (NICs, hubs, and switches) are rated for speed; older devices support 10-megabit transmissions, while newer devices support 100-megabit or 1000-megabit (called gigabit) transmissions. Most NICs and concentrators have the ability to auto-detect the speed of the other hardware on the network and adjust transmission speed so all the hardware can communicate.
- **Base:** This stands for baseband signaling, which means that only Ethernet signals are carried on the cable. Ethernet does not share its cable bandwidth the way telephone cable and electric cable do.
- **T:** This is a code that identifies the physical medium that carries the signal as copper (100Base-F is fiber-optic cable).

CAT-5 cable comes in two types:

- Unshielded twisted-pair (UTP)
- Shielded twisted-pair (STP)

The difference between the two types is pretty obvious — shielded twisted-pair cable has a shield. The shield is made of metal and encases the wires, reducing the possibility of interference from other electrical devices (radar, radio waves, and so on).

I'm not aware of a great difference in performance between UTP and STP cable. UTP is less expensive, and almost all the CAT-5 cable in use is UTP. The only time I've ever installed STP is at client sites in towns that required STP for certain types of cable runs (for instance, if you're running cable through a ceiling that also contains other wiring). If you think the building codes in your town may require STP for the way you're planning to run your cable, check with the local authorities.

Both UTP and STP cable are available in fixed lengths, or *patches.* At either end of the cable is a connector called an *RJ-45 connector,* which you use to connect the computers in your network to the *concentrator,* or hub, of the home network.

Networking consultants buy big rolls of cable, cut each run to the appropriate length, and make their own connectors. That's more work than running precut cable lengths that already have connectors attached.

## Concerning the concentrator

All the lengths of cable share the same home base, a concentrator, which is either a *hub* or a *switch* (routers have switches built in, so if you're using your router as a concentrator, you have a switch). Each cable run goes from the concentrator to a computer (or from a computer to the concentrator, depending on how you like to envision it).

At each end of a length of cable is a connector called an *RJ-45 connector.* One connector attaches to the concentrator, and the other connector attaches to the NIC in a computer.

When you purchase a concentrator, you have a choice between buying a hub or a switch. The difference between them is the way they send data to computers — the switch takes a more intelligent approach. When data is transmitted across the network, the ID of the target (receiving) computer is identified within the data packet.

A hub ignores the computer ID and sends the data to all the computers on the network. The computers check the computer ID, and the computer that's supposed to receive the data accepts it; the other computers ignore it. However, the hub has to split up the bandwidth to send the data to all the computers, so the transmission speed to each individual computer is reduced. A switch notices which computer ID is the target of the data transmission and sends the data only to that computer, using all the available bandwidth for the transmission.

One of the ports on a hub or a switch differs from the others, although it looks the same. That port is an *uplink port,* and you don't use it to connect a computer to the hub. Instead, this port has a special use (see the section "Curing Your Network's Growing Pains," later in this chapter). Look for an icon or label to identify the uplink port, or read the documentation that came with the hub so that you know which port to avoid.

The network arrangement shown in Figure 3-2 is called a *star topology,* although I'm not sure how that name was developed. Personally, I think the resemblance to a star is a little obscure. Perhaps *wheel spokes* is a more accurate description — which would explain the use of the word *hub* (as in the hub of a wheel).

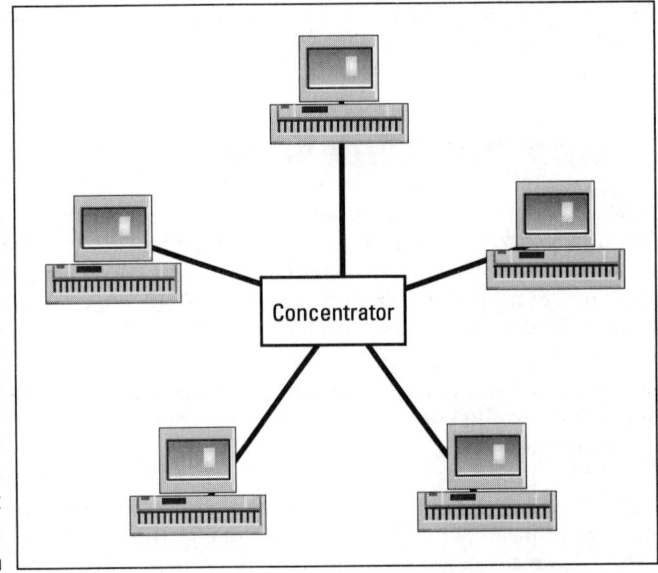


**Figure 3-2:** Notice the multiple cable runs from the concentrator to each computer in an Ethernet network.

# Deciding Where to Put the Concentrator

The concentrator is the core of the network; everything travels to it (and flows from it). You should place the concentrator in a location that reduces the amount of cable you need to schlep through the house. For example, a reasonably logical person can count on the following scenarios:

- If you have two computers on the second floor and one on the first floor, putting the concentrator on the second floor means you'll have only one long cable run.

- If all your computers are on one floor, the logical place for the concentrator is at a midpoint among all the computers.
- If the same number of computers are on the first floor as are on the second floor, find a location that's as close as possible to being equidistant from each computer.

Where you decide to locate the concentrator requires a couple of other important considerations, so logical thinking doesn't always work (much like applying logical thinking to politics or economic theories, or to guessing what "that look" on your spouse's face really means). The following sections help you work through the not-so-logical considerations you need to take into account.

## Concentrators are environmentally fussy

Concentrators have some environmental requirements, and if you don't cater to them, your concentrator will probably get sick and may even die. To ensure that your concentrator is in the correct environment, do the following:

- **Provide good air quality.** After you connect the cables, you don't have to manage the concentrator — no baby-sitting is required. That means you can tuck it away somewhere, but you must provide a dry (not humid), dust-free environment.
- **Avoid covering the concentrator.** Don't place it in a drawer, and don't wrap it in plastic to avoid dust — it needs circulating air to prevent overheating.
- **Avoid excessive heat.** Keep the concentrator away from direct sunlight, radiators, heaters, and any other heat sources.
- **Avoid proximity to other electrical devices.** Don't put the concentrator next to fluorescent lights, radios, or transmitting equipment.

## Concentrators are innately powerless

Ethernet concentrators require electrical power, so they must be located next to an electrical outlet. Unless you want to do some fancy electrical work (or you don't mind the cable(s) keeping you from closing the closet door all the way), a closet — which otherwise would be a great location to hide a concentrator — won't work because there is usually no electrical outlet nearby.

Keep your concentrator plugged into a surge protector. Plug the surge protector into a wall outlet, and then plug the concentrator into the surge protector. Surges travel rapidly through cable, and when they do, they zap everything in the cable's path. A good surge can take out every NIC on the network. A *really*

strong surge can push the damage past the NIC and fry the computer's motherboard. (Remember, every NIC is connected to the connector, and every NIC is also connected to its motherboard.)

## Distance Depends on What You Choose to Measure

Your cable run has to connect every computer to the concentrator, but you can only buy patch cable in specific lengths. The longer the cable, the more you pay. Ethernet networking kits have one piece of cable for each connector in the kit, and each piece of cable is the same length (usually 20 or 25 feet). Given these facts, the word *epicenter* becomes meaningless. For example, if the midpoint between two computers is a distance of 28 feet and you have two 25-foot lengths of cable, put the concentrator within 25 feet of one computer so that you only have to buy one longer cable.

Cable doesn't run from the concentrator to a computer in a straight line. It runs along baseboards, through walls, across ceilings, and sometimes even runs along *all* of these conduits. You can't really measure the amount of cable you'll need between the concentrator and a computer with an "as the crow flies" mentality. The only way to measure properly (and therefore buy the right cable lengths) is to read the sections on running cable later in this chapter. Then, depending on the way you run your cable, you'll have an idea of the length of cable you'll need to connect each computer to the concentrator.

The maximum length of a Cat-5 cable run is 100 meters, which is about 328 feet.

You may have to account for traveling up walls as well as placing the cable across walls, ceilings, or floors. And of course, don't make your measurements too fine — you need to account for some slack. After all, why would you want the cable to come out of the wall in a straight line to the computer? You would have to leap over the cable to cross the room.

In the end, what you're looking for is a location for the concentrator that requires as few very long cable lengths as possible. Make these considerations:

- You're most likely to end up with a concentrator that is very near two computers while being very far from the third computer. In the long run (yeah, the pun was intended), you'll end up saving money, time, and hassle if you accept this fact right now.

- Find a way to position the concentrator near the conduit you're using for the cable run (you may decide to run cable through a wall or a ceiling, or along baseboards). If the cables from all your computers come out of a wall, put the concentrator very close to the wall to avoid the need for longer cables. Some concentrators come with devices that permit wall mounting so that the concentrator doesn't take up table or shelf space.

# Handling Cable Correctly

Be careful about the way you handle cable as you run it through the chase. (A *chase* is the opening through which you place the cable, like inside a wall, in a hollow space above the ceiling, or along the baseboards of a room.) Keep the following tips in mind:

- **The bigger the hole (within reason), the better.** When you drill holes to run cable between rooms or floors, make the holes slightly larger than the connector at the end of the cable. Connectors are delicate, so you don't want to force-feed them through small openings.
- **Keep everything neat, just like your mother taught you.** When you run cable from the entry point in the room (the entrance hole) to the computer, snake the run along the baseboard or the top of the quarter round until you're close to the computer. Keeping the cable tucked off to the side helps to ensure that no one trips over the cable.
- **Be nice to the cable.** Avoid bending cable at a sharp angle. If you have to run the cable around a corner, don't pull it taut.
- **When in doubt, staple like a madman.** You can use cable staples, which are U-shaped nails that act like staples, to attach cable to a surface. Use cable staples that are large enough to surround the cable — do not insert them into the cable.
- **Use an artist's touch.** You can paint the cable to match your baseboard or wall, but don't paint the concentrator.

## Connecting two patch cables

If you need a longer piece of cable, you can connect two pieces of patch cable with a coupler. A *coupler* is a small plastic device with two receptacles (one at each end) that accept RJ-45 connectors — you end a cable run in one receptacle and begin the next piece of cable in the other receptacle. This works just like the similar extension device for telephone lines.

Couplers don't have a terrific history of reliability. Frequently, when you encounter problems with computer-to-computer communication, the blame falls on these connections. Never put a coupler inside a wall or in any other location that's hard to reach, because you need easy access to the coupler if you have to check or replace the connection. The best plan is to use a coupler as a temporary solution while you wait for delivery of a custom-made patch cable that's the correct length.

Even though couplers work similarly to telephone-extension devices, do not use a telephone coupler for your computer cable.

## Making your own patch cables

If you know you have a big networking job ahead of you, you can save a lot of money by making your own patch cables. You can make your own by taking CAT-5 cable, cutting the right length, and attaching an RJ-45 connector at each end. This process is rather easy — I can barely change a light bulb, but I've been making my own cable connectors for years. To make your own patch cables, you need cable, RJ-45 connectors, a wire stripper, and a crimper to seat the connection properly.

You can buy bulk cable inexpensively — a 300-foot roll of cable costs about the same as two 50-foot patch cables. If you buy a larger roll of bulk cable, the price per foot is even lower (sell what you don't use to a neighbor who is installing a home network).

The RJ-45 connectors cost a few pennies each, but you'll probably have to buy at least a 20-pack — I've never seen them sold individually. Buying a crimper should set you back less than $100, and a wire stripper costs a few dollars.

Of course, you can make the investment you of these supplies pay off by offering to install cabled networks for your friends and neighbors.

To make a patch cable, follow these steps:

1. **Cut the length of cable you need.**

   Don't forget to account for climbing up or down walls, running along baseboards, and allowing slack.

2. **Use the stripper to remove about half an inch of insulation from the end of the cable.**

3. **Push the wires into the holes on the RJ-45 connector.**

   You'll find they slide in easily.

4. **Position the crimper where the wires meet the connector, and press firmly.**

   Most crimpers come with instructions, including illustrations, to explain exactly how to crimp the connector. Most crimpers can handle a variety of connector sizes (for example, your crimper can also probably make regular telephone wire connectors, called *RJ-11* connectors), so make sure you use the position marked for RJ-45 connectors.

5. **Repeat Steps 2 through 4 for the other end of the cable.**

# The Chase Is On: Running the Cable

The permutations and combinations of runs depend on the physical layout of your home, of course, but the ideal way to run cable in your home is to find a way to lay the cable in a straight line between the concentrator and each computer on the network. Sounds easy, doesn't it? Good luck! The opening through which you wind and wend the cable is called a *chase*. The chase may be inside a wall, in a hollow space above the ceiling, along the baseboards of a room, or in a combination of these opportunities. If you're lucky, you can find a straight-line chase between the concentrator and each computer.

## Cabling within a room

If you put the concentrator in the same room as one of the computers (or if all the computers on your network are in the same room), you don't need to drill holes in walls or floors. Put the concentrator next to one computer. Connect the closest computer to the concentrator with a short length of cable. Then run a longer piece of cable from the concentrator to the other computer(s). Run the cable along the baseboard, not across the floor.

## Cabling between adjacent rooms

Cabling your network is easy if your computers are located in adjacent rooms on the same floor because you only have to drill one hole between the rooms. Put the concentrator in one room and run one length of cable between the concentrator and the computer. Run another section of cable through the wall to the computer in the other room. You need to drill only one hole, as shown in Figure 3-3.

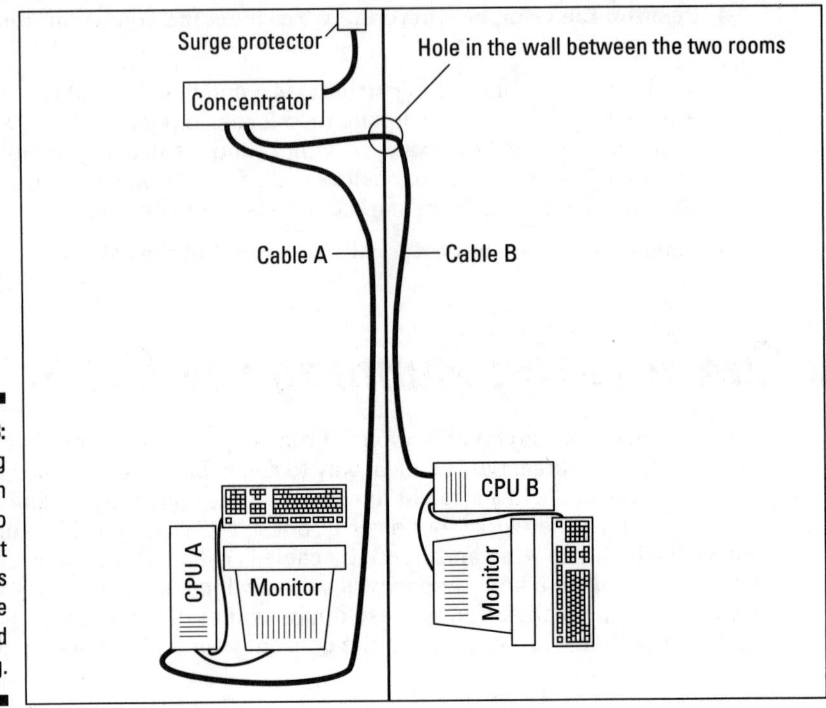


**Figure 3-3:** Cabling between two adjacent rooms requires one drilled opening.

## Cabling between nonadjacent rooms on the same floor

If your computers are on the same floor but aren't in adjacent rooms, you need to do a bit more work. The most direct and efficient cabling route is a chase along your home's beams. Most houses have beams between floors that run straight through the house, either from front to back, side to side, or both. You can usually expect a clear chase from one end to the other.

The logical way to access the chase is to drill a hole in the ceiling or floor (depending on whether the chase is above or below the level you're working on).

I hate drilling holes in the ceiling because, to say the least, the blemish looks crummy. Even if I paint the cable to match the wall, I know it's there. Instead, I use closets or walls to get to the chase.

### Keeping your drill holes in the closet

Wiring through closets is a great way to hide the side effects of cabling. If you have a closet in every room that holds a computer, you're in great shape. It's less important to clean up the hole and touch up the paint when you work in a closet, unless you're some kind of decorating fanatic. If every room doesn't have a closet, don't worry — you can still confine the cabling to the corners of the room.

Drill a hole in the closet ceiling or floor of each room that holds a computer (one room also holds the concentrator). Choose between the ceiling or the floor, depending on the location of the chase.

Bring the cable through the chase to each computer. You can use a *fish* (a tool specially designed for fishing cable that is sold in hardware stores) or a wire coat hanger you've untwisted (the hook at the end grabs the cable).

Of course, a portion of the cable has to run between the closet and the computer or concentrator. If you have enough clearance under the closet door, run the cable under the door and then attach it to the baseboard with U-shaped staples as it moves toward the computers. If you have no clearance under the closet door, drill a hole in the bottom of the doorjamb to bring the cable into the room.

### Cable that's all walled up

For any room that lacks a closet, bring the cable into the room from the chase at a corner. If the cable enters the room through the ceiling from the chase above, bring the cable down the seam of the walls that create the corner (and paint the cable to match the wall). Then run the cable along the baseboard to the computer. If the cable enters the room through the floor from the chase below, run the cable along the baseboard to the computer.

Here are a couple of other schemes to consider if all your computers are on the same floor:

- If your computers are on the second floor, run the cable across the attic floor (or crawlspace above the second floor). Then you can drop the cable down a corner to each computer.
- If your computers are on the first floor, run the cable across the basement ceiling (or crawlspace). Then you can snake the cable up to each computer.

## Cabling Between Floors

If your computers are on different floors, you have more work to do. You need additional cable because your cable length measurement must include the height of the room in addition to the horizontal length required to reach the computer. Here are some tips on what to do if you have a multilevel home network on your hands:

- **Basement/second-floor room arrangement:** If you have one computer in the basement and another on the second floor, you need sufficient cable length to make the trip to the concentrator. Putting the concentrator on the first floor instead of next to one computer may be easier because you may have a problem finding cable that's long enough to span from the basement to the second floor.
- **Stacked room arrangement:** If the rooms are stacked one above the other, you can run the cable through the inside of the walls, near a corner. Use openings around accessible radiators and pipes, and use stacked closets when you can. If the stacked rooms occupy three levels, put the concentrator in the middle level. If you're moving between two floors, put the concentrator on either floor.
- **Kitty-corner room arrangement:** If the rooms are on opposite ends of the house, in addition to being on different floors (as far away from each other as humanly possible), you have to use both walls (or closets) and ceilings. For the vertical runs, use any openings around pipes that are available (houses with radiators usually have lots of space next to pipe runs). If no pipes are available, use the inside of the wall. For the horizontal runs, find a chase above or below the room.

Now, here are some bonus tips to help you run cable across multiple levels:

- **Use gravity to your advantage.** After you drill your holes and find the space in the wall or next to a pipe, work from the top down. Put a weight on the end of a sturdy piece of twine and drop it to the lower floor. Then tape the cable to the weight and haul the cable up. This way is much easier than pushing the cable up through the walls and using a fish to grab it from the top.
- **Use ducts if you can.** You can also use HVAC (heating, ventilation, and air conditioning) ducts, but you should be aware that many municipalities have strict rules about this choice. Some building codes forbid using HVAC ducts to run cable of any type; other building codes just set standards. The advantage of using HVAC ducts is that they go into every room, and they're usually rather wide. The disadvantage is that they rarely travel in a straight line, so you may have to run cable through several rooms to connect a computer to the concentrator. *Never* enter the duct system by drilling a hole. You must use existing entry and exit points, usually through the grate over the point at which the duct meets the wall.
- **Network everything.** Haul some electrical wire, regular telephone cable, and stereo speaker wire through the walls when you run your network cable. Later, if you want your electrician to add outlets for all the computer peripherals you'll probably accumulate, you want to add a phone jack, or you want to add speakers, most of the work is already done. In fact, if you bring several telephone wires along, you have a head start for installing a home security system or a home intercom system. If you think you'll be adding more computers in the future, haul extra lengths of Cat-5 cable.

- **Consider getting more than one concentrator.** If you have a large amount of space to cover, you may actually save money on cable, not to mention saving yourself some trouble, if you use more than one concentrator. And, you'll have a head start if you decide to add computers to your home network later. See the section, "Getting into the Zone," later in this chapter, for more information.

# Beauty Is in the Eye of the Decorator

After you finish all the cabling and the computers are connected to the concentrator, an interesting thing occurs in many households. The person in the household who cares most about the décor (usually Mom) walks around the house muttering sentences in which the word "ugly" frequently occurs. Teenage daughters look at the new high-tech system you installed and react with comments like "Gross!" (Teenage sons don't seem to notice.)

Somebody, perhaps a guest (if not a member of the family), eventually remarks, "We have a network at work, and we don't have holes in the wall that exude cable, and we don't have cable crawling along the floor or the baseboard."

Professional network installers use accessories to make the hardware decorator-friendly, and there's no reason you can't put the same finishing touches on your system. An added benefit is that some of the accessories also make the installation safer, removing cable from places that may cause someone to trip.

## Adding cable faceplates

If you run cable through walls, you can end the cable run at the wall using an Ethernet socket that's attached to the wall with a faceplate, as shown in Figure 3-4. Then, you just need to run a small piece of cable from the computer to the faceplate. You can buy multioutlet faceplates, which you'll need in the room that contains the concentrator.

To use a faceplate to create an Ethernet socket, pull the cable through the hole in the wall and use a cable stripper to remove about an inch of insulation from the cable. If the cable is a patch cable, cut off the connector first. Then insert the wires into the socket, and push against the socket to seal the connection (these are similar to electrical connections that just snap into place). Attach the socket to the faceplate, and attach the faceplate to the wall (pushing the wires back into the wall).

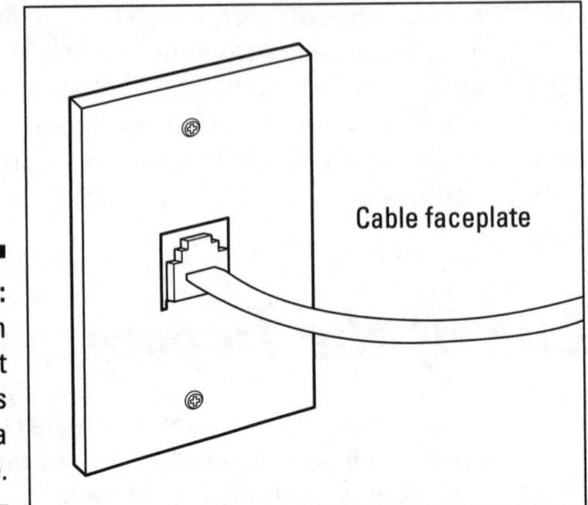


**Figure 3-4:** You can connect computers to a faceplate.

## Using floor cable covers

In any networking situation, a certain amount of cable is exposed because you have to run cable between the wall and the NIC in the computer. The best way to hide as much cable as possible is to put the computer desk against the wall at the point where the cable exits the wall. If that solution isn't possible, cover the cable that runs between the wall and the computer. Floor cable covers can help make your network installation less ugly and can also provide safety by eliminating the chance of tripping over the cable.

Floor cable covers come in two models: covers that lie atop the cable and covers that hold the cable in a channel (see Figure 3-5). Both cover types provide several advantages over loose cable:

- **Cable covers hug the ground and don't move.** You can't accidentally nudge them up into the air as you walk and then trip over the loop you created (which is what frequently happens with Ethernet cable).
- **Cable covers are wide.** And the slope to the top of the cover is very gentle, which lessens the chance that you'll trip.
- **You can use cable covers under a rug.** Don't run cable under a rug because the rubbing of the underside of the rug against the cable can weaken or break the cable's insulation jacket.

Most floor covers are made of plastic or rubber. You can paint the plastic covers, but I find that paint wears away quickly on rubber. If you're running the covers over a carpet, you can even glue carpet strips to the top of the cover, which may help hide the fact that your family room is crawling with cable.

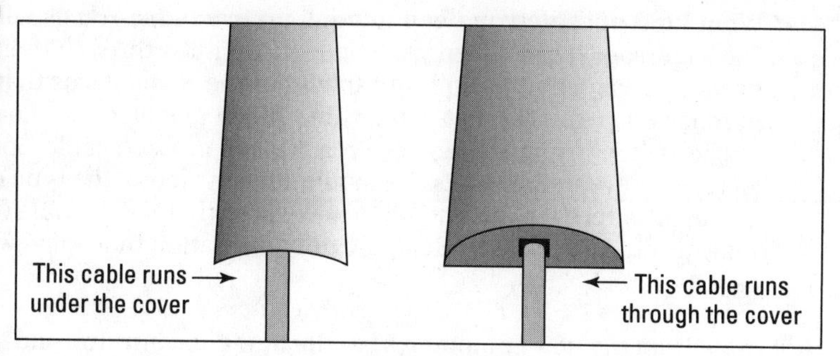


**Figure 3-5:** Cable covers hide ugly cable and reduce the risk of someone tripping over the cable.

# Curing Your Network's Growing Pains

You can be almost certain that your home network will grow — you'll add more computers. (Read how to run cable from the new computer to the concentrator in the section, "The Chase Is On: Running the Cable," earlier in this chapter.) But what happens if you run out of concentrator connections? If you start your home network with a kit built for two computers, where do you plug in additional computers?

You have two solutions:

- Buy a larger concentrator (and sell the original concentrator to a friend who's building a home network).
- Buy another small concentrator and link it to the first concentrator.

You shouldn't need any instructions for carrying out the first solution.

The second solution, however, requires a little bit of homework — you need to read the instructions that came with both concentrators to understand how to link them. Every concentrator has an uplink port, which is specifically designed to connect one concentrator to another concentrator, instead of connecting a computer to a concentrator. (Notice that a concentrator that's meant to accommodate four computers has five ports.) Before you use an uplink port, here's what you need to know:

- **Where the uplink port is:** The uplink port is always at the end of the row of ports (usually next to the place where the power cord goes).
- **What the uplink port looks like:** Notice that the uplink port is usually marked differently from the other ports, either with an icon or the word *uplink.* (If nothing is visible, check the documentation that came with the hub.)

- **What kind of cable you need to hook up two hubs:** You usually need to use a *crossover cable* when you connect two hubs through their uplink ports. You can buy this special cable from the same places that you can purchase regular Ethernet patch cable. Many manufacturers have a toggle switch to change between regular and crossed cable. Some manufacturers have uplink ports that automatically detect the type of cable and make internal adjustments to make sure that patch cable works the same as crossover cable. Read the documentation that came with your concentrator.

Run cable from the new computer(s) to the new concentrator, and connect the old concentrator to the new one via the uplink port (or the other way around). Read the documentation for both concentrators to see whether you need to use a crossover cable and also to see whether the connection from the uplink port goes into a regular port or into the other uplink port. Figure 3-6 is an illustration of a network with two concentrators.

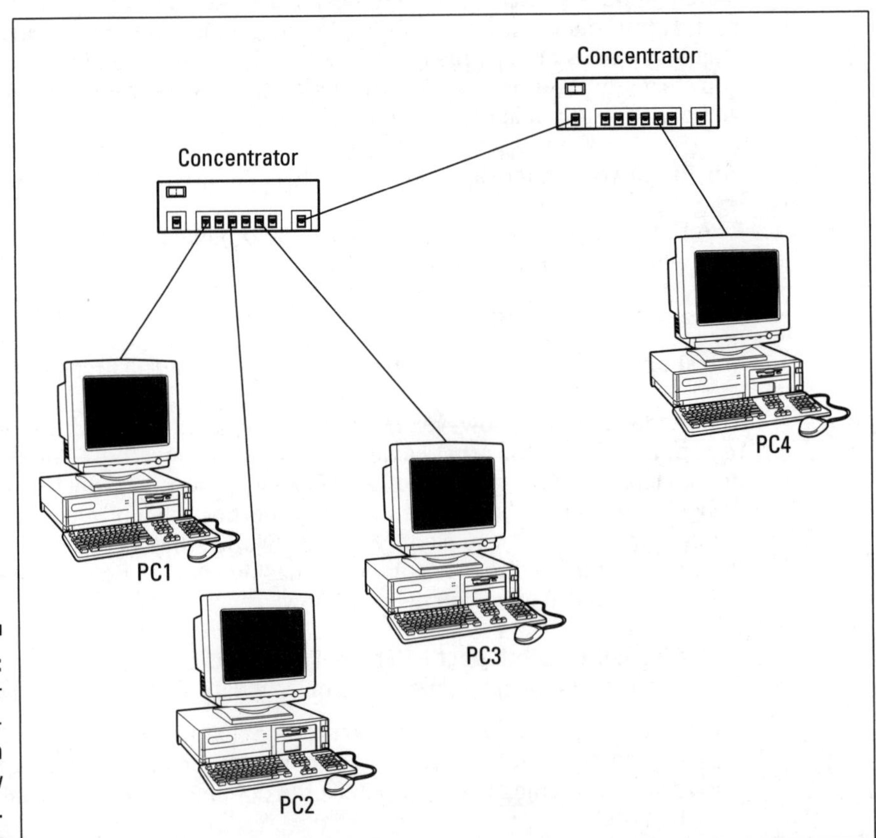


**Figure 3-6:** Add another concentrator when you outgrow the first one.

# Getting Into the Zone

You can gain advantages from linked concentrators, even if one concentrator has enough ports for all the computers on your network. The concept is called *zoning,* and you can zone your network to make cabling easier.

For example, consider that you have two widely separated computers on the first floor. One computer is in the family room at the front of the house, and the other computer is in the kitchen at the back of the house. You have two computers on the second floor, also at opposite ends of the house.

You can place a single concentrator in the family room and run cable across the first floor to the kitchen computer. Then you can run cable down the wall to the computer on the second floor at the front of the house. Finally, you can run cable down the wall and across the house to the computer on the second floor at the back of the house, but doesn't that seem like a lot of cable?

Instead, create zones for your network. For example, you can put two concentrators in the basement or in the attic. Place one near the front of the house and one near the back of the house. Drop the cables from two computers to each concentrator. Then link the concentrators to each other. Because you're using the attic or basement (where beauty doesn't count as much), you can string the cable across rafters, using hooks or duct tape. As you can see in Figure 3-7, zoning is logical and easy, and provides for network growth.

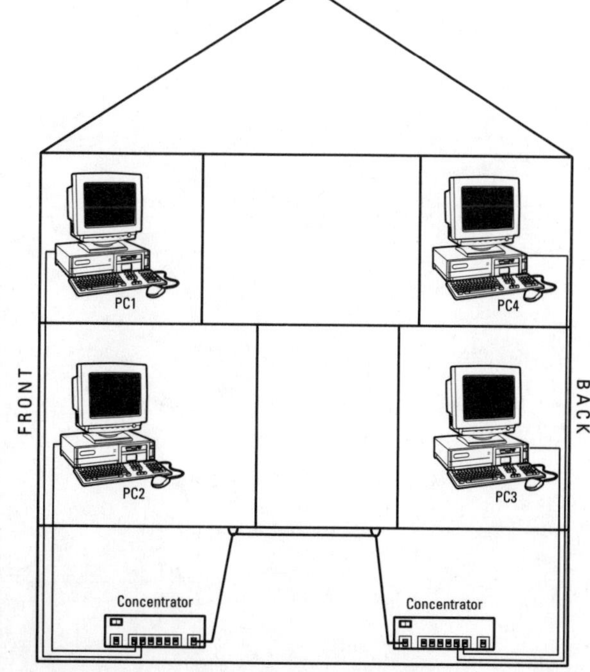


**Figure 3-7:** If your computers are scattered through the house, setting up computer zones makes cabling easier.

# Chapter 4
# Using Wires That Are Already There

*In This Chapter*

- Installing a phone line network
- Using your power lines to create a network

Suppose you don't want to drill holes, climb into the attic, or slither through the crawlspace to drag Ethernet cable through the house. Or suppose you do, but the chief decorator in your house objects strongly. What can you do to get the reliability and easy setup of hard-wired computer networks?

I have the answer. (Of course I do. What author would pose a question if she didn't already know the answer?) You can set up your home networking wiring with wires that already exist in your home — phone and power lines. This chapter covers the instructions that you need to connect all your computers by using the existing cable in your home.

## One Standard, Indivisible, with Liberty and Networking for All

Technical standards are usually developed by groups of manufacturers who come together to form an association for the specific reason of setting standards. Eventually, if enough manufacturers adopt the standards, all the other manufacturers have no choice but to use the new standards. It usually doesn't take long for standards to become universal, global, and totally accepted. At that point, most of the nonstandard stuff disappears from store shelves, and you can feel safe when you shop. (The most dramatic evidence of this is the history of videotape equipment for home use — although you may not be old enough to know people who rushed out to buy Beta equipment and movies on Beta tapes. Beta was introduced first, but VHS won the standards battle.)

If you buy networking equipment that meets standards, no matter what manufacturer's networking hardware you buy, it's going to work with anything else you buy. To check on the manufacturers of the equipment that you need to buy, you need to know about the following standards:

- Telephone line technology (called *phoneline* networking) has been standardized by the Home Phoneline Networking Alliance (`www.homepna.org`).
- The HomePlug Powerline Alliance (`www.homeplug.org`) sets standards for network devices that use household electrical wires.

Manufacturers that are members of these organizations usually have a statement to that effect on their equipment boxes. Their Web sites state that they are members of, or subscribe to the standards developed by, these organizations. Don't buy equipment that doesn't reference these organizations.

# Tapping Into Phone Lines to Connect a Network

If you've chosen to install a phoneline network, you have some easy homework tasks. You need to make sure you get the fastest possible speed for transmitting data across the network. The first version of phoneline equipment, dubbed HomePNA Version 1.0, transferred data at the rate of 1 megabit per second (1 Mbps). Then, phoneline equipment designed for HomePNA Version 2.0 became available, operating at about 10 Mbps. As I write this, manufacturers have begun making plans for equipment based on the standards for HomePNA Version 3.0, which transfers data at the rate of 128 Mbps.

For phoneline networking, adapters are available in the form of internal network interface cards (NICs), Universal Serial Bus (USB) network adapters, and PC card network adapters for laptops. At this point, you should already have installed the phoneline network adapters on the computers. If you haven't, page back to Chapter 2 for installation instructions.

The phone jacks that you use to create your network must all be on the same telephone line. If you have multiple phone numbers in your house, be careful to use only the jacks that are connected to the same phone number. If your house is wired for a second telephone line, but you haven't had the telephone company activate the line with a telephone number, you can still use the jacks that are attached to this inactive line for home networking.

Now it's time to connect the computers so that they can "talk" to each other. To create your phoneline network, just put one end of a regular telephone cable into the network adapter on the computer and put the other end of the telephone cable into the wall jack.

## Whose line is it, anyway?

The telephone lines that run through your walls have a great deal more power than you need for POTS, which is the technical jargon for plain old telephone service. The multiple wires that are inside telephone cables all don't use the same frequency. The wires that provide POTS have one frequency, but other wires use other frequencies. The technical terminology for this is *Frequency Division Multiplexing* (FDM). The different frequencies are described as follows:

- The POTS frequency services telephones, fax machines, and modems. Because all of these devices share the same frequency, you can't receive telephone calls when you're connected to the Internet via a modem.
- A different frequency is available for special devices that provide high-speed Internet access, such as digital subscriber line (DSL) and Integrated Services Digital Network (ISDN) devices, enabling you to use a high-speed device and a POTS device simultaneously.
- The hardware in your telephone line network uses *still another* frequency to communicate among all the computers on your network. POTS and high-speed Internet connection devices continue to operate on their own frequencies and are therefore available to you.

You don't have to worry about which frequency any service or device is using; the network devices and telephone wires automatically know which frequency to use. The only thing you have to do to ensure that your home network operates properly is to connect all the computers to the same telephone number (which isn't a problem unless you have two or more telephone numbers in your home).

Okay, you're done. You now have a network. Well, you have to install the software drivers (the documentation that came with your adapters has instructions, and Chapter 6 of this book discusses installation of drivers), but the hardware stuff is done.

## Where do I plug in phones?

Hello? What? It's not that simple in your house? Oh, I see; you actually want to use a telephone in at least one of the rooms that has a computer. And you want to use a modem and a fax machine?

Don't worry. Your phone line can handle as many devices as it has frequencies. What you have to do is to *gang,* or join, multiple devices so that each device is individually accessible. Each device has to be connected to the telephone line, and I go through the options in the following sections.

## Ganging the network and the telephone

Your phoneline network adapter has two jacks; one is labeled *line* (meaning the wall jack) and the other is labeled *phone*. The labels may use slightly different wording, or may use icons instead of text, but it's not difficult to figure out which jack is for which purpose.

Use the line jack on the phoneline network adapter to connect the computer to the wall jack, using standard telephone cable (which was probably included in the package that contained your phoneline network adapter). Then, plug a telephone into the other jack on the network adapter. Incidentally, on occasion, I've inadvertently put the connections in backward, connecting the phone jack to the wall and the line jack to the telephone — and it all worked! I suspect the wiring is identical in both jacks, but as these devices get more powerful (and more complicated), you may have a network adapter in which the labels on the jacks *do* matter.

You could instead use your wall jack for two devices at the same time by plugging a modular duplex jack (commonly called a *splitter*) into the wall receptacle. The splitter, which you can buy at the supermarket or at an office-supply store, has a standard RJ-11 plug at the front, just like telephone cable. The back end has two RJ-11 receptacles, into which you can plug two devices. Use one receptacle for cable coming from the telephone and the other for cable coming from the phoneline network adapter on your computer.

## Ganging the network, the telephone, and an external modem

If you have an external modem and you also want to have a telephone near the computer that's using the wall jack for network communications, you can easily gang the three devices. All external modems have two RJ-11 receptacles. One receptacle is for the cable that goes from the modem to the wall jack, and one receptacle accepts cable from the telephone. The receptacles are marked, usually with icons (one icon looks like a wall jack, and the other looks like a telephone). If your modem doesn't have icons, it has labels — *line* and *phone*.

Follow these steps to gang the network, telephone, and an external modem:

1. **Plug a splitter into the wall jack.**
2. **Insert the cable from your computer NIC into one side of the splitter.**
3. **Insert the cable from the external modem's line receptacle into the other side of the splitter.**
4. **Plug the cable from the telephone into the telephone receptacle on the modem.**

You probably figured out that this gang arrangement means that the external modem and the telephone don't have their own individual access to the wall jack. A gang arrangement isn't just sharing; it's a highly exclusive, fickle marriage. The modem and telephone are both POTS devices that can't operate simultaneously anyway. (I explain POTS in the sidebar, "Whose line is it, anyway?" earlier in this chapter).

You can't use the modem and the phone line at the same time (and that's true even if you weren't using your telephone lines for networking). If you pick up the telephone while you're using the modem, you do not hear a dial tone. Instead, you hear a lot of strange whistling and beeping noises, which is called *white noise.* (In addition, picking up the phone disrupts the modem communication, so hopefully you aren't downloading an important file at that moment.) Anyone calling your house hears a busy signal, so you won't hear the phone ring when you're online, either. When you're not using the modem, you can use the telephone normally, even though it isn't plugged directly into the wall. The modem's connection to the wall jack provides a pass-through connection to the telephone line.

## Ganging the network, the telephone, and an internal modem

If your computer has an internal modem, the part of the modem that you access at the back of your computer probably includes two receptacles — one for the telephone line and one for a telephone (just like an external modem). Follow the instructions for ganging the network, the telephone, and an external modem in the preceding section.

However, if your internal modem doesn't have a receptacle for the telephone or if you're using a PC card modem on a laptop, you must arrange the gang a bit differently. In fact, you have some choices about how all the devices get to the wall jack. Follow these steps:

1. **Put a splitter in the wall jack and insert the cable from the telephone into one receptacle.**
2. **Join the cables coming out of the NIC and the internal modem.**

   You can choose one of the following methods, which also are shown in Figure 4-1:

   A. Use a Y-connector (conveniently, it looks like a capital *Y*), which accepts both of the RJ-11 connectors (one from the modem and one from the NIC) on one end. Insert the RJ-11 connector (at the other end of the Y-connector) into the empty side of the splitter.

   B. Use a splitter to accept both RJ-11 connections, and then plug the splitter into the empty side of the splitter that's in the wall jack.

C. Use a splitter to accept both RJ-11 connections, and then plug the splitter into a length of telephone cable that has a receptacle at one end and an RJ-11 connection at the other end.

D. Use a splitter to accept both RJ-11 connections, and then plug the splitter into a connector that has a receptacle at each end. Then run cable between the connector and the splitter in the wall jack.

If you're using a USB or PC card network adapter, the principle is the same — just substitute your adapter for the NIC shown in Figure 4-1.

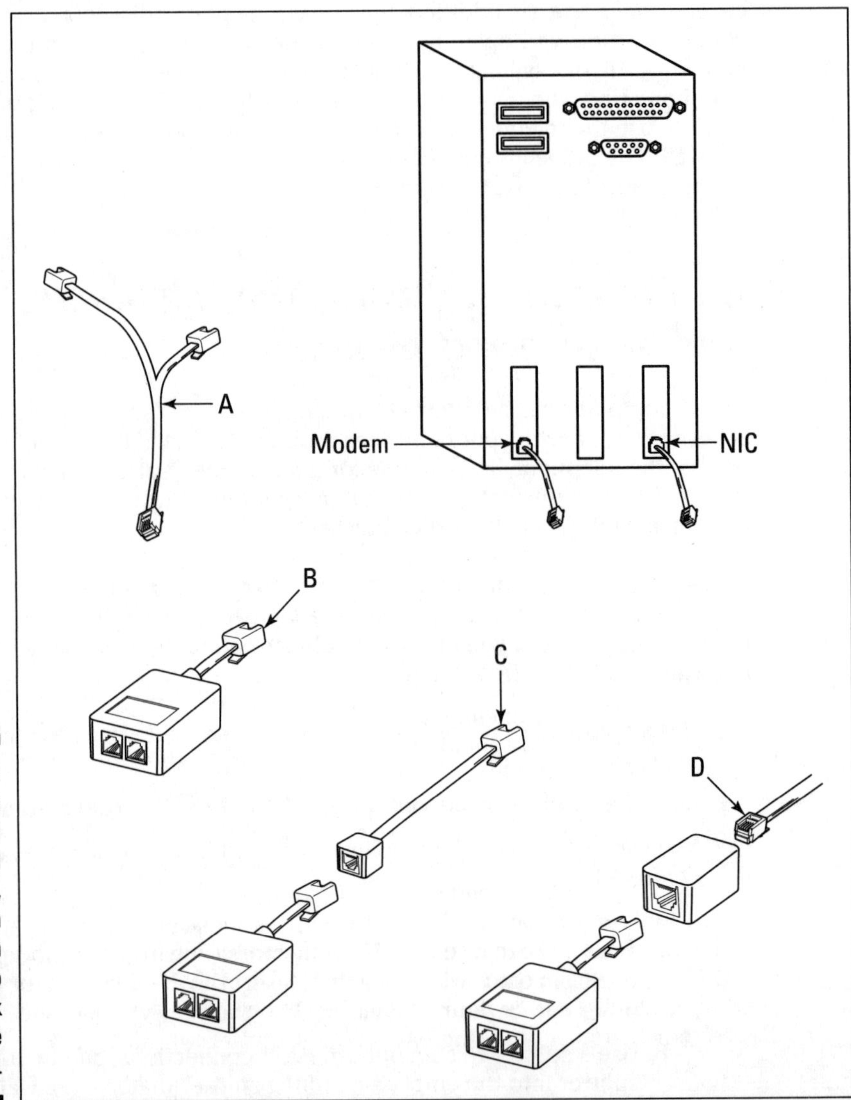


**Figure 4-1:** Gang the internal modem and the NIC, and then send both devices to the wall jack as one connection.

## Too many computers, not enough phone jacks?

Perhaps you have two computers in the same room, but the room has only one phone jack. Maybe you have two computers, each one in its own room, but one of those rooms lacks a phone jack. Relax; it's easy to solve these problems.

If two computers are in the same room, connect one computer to the wall jack and connect the other computer to the second jack in the first computer's network adapter. This is called a *daisy chain,* and it puts both computers on the network. If the computers are in separate rooms, you have to run telephone cable between them. This is easier to do if the rooms are adjacent, but you can buy very long lengths of telephone cable, which means that you can probably connect two computers that are 50 feet apart, or more. If you want to hide the cable, or connect two computers on separate floors, Chapter 3 (which is all about cabling a house for an Ethernet network) is filled with information and tips about getting cable from one place to another in your house.

In fact, you can use the daisy chain approach to attach your whole network to one wall jack, connecting the first computer to the wall jack, connecting the second computer to the other jack in the first computer's network adapter, connecting the third computer to the other jack in the second computer's network adapter, and so on. This frees all the other wall jacks in your house for telephones, modems, and fax machines. A phoneline daisy chain can accommodate up to 25 computers. However, no two computers on the chain can be more than 1,000 feet apart (which shouldn't be a problem, even if you're living in a mansion).

## Phoneline networks and DSL service

You can use your phoneline network even if you've opted to use a digital subscriber line (DSL) modem for Internet access, as long as the DSL service is residential, not business class. Residential DSL is also called *asynchronous* DSL (ADSL), while business-class DSL service is *synchronous* (SDSL). The difference between the two classes of service is the upload speed. ADSL offers fast download speed (when you open a Web page or collect your e-mail, you're downloading) and slower upload speed (when you send files to a server on the Internet or send e-mail, you're uploading). Businesses that need to maintain Web sites use SDSL because they can upload new files and graphics quickly and because SDSL comes with specific IP addresses for their Web servers. In addition, ADSL runs on your existing telephone lines, while SDSL requires the telephone company to bring a separate line into your house.

Even though ADSL uses a different frequency from POTS and computer networking, most DSL providers tell you to put a filtering device on your telephone line to avoid the possibility of interference. These devices are variously referred to as *filters, microfilters,* or *microsplitters,* and they are plugged into a wall jack. Do *not* plug the cable from your network adapter into a filter. Remove the filter, plug in the cable, and then attach the telephone to the second jack on your network adapter. You can use the filter on any wall jack that only has a POTS connection (telephone, fax, or answering machine).

Incidentally, the filter doesn't protect your POTS connections from problems introduced by the DSL connection — it's the other way around. Phoneline technology for POTS is primitive compared to the way technology has learned to use the wires in phone lines in recent years. The filters protect your DSL signal, so the less advanced POTS communications can't interfere with your Internet access.

## Sharing an Internet connection on a phoneline network

Chapter 7 describes the steps required for setting up your Internet connection so that all the computers on the network can share the connection. However, for each networking connection type (Ethernet, phoneline, powerline, or wireless), you must bear in mind, and contend with, specific considerations. In this section, I present an overview of those considerations for phoneline networks.

For any connection type, the technical challenge is to connect the network to the Internet device. If the Internet device uses the same type of wiring, there's no problem. If the Internet device uses a different type of wiring, you have to get from here (your network) to there (the Internet device).

If your Internet device is a telephone modem that's attached to one of the computers on your network, then, by default, your Internet device is using the same type of wiring as your network. Read Chapter 7 to find out how to set up Internet Connection Sharing.

If your Internet device is a DSL/cable modem that is using an Ethernet connection, you get from here (phoneline) to there (Ethernet) by using a bridge. Because bridges cross chasms, that's an apt name for the device, isn't it? A network *bridge* is a device that sits in the middle between two topologies. The bridge has at least one connector that matches the network wiring (let's call it the on ramp) and at least one connector (the off ramp) that matches the wiring of the Internet connection device.

Phoneline bridges have multiple connectors (ports), and the number of connectors varies by manufacturer. All the connectors look the same, so you have to pay attention to the labels.

At least one port is an RJ-11 (telephone line) port that lets the bridge connect to your network. The port may be labeled *phoneline, wall,* or *HPNA.* Connect telephone cable (which is probably included with the bridge) from this port to a wall jack or to the second jack on any network adapter. This connects your bridge to your network. If a second RJ-11 port exists, it's probably labeled *phone,* and you can use that to connect a telephone, modem, or fax machine to the network.

To connect the bridge to your Ethernet modem, look for a port labeled *LAN, Uplink,* or *Ethernet.* This is an RJ-45 connector. Connect that port to your modem using Ethernet Category 5 cable (which is probably included with the bridge). If there's a second RJ-45 port on the bridge, it's to connect the bridge to an Ethernet hub, bridging two networks (one phoneline and one Ethernet). You probably don't need this port, because it's unlikely that you have two disparate networks in your home.

If your Internet connection device is DSL, there's good news. Recently, because of the rising popularity of phoneline networks, manufacturers began offering phoneline DSL modems in addition to the standard Ethernet DSL modems. Your DSL provider may have a kit that you can buy. The kit contains all the equipment you need to create the network and share the Internet connection with all the computers on the network. In fact, some of these devices offer tons of features in addition to home networking and shared Internet access. Those features take advantage of all the nifty things you can do using telephone lines, such as setting up intercom systems and room-to-room dialing, forwarding calls from one extension to another, and lots more.

## Troubleshooting phoneline networks

If your telephone lines generate a lot of static, the problem not only affects regular telephone communication, but it also affects your network communication. For voice services, static is annoying, but it doesn't prevent you from using the telephone. For network communication, static can have a more serious effect. Static can prevent computers from communicating, or it can corrupt the data that's being exchanged across the network.

Static is almost always the telephone company's fault, because its source is almost always the telephone lines entering your house. Telephone cable doesn't age well, because the insulation that protects the cable erodes over time. If the insulation isn't doing its job, the wires can touch each other or be affected by moisture. If your telephone cables are underground, water can be in the duct. If your telephone cables are above ground, the problem with eroding insulation is often compounded by squirrels and other varmints who love to chew on the insulation.

It's been my experience that phone companies aren't terribly cooperative about replacing telephone lines that are deteriorating and causing static. First of all, when you call to complain about static, the technician usually takes the approach that the problem is in the wiring that's inside your house (which most telephone companies won't work on without charging you) or in the telephone you're using. If you have static regardless of the extension you use, and if you've checked with neighbors who report occasional (or constant) static problems, you can be insistent that the problem is in the telephone company's wires, not in your house wiring.

Even when the telephone company admits that its wires are causing the problem, it often replaces one section of wire (perhaps the direct connection between your home and the nearest junction box), but not the wires that run from the junction box back to another box on the system. If static continues, or returns after a short time, you may have to fight to get insulated telephone cable delivered to your house. Your state has a commission that regulates and oversees public utilities such as the telephone company, and the commission has procedures for customers who want to force utility companies to "do it right."

One clue that your telephone lines have static is that telephone modems operate at speeds well below their rating, and even occasionally lose the connection. You can also hear static by picking up the phone, pressing one digit, and listening to the "silence" for a moment — at least it's supposed to be silence.

If your phone lines and phone service are fine, but one or more computers can't communicate with the network, check your phoneline network adapters (and bridge, if you're using one). Read the documentation that came with your phoneline hardware to see which indicator lights should be working and what color the light(s) should be. For example, most phoneline devices have an indicator labeled *link* that displays a green light when the device is working properly. If the green light isn't glowing on one of the network adapters, you need to figure out whether the adapter is broken or whether something is interfering with its ability to function.

To see if the adapter is faulty, change its connection. The best test is to move this adapter to a computer that has a working adapter — just switch the two adapters. This is easier to do if you're using USB adapters, and I doubt that I would want to use this test if I had to open two computers to switch adapters. (This is another reason to buy USB devices.) However, if none of the other tests are conclusive, this is the only way to tell whether the adapter is bad or whether a connection to your phone lines isn't working properly.

Another test is to move the connection point for that adapter. For example, if the adapter is plugged into a wall jack, move it to another wall jack or to the second port on a working adapter (you may have to use a longer telephone cord). If this works, the wall jack may have a problem. If the adapter is plugged into a splitter on a wall jack, remove the splitter and plug the telephone cable directly into the wall. If this works, the splitter is bad. If the adapter is on a USB port, plug another USB device into the port (you may have to borrow one if you don't have any other USB devices). If the new device doesn't work properly, the problem is with your USB port. If the new device works, you can eliminate the USB port as the source of your problem. If you have an internal phoneline NIC, try moving the NIC to another PCI bus.

If none of these tests are conclusive, read the troubleshooting directions in the documentation, check the support pages on the manufacturer's Web site, or call the manufacturer's technical support department.

# Powering Up Your Network with the Electric Company

If you choose your home's power lines for your network, you don't need to run cable through the walls, the floors, or anywhere. Each network adapter plugs into the power outlet on the wall. The manufacturers that make network devices for electrical lines refer to their products (and the topology) as *powerline* devices.

The more I've worked with powerline networks, the more I appreciate this technology. It offers the portability of wireless networks without the annoying hassles that wireless technology introduces. You can put a computer anywhere in the house (or, for that matter, on the porch or the deck), just as wireless users can. The speed of powerline communications is higher and more consistent (it doesn't suffer serious degradation as you move computers farther apart the way wireless does). Nothing interferes with the signal, so you don't have to worry about locating your computer away from anything metal or operating on the same frequency. And, with powerline networking, you escape the annoying "tweaking" of the antennas and computer locations.

## Using USB powerline adapters

Most powerline network adapters are USB devices, which makes installing the network adapters a piece of cake. You don't have to open the computer. Merely plug the USB connector into the USB port on your computer, and then plug the network adapter into the wall outlet. You're done.

Because Windows automatically sees a USB device when you connect it, the operating system launches the process of installing drivers automatically. Walk through the wizard, referring to the documentation that came with your powerline adapter. If your version of Windows doesn't have drivers for your adapter, use the driver(s) on the disk that came with the adapter. Details on performing these tasks are available in Chapter 6.

## Using your built-in Ethernet adapter

Because almost all computers come with a built-in Ethernet adapter, some manufacturers of powerline equipment have come up with a nifty way to use that adapter for powerline networking. You can buy a powerline adapter that connects to your existing adapter. This means you can spare a USB port for other USB devices (such as printers and scanners).

Essentially, these powerline adapters are bridges, because they connect your Ethernet adapter to the powerline adapter with a short Ethernet cable (which comes with the device). The powerline adapter also has a standard plug, which connects to the wall outlet.

## Powerline networks and Internet Connection Sharing

If your Internet device is a telephone modem that's attached to one of the computers on your network, then, by default, your Internet device is using the same type of wiring as your network. All the computers reach the modem over the network, accessing the computer that has the modem, and there's no separate wiring for the modem. Read Chapter 7 to find out how to set up Internet Connection Sharing.

If your Internet connection is a DSL or cable modem, those are Ethernet devices, and you need to connect your powerline network to the Ethernet connection on the modem. The hardware device that accomplishes this trick is a *bridge*. See the discussion about phoneline bridges earlier in this chapter to understand how bridges work and how to make the connections. The only difference is that for powerline networks, you need to connect one end of the bridge to a wall outlet and the other end of the bridge to your DSL or cable modem.

## DSL powerline kits

In addition to powerline adapters and bridges, you can buy powerline devices that combine routers and modems. One device, connected to your DSL telephone line, hooks the entire powerline network into the Internet.

## Powerline security

A potential security problem exists with powerline networking, because a neighbor who is also running a powerline network could access your computers and files. Your immediate neighbors probably share the same transformer that your house uses and may even share some of the same physical wires. This means that network communication within your house could travel to your neighbor's house. The solution to this potential security breach is to create a network password and to encrypt all transmissions between computers on the same network.

Your powerline network adapter has a software CD that contains a security software application that takes care of the potential security problems. Install the software on every computer on your network.

When you install your first powerline adapter software, create a network password by changing the default password (most manufacturers use *HomePlug* as the default password). Enter the new password using any combination of letters, numbers, and capitalization (passwords are case sensitive). Write the password down and don't lose the piece of paper. When you install the other powerline adapters, enter the same password in the security dialog box.

After the software is installed on all the network computers, the computers find each other (because they all have the same password), and all communication across the network is encrypted.

## Troubleshooting powerline communications

I've installed many powerline networks, and they generally run smoothly. However, I've received a couple of troubleshooting calls from families who report that one computer cannot find the network. The same problem existed with each call — the powerline adapters were plugged into surge protectors.

Don't plug adapters into surge protectors. You can use a power strip (handy because the two outlets on the wall plug may not be enough for a computer, monitor, and powerline adapter). However, power strips that have surge protection features don't work properly with powerline network adapters because the technology that provides surge protection can interrupt the flow of data.

Most powerline adapters have built-in surge protection — check the specifications before you buy.

# Chapter 5

# Look Ma, No Wires

### In This Chapter

- Understanding wireless technology
- Positioning computers
- Wireless network security issues
- Finding wireless hotspots for public use

If you opt to use wireless technology, you don't have any cables to run through the walls or the floors, or even from the computer to an outlet. All you have to do is install the wireless network adapters, and their attendant software files (covered in Chapter 6), and you have a network. Of course, you have to perform all the other tasks required to enable file, printer, and Internet sharing, but this book deals with all of that, and it makes it all easy to accomplish.

Sounds cool, doesn't it? Well, it is, most of the time — but not all networks perform well with wireless topology. In this chapter, I explain what you need to know, and also what you need to think about, as you plan and install your own wireless network.

Wireless networks are much easier to install, run, and maintain if all your computers are running Windows XP. Its built-in support for wireless networking makes everything you have to do operate on automatic pilot, saving you all the setup headaches you may encounter in earlier versions of Windows.

## Translating the Geek-Speak of Wireless Technology

To set up a wireless network that works, you have to understand how radio frequency (RF) communications work, and you also have to gain some understanding of the variety of wireless communication standards. Purchasing hardware without this knowledge puts you at risk for incompatible nodes on your network.

## Radio frequency: Hello, den? Kitchen here

The computers on the network communicate via radio waves sent through the air. Attached to the network adapter you installed on each computer is a device called a *transceiver.* It's a thin rubber antenna that pokes out from the adapter. As its name implies, a transceiver both transmits and receives radio waves. The distance the transceiver is certified to traverse varies depending on the wireless technology you've adapted. Check the manufacturer's documentation to find out how far apart you can place computers.

The transceiver that's included with wireless network adapters sends radio waves in a wide arc; it isn't point-and-shoot technology. Each computer is unaware of the location of the other computer(s), and each computer spins its radio waves up, down, and around in the hope of finding a soul mate to talk to.

## Wireless standards — alphabet soup

Wireless network standards are changing faster than any other set of standards in the network communications market. This phenomenon is the result of the growing popularity of wireless network communications. For example, corporate network administrators want to be able to let mobile warriors log on to the main network (cabled with Ethernet) when they show up at the office, without having to provide Ethernet equipment hookups for them. Corporate workers want to be able to amble over to the company's mail server and pick up their e-mail on their handheld devices. The use of wireless technology will result in more (and cleverer) applications for this convenient connection method.

The Institute of Electrical and Electronics Engineers (IEEE) is responsible for setting the standards for wireless local area networks, and the family of specifications is contained in the standards known as 802.11. Currently, the 802.11 family contains three sets of standards for you to choose from: 802.11a, 802.11b, and 802.11g.

### 802.11a

The 802.11a standard is fast, but it often requires more complicated devices and is sometimes more difficult to configure (depending on the type of hardware devices you use on your network). It's most often found in large corporate networks, where it serves its wireless purpose in the midst of wired Ethernet enterprises. Technically, 802.11a can transmit data at a speed of 54 Mbps ("technically" means that speed is rarely achieved in the real world). It uses the 5-GHz band, which is less likely to run into other devices that cause interference problems.

### 802.11b

The 802.11b standard is the standard that was originally called *Wi-Fi* (which stands for wireless fidelity, but almost nobody who uses the term Wi-Fi knows that, because Wi-Fi has become a term that means "network wireless"). Wi-Fi hardware devices are widely available, and they're all reasonably priced. All manufacturers of network devices make Wi-Fi products.

This standard can technically communicate at a speed of 11 Mbps, but I would be surprised if you achieved that speed consistently. One thing I did notice, however, is that 802.11b devices tend to maintain their speed (even if it's less than 11 Mbps) better over long distances than do 802.11a devices.

The 802.11b devices operate on the 2.4-GHz band, which is also used by other radio frequency devices. This could give you a problem with interference. See the section "Detouring around obstructions," later in this chapter, for information about interference.

You may also see devices that are marked as 802.11b+. This is a slightly faster version of 802.11b, but I've read about some problems with compatibility between the two "b" standards if you use equipment from different manufacturers.

To make sure you can purchase Wi-Fi products from multiple manufacturers that can "talk" to each other, a group exists to certify compatibility. WECA (Wireless Ethernet Compatibility Alliance) was formed in 1999 to certify interoperability of wireless local area network products that are built on the IEEE 802.11b specifications. Look for the Wi-Fi certification logo when you buy hardware. However, keep in mind that while hardware compatibility ensures communication, different manufacturers may implement security measures differently (and that's not covered by Wi-Fi certification).

### 802.11g

The 802.11g standard is the new kid on the block, and has become the latest standard for wireless networks. Manufacturers of 802.11g devices advertise communication rates of 54 Mbps, using the same 2.4-GHz band that 802.11b uses.

Some 802.11g devices are marked G+B. This means that they automatically recognize, and communicate with, both 802.11b devices and 802.11g devices. The term used to describe these devices is *dual-band.* Dual-band devices provide a way to expand your existing wireless network without starting all over. (G+A devices are also available for corporate users.) When a G+B device communicates with a device using 802.11g, communication is established at the higher speed possible with 802.11g. However, when a G+B device communicates with a device using 802.11b, the speed drops to that of 802.11b device.

### 802.11i

At the time of writing, the 802.11i standard is still in the development and testing stages. It's Wi-Fi with better security.

# Positioning Computers

You have two issues to consider when deciding where to place computers on a wireless network: the distance between the computers and the need to avoid potential sources of interference with the wireless radio signals.

## How far can you go?

Distance is a serious problem for wireless home networks. Most manufacturers rate the range of wireless adapters at a couple of hundred feet indoors and over a thousand feet in open spaces. But those are technical possibilities, and it's unlikely you'll be able to count on those numbers as you decide on placement for your computers. In fact, many home wireless networks don't achieve half those distances, and some don't achieve a third of them. The distance problem is aggravated (or mitigated, depending on how you look at it) by whether the computers are in a "line of sight" of each other.

If you've planned a nifty wireless network that covers several floors of your home, you'll probably have to redo your plan. You can usually extend the distance of the signals with a hardware device, either a router or an access point. (See the section "Empower Your Network with Hardware Doohickeys," later in this chapter.)

You don't have to move your entire network onto your front lawn to achieve maximum distance, because "open space" means that computers aren't separated by solid structures. For example, if you have a computer in the kitchen and a computer in the family room, and you have one of those "designed for open living space" houses, it's probably fine that the computers are 100 feet or more apart. The separations between the rooms are probably not much more than archways, or even furniture, instead of a solid wall (containing pipes and ducts) with a small doorway.

The farther an RF signal has to travel, the slower it moves. So, you need to decide whether distance or speed is more important to you.

## Detouring around obstructions

Radio waves travel freely in the air until they run up against metal or water. Both elements stop radio waves in their tracks. The water problem probably isn't something to worry about in your house, unless you plan to store your computer under a waterbed. However, the metal problem can be serious.

Plaster walls with metal lath, and walls that hold cast-iron plumbing pipes, frequently interfere with the ability to run a wireless network in a home. Of course, you could replace all the plaster with drywall and replace the drainpipes with PVC pipes, but that seems like a bit much just to have a wireless network. Some people have reported that the metal ducting for heating and air-conditioning systems also interferes with wireless communications.

The problem of metal isn't restricted to what's in your walls. You can't put your computer under a metal desk or in a place where a metal file cabinet or bookcase is between the computers that need to talk to each other.

Another (actually, more common) obstruction that your wireless network may encounter is radio-signal interference. For example, the 2.4-GHz frequency that's used by 802.11b and 802.11g devices is also used by most cordless telephones. In fact, you should always avoid putting a computer near the phone's base station (which is an extremely active transceiver). Microwave ovens also "broadcast" in the 2.4-GHz band, so keep your computers away. In addition, you can experience interference from fluorescent lights.

Incidentally, it's not necessarily only the network communications that bear the brunt of interference; the other device (such as the phone) frequently shares the problem. I have friends with wireless networks who send me rather loud, and extremely annoying, clicking noises when they talk to me on their cordless telephones. They usually don't hear the loud clicks; the clicks only sound like a little bit of static on their end. On my end, the loud clicks drive me crazy. The network problems drive *them* crazy, because a file transfer can suddenly fail because the connection was interfered with.

A less disastrous form of interference comes from any dense obstruction that might be in the path of your wireless signal. By less disastrous, I mean that communications aren't stopped dead, but they're slower and travel only a short distance. For example, a pile of books near the antenna can mess up your wireless signal.

Regardless of the jokes or rumors you may have heard about your electric garage door unexpectedly opening when you transfer files across your wireless network, interference isn't a problem. Garage doors operate in the 433 MHz range, far away from the ranges used by computer network devices.

# Empower Your Network with Hardware Doohickeys

Suppose that you want to share a digital subscriber line (DSL) or cable modem with all the computers on your wireless network. Suppose that you have two computers on the first floor, and you're dying to do work on your wireless-equipped laptop while you relax in your bed (on the second floor), but the signal doesn't reach. Don't worry; manufacturers have come up with some clever hardware devices to overcome your problems. In this section, I give you an overview of some of these doohickeys.

## Wireless routers

By definition, a *router* transfers data between multiple networks. In home networks, you can use a router to move data from one network (your home network) to another network (the Internet). This is how you share a DSL or cable modem Internet connection with all the computers on the network.

A wireless router (frequently called a wireless local-area network (WLAN) router) has an antenna that captures the signals from all the computers on your wireless network, effectively acting like a hub or a switch.

The router also has ports for Ethernet connections. For most wireless home networks, the Ethernet port is used to connect the DSL or cable modem to the router. However, you can also use those ports as a hub for an Ethernet network, essentially combining three networks: the wireless network, an Ethernet network, and the Internet.

A router also provides IP addresses to the computers on the local network. Because it does so, it's acting as a Dynamic Host Configuration Protocol (DHCP) server. The router provides a single point of communication with your DSL or cable Internet service provider (ISP). (The ISP only sees the router, not the individual computers that are on the network.) Some routers even come with built-in firewall capabilities.

WLAN routers are easy to install and configure. You must physically connect the unit to a DSL or cable modem using Ethernet cable. The port is usually labeled *WAN* (for wide-area network) or *Ethernet*. The manufacturer's instructions can help you make the connections.

## Access points

An *access point* is a hardware device that connects the computers on a wireless network to each other (like a hub on an Ethernet network) and to a single access point on an Ethernet network. You can connect an access point to a router, to a hub or switch that connects an Ethernet network, or to an Ethernet adapter in a computer that has connected that adapter to a DSL or cable modem. You use Internet Connection Sharing (ICS) to share the connection). The access point antenna is more powerful than the antennas on your wireless network adapters and provides a way to extend and speed wireless communications.

It's unusual to find an access point in wireless home networks because a router usually serves your purposes better (wireless routers have built-in access points). It's certainly more efficient to share a broadband Internet connection through a router rather than to set up ICS. The computer that holds the Ethernet adapter that connects the modem also has to have a wireless adapter to connect to the network, so you have to install and configure two adapters.

I found one access point (from D-Link) that has the capacity to provide DHCP services, along with other features usually found only in routers. This means you can use the access point instead of a router, and share a broadband connection without having to resort to ICS. You just connect the access point to the cable/DSL modem, using Ethernet cable. (The computers connect to the access point via wireless signals.) I suspect that if this access point sells well, other manufacturers may offer the same enhanced access points.

## Signal boosters

Some manufacturers offer devices called *signal boosters,* which are specifically designed to enhance the wireless signals on your network. Boosters make your transmissions faster, or let them travel further.

However, signal boosters have to be plugged into an access point; they can't stand alone. Manufacturers also offer wireless bridges, which must also be plugged into an access point. These devices aren't generally useful for a home network; they are used in corporate environments that maintain multiple topologies.

# Understanding Wireless Network Security

In a cabled or wired network, you have a built-in method for preventing unwanted visitors from joining your network. All you have to do is keep your eyes open. To join your wired network, a user has to come into your home and plug a computer into one of your network ports. That port may be an RJ-45 connector on an Ethernet hub, a telephone jack, or an electric plug. If somebody came into your house and plugged a computer into a network device, you'd certainly notice.

Your wireless network, however, uses radio waves that can move through walls, ceilings, and doors to receive and transmit data. As a result, any wireless-equipped computer within transmitting distance may be able to join your network. Unless a user yells "Hi, I'm plugging in," you won't know a new node has been added to your network. If your next-door neighbor decides to work on her front lawn on a nice day, her wireless-equipped laptop could inadvertently become a node on your network. A more sinister laptop user could deliberately lurk nearby to grab information from your network computers. At best, the interloper becomes a parasite, getting Internet access from your shared Internet connection. At worst, he gets to the files on your network, or plants viruses on your network computers.

Lacking a direct-port requirement for plugging into your network, you have to find another way to secure your network, and the data it holds.

In small networks (home networks or small business peer-to-peer networks), wireless security is enabled by using two security components: Service Set Identifiers (SSIDs), and data encryption.

The steps required to install and set up these security features are covered in Chapter 6, but in the following sections I'll give you an overview of the wireless security issues and components. My explanations are simplified, in fact over-simplified (this subject is the basis of very thick books), but they should help you understand what your options are as you configure your wireless network components.

## SSIDs

SSIDs are required before your wireless network adapter can talk to other computers on your network. If you're using Windows XP, configuring the SSID is automatic. If you're using an earlier version of Windows, you must go through a configuration process. The configuration steps depend on your version of Windows, and the network hardware you purchased, so check the documentation that came with the hardware. I hate to sound like a nag (even though I've perfected the art of nagging by raising children), but again I'm telling you that if you want a wireless network, you should be running Windows XP. In fact, Windows XP is best for any type of home network.

OS X for Macintosh computers also natively supports wireless networks and installs an SSID.

SSIDs are nothing more than an imitation of the requirement for naming your workgroup — all the wireless computers have to have the same SSID to communicate with each other. Because it's possible for an interloper to configure a computer with the SSID you're using, this doesn't really qualify as a great security measure, but it can prevent accidental intrusions.

If you use the default SSID that's built into your network hardware, anybody can join your wireless network. (In a wired network, if an intruder wanted to join your network by configuring his computer with the same name you applied to your workgroup, he would still have to plug his computer into a port within your home — and that's something you'd notice). To make it difficult for unseen intruders to join your network, you must create a unique SSID for your network, and configure every computer to look for that SSID during startup.

As an experiment (well, to be honest, to win a bet I made with a colleague), I once took a wireless laptop computer configured with the default SSID around a neighborhood. As I wandered across the front lawn of several houses, my laptop found, and joined, the wireless network installed in each house. None of those households had changed the default SSID. I was able to see every shared drive, and could have opened any document in any shared folder. I also could have transferred any file from my computer to the network (including a virus).

If you want some extra income as a computer consultant, perform the same experiment, and then knock on each door, explain you know how to secure wireless networks (because you've read this book), and sign up each household as a client. The extra income will provide a really nice vacation, or even a new car.

## Broadcasting across the airwaves

Most access points (including the access points contained within wireless routers) have a configuration option that lets you determine whether your router broadcasts your SSID. By default, all access points send out a broadcast signal, announcing the network name (the SSID). This makes it easy to find the network when you're attaching a new computer to the network.

However, broadcasting also makes it easy for anyone else within RF range to learn the name of your network, eliminating one of the steps needed to invade your network. For example, I recently set up a wireless network at a friend's house. Immediately after installing a wireless network adapter on one of the computers, the dialog box seen in Figure 5-1 appeared.

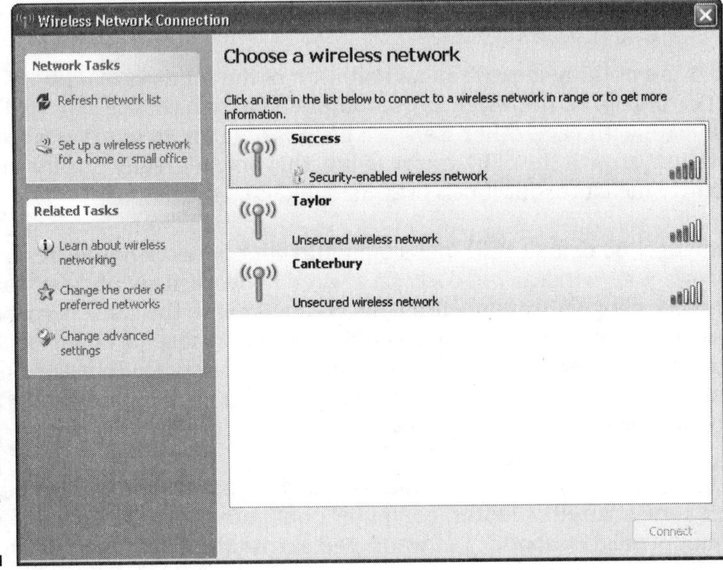


**Figure 5-1:** Look at all the wireless networks available to this computer!

None of the network SSIDs displayed in the dialog box matched our network (we had turned off broadcasting). My friend examined the names, and told me these were his neighbors. Notice that two of his neighbors were not only broadcasting their SSIDs, but were running unsecured networks. With a click of the mouse, I could have joined those networks, giving me access to files, and the opportunity to wreak havoc. To invade the neighbor with the secured network, I would have to know the password. Unlike malicious computer users, I don't have a password-breaking software application on my computer, so I was totally locked out of that network.

Of course, the down side is that if you turn off broadcasting, you have to type in the network SSID every time you add a computer or network device to your network. Big deal! How hard is that?

Turning off broadcasting doesn't turn off the process of sending a broadcast signal every few seconds. Instead, it tells the access point to turn off the display of the SSID during the broadcast. The signal continues to pulse so that you can connect computers to the network.

## Data encryption

You can encrypt data as it passes among the computers on your wireless network. Only the computers you configure as members of your own network can decrypt the data transmissions. The theory is that anyone glomming on to your wireless network won't be able to capture the data that's moving through the network (but the theory is fallible — read on). Two encryption schemes are available for wireless home network equipment: Wired Equivalent Privacy (WEP), and Wi-Fi Protected Access (WPA).

### WEP

WEP is designed to encrypt data as it travels among the computer on your network. To make sure that the computers are entitled to get encrypted data, WEP uses features that verify a computer's participation in the network, such as the SSID, or the specific hardware ID of a network adapter (all computer hardware has a built-in unique ID). Those features are usually called *encryption management functions*.

The network computers can encrypt and decrypt data because the sending and receiving computers have been assigned encryption verification keys (called *shared keys*) during configuration.

Unfortunately, the transmission of the management data, such as the shared keys, the SSID, and even the workgroup name, isn't encrypted — it's clear text that any eavesdropping computer can read (assuming the user has the software required to eavesdrop). Once an eavesdropper has the authentication information, it's a simple task to configure a computer to participate in data exchanges.

WEP doesn't provide a serious, strong, identification challenge for a computer or user that's attempting to receive data. The IDs and the keys are set up during configuration of the network adapters and access points, and they don't change (unless you go to the trouble of changing them manually on every computer). This makes it easy for interlopers to pretend to be authenticated members of the network.

Now that I've disparaged WEP as an encryption device, I urge you to use it if you don't have any way to use WPA, which is stronger (and is covered next). I'm not retracting my opinion, but for home networks, WEP is certainly a feasible and useful security device. It's unlikely that network interlopers are trying to gain your shared keys, or determine the hardware IDs of your adapters, because it's unlikely that you have data on your computers that makes it worth all that effort. WEP prevents casual or inadvertent eavesdropping.

An attacker has to be rather dogged in his efforts if he wants to break WEP security. Of course, if you're in charge of the wireless network at the Pentagon, or at some corporation that is developing a secret formula for making everyone thin without dieting, you should move to WPA. After all, for the kind of information available on your network, interlopers would make the effort to eavesdrop on your network data exchanges. It's unlikely they would do all that work to get into a home network.

### WPA

A new security model, called Wi-Fi Protected Access (WPA), which is approved by the Wi-Fi Alliance, provides more security than WEP.

WPA also works with authentication and keys, but it eliminates many of the security soft spots that WEP contains. All transmissions, including the exchange of management data, are encrypted.

In a corporate network, WPA works with central authentication features, which strengthens the security even more. In a small peer-to-peer network (such as a home network), where no central authentication servers are available for storing keys and other authentication functions, WPA runs in *home mode.* Home mode is also called *Pre-Shared Key (PSK)* mode, and it uses manually-entered keys or passwords that are easy to set up. You set up your keys when you configure your network devices (the steps are covered in Chapter 6).

All you need to do is enter a password (also called a *master key*) for each of your network nodes (computers, access points, and router). WPA runs your security from that point on. The master key allows only devices with a matching master key to join the network, which keeps out eavesdroppers and other unauthorized users. Then, WPA uses encryption algorithms that are more powerful than those provided in WEP.

However, WPA presents a small problem for people who have already installed Wi-Fi hardware — either WEP or WPA security is built into the hardware chips. If your network hardware doesn't support WPA, most manufacturers offer what's called a "firmware update" to move existing wireless hardware to the new security standard. A firmware update is a small software program that applies itself to the chipset (the process is called *burning*). If you have older WEP equipment, you should be able to download the update from the manufacturer at no cost.

Firmware updates are specific to manufacturer and model. You cannot update your model number with a "similar" model number. Installing the wrong firmware turns your hardware into a useless piece of metal. If your model has been discontinued, don't use the firmware for the replacement model. Instead, contact the manufacturer to see if firmware is available for your hardware. If not, continue to use WEP, or buy a new device.

### Mix and match WEP and WPA

If some of your network devices support WEP, and other (newer or updated) devices support WPA, you can mix those devices on your network. However, your network security drops to the level of the weakest security feature, which is WEP. If running WEP makes you nervous, or makes you feel "ungeeky," eventually you should update your network hardware to gain WPA support.

Windows XP, which natively supports wireless communication, has been supplying security patches for users, including the files required for applying WPA (as long as your network hardware supports it). This is just one more reason for using Windows XP exclusively for wireless networks.

Experts claim that WPA isn't a total security solution; it's just better than WEP. Wireless devices that will run on the upcoming 802.11i standard have even stronger security functions. Security for wireless networks is an emerging technology, and as more wireless devices become popular, security will continue to improve.

A real problem with these security features is the way they're applied — some manufacturers only apply higher-level security measures in access points (or in routers, which have built-in access points), instead of applying security features in network adapters. If you're not using an access point, check with your manufacturer to see if you can apply security with your network adapters.

# Wireless Hotspots for Public Use

Throughout the world, companies are setting up public-use wireless networks, called *hotspots,* enabling anyone with a wireless network adapter on a laptop to get to the Internet. You'll find hotspots at airports, chain stores (especially coffee shop chains), and all sorts of other locations.

An up-to-date list of hotspots is available at `www.wi-fihotspotlist.com`. You can search by country, state, or city.

Hotspots are either commercial (you pay a fee to use the network) or public (free). Free hotspots are often available from nonprofit organizations that are committed to eliminating the digital divide that exists among economic levels.

Some corporations provide membership in commercial hotspots to let their mobile warriors join the company network while they're on the road. Goodness, we wouldn't want an employee to have an hour's free time in an airport when she could be working! Two popular commercial hotspot companies are Boingo (`www.boingo.com`) and T-Mobile (`www.tmobile.com`). These companies offer thousands of hotspot locations, and you can enroll online (or start your own hotspot branch as a franchise business).

To use a hotspot, your laptop must have a wireless adapter as well as software that can join the hotspot network. If you're running Windows XP, the operating system discovers the network automatically and asks you if you want to join it. If you do, the operating system automatically finds the technical information it needs and configures your adapter. If you're running an earlier version of Windows, you must have the software and you must know what the software configuration options are; you then must perform a manual setup. That means you must know the network's SSID, which isn't always readily available. Some public hotspots post the SSID on a sign, but if you don't see a sign, you have to ask someone. In an airport, no one may be available (or the person "minding the store" hasn't the vaguest idea what an SSID is). Don't assume that an employee of the coffee-shop hotspot you're using knows the SSID either (trust me).

Some of the hotspot vendors (for example, Boingo) let laptop users who don't have Windows XP installed download software that lets the older versions of Windows operate similarly to Windows XP. The software looks for a wireless signal, notifies you when it finds one, asks you if you want to join the network, and automatically configures your network adapter.

To join the hotspot network, you need to fill out a logon dialog box (just as you do with your own home network). If you have a membership with the hotspot operator, you just fill in your logon name and password. If you don't have a membership, you're asked to fill in credit card information. (Free hotspots tell you the logon name and password to use.) You use your browser to log on, and specific instructions are available from the hotspot provider.

Here are some guidelines for using hotspots:

- You must be using an 802.11b or 802.11g adapter — I know of no hotspots that support 802.11a.
- Some hotspots don't use encryption, so you may have to reconfigure your adapter to turn off encryption. However, more and more hotspots are using WPA.
- Don't use a hotspot that doesn't apply encryption unless you're running a firewall on the computer.
- Even if you're running a firewall, don't send sensitive data through a hotspot because the firewall can't protect data during transmission.
- Be sure to log off when you're done, because the clock that's watching your session and determining the fee you'll pay isn't shut off until a log off closes your session record.

# Part II
# Configuring Computers for Networking

"If it works, it works. I've just never seen network cabling connected with Chinese handcuffs before."

## In this part . . .

After you've installed all the hardware and connected all the computers, you have to perform a few software-based chores. You can put away your tools because you do the rest of the setup stuff at the computer. The only tools you need are keyboards and mice.

The chapters in this part of the book walk you through the tasks required for setting up the software side of networking. None of the tasks are complicated and many of them are automated or semi-automated — the computer does most of the work for you, which is what computers are supposed to do.

Some of the stuff you have to do is routine technical stuff, like installing *drivers* (software files that control hardware devices like NICs). You also have to set up each computer so it's willing to share some of its contents with the rest of the network.

The information in the chapters in this part goes beyond simple networking procedures, because you also learn how to share your Internet connection among all the computers on your network. Installing shared Internet access probably cures more family problems than an expensive therapist. You don't have to set rules about time limits, and you won't hear the whines and yells that echoed through the house when somebody stayed online too long.

# Chapter 6

# Installing Networking Software

*In This Chapter*

- Installing drivers — the software that drives the hardware
- Configuring services — the settings that control communication
- Understanding the Windows home networking wizards — automating all the tasks
- Setting up laptops to switch between home and office networks
- Letting your Macintosh join the party

Simply connecting cable (or antennas) to your home computers doesn't create a network. It's like attaching a VCR to your TV set: After the cable is connected, you still have to set up the system before you can do anything with it, such as record programs. On a computer network, you have to set up everything by installing the software that controls the communication features. This chapter shows you how to do this.

## Install Wireless Doohickeys First

The instructions in this chapter are for installing network adapters, but if you're hooking up a wireless network, you have to install your wireless router or access point first. Then, when you install your wireless network adapters, they'll be able to find the wireless network. The specifics for installation and configuration vary among manufacturers, but I'll go over the general tasks you need to perform.

### Installing the software

Most routers and access points require you to install software before you connect the device to a computer. Follow the instructions included with the device, which either tell you to install a software application, or install drivers.

## Some computers have two NICs

If you had a digital subscriber line (DSL)/cable modem before you created a home network, your computer already has a network interface card (NIC), because you need a NIC to connect to the modem. Some people decide to keep that NIC dedicated to the modem and install a second NIC for the network. Other people switch the NIC to the network and then let the network join the modem, either through the hub or through a router. You find advantages and disadvantages to each decision, and I discuss these issues in Chapter 7.

In the meantime, throughout this chapter, you find out about settings for NICs. So, if you have two NICs in your computer, you need to know which NIC to work on when I tell you to open the Properties dialog box for your NIC or when a networking wizard wants to apply settings to a NIC.

When you're following the steps in this chapter for configuring the network, perform all the tasks on the NIC that's dedicated to the network — not the NIC that's connected to the modem (which is your Internet-connection NIC). In Chapter 7, I walk you through the steps for configuring the Internet-connection NIC.

If you're using one of the Windows wizards to set up your network, you'll be setting up both the network and the Internet connection. The wizard asks you to identify the networking NIC and the Internet-connection NIC because the wizard needs that information.

### *Connecting to an Ethernet adapter*

Here's the dilemma — to install and configure a wireless router or an access point, you must connect to the device with Ethernet cable. After the device is set up, you can disconnect the Ethernet connection, and let the device perform its tasks wirelessly. Your router or access point has an Ethernet cable in the box, along with a software disk, and instructions.

If you're connecting wireless computers to an existing Ethernet network, just plug the access point into your concentrator. You can access the device from any computer on the network that's attached to the concentrator.

Most computers come with an Ethernet adapter built in, and if one of your computers has one, you can connect the router/access point to it. Check the back of your computer to see if you have one. Don't confuse an Ethernet adapter with a telephone modem (also built in to many computers). Here are some clues to telling which is which.

- The documentation that came with your computer should have information about the devices installed in the computer.
- A telephone modem adapter usually has two connectors — one for the modem and one for a telephone.

- The Ethernet connector at the end of the cable is an RJ-45 connector, which is slightly larger than the RJ-11 connector for telephone wire. A telephone wire connector falls out of an RJ-45 port, and an Ethernet cable connector doesn't slide into an RJ-11 port easily.
- The Device Manager dialog box includes an Ethernet adapter in the list of devices if you have one. (Right-click My Computer, and choose Properties to find the Device Manager — the exact location varies depending on your version of Windows. Chapter 15 has information about using Device Manager.)

If you have no Ethernet adapters on any computers on your network, take the router/access point to a friend who has a computer with an Ethernet adapter. Set up the device, and bring it home.

## Configuring the device

Open the browser on the computer attached to the device and enter the device's IP address in the Address Bar. Then enter the User ID and password noted in the documentation.

When the configuration window appears, use the tabs to set up the device, using the information from your ISP and from the documentation that came with the device.

For routers, you must use the settings provided by your ISP, including (but not necessarily limited to):

- The subnet mask.
- The IP address of the ISP's gateway.
- The IP address of the ISP's DNS server (or multiple DNS servers).

### Ad-hoc mode versus infrastructure mode

Wireless networks can be established in two ways: using Ad-hoc mode, or using infrastructure mode. Ad-hoc mode is used when you just want two or more wireless computers to find each other. This is useful if all you want to do is access the other wireless computers (for exchanging files). Infrastructure mode means you've installed an access point or a router (or both) so that you can take advantage of security features (such as assigning an SSID and encrypting communication as explained in Chapter 5), and can share an Internet connection. Throughout all my discussions of wireless networks in this book, I'm assuming you're using infrastructure mode.

The documentation for the device provides information for the router's settings, including (but not necessarily limited to):

- Entering a new password to replace the default password.
- Setting up DHCP services.
- Setting security values.
- Setting firewall options (if the router includes a firewall).

After your router is set up, you can disconnect the Ethernet cable and let the antenna connect to the wireless adapters you'll be installing (covered next).

# Installing Drivers for Network Adapters

Your network connectors — network interface cards (NICs), Universal Serial Bus (USB) connectors, and so on — are hardware devices, and every hardware device on a computer needs a *driver.* Drivers are files that the operating system uses to communicate with the hardware, telling the hardware what to do, when to do it, and how to do it.

After you physically install the network adapter, Windows should discover it automatically the next time you start your computer. The Windows Plug and Play feature goes to work while the operating system is starting up and begins installing the software drivers immediately. If Windows doesn't automatically find the hardware and offer to install the software, your hardware is not Plug and Play compliant, and you have to install the driver software manually. The following sections detail how to install drivers for either scenario.

Windows discovers USB devices as soon as you connect them. You don't have to turn off your computer to connect a device to a USB port.

## The Plug and Play way

The Plug and Play feature is like a little elf that looks at all the hardware in your computer during startup, and when a new Plug and Play hardware component is detected, he notifies Windows. As soon as Windows hears about the new hardware, it wants to begin installing the software drivers immediately.

Windows sends a message to your screen to tell you that it has found the new hardware you added, and asks if you want to install it. Say Yes to begin the installation, which is accomplished via a Windows wizard named, appropriately enough, the Add New Hardware Wizard.

If your network connector is a USB device, and you installed it while your computer was running, the Windows Plug and Play elf was watching and offered to install the software as soon as you installed the connector — you didn't have to restart the computer. This ability to install a device without shutting down the computer is called a *hot installation,* and it's one of the coolest things about USB devices (yes, that's a pun).

When you tell Windows you want to install the network hardware that the Plug and Play feature discovered, a wizard shows up to walk you through each step of the process. Figure 6-1 shows the first window of the wizard, but the graphics and text you see may differ, depending on the version of Windows you're using. However, the graphics and text are just the glitzy stuff, and the wizard's behavior is the same across all versions of Windows, except Windows XP. (Read on, I explain the differences in the way Windows XP works throughout these sections.)

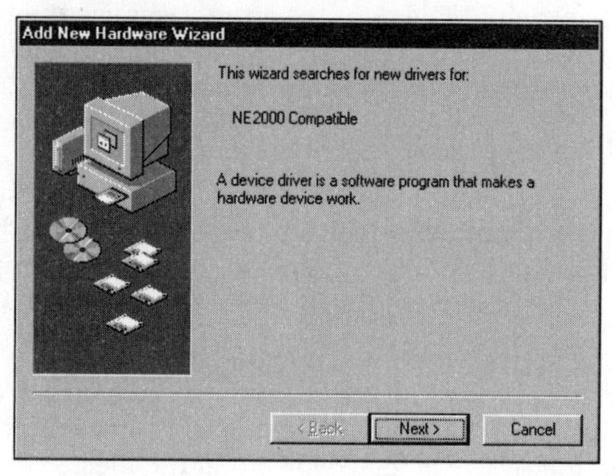


**Figure 6-1:** It's easier to install drivers when a wizard shows up to hold your hand.

The wizard works by asking questions and offering choices. As you complete each step, click the Next button to move to the next wizard window. You can also click the Back button if you want to return to a previous window and change your answers.

For this particular task (installing drivers for your network hardware), the wizard has only a few questions. Essentially, the wizard is trying to figure out where to find the files it needs. You have a crib sheet you can check before you give the wizard any answers; it's in the documentation that accompanied your network hardware.

Luckily, this stuff isn't overly complicated, because you have only three choices.

- **Drivers built into Windows.**

  Windows has built-in drivers for lots of models from many manufacturers. The list of built-in drivers varies among the versions of Windows (more drivers are included in the more recent versions of Windows). If Plug and Play found your hardware, your version of Windows probably has the drivers you need.

  The drivers for your adapter may have been copied to your hard drive when Windows was installed, or they may be on the original Windows CD, so you should have the CD at hand just in case you need it.

  If you purchased your computer from a manufacturer that preinstalled Windows, you may not have a Windows CD with drivers. However, the manufacturer installed all those files in a folder on your hard drive.

- **Drivers included by the hardware manufacturer.**

  Many manufacturers provide their own drivers, enclosing a CD or a floppy disk in the packaging. They do this either because they know that Windows doesn't provide the drivers, or they've updated and improved the drivers since your version of Windows was released.

- **Drivers you downloaded from the Web.**

  Manufacturers update drivers periodically, and you can find their Web site information in the documentation that came with the hardware. Look for a link on the manufacturer's home page that says support, drivers, or software.

  Microsoft also keeps up with drivers, and you can travel to `www.microsoft.com/windows/default.asp` to see if new drivers for your adapter are available there. Click the link to your version of Windows, and then follow the links to download the files.

The following three sections offer further details on how to complete the Add New Hardware Wizard, based on the drivers you're using.

### Using Windows drivers

The wizard offers to search for the best driver for your hardware and displays a message that says this is the recommended option. If the documentation for your adapter indicates that you can (or should) use Windows drivers, let the wizard do the searching for you.

The wizard starts by checking the driver files that were transferred to your hard drive when you installed Windows. If the files are there, the wizard moves on, displaying the name of the adapter for which it has a driver and inviting you to click Next to install the driver.

If you're running Windows XP, no wizard appears if the drivers are available on your hard drive. Windows just installs the drivers and displays a message telling you that your new hardware has been installed. The procedure takes only a few seconds. This is called a *silent install,* and it's one of the features that makes Windows XP so efficient. In fact, during installation, Windows XP copies more drivers to the hard drive than any previous version of Windows, so you almost always have a silent install of new hardware devices.

If the files aren't on the hard drive, the wizard asks you to insert the Windows CD in the CD-ROM drive. If your Windows operating system was installed by the computer manufacturer, the files you need are probably already on your hard drive and no CD exists for you to insert. You need to know the path of the folder that holds the operating system files. (Look for a folder named Win98, WinMe, WinXP, or WinCabFiles.)

Press and hold Shift when you insert the CD to prevent the disk from starting the Setup program automatically.

### *Using the manufacturer's drivers*

If the documentation for the NIC indicates that you should use the drivers supplied by the manufacturer, insert the disk that came with your NIC. Depending on the version of Windows you're using, the wizard options for using the manufacturer's drivers vary. In some versions of Windows, the wizard offers an option to display a list of drivers in a specific location. In other versions of Windows, the wizard offers a Have Disk button. Both options get you to the same place — a wizard window that asks you where the drivers are.

In the window that asks for the location, type the drive letter for the disk that holds the software drivers. For a floppy disk, type **A:**. For a CD, enter the drive letter assigned to your CD-ROM drive (usually **D:**).

### *Using downloaded drivers*

If you want to use drivers you downloaded, remember that most of the time the file you download isn't a driver — it requires you to run the program you downloaded in order to extract the drivers. After the drivers are extracted, the process is the same as using the manufacturer's drivers. Select the option to search a specific location, or click the Have Disk button. Then enter the location where you saved the driver files on your hard drive. If you don't remember the name of the folder, click the Browse button and select the correct drive and folder, as shown in Figure 6-2.

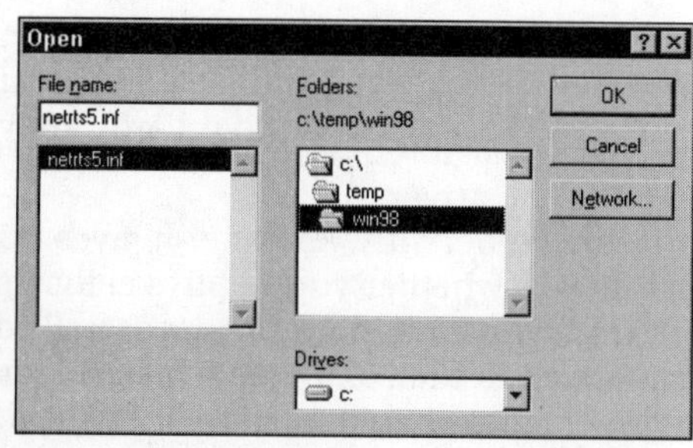


**Figure 6-2:** Select the drive and folder in which you saved your downloaded drivers.

After the files are transferred to your hard drive, Windows displays a message telling you to restart your computer to have the new settings take effect. Click Yes to restart Windows.

## Doing it yourself

If your network hardware isn't Plug and Play, or if Windows fails to detect it during startup, you need to install the drivers manually. Relax, it's easy. In fact, you're performing the same tasks that the Add New Hardware Wizard performs, except that you have to select options instead of letting the wizard roll along on automatic pilot.

If your version of Windows doesn't have a driver for the hardware in its driver's database, Plug and Play may not detect it.

Manual installation of hardware starts with the Add New Hardware Wizard, but instead of running on automatic pilot, the wizard expects you to point the way. You can use this method to install Windows drivers, manufacturer's drivers, or drivers you downloaded from a Web site. Here's how:

1. **Choose Start⇨Settings⇨Control Panel.**

   The Control Panel window opens.

   (In Windows XP, choose Start⇨Control Panel.)

2. **Double-click the Add New Hardware icon.**

   The Add New Hardware Wizard window opens.

   (In Windows XP, click Printers and Other Hardware, and then, in the left pane, click Add Hardware.)

3. **Click Next to begin.**

   The wizard tells you it's going to look for new hardware devices. It doesn't matter that you know it's probably not going to work — if your new device were Plug and Play, it would have been detected when you started your computer. However, this wizard is obstinate and offers no option named "don't bother."

4. **Click Next to start the search for Plug and Play hardware.**

   Wait for the wizard to give up. After the fruitless search ends, the wizard offers to search for hardware that isn't Plug and Play. This search is a silly waste of time, because you know exactly what hardware you want to install.

   The Windows XP wizard works differently, and after it gives up the search for new hardware, it asks whether you've physically installed the hardware yet. Select Yes if you have. Selecting No installs drivers before the hardware is attached to the computer, which is handy for manufacturer-supplied drivers that should be installed before the hardware is installed (the documentation that comes with the hardware explains the procedure). Then, after you install the hardware and restart the computer, the drivers are on your hard drive, and Windows XP performs a quick silent install.

5. **Select the No, I want to select the hardware from a list option, and click Next.**

   The Hardware Types list appears.

6. **Select Network Adapters, and click Next.**

   The Select Device dialog box opens to display a list of manufacturers and models, as shown in Figure 6-3.

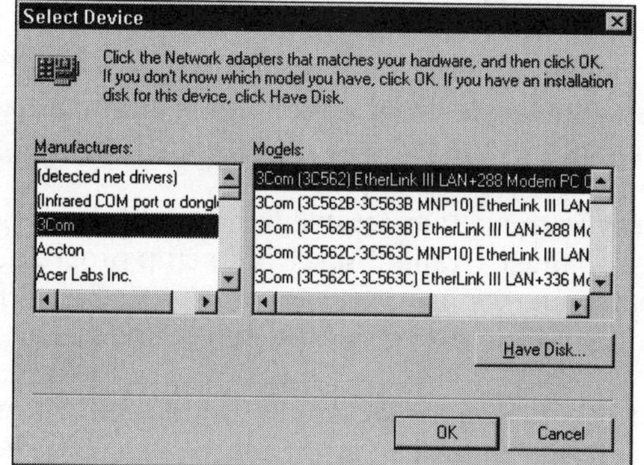


**Figure 6-3:** Choose the manufacturer and model of your network adapter, or opt to install your own drivers.

7. **If your network adapter is listed and you're planning to install drivers from the Windows CD, select the adapter's listing and click Next.**

   Windows finds the drivers on your Windows CD and copies the files to your hard drive.

8. **If you have drivers from the manufacturer or from a Web site, click Have Disk.**

   The Install From Disk dialog box appears, as shown in Figure 6-4. Enter the drive letter for the location of the manufacturer's disk, or click Browse to find downloaded drivers on your hard drive.

**Figure 6-4:** Direct the wizard to the drive that holds the files.

9. **Follow the wizard's instructions to finish installing the drivers.**

   After the files are copied to your hard drive, the System Settings Change dialog box appears, informing you that you must restart the computer to have the new settings take effect. Click Yes to restart the computer.

## Special tasks for installing ISA NICs

If you purchased a NIC for an Industry Standard Architecture (ISA) bus on an older computer, you may have to do some extra work to install the NIC properly. The manufacturer should have included instructions for performing these tasks, but frequently they're not very clear. This section presents an overview of the chores that you face.

If your NIC is installed on a Peripheral Component Interconnect (PCI) bus, the bus and the operating system take care of setup chores automatically. See Chapter 1 for a discussion of ISA and PCI bus types.

Some NICs have software programs that establish the settings you need; other NICs have jumpers that you must arrange. Many NIC setup programs run in an MS-DOS session; the documentation instructs you to choose Start⇨Run and then type a command in the Open text box of the Run dialog box.

Most of the time, the setup program can determine which settings are available for the NIC. These settings involve an interrupt request (IRQ) level and an input/output (I/O) address, which are technical specifications that guarantee that your NIC has a unique position in the technical scheme of things for your computer. (I won't bother you with all the technical explanations, because it's only important to know that they're unique to this piece of hardware.)

You can use the setup program that comes with the NIC to specify a particular IRQ level and I/O address. Some NICs don't use software to configure the settings. Instead, they use jumpers. A *jumper* is a small piece of plastic that "jumps" across pins, and whether the pins are "jumpered" determines the settings. The NIC comes with documentation that explains all the possible settings and how to position the jumpers to create the setting you need.

Sometimes you need to wait until you've finished the installation (with incorrect specifications) and then correct the specifications, such as when the default settings for the NIC conflict with the settings for another device on your computer.

### Determining which settings are available

Determining the unused IRQ and I/O settings before installation is faster and more efficient than waiting until later. You can determine the unused IRQ and I/O settings by following these steps:

1. **Right-click the My Computer icon on the desktop, and choose Properties from the shortcut menu that appears.**

   The System Properties dialog box opens.

2. **Click the Device Manager tab.**

   A list of all the devices in your computer appears.

   (In Windows 2000 and Windows XP, click the Hardware tab and then click the Device Manager button.)

3. **Click Print (or click the Printer icon).**

   The Print dialog box for Device Manager opens.

4. **Select System Summary, and click OK.**

   A summary report of the resources in your computer prints. These reports are usually about three pages long.

The IRQ Summary section of the report lists all the IRQs currently in use, and any missing number is considered to be available (numbers range from 0 to 15).

The I/O Port Summary section of the report lists all the I/O addresses currently in use. When your NIC setup program presents possible I/O addresses, select one that isn't being used by another device. Then follow the instructions that came with your NIC to set the IRQ and I/O specifications.

### Checking the installation settings

During the installation of the drivers, Windows determines the settings of your NIC. The determination may or may not be accurate. After installation, you need to check the settings attached to the NIC to make sure that they're accurate, which you can do by following these steps:

1. **Right-click the My Computer icon on the desktop, and choose Properties from the shortcut menu that appears.**

   The System Properties dialog box opens.

2. **Click the Device Manager tab.**

   (In Windows 2000 and Windows XP, click the Hardware tab and then click the Device Manager button.)

3. **Click the plus sign next to the listing for Network Adapters.**

   Windows reveals the specific entry for your NIC when the Network Adapters category expands.

4. **Right-click the listing for your NIC, and choose Properties.**

   The Properties dialog box for your NIC opens, with the General tab in the foreground.

If everything is fine, the Device Status section of the dialog box displays a message that says the device is working properly. If a problem exists, the message warns you that the device is not working properly.

If a problem exists with the NIC settings, the Network Adapters listing is probably already expanded when you select the Device Manager tab. The listing for your NIC probably has a symbol over its icon, either an exclamation point or an *X*. The symbol indicates that a problem exists with the settings for the NIC.

In either case, you should check the specific settings. Click the Resources tab to see the settings (see Figure 6-5). If the dialog box indicates there's a problem, see the next section, "Changing the NIC settings."

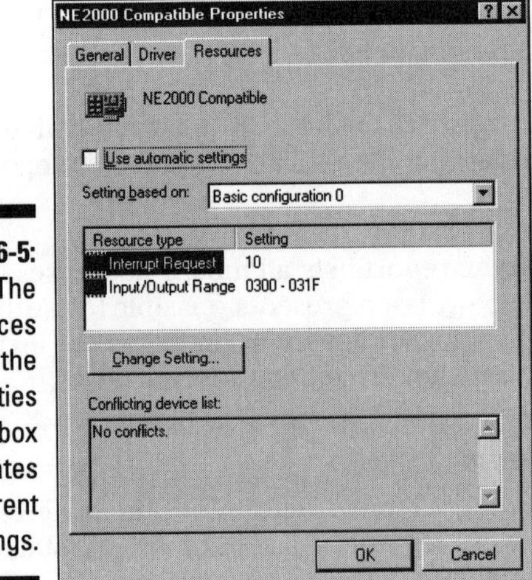


**Figure 6-5:** The Resources tab of the Properties dialog box enumerates the current settings.

## *Changing the NIC settings*

You may need to change the NIC settings if you couldn't successfully install the NIC or if Windows couldn't correctly identify the NIC, the IRQ level, or the I/O address.

If everything didn't work properly and the settings are incorrect, you must correct them. This process is sometimes complicated and sometimes easy. Sorry, but I can't be more specific than that. Follow along to see which set of circumstances matches your situation.

### *When IRQ and I/O settings don't match the NIC settings*

You know what the IRQ and I/O settings are, either from the documentation that came with the NIC or from the preinstallation setup program that you ran. To set the IRQ and I/O settings to match the NIC settings, follow these steps:

1. **Select the incorrect setting.**

   If both the IRQ and I/O settings are wrong, select each one, one at a time.

2. **Click the Change Setting button.**

   **You may first have to deselect the option Use automatic settings.**

   The Edit Interrupt Request dialog box or the Edit Input/Output Range dialog box opens.

3. **Change the setting to match the physical setting of the NIC.**

   Type the correct number, or use the arrows to select a new setting.

4. **Click OK three times to close all the open dialog boxes.**

   You'll probably be told to restart the computer to have your changes take effect.

### When the settings match but have a conflict

If the settings that appear match the settings you configured for the NIC but the installation still isn't working properly, you may have a conflict with another device. You need to rerun the preinstallation program for your NIC to change the setting that has a conflict.

Don't rerun the preinstallation program for your NIC blindly. You could spend half your life guessing the settings. Refer to the section "Determining which settings are available," earlier in this chapter, to make sure you know which IRQ or I/O settings are available and are not being used by another device.

# Installing Network Protocols and Services

If you're running Windows XP or Windows Me on any computer, you can automate all the steps in this section for every computer on the network (except Windows 2000 Professional, which won't work with the Windows Home Networking Wizard). This magic is accomplished with the Windows Home Networking Wizard. See the section "Using the Windows Home Networking Wizards," later in this chapter.

Computers that are connected in a network have to talk to each other. That's how they find each other and exchange files. In order to talk to each other, all the computers must speak the same language. The computer jargon for the language that computers use to communicate is called *networking protocol.* You need to install at least one networking protocol on each computer on your network.

The "mouthpiece" for communications between computers is the network adapter. The process of connecting the language to the mouthpiece (the protocol to the adapter) is called *binding.* After the protocol is bound to the NIC, your computers can talk to each other.

Once the computers can communicate, you can do stuff between computers. Each task you want to perform is a *service.* Services include sharing files, sharing printers, and logging on to the network.

## Deciding on a protocol

Windows provides a number of protocols, including these two commonly used protocols:

- **NetBIOS Extended User Interface (NetBEUI):** This protocol is a simple, efficient one that works on peer-to-peer networks and client/server networks running earlier versions of Windows (such as Windows NT). See Chapter 1 to find out about the different types of networks.
- **Transmission Control Protocol/Internet Protocol (TCP/IP):** This protocol is used on the Internet and is also used by many companies for running large networks.

On older versions of Windows, when you install a NIC as described in the previous sections, Windows may automatically install another protocol, IPX/SPX (Internetwork Packet Exchange/Sequenced Packet Exchange). Novell developed this protocol for its NetWare network operating system. Microsoft also has its own flavor of IPX/SPX, and for some reason, it's part of the installation of a NIC in some earlier versions of Windows. Unless you have a NetWare server on your home network (which would certainly be surprising), you won't be using this protocol, so you can safely remove it.

Making a decision about which protocol to use for your home network isn't always easy. The two choices to consider, NetBEUI and TCP/IP, each have pros and cons. However, the version of Windows and the hardware on your network may force a decision. Following are the things you need to know to make a decision about the protocol for your network:

- Sharing an Internet connection with a DSL or cable modem requires TCP/IP.
- Windows XP automatically assumes TCP/IP, and it requires some rather complicated extra steps to configure it for NetBEUI. In fact, if any computers on your network are running Windows XP, you should use TCP/IP and forget NetBEUI.

- If you're using a telephone modem, you can share an Internet connection with NetBEUI, and the Internet Connection Sharing feature takes care of the TCP/IP details (see Chapter 7). However, you have to take the time and effort to install NetBEUI on any Windows XP computer on your network.
- NetBEUI is easier to install, because TCP/IP requires some extra steps.

Want my advice? Here's my list of criteria for making this decision:

- If any computer on your network is running Windows XP, use TCP/IP.
- If you use a DSL or cable modem (or plan to in the near future), use TCP/IP.
- If you're going to be buying a new computer in the near future, it will be running Windows XP, so use TCP/IP.
- If your network is made up entirely of computers running Windows 98 Second Edition and Windows Me, and you're never going to buy another computer, use NetBEUI. When you configure your modem and create a Dial-Up connection, Windows automatically adds TCP/IP to that connection.

## Adding a protocol

Depending on your version of Windows, when you installed the software (drivers) for your network adapter, either NetBEUI or TCP/IP may have been installed automatically. That means if you've decided to use TCP/IP, you may have to add that protocol to your Windows 98 computers. If you've decided to use NetBEUI, you may have to add it to your Windows XP computers.

You'll probably need the Windows CD to access the files for the protocol you're installing, so put it in the CD-ROM drive (unless your Windows files were preinstalled on your hard drive, in which case the installation program finds them automatically). Then follow these steps:

1. **Choose Start⇨Settings⇨Control Panel.**

   In Windows XP, choose Start⇨Control Panel. The Control Panel window opens.

2. **Double-click the Network icon.**

   In Windows XP, choose Network and Internet Connections and then click the Network Connections icon. Right-click the Local Area Connection icon, and click Properties in the menu that appears.

   The Network dialog box opens, with the Configuration tab in the foreground (the General tab in Windows XP).

(In Windows 2000 Professional, the icon is named Network and Dial-up Connections. When you double-click the icon, a new window opens. Double-click the Local Area Connection icon, and then click the Properties button.)

3. **Click Add or click Install.**

   The button labels differ, depending on the version of Windows.

   The Select Network Component Type dialog box opens. The items listed in the dialog box differ, depending on the version of Windows you're running. However, all versions of Windows display a choice named Protocol.

4. **Select Protocol and then click Add.**

   The Select Network Protocol dialog box opens. If you're running Windows 98, select Microsoft from the Manufacturer list. Newer versions of Windows don't offer any choices except Microsoft.

5. **Choose NetBEUI or TCP/IP from the Network Protocols list.**

   Windows XP does not display a listing for NetBEUI — see the sidebar "Installing NetBEUI in Windows XP," later in this chapter.

6. **Click OK.**

   You return to the Network dialog box.

7. **Click OK in the Network dialog box.**

   The necessary files are transferred to your hard drive. The Systems Settings Change dialog box opens and prompts you to restart your computer.

8. **Restart your computer.**

If you want to install both protocols, repeat these steps for the second protocol.

# Configuring TCP/IP

If you install TCP/IP, you have to do some additional setup work. TCP/IP requires each computer on the network to have its own address, called an IP address. An *IP address* is a string of numbers that identifies the computer. No two computers on your network can have the same IP address. (The same thing is true on the Internet, where every Web site you visit is on a computer with a unique IP address.)

## TCP/IP and shared Internet connections

You can share an Internet connection by letting all the computers on the network access a modem that's attached to one computer. To do this, you must run the Internet Connection Sharing program, called ICS, which is available on all versions of Windows since Windows 98 Second Edition.

## Installing NetBEUI in Windows XP

Windows XP doesn't list NetBEUI as an available protocol. It's not that you can't run NetBEUI on Windows XP; you certainly can. Microsoft just decided that because TCP/IP is its protocol of choice, they would make it harder for you to use the NetBEUI protocol on their newer versions of Windows (this is called a psychological deterrent).

The Windows XP CD has the files you need to make NetBEUI available. Insert the CD in the CD-ROM drive, and follow these steps to install NetBEUI:

1. **Choose Start⇨My Computer.**
2. **Click the Folders icon on the toolbar to display drives and folders in the left pane.**
3. **In the left pane, expand the folder listings for the CD and select the Valueadd\MSFT\Net\NetBEUI subfolder.**
4. **In the right pane, right-click `Nbf.sys` and choose Copy.**
5. **In the left pane, expand the folder listings for drive C and right-click the Windows\System32\Drivers folder.**
6. **Choose Paste to copy the Nbf.sys file to the Drivers folder.**
7. **In the left pane, return to the Valueadd\MSFT\Net\NetBEUI folder.**
8. **In the right pane, right-click Netnbf.inf and choose Copy.**
9. **In the left pane, right-click the C:\Windows\Inf folder.**
10. **Choose Paste to copy the Netnbf.inf file to the Inf folder.**

By default, the Windows\Inf folder is hidden in My Computer and Windows Explorer. To see it, choose Tools⇨Folder Options, click the View tab, and select the option Show Hidden Files and Folders.

Now, when you want to add a protocol to your Windows XP computer, NetBEUI is listed as an available protocol.

If you have a telephone modem, ICS is your only option, because you cannot let each computer on the network connect to the modem individually. The computer that has the modem becomes the *host computer,* and all the other computers are called *client computers.* The clients connect to the host to share the modem's connection to the Internet. If the host computer isn't running, the clients can't get to the Internet.

However, if you're using a DSL or cable modem, it's easier to share the Internet connection through a router, which is a hardware device that connects multiple computers to the modem. In fact, if you buy a router with multiple connectors for computers, you don't have to buy a concentrator, because the router is also a switch (in addition to providing shared Internet access). The router becomes the host, and all computers on the network are clients. It doesn't matter if any computers on the network aren't running — every computer connected to the router can access the Internet. Chapter 7 has detailed instructions about using routers.

### Setting the IP addresses

The host provides the IP addresses for all computers on the network (*all* is explained in Chapter 7), so you must configure each computer's IP address with that in mind, using the following steps:

1. **Open the Network icon in the Control Panel, as described in the preceding section.**
2. **In the Components list, select TCP/IP and click Properties.**

   Don't select the TCP/IP-Dial-up adapter listing (if one exists). Instead, select the TCP/IP listing that's linked to the name of your network adapter. Doing so opens the TCP/IP Properties dialog box.
3. **Select the option Obtain an IP address automatically.**

   The option may already be selected (it's commonly the default selection).
4. **Click OK.**

## Adding network services

The first service that you probably want to add is File and Printer Sharing for Microsoft Networks so that you can share your files and your printer with users on the other computers. Then, if you want to log on to your network with a user name, you can add one of the client services. I discuss these options in this section.

For Windows 98/Me, you need to have your Windows files available, so make sure the Windows CD is in the CD-ROM drive before you begin.

### Adding the File and Printer Sharing service

Because the File and Printer Sharing service is so common, you don't have to go through the Add Services dialog box to install it — Microsoft provides a button for quick access to the installation of this service. Follow these steps to add the File and Printer Sharing service to your system:

1. **Open the Properties dialog box for your NIC, as described earlier.**
2. **Select the File and Print Sharing option.**

   In Windows 98, you must first click the File and Print Sharing button and then select the option.

### Adding network client services

Client services are added to networks to provide a way for individuals to log on to the network. In a client/server network (where all the computers on the network are connected to one server computer), the server authenticates the logon name and password. In a peer-to-peer network (where all the computers on the network can access all the other computers), the logon provides a method of keeping track of users and their preferences. See Chapter 9 for more information about users and logon names.

When you open the Properties dialog box for your NIC, as described in the following steps, you should see a listing for Client for Microsoft Networks. If not, you must install it, using the following steps:

1. **Choose Add or Install.**

   The Select Network Component Type dialog box opens.

2. **Choose Client, and click Add.**

   The Select Network Client dialog box opens. In Windows 98, select Microsoft in the Manufacturer's list. Windows Me/2000/XP offers no manufacturers except Microsoft.

3. **Choose a client service from the right pane.**

   Choose Client for Microsoft Networks to log on to the network with your user name.

4. **Click OK.**

   The necessary files are transferred to your hard drive, and you return to the Network dialog box.

5. **Click OK in the Network dialog box.**

   The Systems Settings Change dialog box opens, prompting you to restart the computer.

6. **Restart your computer.**

## Naming computers and workgroups

The Microsoft networking system is fussy about keeping things straight. The networking services want to know who's who, who's where, and what's what. Because of this compulsive attitude, you must give each computer on your network a unique name. In addition, you must name the group that exists when all the computers that are linked on the network get together.

### *Naming names in Windows 98 and Windows Me*

To set computer names and workgroup names in Windows 98/Me, follow these steps:

1. **Choose Start⇨Settings⇨Control Panel.**

   The Control Panel window opens.

2. **Double-click the Network icon.**

   The Network dialog box opens.

3. **Click the Identification tab (see Figure 6-6).**

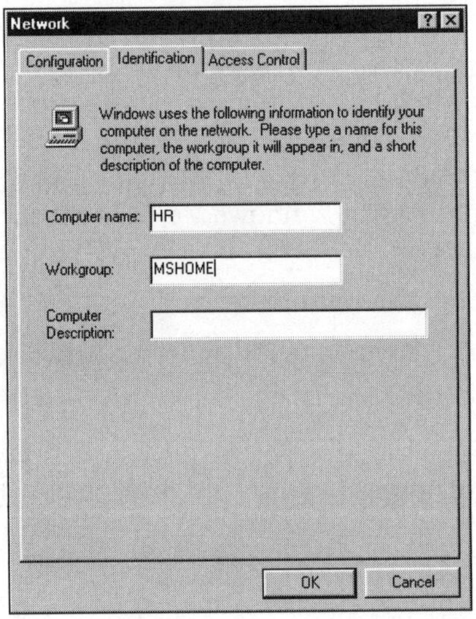

**Figure 6-6:** Use the Identification tab to identify each computer on the network.

4. **Enter a unique name for this computer.**

   You can use up to 15 characters for the name, but the name cannot include any of the following characters: / \ * , . @. A space is also not permitted as part of a name.

5. **Enter a workgroup name.**

   The *workgroup name* is the name you use for the group of computers that comprise your home network. You can use the default name or invent a different name.

   The default name for a workgroup in Windows 98 is Workgroup; for all later versions of Windows, the default name is MSHOME. You can use any name you want, but every computer on the network must use the same workgroup name.

6. **Optionally, enter a computer description.**

   Other viewers can view the description you enter if they use the Details view in Network Neighborhood (covered in Chapter 10).

7. **Choose OK.**

   Your computer is ready to participate in the network.

   The Systems Settings Change dialog box opens, prompting you to restart your computer.

8. **Restart your computer.**
9. **Repeat these steps for each computer on the network.**

### Naming names in Windows 2000

To set computer names and workgroup names in Windows 2000, follow these steps:

1. **Right-click on My Computer, and choose Properties from the shortcut menu.**

   The System Properties dialog box opens.

2. **On the Network Identification tab, click the Properties button.**

   The Identification Changes dialog box opens.

3. **Enter a computer name and workgroup name as needed.**

   Be sure you select the Workgroup option to avoid having the computer try to log on to an authenticating domain.

### Naming names in Windows XP

To set computer names and workgroup names in Windows XP, follow these steps:

1. **Right-click on My Computer, and choose Properties from the shortcut menu.**

   The System Properties dialog box opens.

2. **On the Computer Name tab, click the Change button.**

   The Computer Name Changes dialog box opens.

3. **Enter a computer name and workgroup name as needed.**

   Be sure you select the Workgroup option to avoid having the computer try to log on to an authenticating domain.

# Using the Windows Home Networking Wizards

Both Windows Me and Windows XP have a wizard that walks you through the process of setting up your network; this wizard also sets up a shared Internet connection. Using the wizard means that you don't have to set the configuration options manually. However, many people feel that manual configuration is easier than working their way through a wizard. And, people who are fairly comfortable with computers and Windows often tend to avoid wizards (in fact, many sneer at wizards).

Just to keep things simple and organized, in this chapter, I discuss only the steps you follow to set up the network. I cover the Internet Connection Sharing options in Chapter 7. However, you may want to read Chapter 7 now and do everything at once.

The wizard configures all the options discussed in the previous sections. It creates a small program that you put on a floppy disk and carry to the other computers on the network. Running that program on each computer sets the configuration options discussed in the previous section.

If you have both Windows Me and Windows XP computers on your network, you must use the Windows XP Home Networking Wizard. Then use the floppy disk the wizard creates to set up your Windows Me computer.

The wizard's floppy disk program doesn't work in Windows 2000. After you finish with the wizard, use the manual steps described in the previous sections to configure your Windows 2000 computer.

# Windows Me Home Networking Wizard

To launch the Windows Me Home Networking Wizard, double-click the My Network Places icon on your desktop and then double-click the Home Networking Wizard icon. The first wizard window is a welcoming message that requires no action on your part except clicking Next to get started on the real work. The next window sets up Internet Connection Sharing, which I discuss in Chapter 7.

The following few sections lead you through the remaining windows of the wizard for Windows Me.

### Choosing names

Click Next to move through the wizard to the Computer and workgroup names window, as shown in Figure 6-7.

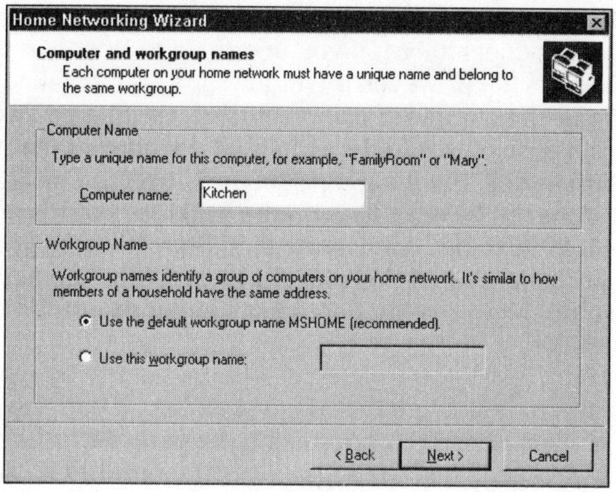

**Figure 6-7:** Name this computer, and name the workgroup that all the computers on the network are to use.

Enter a name for this computer, and enter a name for the workgroup. The computer name must be unique for the network, but all the computers on the network must use the same workgroup name. The wizard preselects the name MSHOME for the workgroup and indicates that's the recommended name for your network. That recommendation isn't made for any particular reason, and you can select the option to give the workgroup a name of your own choosing.

### Share and share alike: Setting up file- and printer-sharing services

The next wizard window (see Figure 6-8) sets up file- and printer-sharing services. When you share a folder, network users can get to any file in that folder, using any computer on the network. When you share a printer, everyone can use it, from any computer on the network.

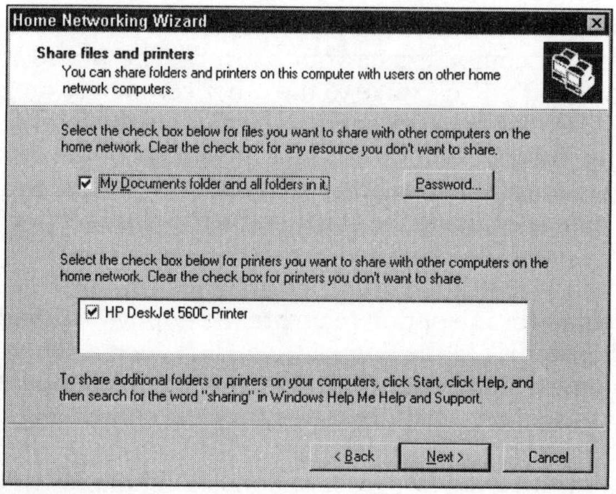

**Figure 6-8:** The wizard assumes you want to share your documents folder and any printer that's connected to this computer.

Your wizard window may display an additional folder, named Shared Documents. This folder doesn't exist if you upgraded to Windows Me from Windows 98 or Windows 95. However, if Windows Me was installed on a blank hard drive (usually by the computer manufacturer), the Shared Documents folder exists. The purpose of this folder is to hold documents that were created specifically for sharing, but it's not particularly useful. The Shared Documents folder does not have an icon on the desktop, and it's not all that easy to locate if you want to put documents in it. Depending on your system configuration (or perhaps it's just the wizard's mood of the moment), this folder is either a subfolder in the My Documents folder or a subfolder in the \Windows\All Users folder.

You don't have to share the folders that the wizard lists if you don't want to, and failing to share them doesn't interfere with the wizard's tasks — your network configuration proceeds just the same. After the network is configured, you can share manually any folder on any computer, including these folders, so you don't have to make the decision now. (I discuss creating shared folders in Chapter 8.)

The Password button next to the folder name exists so that you can create a password for each folder. This action limits other users' access to the folders, because anyone who doesn't know the password isn't permitted to open the folder from a remote computer. Chapter 8 offers detailed instructions for creating password protection for shared folders.

If you select the option to share the folders and you also decide to skip the password option, when you click the Next button, Windows Me displays a message urging you to enter a password. Click OK to make the message go away — you can password-protect any folder at any time, and you don't have to complete this task now.

### *Creating a networking setup disk for all the other computers*

The next wizard window asks whether you want to create a home networking setup disk for the other computers on your network. The wizard transfers files to a floppy disk that you can take to the other computers on your network to configure them for network services (including the Internet Connection Sharing feature). You should take advantage of the disk, because if you don't run the wizard on your other computers, you have to set up those computers manually, using the steps in the previous section of this chapter.

Click Next after you select the option to create the floppy disk, and put a blank formatted floppy disk in the floppy drive. Click Next again to create the disk, which takes only a moment or two. Then remove the floppy disk from the drive, and put a label on it that indicates it's your networking setup disk.

Click Finish in the wizard window — you're done. Windows Me transfers all the files required to run networking services to your hard drive (you may be asked to put the Windows Me CD in the CD-ROM drive if it isn't already inserted). You must restart your computer to put the network settings into effect. When your computer reboots, it's part of a working network!

### Using the networking setup disk on all the other computers

The floppy disk you created is an easy-to-use tool for configuring the other computers on your network. Go to each computer, and insert the floppy disk in the floppy drive. Then double-click the My Computer icon on the desktop. Double-click the floppy drive icon, and double-click the file named Setup.exe.

The same Home Networking Wizard you used on your Windows Me computer opens, and you merely walk through each window, answering questions and making selections. Give this computer a unique name, and use the same workgroup name you entered for your Windows Me computer. Say No to the wizard's offer to create a setup disk (you don't need another one).

Select the sharing options for the folders and printers that are on this computer. You don't have to share the suggested folders — you can decide which folders you want to share (see Chapter 8). However, if this computer has a printer, you need to share it.

## Windows XP Network Setup Wizard

The Windows XP Network Setup Wizard works a bit differently from the Windows Me Home Networking Wizard, but the end results are the same. To launch the Windows XP Network Setup Wizard, follow these steps:

1. **Choose Start⇨Control Panel.**

   The Control Panel window opens.

2. **Click Network and Internet Connections.**

   The Network and Internet Connections window opens.

3. **Click Network Setup Wizard.**

The first wizard window is a welcoming message that requires no action on your part except clicking Next to see a window that tells you to check a list of tasks before running the wizard. The tasks referred to are the installation of your network hardware and the installation of the hardware's drivers. Because you've done that, click Next again to get started. In the following sections, I discuss the options and actions you face in the remaining wizard windows.

### Select a connection method

The next wizard window asks you to select a connection method, which means it's setting up your Internet connection. I cover the details for these settings in Chapter 7, so in this section, I move past the Internet connection stuff and walk you through the wizard windows that are devoted to network configuration options.

### Identify the computer

The wizard asks you to enter a description of the computer and to give the computer a name. The description is optional, but the computer name isn't. The name must be unique on the network and should consist of a single word. Click Next after you've named the computer.

### Name your network

In the next window, you must name your network. By default, the wizard selects the name MSHOME, but you can change it to any name you want (some people use the family name). The network name must be the same on every computer in the network. Click Next to continue.

### Confirm the settings

The wizard shows you the network settings it's going to apply to the computer, and when you click Next, it applies the settings.

### Make a floppy disk (if you want to)

The wizard offers to make a floppy disk you can use to run this wizard on all the other computers on your network (except any computers that are running Windows 2000, which must be configured manually). Accept the offer, or politely decline, by choosing the appropriate option.

## Windows XP SP2 Wireless Network Setup Wizard

If you're setting up a wireless network, and if you're running Service Pack 2 for Windows XP, you have a network setup wizard specifically designed for you. To launch it, choose Choose Start➪All Programs➪Accessories➪Communications➪Wireless Network Setup Wizard.

The Wireless Network Setup Wizard assumes you're setting up your network in infrastructure mode (see the sidebar earlier in this chapter that explains infrastructure mode). It provides the basic configuration options for security — to set up file and printer sharing you must run the "regular" network wizard, or set up each adapter manually.

### Setting Basic Configuration Options

Walk through the wizard windows, starting with the window that asks you to create an SSID for your wireless network, and select an encryption option (see Figure 6-9). For more about SSIDs and encryption, read Chapter 5.

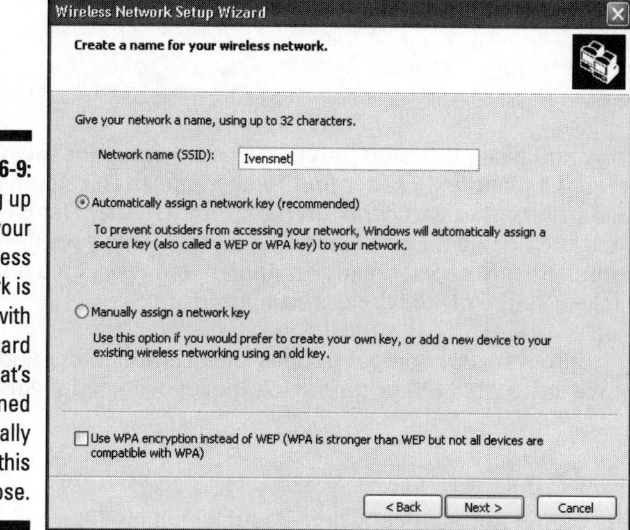


**Figure 6-9:** Setting up your wireless network is easier with a wizard that's designed specifically for this purpose.

### Transferring Settings to the Other Computers

The other network wizards I discussed in this chapter offer the option to save the network settings to a floppy disk, which you can use for the other computers on your network. This is the way to make sure that all the computers have the proper settings.

The settings for wireless networks that are using SSIDs and encryption won't fit on a floppy disk. The wizard offers you two ways to save the settings so you can use them on the other computers: Save the settings to a USB flash drive, or set up the other computers manually.

A USB flash drive is a cute little storage device, that is sometimes called a keychain drive (because you can hang it on a keychain). You plug the device into a USB port, and have instant access to the drive. You can save files, or copy files to from the drive to a computer. Flash drives come in a variety of sizes, but the most common sizes hold 128MB or 256MB data.

If you don't have a flash drive, the wizard offers the option to print all the settings and then use the printed document to enter data in the other computers.

There's another option, which I came up with when I realized I didn't want to type in those long, arcane, settings. Here's a typical printout, and I'll bet you don't want to type all this stuff in either:

```
Network Name (SSID): Ivensnet
Network Key (WEP/WPA Key):
75101c23af79474ab9ad12165b2591cb6f04824b139c4480199b91cd87a1e
Key Provided Automatically (802.1x): 0
Network Authentication Type: WPAPSK
Data Encryption Type: TKIP
Connection Type: ESS
```

To be able to copy and paste this stuff into the wireless setup for the other computers, I created a plain text printer file. To accomplish this, I had to install a plain text printer that was configured to print to a file. Then, when the wizard printed the document, I selected that printer. This gave me a text file that can be opened in Notepad on any computer, and it fits on a floppy disk so I could take it to the other wireless computers.

To install a text printer on your computer, open the Printers folder and start the Add Printer Wizard. Install the printer using the following configuration options:

- Specify a local printer
- Deselect the option Automatically detect and install my Plug and Play printer (there's no text printer plugged into any port)
- Select FILE (Print to File) as the port
- In the Manufacturer list, select Generic
- In the Printers list, select Generic/Text Only
- Use the default printer name (Generic/Text Only)
- Don't make this printer the default printer
- Don't share the printer
- Don't print a test page

When it's time to have the wizard print the wireless network settings, select the Generic/Text Only printer in the Print dialog box. You don't have to select the option Print to File, because the printer is already configured to print to a file. Just click the Print button. When the Print to File dialog box opens, enter a filename, and add the extension .txt to the filename (so it automatically opens in Notepad). Copy the file to a floppy disk, double-click it to open it, and copy and paste the information into the wireless network wizard on the other computer.

# Accommodating Road Warriors

A *road warrior* is an employee who often works off-site (usually visiting customers) and communicates with his employer via a laptop computer. Using the laptop, road warriors can collect their e-mail, dial in to company inventory records and customer records, or access other company databases. When road warriors show up at the office, they use a PC card NIC to plug into the company network.

If you bought a laptop for a family member who was headed for college, your student qualifies as a road warrior during school breaks, when the laptop returns home.

Most road warriors bring their laptops home and want to join their home network. This scenario presents a special challenge for Windows, because the settings for each network differ. For some people, an additional complication exists — the connection type (the topology) isn't the same. In this section, I discuss some of the things you face if you want to move a laptop between networks.

## Bridging the topology gap

One problem you face is different topologies, unless your home network is using Ethernet (which is the topology of choice for business networks). If both your home and company networks are connected by Ethernet, you can plug into either network at will. You can use your network adapter for both your home and corporate network (although you need to change settings to match the network you're logging on to).

If your home network is using anything other than Ethernet, you need to find a way for the laptop to join the home network. You have two ways to accomplish this:

- Buy a NIC for the laptop that matches the topology of your home network.
- Buy a device that bridges the gap between your network topology and the Ethernet NIC that's already on the laptop. The device is called a *bridge.*

If your home network is running any topology except Ethernet and you're using a DSL or cable modem for your Internet connection, you may already have a bridge to connect the modem (an Ethernet device) with your network (see Chapter 7 for details).

Bridges connect separate topologies by offering two connector types. One is Ethernet and the other is wireless, phoneline, or powerline. The data moves from one topology to the other by passing through the bridge. All manufacturers of network devices offer bridges.

## Managing multiple settings

It can be difficult to manage the different settings you need for your NIC as you move between networks. The configuration settings for logging on differ, because at work, you're almost certainly logging on to a domain (a client/server network), while your home network is designed as a workgroup (a peer-to-peer network). You have several ways to adjust your settings as you switch between networks, including the following:

- Manually change the settings.
- Buy software that switches between settings.
- Use a built-in command-line tool to save and load settings (this is only available in Windows 2000 and Windows XP).

I go over all of these methods in the following sections. I think it's important to know the manual solution, because if you use either of the other solutions and something goes wrong, you then know how to identify and fix the problem.

## Changing settings manually

Manual changes aren't complicated or geeky, because you're essentially doing the same things I covered earlier in this chapter when I explained how to configure your network settings.

Make the change just before you shut down your computer, when you know that the next time you boot your computer, it will be joining the "other" network.

Any or all of the following settings may need to be changed (the specific dialog boxes are described earlier in this chapter):

- The workgroup or domain selection, along with the name of the workgroup or the domain.
- The TCP/IP settings on the NIC. Often, the settings are the same for both work and home — Obtain an IP Address Automatically.
- The gateway or Domain Name System (DNS) server for a shared Internet connection (see Chapter 7 for more information about these settings).

### Windows XP stores two sets of configuration options

Windows XP has a nifty feature for NIC configuration called an *alternate configuration.* It's only available if your main configuration is for obtaining an IP address automatically (a Dynamic Host Configuration Protocol (DHCP) server exists on the network) and the alternate configuration (the other network) doesn't have a DHCP server. The alternate configuration can be set up for either an Automatic Private IP Address (APIPA) or fixed IP addresses. Click the Alternate tab to enter the information for the alternate IP information, and Windows XP switches to it if it can't find a DHCP server when you boot into the other network.

## Using software to move between networks

Several software programs are available that let you save the configuration settings for each network and then load the setting you need to log on to a network. In this section, I discuss two of these applications, because they're the ones that get the best reviews.

Netswitcher saves your network settings so you can load them as you need them. When you install Netswitcher, the program immediately asks if you want to save the current configuration so that you can restore it later. After you've completed that task, select the command to define a different set of network settings and enter the configuration for your "other" network. Each set of configuration settings is called a *location.* When you boot the computer, you select the location you need for the network you're joining. You can find out more about Netswitcher at `www.netswitcher.com`.

Mobile Net Switch works similarly to Netswitcher. However, Mobile Net Switch supports only Windows 98 Second Edition and later versions of Windows (not plain old Windows 98). For Windows 98 SE, you must install the Windows Management Instrumentation (WMI) component, which is not installed by default. The WMI component is available for installation in the Windows Setup tab of the Add/Remove Programs applet in the Control Panel. Highlight Internet tools, click Details, and then select Web-Based Enterprise Mgmt. After the component is installed, reboot the computer. You can find out more about Mobile Net Switch at `www.mobilenetswitch.com`.

## Using the netsh command-line tool

If you're more experienced in working with computers, and you understand the power of the command line, you can save and retrieve network settings with a powerful tool named netsh.exe. This utility is only available in Windows 2000 and Windows XP. Using netsh.exe falls in the middle between the inefficiency of resetting your network configuration manually and using a third-party software tool to automate the process. You have to record the settings to store them, which means you have to manually change the settings once. After that, you can retrieve either set of configuration options.

I'm a command-line junkie, so this is my method for network switching. You can read all about netsh.exe in the help files, but you need the following commands to store and retrieve settings.

To store a copy of the current settings, use the following syntax:

```
netsh -c interface dump > c:\foldername\filename.txt
```

To load a copy of the settings that you'll need next, use the following syntax:

```
netsh -f c:\foldername\filename.txt
```

I created a folder named c:\configurations to store my settings. Then I logged on to my office network (with the correct settings loaded, of course) and entered the following command to save the settings in my configurations folder:

```
netsh -c interface dump > c:\configurations\office.txt
```

Before I logged off, I manually changed my settings to the ones need for my home network and shut down the computer. After I successfully logged on to my home network, I entered the following command:

```
netsh -c interface dump > c:\configurations\home.txt
```

Now, both sets of settings are saved, and I don't have to make manual changes anymore. When I'm going to move my laptop, just before I log off the office network, I get ready to log on to my home network by entering the following command to load my home network settings:

```
netsh -f c:\configurations\home.txt
```

When my next logon is going to be at the office, just before I log off my home network, I enter the following command to load my office network settings:

```
netsh -f c:\configurations\office.txt
```

# Macintosh Can Join the Family, Too

If you have a Macintosh in the house, you can add it to your network, but the process is not a cakewalk. It won't work unless you've chosen an Ethernet solution for your home network.

New Macs (and some older Macs) have built-in Ethernet adapters. You can buy NICs for the older Macs that lack adapters.

If you installed a NIC, use the installation CD that came with the NIC to install drivers. A simple installation program accomplishes this (follow the manufacturer's instructions). When all the software is transferred to the Mac, you need to restart the computer.

AppleTalk and EtherTalk (the protocol that runs AppleTalk over an Ethernet network) are preinstalled on most Macs. Make sure that AppleTalk is active — check the Active radio button in Appleshare. Also, make sure that the right network connection is selected. In the Apple menu, select Control Panels and select the Network or AppleTalk option. Then select the Ethernet or EtherTalk option (the default in OS X), and close the window.

MacTalk is the default networking mechanism for Mac OS machines. Unfortunately, MacTalk doesn't know about Windows; PCs don't speak MacTalk. Your challenge is to convince the Mac to communicate using Windows-compatible networking protocols. You can meet the challenge by using TCP/IP as the network protocol. In a way, you're creating an environment in which the Mac interacts with the PC as if both of them were communicating over the Internet.

Set the TCP/IP configuration in the TCP/IP Control Panel, entering a TCP/IP address for the Mac. In addition, the Mac must be configured for sharing, which is like selecting File and Printer Sharing in the PC. Open the Apple Menu and select Control Panels, and then double-click the Sharing Setup option. Enter your name, a password, and the name of the computer. In the File Sharing section, check the label on the File Sharing button. If the label is Start, click the button to activate file sharing. If the label is Stop, the service is already running.

If you're running OS X, the ability to connect to Windows computers is built in. If not, and you've purchased software to assist your efforts to join a peer-to-peer network that includes Windows machines, follow the instructions to complete the installation of networking protocols provided by that software.

# Chapter 7

# Setting Up Shared Internet Connections

*In This Chapter*

- Taking a look at Internet connection hardware options
- Configuring dial-up networking connections
- Sharing Internet connections
- Examining hardware devices that provide connection sharing

To use the Internet, including for e-mail and Web surfing, you need a hardware device that can connect to an Internet service provider (ISP), software that drives the connection to the ISP, e-mail software, and a Web browser. Wait, don't panic; everything except the hardware comes with Windows.

You can share an Internet connection around the network, and the way you design your sharing scheme depends on the hardware equipment you use. This chapter covers the steps you need to take to set up both the hardware and the network settings.

## The Internet: From Your House to the World and Back

The Internet works by using communication hardware to move data from server to server, all over the world. A hierarchy of computers operating on multiple levels accomplishes this massive feat. For you, sending and receiving data starts and ends with your hardware, which is responsible for moving data between your computer and all the other computers on the Internet.

You're not hooked up directly with the computer you want to communicate with — your data moves through a bunch of computers to get to your target. The hierarchy of computers that runs the Internet starts (or ends, depending on the way you look at it) with a group of computers called the *backbone*.

Backbone servers are strategically placed throughout the world, and they communicate with the next layer of servers, all of which communicate with the next layer, and so on.

As Figure 7-1 shows, you use a hardware device to communicate with an ISP, which is a company you connect to in order to move through the Internet. The ISP uses a hardware device to communicate with the next layer of servers, and each layer moves data to the next until the packet of information reaches the target server (the Web page you want to see, or the mailbox of the recipient of your e-mail message). Each time a server moves data to another server, it's called a *hop.* If you want to see how many hops it takes to get from your computer to a particular place on the Internet, check out the sidebar "Tracing the route to a Web site."

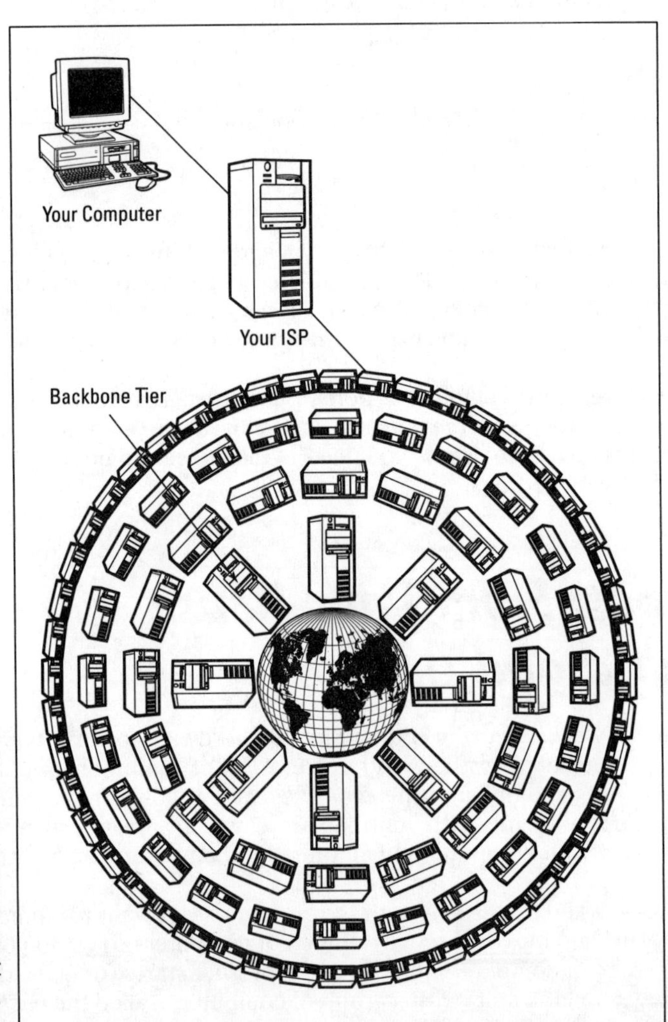


**Figure 7-1:** Your data hops from server to server to reach the right destination.

## Tracing the route to a Web site

Windows has a nifty utility that lets you trace the route from your house to a Web site, and you can use it while you're connected to the Internet. It's a command-line utility, so you need to open an MS-DOS command window to use it. Here's how:

- In Windows 98 and Windows Me, choose Start⇨Programs⇨MS-DOS Prompt.
- In Windows 2000, choose Start⇨Programs⇨Accessories⇨Command Prompt.
- In Windows XP, choose Start⇨All Programs⇨Accessories⇨Command Prompt.

In the command window, type **tracert *WebSite*** (substitute the name of the Web site you want to track down for *WebSite*) and press Enter. (Tracert stands for *trace route.*) The tracert utility tracks the hops between your computer and the target server. For example, I wanted to see the number of hops involved in communicating with one of my own Web sites from my office. Here's what appeared on my screen after I entered **tracert ivens.com**:

```
Tracing route to ivens.com
    [64.226.173.212]
over a maximum of 30 hops:
1 10 ms 10 ms 10 ms
    dsl092-230-065.phl1.dsl.spe
    akeasy.net [66.92.230.65]
2 10 ms 10 ms 10 ms
    dsl092-239-001.phl1.dsl.spe
    akeasy.net [66.92.239.1]
3 10 ms 10 ms 10 ms
    border1.fe5-14.speakeasy-
    27.ext1.phi.pnap.net
    [216.52.67.91]
4 10 ms 10 ms 10 ms
    core1.fe0-1-
    bbnet2.phi.pnap.net
    [216.52.64.65]
5 10 ms 10 ms 10 ms
    p3-3.phlapa1-cr1.bbn-
    planet.net [4.25.93.33]
6 10 ms 10 ms 10 ms
    p4-0.phlapa1-br1.bbn-
    planet.net [4.24.11.82]
7 10 ms 10 ms 10 ms
    p15-0.phlapa1-br2.bbn-
    planet.net [4.24.10.90]
8 10 ms 20 ms 10 ms so-0-0-
    0.washdc3-
    nbr2.bbnplanet.net
    [4.24.10.185]
9 10 ms 20 ms 10 ms so-7-0-
    0.washdc3-
    nbr1.bbnplanet.net
    [4.24.10.29]
10 30 ms 30 ms 30 ms so-0-0-
    0.atlnga1-br1.bbnplanet.net
    [4.24.10.14]
11 30 ms 30 ms 30 ms so-0-0-
    0.atlnga1-
    hcr9.bbnplanet.net
    [4.0.1.250]
12 30 ms 30 ms 30 ms giga-
    bitethernet0.nethostatl-
    gig.bbnplanet.net
    [4.0.36.14]
13 30 ms 30 ms 30 ms
    64.224.0.67
14 30 ms 30 ms 30 ms
    64.226.173.212
Trace complete.
```

The trace started with my ISP, Speakeasy.net, and then Speakeasy moved me through the Internet to the servers of the company that hosts my Web site. Note the time lapses displayed on the screen, which are calculated in milliseconds (ms). I'm using a high-speed Internet device — digital subscriber line (DSL) — and if you try this with a telephone modem, you'll probably see much higher numbers, indicating slower communication rates.

# Understanding Your Hardware Options

To reach the Internet from your home computer, you need a hardware device that can communicate with an Internet server. Depending on where you live, you have some choices about the type of hardware you can use. Your options may include

- A telephone modem
- A cable modem
- A DSL (Digital Subscriber Line) modem
- A satellite dish

Each of these connection options has its individual pros and cons — and some options aren't as widely available. Read on for more information that can help you determine which connection is the right one for your home network.

The more time you spend on the Internet, the more you realize how much speed counts. If you have to make 15 hops to get to a server with a Web site you want to view, the Web page has to make 15 hops back to you before it can display its contents. Add to that the amount of time it takes for the graphics on the Web page to unfurl on your screen, and you realize that Internet communication is largely a matter of "waiting for something to happen."

When you make your decision about Internet hardware, make speed a priority. Go for the fastest solution you can afford.

## Telephone modems

A telephone modem works by taking computer data (digital data) and translating it into a form that the telephone line can handle (analog data). This process is called *modulation.* At the receiving end of your modem transmission, another modem receives the analog data from the phone line and translates it into digital data that the computer can understand. This process is called *demodulation*. The modulate-demodulate functions that modems provide led to the word *modem.*

A modem uses the part of the telephone line's circuitry calls POTS (plain old telephone service), which it shares with telephones and fax machines. This is analog circuitry, and the maximum speed you can attain is 56 Kbps (56,000 bits, or 56 kilobits, of data transferred per second). Therefore, the fastest modem you can buy is referred to as a 56K modem. In fact, today it's probably the only modem speed available.

When you use a modem to access the Internet, you dial out to your ISP. The ISP's servers provide you with access to the World Wide Web and provide access to e-mail. Your e-mail address generally has the name of the ISP, à la `JohnDoe@MyISP.com`.

Here are some of the pros to using a telephone modem for connecting to the Internet:

- It's the cheapest Internet connection.
- If your computer has a modem built in, you don't have to buy hardware.
- Dial-up access is available everywhere.

Here are some of the cons:

- It's slow.
- You have to dial out each time you want to use an Internet service. Most ISPs don't permit you to dial in and just stay online all the time, so getting a separate telephone line for the modem doesn't give you a permanent Internet connection.
- A modem connection ties up your existing phone line.
- If you want a dedicated modem line, you have the added cost of paying for a second phone line. One the other hand, a dedicated modem line does stop a lot of the family arguments when Dad wants to make a phone call at the same time the kids are playing games on the Internet.

## Cable modems

Cable modems send data over your cable television company's line. The device connects to your system with Ethernet cable, so you need a router (for shared Internet access), or a network interface card (NIC) in a computer to which you attach the modem. The cable modem itself splits its connection between the network (or PC) and the television cable box. Your data goes back to your local cable TV company, where the cable company maintains a Cable Modem Termination System (CMTS) at the local office (which is called the *headend*). The CMTS is like a giant hub, where all the people who use this cable company's modems meet. You and your neighbors are basically participating in a computer network. The CMTS also provides the pass-through to the Internet.

Here are some of the advantages to using a cable modem:

- **Cable modems are always on, and you are always connected to the Internet.** Like any network, the cable company network is (or should be) always up and running. That's certainly much easier than operating with a telephone modem, where you have to dial out each time you want to use an Internet service. And you're not tying up your telephone line.
- **Cable modems download data much faster than telephone modems can.** Technically, a cable modem can reach speeds of over 1 million bits per second (1 Mbps). However, the cable company's own connection to the Internet may be slower than that, so the speed of transmission you actually realize is more likely to be in the range of several hundred-thousand bits per second.
- **You don't have to perform any configuration chores to get your cable modem to connect to an ISP.** The installation process the cable company performs hooks you up with its ISP automatically.

Here are some of the cons:

- **As any network grows, each node on the network operates a little slower.** If you add ten more computers to the Ethernet concentrator of your own home network, each computer on the network operates more slowly — as the available bandwidth is shared, each participant gets a little less of it. As more people sign up with your cable company, each of you loses some speed.
- **The speed for file uploads is not nearly as fast as the speed of downloads.** In fact, uploading is frequently as slow as 56 Kbps, the same as a telephone modem. However, you probably won't notice the difference between the upload and download speeds, because the only important speed is downloading. For most users, the only time you upload is when you send e-mail. Viewing a Web page is a download process. With a cable modem, Web pages pop up quickly on your screen, so you don't have to watch each page unfold its graphics slowly, the way modem users do.

## Digital subscriber line (DSL) modems

A digital subscriber line (DSL) modem is a digital device (telephone modems are analog devices) that uses your telephone lines. DSL uses a separate frequency range (one that can handle digital transmissions) in your telephone wires, so you can continue to use your telephone and fax over the POTS range.

Like a cable modem, a DSL modem connects to a computer via Ethernet cable, so you need a NIC in the computer that's hosting the modem.

More versions of DSL are available than I can keep track of, and DSL providers keep inventing new versions. For your home network, however, you're probably going to want ADSL service, which stands for Asymmetric Digital Subscriber Line service. Because ADSL is the most common form of DSL service, most people ignore the *A,* and when they talk about DSL, they usually mean ADSL.

Technically, ADSL can support download speeds of 8 Mbps and upload speeds of 1.5 Mbps. That's beyond blazing fast. But, don't get excited; you're not likely to meet anyone who has achieved anything near that technically possible level. In fact, unless you're prepared to spend a great deal of money each month, you won't operate at a fraction of the technically possible speeds.

The fact that the upload speed differs from the download speed is the reason the service is called *asymmetric.* Symmetric DSL (SDSL) provides upload speeds that are the same as download speeds. This service is much more expensive, and it's overkill for home users. Companies that maintain busy Web sites that must constantly update the information on their sites use SDSL technology.

Here are some of the pros to using a DSL device:

- You can use your telephone and fax at the same time you use DSL.
- Like a cable modem, a DSL device provides an always-on connection to the Internet.
- Unlike a cable modem, your connection is private — you're not part of a network.
- You don't have to do anything to configure the DSL device to communicate with your ISP; it's all part of the setup performed by the technician who installs the device.

  A professional installs the DSL device, because the phone line has to be split to accommodate the technology. To make the split, the telephone company does something technical to your line before the installer arrives. However, a new DSL technology, called DSL-Lite, is available in many communities, which makes it possible for you to install your own device.

Here are some of the cons to using a DSL device:

- **Fast speeds command high prices.** DSL services are purchased from providers on a monthly-fee basis, and the fees can be rather hefty. The higher the speed, the higher the monthly cost.

- **You must meet certain requirements.** Before you can rush to order DSL services, you have to answer Yes to both of the following questions:
  - Does your telephone company provide the technology that DSL requires in its lines?
  - Do you live within 18,000 feet of a telephone company central switching office?

The central switching office for a telephone company is called the *CO* (for central office).

You don't have to get out your tape measure and walk from your house to the CO; any DSL service provider can tell you if you qualify. In fact, telephone companies are becoming direct DSL service providers, which give you one-stop shopping.

## Fiber-optic DSL

Telephone companies across the United States are beginning to install fiber-optic cable, and when your phone lines are converted, DSL connections of unparalleled speed will be available.

Instead of copper, fiber-optic cables contain bundles of glass strands, each of which is thinner than a human hair. Laser-generated light transmits signals down the fiber at speeds that far exceed those of copper. In addition to voice and data, fiber-optic technology is capable of transmitting video. As a result, after fiber-optic lines come to your neighborhood, you can expect to see all sorts of interesting services offered.

DSL providers that use these fiber-optic lines will offer packages similar to those currently available — a rate of speed that depends on what you're willing to spend each month. For example, if your DSL provider currently provides monthly plans for about $30, $50, and $70, for download speeds that range from about 360 Kbps to 1 Mbps (with slower upload rates), the same price ranges should buy you the following download/upload speeds:

- 5 Mbps/2 Mbps
- 15 Mbps/2 Mbps
- 30 Mbps/5 Mbps

Contact your phone company to find out if and when your neighborhood is scheduled for conversion to fiber-optic cable.

## Satellite connection

If you live too far from a phone company office for DSL and there is no cable TV on your street, you might want to consider satellite Internet access. A satellite Internet connection works by sending and receiving data through a satellite.

Satellite communications are much faster than telephone modem exchanges, but not as fast as DSL or cable. The service is more expensive than any other type of Internet connection, but if you can't put up with the slow speed of a phone modem, it's an alternative worthy of consideration.

The hardware you need includes a satellite dish (which contains an antenna), and a transceiver (transmitter/receiver) modem. Until recently, you had to purchase two modems, one for transmitting, and one for receiving, but today's satellite providers sell transceiver modems.

You can buy satellite modems with built-in routers (four ports). I don't know of any satellite provider who supports equipment if you connect the modem to a standard router. None of the equipment requires you to install drivers, or go through a configuration setup process, and all satellite providers send installation technicians to install the equipment.

You can get more information from any satellite provider, and the two most popular (and most reasonably priced) are the following:

- Direcway (which used to be called DirecPC), which is at `www.direcway.com`.
- StarBand, which is at `www.starband.com`.

# Configuring Telephone Modem Connections

If you're using a telephone modem to connect to the Internet, you need two things:

- **An account with an ISP:** To find an ISP that you can trust, ask friends or check reviews in computer magazines.
- **A software connection to the ISP:** The software connection to the ISP is part of the Dial-Up Networking (DUN) feature that's built into Windows.

If you're going to share a telephone modem connection across the network, the modem, the DUN, and the sharing software should be installed on the computer that has the latest version of Windows because the setup, configuration, and technology gets better with each Windows version.

After you configure the DUN connection, your modem can dial out and connect to your ISP, which passes you on to the Internet. You can have as many DUN connections as you need (one for each ISP you use). Most people have only one ISP, but some families have both an ISP and an AOL account, for example. Additionally, some people have accounts through their employers.

If you're going to share your Internet connection across the network, install a DUN connection on the computer that acts as the host or server for your modem-sharing software. Setting up a DUN connection is quite simple. Before you start, be sure you have the following information at your fingertips (it's all provided by your ISP):

- The local phone number that you dial to log on to your ISP.
- Your online account user name. (You choose this name, and you must give it to the ISP when you sign up.)
- Your online account password. (Some ISPs give you a password. Others let you choose the password yourself, and you must give it to the ISP when you sign up.)
- The TCP/IP settings needed to communicate with your ISP's server.

Your ISP also provides information about setting up your e-mail software so that you can get your messages and send messages to others.

In the following sections, I show you how to set up your DUN connection to your ISP. I'm assuming you want to share your Internet connection so that everybody in the household can surf the Net simultaneously. That means you must have your modem attached to a computer that's running Windows 98 Second Edition (Windows 98 SE), Windows Me, Windows 2000, or Windows XP. The setup is different for each operating system, so refer to the appropriate section. The following sections assume you've already installed your modem. To find out about setting up modems, check out *Windows 98 For Dummies, Microsoft Windows Me Millennium Edition For Dummies, Windows 2000 Professional For Dummies,* or *Windows XP For Dummies,* 2nd Edition, all published by Wiley Publishing, Inc.

## Creating a DUN connection in Windows 98 SE and Windows Me

With the information from your ISP at hand, follow these steps to create a Dial-Up Networking (DUN) connection in Windows 98 SE or Windows Me:

1. **In Windows 98 SE, double-click the My Computer icon and then double-click the Dial-Up Networking folder; in Windows Me, choose Start⇨Settings⇨Dial-Up Networking.**

   In the Dial-Up Networking folder, you should see the Make New Connection icon. If any other objects are in the folder, you have already created a Dial-Up Networking connection.

2. **Double-click the Make New Connection icon.**

   The Make New Connection Wizard launches to walk you through the process of installing your Internet connection (see Figure 7-2).

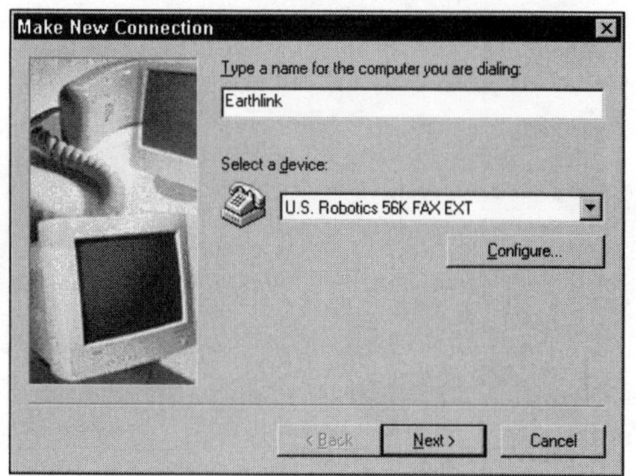


**Figure 7-2:** The wizard's first question is "What's my name?"

3. **Enter a name for this DUN connection, and then click Next.**

   It's a good idea to give the connection a name that makes it easily identifiable — the name of your ISP is usually a good choice.

   This wizard screen also shows the name of your modem, which you should have installed before this. If you didn't install a modem, the wizard automatically goes into "install a modem" mode and walks you through the necessary steps.

4. **Enter the area code and phone number for your ISP, and then click Next.**

5. **Click Finish.**

   You are returned to the Dial-Up Networking window, where an icon for your new DUN connection appears.

Unfortunately, you're not finished. The programmers created the Finish button to amuse themselves — they apparently have weird senses of humor. You have more tasks, and these are the tasks that require the technical information you acquired from your ISP. Follow these steps to finish setting up your DUN connection:

1. **Right-click the icon for your DUN connection and choose Properties from the shortcut menu.**

   The Properties dialog box opens.

2. **In Windows 98 SE, click the Server Types tab; in Windows Me, click the Networking tab.**

   The Server Types tab displays the settings for your ISP's server, which should be similar to those shown in Figure 7-3.

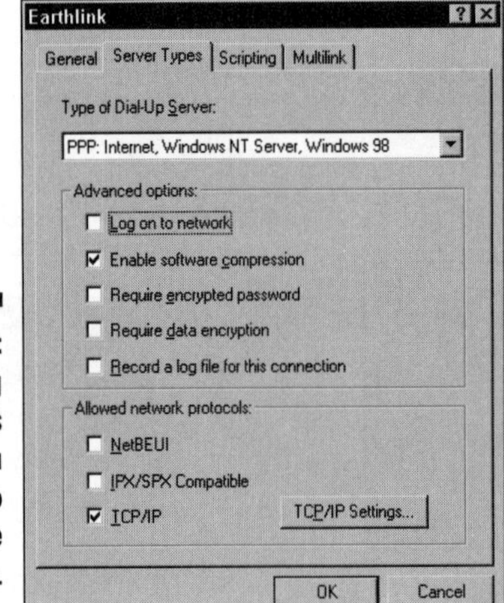


**Figure 7-3:** This dialog box is where you begin to configure settings.

   In Windows 98 SE, your settings should be the same as those shown in Figure 7-3. If your ISP instructed you to select the encrypted password option, select that check box (this would be unusual, however). In Windows Me, the encrypted password option is on the Security tab.

3. **Click the TCP/IP Settings button.**

   The TCP/IP Settings dialog box opens, as shown in Figure 7-4.

   Most ISPs assign an IP address when you log on. If your ISP wants you to enter a specific IP address, follow the instructions you received to fill in the requisite fields.

4. **Click OK twice to close the DUN connection dialog box.**

   Now you're really finished!

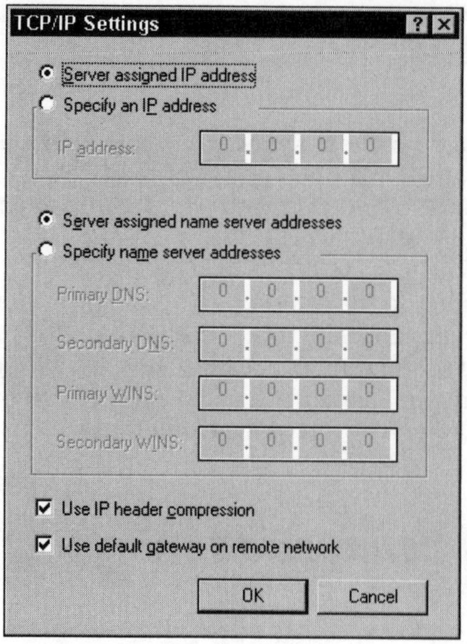

**Figure 7-4:** To complete this dialog box, refer to the instructions from your ISP.

When you want to connect to the Internet, follow these steps:

1. **Open the Dial-Up Networking window (in Windows 98 SE, you must first open My Computer).**
2. **Double-click the icon for your DUN connection to open the Connect To dialog box, as shown in Figure 7-5.**

   By default, Windows 98 SE puts your name in the User Name field, but your ISP may have instructed you to use your e-mail address instead.

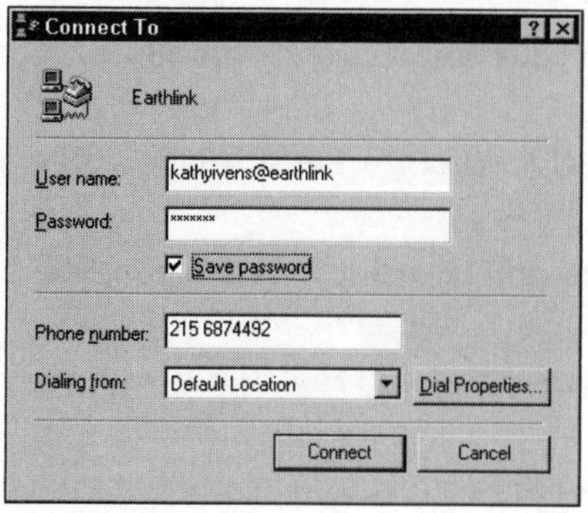

**Figure 7-5:** Make sure that the dialog box is filled out to match the requirements of your ISP.

3. **Enter your ISP password, and then select the Save Password check box so you don't have to enter it every time you dial out.**
4. **Click Connect.**

   Your modem dials out, and you hear some squawking noises as your modem and your ISP connect. Now you and everybody else on the network can open your browsers and visit Web pages, or open your e-mail software and correspond with the world.

If you want to be able to connect to the Internet with a single click instead of opening all those windows, right-click and drag the DUN icon to your Quick Launch bar (which is located to the right of the Start button). When you release the mouse button, a menu appears. Choose Create Shortcut(s) Here from the menu to add the DUN icon to the Quick Launch bar.

## Creating a DUN connection in Windows 2000

Follow these steps to set up a DUN connection in Windows 2000 Professional:

1. **Choose Start⇨Settings⇨Network and Dial-up Connections.**

   The Network and Dial-up Connections window opens.
2. **Double-click the Make New Connection icon.**

   The Network Connection Wizard opens. Click Next to move past the window with the welcoming message.
3. **Select the Dial-up to the Internet option, and then click Next.**

   The other options appear because Windows 2000 uses the same wizard for all types of connections, including network connections.
4. **Select the option to set up your connection manually, and then click Next.**
5. **Select the option to connect to the Internet through a phone line and a modem, and then click Next.**
6. **Enter the phone number to dial in order to reach your ISP, and then click Next.**
7. **Enter the user name and password you registered with your ISP, and then click Next.**
8. **Enter a name for this DUN connection, and click Next.**

9. **If you want, select the option to set up an e-mail account.**

   If you opt for e-mail setup, you're off and running on a configuration process for Outlook Express. If you were going to use Outlook Express as your e-mail software anyway, you may want to do it now. Or you may want to worry about all that work later and just get your DUN connection out of the way for now.

   For this discussion, I'm choosing not to set up e-mail.

10. **Click Finish.**

    If your ISP instructed you to enter an IP address instead of obtaining an IP address from the server, deselect the option to connect to the Internet immediately before you click the Finish button. Then right-click your DUN connection icon and choose Properties from the shortcut menu. Click the Networking tab and fill in the IP address information according to the instructions from your ISP.

To connect to the Internet, choose Start⇨Settings⇨Network and Dial-up Connections. Double-click your DUN connection, and choose Dial.

If you want to be able to connect to the Internet with a single click, right-drag the DUN icon to your Quick Launch bar. When you release the mouse button, a menu appears. Choose Create Shortcut(s) Here from the menu to add the DUN icon to your Quick Launch bar.

## Creating a DUN connection in Windows XP

Use the following steps to set up a dial-up connection in Windows XP:

1. **Choose Start⇨All Programs⇨Accessories⇨Communications⇨New Connection Wizard.**

   The New Connection Wizard opens. The first window is an introduction to the wizard, and there's nothing for you to do, so click Next to begin.

2. **Select the Connect to the Internet option, and then click Next.**

3. **Select the Set Up My Connection Manually option, and then click Next.**

   This wizard window offers three options (see Figure 7-6). I'm assuming that you've already contacted an ISP and received instructions. You could also select the option to use a CD you received from your ISP, but most of the time this is just a longer method of entering the information you'd enter by selecting the Set Up My Connection Manually option. In addition, many ISP CDs make assumptions about the e-mail software you want to use, or they install an e-mail program automatically (which may not be the e-mail program you'd planned to use).

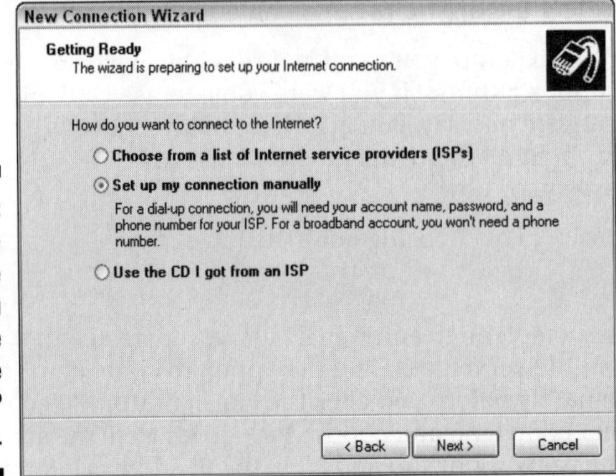


**Figure 7-6:** Tell the wizard the method you want to use to configure your ISP connection.

4. **Select the Connect Using a Dial-up Modem option, and then click Next.**
5. **Name the connection, and then click Next.**

   The wizard tells you to enter the name of your ISP, which is a good choice. The name you enter becomes the label under the icon for this connection.
6. **Enter the phone number you dial to make the connection, and then click Next.**

   Your ISP provides the number, and it should be a local number. If it's not, don't forget to enter a 1 and the area code. Even if it is a local number, enter the local area code if your area has 10-digit dialing (that is, where you have to dial the local area code for local calls).
7. **Specify whether this DUN connection is exclusive to you or can be used by others who use this computer.**

   Select the Anyone's Use option if you want this DUN connection to be available to any user who logs on to this computer. Select the My Use Only option if you want this DUN to be part of your personal profile and be unseen by any other user who logs on to this computer.
8. **Enter the account information and specify the way it should be configured (see Figure 7-7).**

   Enter the user name according to the instructions you received from your ISP. Some ISPs use just a logon name, and other ISPs require your mailbox name, such as `myaccount@myisp.com`.

   If everyone in the household logs on to the ISP with the same account (the common scenario), select the option Use This Account Name and Password When Anyone Connects to the Internet from this Computer. If each user in your household has his or her own account, clear the check box.

**Figure 7-7:** The wizard needs to know how you want to sign on to your ISP's server.

If this connection is your primary (or only) way to connect to the Internet, leave the option Make This the Default Internet Connection selected. If you're creating the connection as a backup, in case your DSL or cable modem isn't working, clear the check mark from the check box.

If you want to use the built-in Windows XP firewall to block access from the Internet, leave the check mark in the Turn On Internet Connection Firewall for this Connection check box. If you'll be setting up a software firewall, remove the check mark. See Chapter 13 to find out about firewalls.

9. **Review the settings, and then click Finish.**

   If anything is incorrect, click the Back button to return to a previous page and make the necessary changes. Otherwise, click Finish to create the connection.

Select the option to add a shortcut for this connection to your desktop so that you don't have to navigate your way through menu items to find the connection when you want to use it.

# Sharing a Telephone Modem Connection

After you have set up a communications line to an Internet service provider, you have to share that line with all the other computers on the network. This process requires each computer to attach itself to an IP address, which in turn requires TCP/IP (see the sidebar, "Understanding TCP/IP"). If you chose NetBEUI as your network protocol, now you have two protocols — the process of setting up your modem, cable modem, or DSL device automatically added TCP/IP to your network protocols. (See Chapter 6 for more on protocols.)

## Understanding TCP/IP

Although TCP/IP is the acronym for Transmission Control Protocol/Internet Protocol, you may find a number of folks who claim it really stands for Terribly Confusing Proposition/Irritating and Perplexing. I say pay them no mind. They're just a little cranky because they haven't yet found a simple, straightforward explanation of TCP/IP. To ensure that you don't join their ranks, let me quickly explain TCP/IP.

Think about the fact that you can send a letter to someone in Paris, London, Tokyo, or Sydney and be reasonably sure that he or she will get it (as long as you address the letter properly). That's a pretty amazing feat when you realize that each country has its own language, its own customs, and its own unique postal system. The reason your letter makes it to its destination is because of the existence of a standardized set of rules for the manner in which mail is transmitted.

That, in a nutshell, defines TCP/IP — a set of standardized rules for transmitting information. In the case of TCP/IP, the information is in electronic rather than paper form. TCP/IP enables computers to communicate with one another by using each computer's address, which is called an *IP address.*

E-mail, Web pages, files, and other data are transmitted over the Internet in *packets,* which are nothing more than small electronic parcels of information. The computer doing the transmitting takes a large amount of information and breaks it into small, manageable individual packets to send it across the Internet. The receiving computer collects each of the packets and puts them back together to reconstitute the original piece of information. Both computers follow the rules built into TCP/IP to know how to break up and reconstitute the data.

While it's possible to share a modem connection on a Windows 2000 computer, I'm not going to cover it here. It's rarely necessary to perform this task on a home network. First of all, most Windows 2000 computers on a home network are laptops ("borrowed" from employers), and laptops wouldn't be host computers. Second, sharing a connection on a Windows 2000 computer is quite complicated because everything has to be configured manually (on both the host and the clients). If you need to use a Windows 2000 computer as an Internet Connection Sharing (ICS) host, read the help files or check out *Windows 2000 Professional For Dummies* by Andy Rathbone and Sharon Crawford (Wiley) to get all the information you need.

# Windows 98 SE Internet Connection Sharing

If Windows 98 SE is the latest version of Windows on your network, that's where your modem and DUN connection must be installed. Now you need to use the Internet Connection Sharing (ICS) software to set up Internet access across the network. Unfortunately, when you installed Windows 98 SE on the computer, the ICS software wasn't installed by default. If you (or whoever installed the operating system) performed a custom installation, ICS may have been installed. Consider this neat feature of ICS: The steps you take to see if ICS is already installed are the same steps you use to install it, in case it isn't there.

### Installing and configuring the host computer

Before completing the following steps, make sure that you have your Windows 98 SE CD on hand (unless the files were installed on your hard drive by a manufacturer who preloaded the operating system before you bought the computer).

Here's how to determine if ICS is already installed, and how to install it if it's missing:

1. **Choose Start⇨Settings⇨Control Panel.**

   The Control Panel window opens.

2. **Double-click the Add/Remove Programs icon.**

   The Add/Remove Programs Properties dialog box appears.

3. **Click the Windows Setup tab.**

   This tab displays a list of operating system components that have been installed. The system inspects your computer to see what's there, so it may take a few seconds before the list appears.

4. **Scroll through the list and click the listing — not the check box — for Internet Tools.**

   The state of the check box can be a clue to the status of installed Internet features (see Figure 7-8).

   - If the check box is blank, no Internet tools have been installed, and you have to install ICS.
   - If the check box is white and contains a check mark, all the Internet tools are installed, and you don't have to install ICS.
   - If the check box is gray and contains a check mark, some Internet tools are installed, but you don't know yet whether ICS is one of them.

5. **If the check box is blank or gray, click the Details button.**

   A list of Internet tools displays, with a check mark next to any that are already installed.

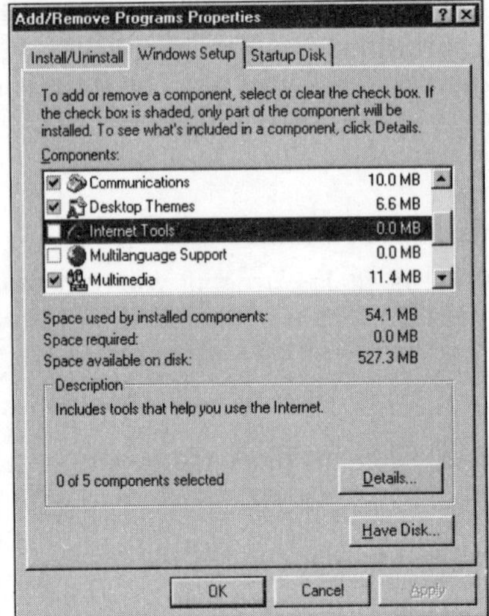


**Figure 7-8:** This computer has no Internet Tools installed.

6. **Click the Internet Connection Sharing check box to place a check mark in the box.**

   The check mark sends a signal to the operating system that you want to install ICS.

7. **Click OK to close the Internet Tools window, and then click OK again to close the Add/Remove Programs Properties dialog box.**

   Windows copies the ICS software files to your hard drive, and then launches the Internet Connection Sharing Wizard.

8. **Click Next to move past the Welcome window.**

9. **Tell the wizard whether you're using a modem or a high-speed connection, and then click Next.**

10. **Click Next to create the client software.**

    Put a blank floppy disk in your floppy drive. You'll use this disk to install the client software on all the other computers. When Windows finishes copying files to the floppy disk, a message appears to tell you to remove the disk and click OK.

11. **Click Finish.**

    A message appears to tell you that you must restart your computer. Click Yes to have Windows restart.

### *Setting up the client computers*

You can use the client software on any Windows 98 or Windows 95 computer. To set up the client computers, follow these steps:

1. **Insert the floppy disk you made into the floppy drive of a client computer.**
2. **Choose Start➪Programs➪Windows Explorer.**

   The Windows Explorer window opens.
3. **Select the floppy drive in the left pane.**

   The right pane displays the contents of the floppy disk.
4. **Double-click the `icslet.exe` file.**

   The Connection Setup Wizard opens, displaying a welcome message. Click Next to move to the next wizard window, which explains that when you click Next again, the wizard makes the appropriate changes to your settings.
5. **Click Next.**

   The wizard announces that your system is configured for Internet Connection Sharing.
6. **Click Finish.**

   If the host computer is connected to the Internet, select the option to head for the Web when you click the Finish button. Or connect to the Internet on the host computer before you click the Finish button. Or wait until later to open the browser on the client computer and go to your favorite Web page.

# Windows Me Internet Connection Sharing

If your Windows Me computer has the modem, then this computer is the host. You have to configure the computer for hosting, and you also have to create the software disk you'll use to configure the client computers.

## Installing and configuring the host

In Chapter 6, I go over the Windows Me Home Networking Wizard, including the stuff you have to do to share an Internet connection — that wizard is a total solution. If you only used the wizard to set up your network, you can rerun it to set up Internet Connection Sharing. Here's how:

1. **Choose Start➪Programs➪Accessories➪Communications➪Home Networking Wizard.**

   The first window of the Home Networking Wizard opens. Click Next to get started.
2. **Tell the wizard that this computer has a connection to the Internet (see Figure 7-9).**

The wizard finds your DUN connection, if you have one. If you have a cable modem or a DSL device attached to a NIC, the wizard finds and displays the NIC. Click Next.

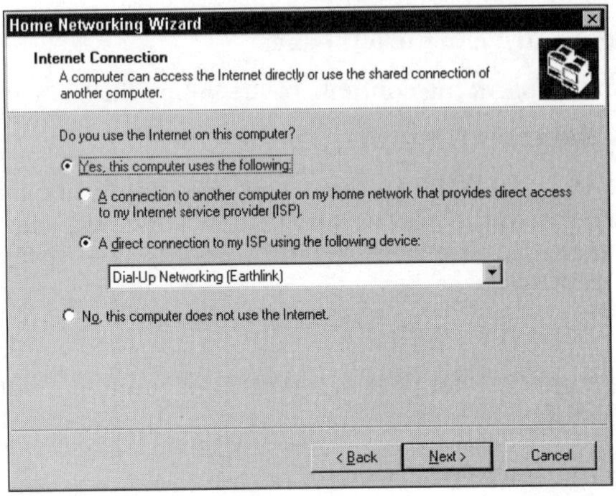

**Figure 7-9:** The wizard needs to know that this is the computer with a connection to the Internet.

3. **Tell the wizard you want to share this connection with the other computers on the network.**

   The wizard finds the NIC that connects the computer to the rest of the network (see Figure 7-10).

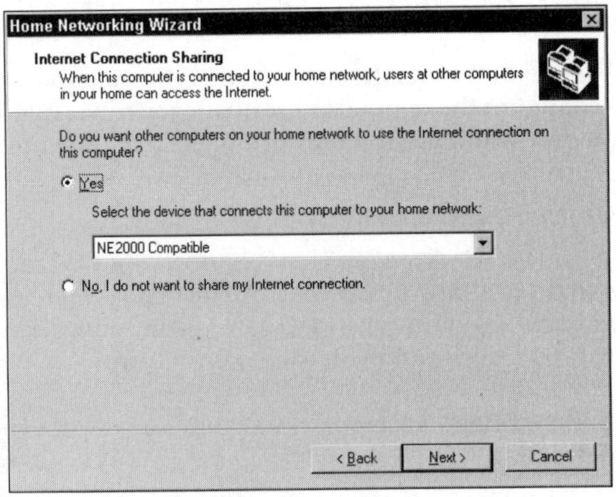

**Figure 7-10:** Tell the wizard you're willing to share.

4. **Decide on automatic connections.**

   This window (shown in Figure 7-11) appears only if your Internet connection is a dial-up affair (instead of an always-on connection). Choose

Yes to automate the launching of the DUN connection whenever anyone on the network opens a browser or opens e-mail software when the connection isn't active. Selecting this option means that the person who is working at the host computer doesn't have to launch the connection every time someone on the network wants to get to the Internet. It also means that other users don't have to come to the host computer (if no one is using it) to launch the DUN connection.

If you prefer to keep control of when the DUN connection is used, choose the option that starts with No.

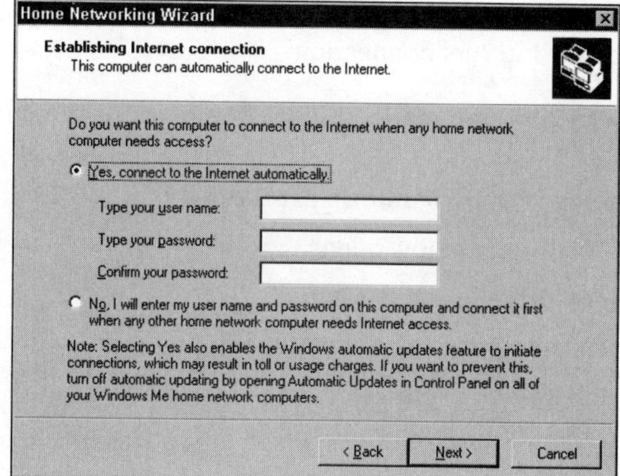


**Figure 7-11:** If you want to automate opening the DUN connection, fill in the information for the ISP.

5. **Go through the rest of the wizard windows, supplying the information the wizard needs.**

   The remaining windows contain the information you filled out when you set up your network with the wizard — the computer's name and your options for sharing folders and printers. The information you previously entered is still there — just check it for accuracy and click Next to keep moving.

6. **In the Setup Disk window, choose Yes to create a setup disk for the other computers.**

   Insert a blank floppy disk in drive A, and click Next.

7. **Click Finish.**

   You may see a message telling you to restart your computer. Take the floppy disk out of the drive, and click Yes to restart.

### *Setting up the client computers*

If any client computers are also running Windows Me, you don't need to use the floppy disk you made. Just run the Home Networking Wizard on each of those computers and answer the wizard's questions appropriately. This means instead of saying "Yes, the modem is here," you say, "Use the network to connect me to the modem."

You cannot use the floppy disk on a computer running Windows 2000; you must set up that computer manually. The TCP/IP configuration must be set to obtain an IP address automatically.

For client computers that are running Windows 98, use these steps to set them up for sharing the Internet connection:

1. **Insert the floppy disk you made into the floppy drive of a client computer.**
2. **Choose Start⇨Programs⇨Windows Explorer.**

   The Windows Explorer window opens.
3. **Select the floppy drive in the left pane.**

   The right pane displays the contents of the floppy disk.
4. **Double-click the `Setup.exe` file.**

   The Connection Setup Wizard opens, displaying a welcome message.
5. **Click Next.**

   The Home Networking Wizard (yep, the same one that is built into Windows Me) is installed on this computer. The wizard automatically starts the Internet Connection Sharing part of the program. Go through the wizard, answering the questions as if you were running the wizard on a Windows Me computer.

   Remember that you're telling the wizard that the Internet connection is installed on the host computer, not the computer on which you're running the wizard.

## Windows XP Internet Connection Sharing

If your Windows XP computer has the modem, then this computer is the host. You have to configure the computer for hosting, and you also have to create the software disk you'll use to configure the client computers. In Chapter 6, I go over the Windows XP Home Networking Wizard, which is a total solution for setting up a network and sharing your Internet connection. If you only used the wizard to set up your network, you can rerun it to set up Internet Connection Sharing and to create a floppy disk for the client computers. Use the following steps to accomplish this:

1. **Choose Start➪All Programs➪Accessories➪Communications➪Network Setup Wizard.**

   The Network Setup Wizard opens. The first window is an introduction to the wizard, so click Next. The next window is a reminder of things to do first (you've already done them), so click Next again.

2. **Select the connection method for a host computer, and then click Next.**

   The wizard offers several choices, but because you're setting up the host computer for Internet Connection Sharing, you must choose the option that indicates that this computer connects directly to the Internet.

3. **Select the DUN connection you created, and then click Next.**

4. **Name the computer, and then click Next.**

   If you already ran the wizard to create your network (as described in Chapter 6), the name is already there, as is any optional description you entered.

5. **Name the workgroup, and then click Next.**

   If you already ran the wizard to create your network (as described in Chapter 6), the workgroup name is already entered.

6. **Approve the configuration settings.**

   If something seems wrong, click Back to correct the error. Otherwise, click Next and wait for the wizard to apply the configuration settings to your system.

7. **Select the option to create a setup disk, and then click Next.**

   Follow the wizard's prompt to create the disk.

If any client computers are also running Windows XP, you don't need to use the floppy disk you made. Just run the Home Networking Wizard on each of those computers and answer the wizard's questions appropriately. This means instead of saying "Yes, the modem is here," you say, "Use the network to connect me to the modem."

For computers running versions of Windows earlier than Windows XP, insert the disk in the floppy drive and follow the instructions the wizard provides to run the software.

You cannot use the floppy disk on a computer running Windows 2000; you must set up that computer manually. The TCP/IP configuration must be set to obtain an IP address automatically.

# Sharing DSL or Cable Modems

You can share your DSL or cable modem with all the computers on your network, and it's easy to do so. However, you may have to install some hardware to make sure that all the computers can connect to the modem. In addition, you need to decide whether to use a router to effect sharing. I'll go over all these choices in the following sections.

## Bridging the wiring gap

DSL and cable modems are Ethernet devices. If your network is connected with Ethernet cable, you don't have to bridge the wiring gap, and you can move on to making a decision between multiple NICs or a router (covered in the next section).

If your network is connected by phoneline, powerline, or wireless connections, you have to create a bridge for the network so that it can cross over to the Ethernet modem. For phoneline or powerline networks, the device is called a *bridge,* and for wireless networks, the device is called an *access point* (AP), but it's actually a bridge. In addition, some routers are also bridges, or is the correct way to say that "some bridges are also routers"? A wireless router is an example of this type of device.

Confused? I define the terminology in the following paragraphs.

A bridge is a hardware device that accepts connections for two different topologies. One connection type is a non-Ethernet connector, and you purchase the bridge for the specific type of wiring you need. For example, a phoneline bridge has a phoneline connector.

The other connection type is always Ethernet, which means the device has an RJ-45 port that accepts a connector at the end of Ethernet cable. The other end of the Ethernet cable is connected to an Ethernet device, usually a DSL or cable modem. However, you could connect the other end of the Ethernet cable to a hub or switch that's being used to create an Ethernet network. That's a way to join a non-Ethernet network to an Ethernet network. Joining disparate networks is what bridges do. Figure 7-12 illustrates the way a bridge works. Of course, if your network is wireless, instead of wires on the network and the bridge, you have antennas.

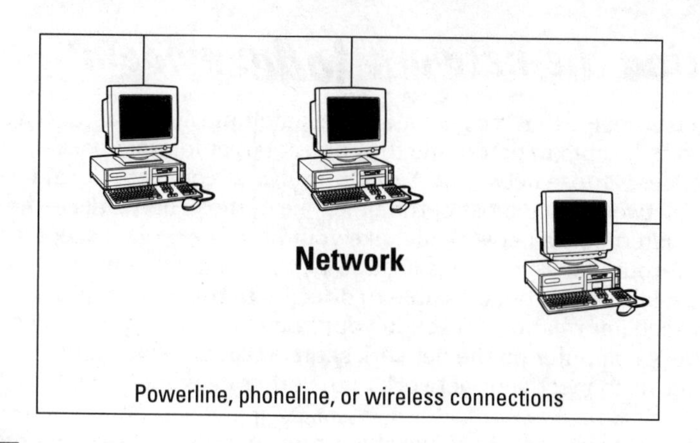


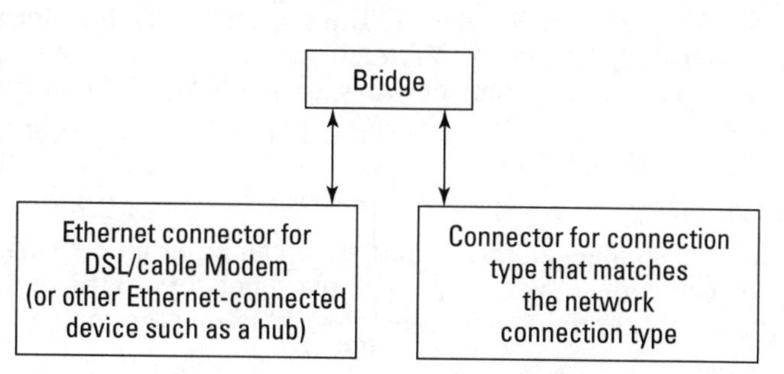


**Figure 7-12:** A bridge has two connection types so that it can merge disparate connectors.

The documentation that comes with the bridge provides detailed instructions for making connections and configuring the device, but here's a quick overview:

- If your network is wireless, connect Ethernet cable between the RJ-45 connector on the AP or the wireless router (look for a port labeled *LAN, WAN,* or *RJ-45*) and the DSL/cable modem.
- If your network is powerline, connect Ethernet cable between the RJ-45 connector on the bridge (which is probably labeled *LAN, WAN,* or *RJ-45*) and the DSL/cable modem. Plug the wire that's attached to the bridge into an electrical outlet.
- If your network is phoneline, connect Ethernet cable between the RJ-45 connector on the bridge (which is probably labeled *LAN, WAN,* or *RJ-45*) and the DSL/cable modem. Use telephone cable to connect the bridge phoneline connector (probably labeled *PNA* or *Line*) to a phone jack.

## Routing the network to the modem

A *router* is a device that moves data across multiple networks, and it's designed to be able to determine the correct target for data packets that are moving across those networks. A router is always connected to at least two discrete networks, and most of the time, one of those networks is the Internet (yes, the Internet is a network just like your home network, except it's much bigger). A router always acts as a gateway: the connection point between two networks. In that position, it's able to direct data traffic, deciding which way to send each information packet. In your home network, you can use a router to let every computer on the network share a DSL or cable modem, setting up the router to connect your network to the other network (the Internet).

Acting as a gateway, routers have at least two connectors — one for your network and one for the Internet network. The connector for the Internet side of the gateway is usually labeled *WAN* (which stands for wide area network), and the connector for your home network is usually labeled *LAN* (for local area network).

### Ethernet routers

Ethernet routers connect all the computers on an Ethernet network to the Internet. You can connect your already in-place network to the router, or you can use the router to connect the network (letting the router act as a concentrator).

The following instructions apply to the following scenarios:

- Your Ethernet network is already connected to a concentrator.
- Your non-Ethernet network is connected to a bridge.

Use the following steps to share your DSL/cable modem with all the computers on your network:

1. **Connect Ethernet cable between the hub/Ethernet connector on the bridge and the LAN connector on the router.**

   Consult the documentation for the router to find the technical specifications for that connection. You may have to use a crossover cable instead of a regular patch cable, and you may have to use the Uplink port on the hub instead of a regular computer port.

2. **Connect Ethernet cable between the modem and the WAN connector on the router.**

   Consult the documentation for the router to find out whether you need to use a crossover cable or a regular patch cable.

Follow the instructions in the manufacturer's documentation to configure the router. The router accepts IP addresses from your ISP and then distributes IP addresses to the computers that are on the network. Your ISP only sees the router, and the individual computers on the network are invisible to the Internet (which includes your ISP).

### Ethernet routers can be concentrators, too

If you're still in the planning stages for your network, and you've decided to use Ethernet, you can omit the purchase of a concentrator. Instead, buy a router with multiple LAN connections and use those connections as the concentrator.

In fact, if you already have a concentrator-connected network and then decide to use a DSL/cable modem, you can buy a multiport router and use it in either of the following ways:

- Replace the concentrator and sell it to a friend who is building a home network.
- Leave the concentrator in place and use the router to expand your network when you add more computers (and your original concentrator is out of ports).

In fact, a multiport router can accept connections from multiple concentrators.

### Non-Ethernet routers

New on the market are routers for wireless and phoneline networks. These routers act as both bridges and routers, and the word *brouter* is now occasionally heard when techies speak about these devices in computerese.

If you have a wireless network, the router has antennas to manage data to and from the wireless network (the LAN) and an RJ-45 connector to manage data to and from the DSL/cable modem. Of course, if you read the information about bridges earlier in this chapter, you're saying, "That's just a bridge." No it's not, because the router has two important capabilities that a bridge lacks — it manages IP addresses for the network computers and it acts as a gateway (which means that the individual computers on the LAN are invisible to the Internet).

For phoneline networks, a phoneline router connects to your LAN the same way your computers do — by running a telephone wire between the PNA port and a telephone wall jack. The phoneline router connects to the DSL/cable modem by running Ethernet cable between the router's WAN port and the modem. Because it's a router, not a bridge, the phoneline router provides IP addresses for the network computers and acts as a gateway to make the LAN invisible to the Internet.

## Configuring the router

A router requires configuration to perform its tasks. It doesn't have a keyboard or screen, so you must configure it from one of the computers that it's connected to. Some routers have software programs that you install on the computer. When you run the program, the software finds the device and lets you configure it. Other routers have built-in Web servers. Just open the browser on your computer and type in a special address (like `http://192.168.0.1`), and then configure the router in your Web browser.

You must enter the same type of information as you would have entered if your DSL device or cable modem had been connected to a single computer. That means entering an IP address or telling the router to obtain an address automatically from your ISP. Use the instructions from your ISP in addition to the instructions that came with the router.

## Configuring client computers for a router

On the client side, the router's IP address becomes the gateway. Depending on the instructions that came with your router, you may have to enter that IP address in the Gateway field of the NIC Properties dialog box on each computer. The gateway information is part of the TCP/IP properties.

In Windows 98 and Windows Me, use the following steps to configure the computer to find the router:

1. **Choose Start⇨Settings⇨Control Panel.**

   The Control Panel window opens.

2. **Double-click the Network icon.**

   The Network dialog box opens, with the Configuration tab in the foreground.

3. **Select TCP/IP, and then click the Properties button.**

   The TCP/IP Properties dialog box appears.

4. **Click the Gateway tab.**

5. **In the New Gateway field (see Figure 7-13), enter the IP address for the router, and then click the Add button.**

   The IP address appears in the Installed Gateways list.

6. **Click OK twice.**

   After Windows copies files and saves the new information, reboot the computer.

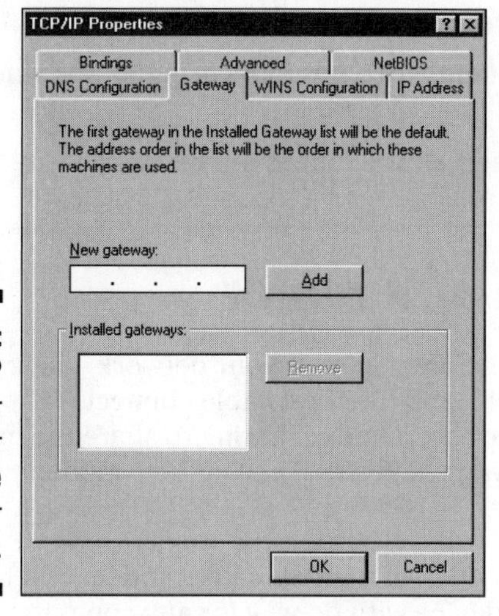


**Figure 7-13:** Enter the IP address for the router so that the computer can find it.

In Windows 2000 and Windows XP, take these steps to configure the computer to access the router:

1. **In Windows 2000, choose Start➪Settings➪Network and Dial-up Connections; in Windows XP, choose Start➪Show All Connections.**

   A window displaying your network and Internet connections appears.

2. **Right-click the icon for Local Area Connection and choose Properties from the shortcut menu.**

   The NIC Properties dialog box appears.

3. **Select TCP/IP, and then click the Properties button.**

   The TCP/IP Properties dialog box appears.

4. **Click the Advanced button.**

5. **In the Default Gateway section, click the Add button.**

   The TCP/IP Gateway Address dialog box appears (see Figure 7-14).

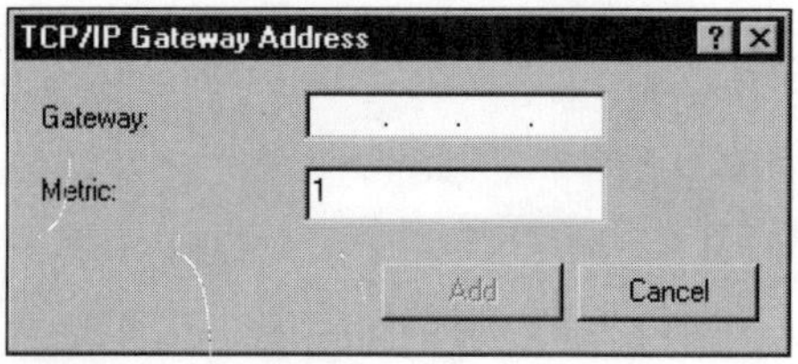

**Figure 7-14:** Enter the router's IP address.

6. **Enter the router's IP address, and click the Add button.**

   You can ignore the Metric field — it's for configuring routes when there are multiple gateways.

7. **Click OK until you've closed all the dialog boxes.**

## Two NICs instead of a router

If you had a DSL/cable modem before you built your network, one computer on the network already has a NIC, and Ethernet cable connects that NIC to the modem. You can use Internet Connection Sharing to share the modem over the network in the same way you'd share a telephone modem with the other computers on the network.

To make this work, you have to think of the DSL/cable modem as a telephone modem — it's an independent device with no way for any computer on the network to attach to it directly. The client computers "talk" to the modem by connecting to the computer that holds the modem.

The computer that holds the modem becomes the gateway, with a connection to the modem and a separate connection to the network. This configuration requires two NICs — one for the network and one for the modem. The network NIC matches the wiring type of the network (Ethernet, wireless, phoneline, or powerline).

# Chapter 8

# Configuring Computer Sharing

### *In This Chapter*

- Creating shares on each computer
- Protecting shared resources with a password

After you install the network hardware, install the cable to connect the computers, and *configure* (set up) the operating system to recognize and use those items, your computers are members of the network. Each computer can *see* the other computers on your network. You can view the computers that are connected to your network by opening the network window, which is Network Neighborhood in Windows 98 and My Network Places in later versions of Windows. Figure 8-1 shows the network window for a home network with two computers.

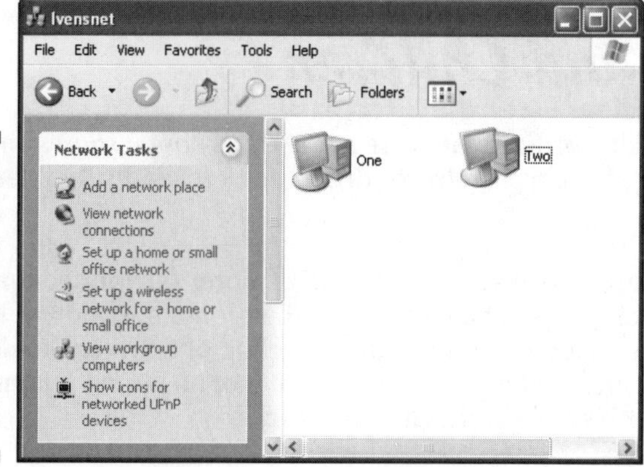


**Figure 8-1:** The computers on the network are displayed in the network window.

The list of computers you see includes the computer you're using, which of course you don't access through the Network Neighborhood or My Network Places window because you're already there.

Seeing a computer in Network Neighborhood or My Network Places means that the computer is up and running and is physically connected to the network. It doesn't mean that you can look inside the computer to see the files that are contained within it or that you can copy files from one computer to another. Computers don't share any resources until you configure them for sharing. I cover how to do that in this chapter.

The word *share* is used a lot in network computing:

- As a verb, *share* means configuring a resource on one computer so that people working on other computers can use it.
- As a noun, a *share* is a resource that's configured for access by users on other computers. If you configure your C drive for sharing, that drive is known as a share.

You have to create the shared resources that you want to offer to remote users. The most common shares are hard drives and folders, because those are the containers for files. However, you can also share peripheral devices, such as a printer or CD-ROM, Zip, and floppy drives.

Every share you create shows up in Network Neighborhood or My Network Places when you open (double-click) the computer's icon.

# Understanding Hierarchy: Shares Have Parents and Children

Shares have a pecking order. Shares are made up of *parent shares* and *child shares.* This matches the hierarchy for drives, folders, and subfolders on your computer.

In the normal hierarchy you see in Windows Explorer on your computer, a parent is any container that can contain another container. A drive is the parent container for a folder, and a folder is a child of a drive. A folder can be a parent of a subfolder, and a subfolder is a child of its parent folder (and, by extension, I guess it's also a grandchild of a drive).

Having trouble? Think of the way the filing cabinet in your home office holds all your tax files or a manila envelope in your filing cabinet holds all the tax information for last year — both the filing cabinet and the manila envelope are parents, although the filing cabinet could be considered more of a grandparent. The bottom line is that parents exist at every level of the hierarchy. You can remember this pretty easily if you figure that the youngest generation is the one that's least likely to have children of its own.

Figure 8-2 demonstrates the order in which containers and contained items are stored on your computer. This ordered pattern is called the *hierarchy.*

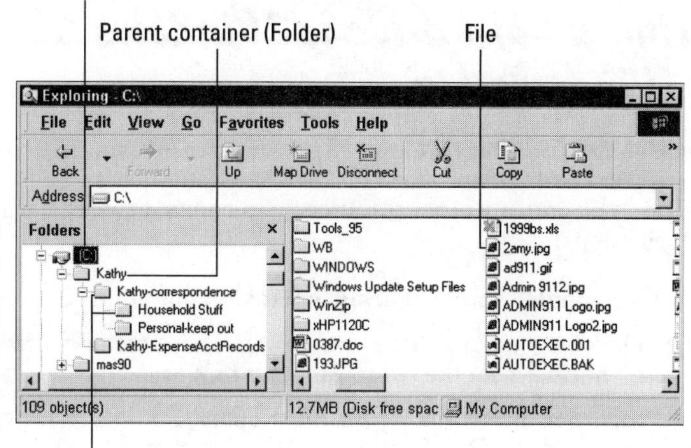


**Figure 8-2:** The hierarchy of computer components.

Drives are the top of your computer's hierarchy and may contain folders or files, or both. Folders can contain other folders or files, or both.

When it comes to shares, however, the parent-child relationship begins on the level at which you create a share. For example, consider that you want to allow all the users in your home network to be able to share a drive. The drive that's being shared is a parent share. The same goes if you decide not to share a drive, but instead share specific folders. When you share a folder, that folder is a parent share, and any subfolder is a child share. Memorize this rule, because it's important to the way you maintain control over shares: *Every child in a parent share is automatically shared.*

The hard drive is also called the *root,* and the folders and files that are displayed when you look at the drive in Windows Explorer or My Computer are said to be located on the root.

# Sharing a Hard Drive

Home networks commonly share all the folders and files on the hard drives of every computer. Sharing a drive is a convenient way to make sure that you can find and use files, no matter where they are on a computer. You don't automatically see the contents of a hard drive on another computer. First, you have to configure the hard drive for sharing. This works differently, depending on the version of Windows running on the computer you're setting up for sharing.

## Sharing a hard drive in Windows 98 and Windows Me

When you share a drive in Windows 98 or Windows Me, you also have the opportunity to create permissions for the share (and that's true for sharing folders, printers, and any other resources). To create a shared hard drive, follow these steps:

1. **On the computer you're sharing, open My Computer.**
2. **Right-click on the hard drive you want to share (usually drive C) and choose Sharing from the shortcut menu that appears.**

   The Properties dialog box for the drive opens, and the Sharing tab is in the foreground. The Not Shared option is selected, and all the other options in the dialog box are grayed out and inaccessible.
3. **Select the Shared As option.**

   The options in the dialog box are now available, as shown in Figure 8-3.

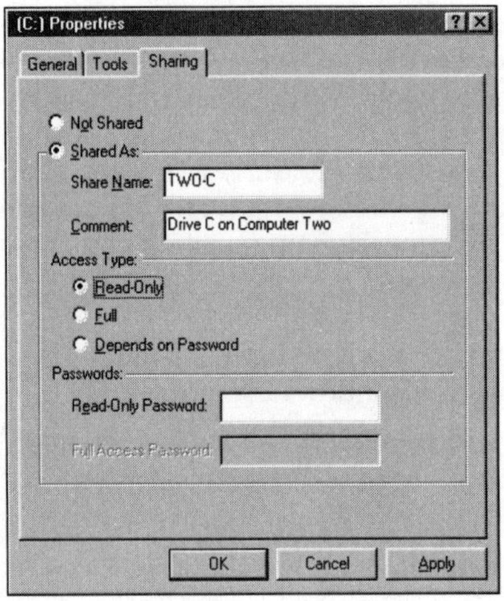

**Figure 8-3:** Set the controls for this share and give it a name.

4. **Type your own name for this share (Windows automatically calls it *C*) in the Share Name text box.**

   Choose a name that describes the share. For example, for the computer in the den, Den-C is a good name.

5. **If you want to provide a more complete description of the drive, you can type a descriptive phrase about this share in the Comment text box.**

   You can use the Comment text box to add more description about this share (for example, "Hard drive on the den computer"). The text in the Comment text box appears to remote users if they use the Details view of Network Neighborhood or My Network Places. (By default, Windows displays an icon view instead of the Details view.)

6. **Configure the Access Type and Passwords.**

   See the next section, "Controlling user actions in Windows 98 and Windows Me," for information about these options. By default, Windows makes the access type Read-Only, but unless you have a good reason not to, change the access type to Full.

7. **Click OK.**

   If you opted to require a password in Step 7, a Password Confirmation dialog box appears so that you can type the password again to confirm it. If you don't type the password correctly in the Password Confirmation dialog box, a message appears indicating that you've typed an incorrect password. Click OK to return to the dialog box, and retype the password. If your entry is incorrect again, choose Cancel and start over with a password you can type without making typos.

You are returned to the My Computer window, where a hand appears under your hard drive icon. The hand indicates that the drive is a shared resource. All the shares that you create display that hand icon.

## Controlling user actions in Windows 98 and Windows Me

Every time you create a share in Windows 98 and Windows Me, you have three choices of access types for that share. The following controls describe what you can do to limit the power of users on your network:

- **Read-Only:** Remote users can open and copy documents from the share but can't make changes to or delete the documents. If you choose this option, you can either require a password to admit only certain users to the share or skip the password to give read-only access to every remote user.

- **Full:** Remote users can manipulate and use folders and files on your hard drive as though they were working directly at your computer. If you choose this option, you can either require a password or let all remote users have full access to your hard drive.
- **Depends on Password:** The passwords that you create contain one of the access rights. As a result, the actions that users can perform depend on the passwords they use. If you choose this option, you must create a password for each type of access.

Remember that if you want to work on your own files from another computer, you're a remote user just like any other remote user. You have to know the password to get into your own files.

If you opt to use passwords to admit only certain users to this share, or to separate users who can only read files from users who can write files, create the password or passwords as needed. Then give the appropriate password only to certain users.

For example, you may decide to create a shared resource for the folder that contains the files for your household budget. You only want your spouse to have access to the files, and of course he should have full access. Select the Full option, and enter a password in the Full Access Password field. Give your spouse the password (and you'll need it, too, if you want to work on the files from a remote computer).

On the other hand, suppose that you want to let everybody view that novel you're writing, but when you're working at a remote computer, you want to be able to create and modify the files. Select the Depends on Password option, and give everybody the Read-Only password. Keep the Full Access Password to yourself.

If you don't want anyone to access a share except you (when you're working at a remote computer), invent a password and don't tell anybody what it is.

When a remote user looks at the shares on a Windows 98/Me computer in Network Neighborhood or Windows Explorer, the user has no indication that a share is password-protected. The first clue comes when the user tries to open the share and sees a dialog box asking for the password.

## Sharing a hard drive in Windows 2000

If you're running Windows 2000, the basic steps for sharing a hard drive are the same as those for Windows 98 and Windows Me, but your options are different. Here's the way to share a drive in Windows 2000:

1. **On the computer you're sharing, open My Computer.**
2. **Right-click on the hard drive you want to share and choose Sharing from the shortcut menu that appears.**

   The Properties dialog box for the drive opens, and the Sharing tab is in the foreground. The Do Not Share This Folder option is selected, and all the other options in the dialog box are grayed out and inaccessible.
3. **Select the Share This Folder option.**

   By default, Windows 2000 creates a hidden administrative share named C$ (unless you're sharing drive D, in which case it's named D$). Administrative shares are for system administrators, and because Windows 2000 is designed for business use where sharing and security are the norm, this automatic action occurs. (The $ character at the end of a share name hides the share from Network Neighborhood and My Network Places. You can take advantage of this nifty trick yourself — see the section "Using Hidden Shares," later in this chapter.)
4. **Click the New Share button to create a new share for the drive.**

   The New Share dialog box opens, as shown in Figure 8-4.

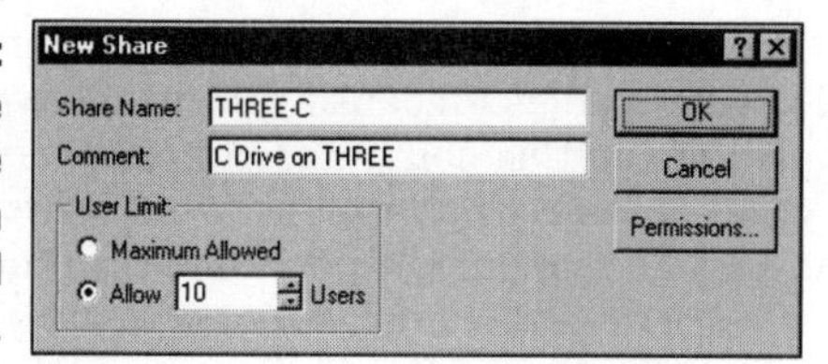


**Figure 8-4:** Name the new share and enter an optional description.

5. **Name the share, and optionally, enter a description in the Comment field.**

   If you're running NTFS, a Permissions button is visible. Users from other computers can access the share if they exist as users on the local machine. The way to keep a specific user out of the share is to omit that user's name in the list of local users. When a user is recognized on the Windows 2000 local computer, he or she can access any share you create. If you want to restrict user actions, you must use the NTFS security settings for the drive or folder.

   Set up a user account on the computer for each user on the network. Then, in the Permissions dialog box for the share (not the Permissions dialog box for the folder), add the name of each user and give Full Control.

   To find out more about drive and folder security in a Windows 2000 computer running NTFS, read *Windows 2000 Professional For Dummies* by Andy Rathbone and Sharon Crawford (Wiley Publishing, Inc.).

### Sharing a hard drive in Windows XP

Sharing a hard drive on a computer that's running Windows XP Home Edition is slightly more complicated than it is on other versions of Windows. To accomplish this deed, you have to engage in a small skirmish with the operating system, which doesn't like the idea of sharing a drive. Use the following steps to share a drive:

1. **On the computer you're sharing, open My Computer.**
2. **Right-click on the hard drive you want to share and choose Sharing and Security from the shortcut menu that appears.**

   The Sharing tab appears, displaying a message that warns you that sharing a drive isn't a good idea. Beneath the message is a link you can click to indicate you understand the risk, but you want to share the drive. Then the Sharing tab changes to reveal the options that allow you to share the drive.
3. **Select the Share This Folder on the Network option.**
4. **Enter a name for the share.**
5. **Select the Allow Network Users to Change My Files option.**

   If you don't select this option, network users can view files but can't create new files or modify existing files. Because you're a network user when you want to work on a file on this computer from a different computer, there's not much point in restricting what network users can do. However, it isn't really as easy as this paragraph makes it sound. The security in Windows XP is rather complicated, and it gets more complicated when you share folders. See the section, "Windows XP Security — Sorting Out the Confusion," later in this chapter.
6. **Click OK.**

## Sharing Removable Drives

You use the same steps that you used to share a hard drive when you want to share a peripheral (removable) drive. Peripheral drives are considered external to your computer (your hard drive is internal), such as your floppy drive, a CD-ROM drive, or a Zip drive.

However, the results of sharing are a bit different because all your peripheral drives are also removable drives — the contents change depending on which disk is currently inserted in the drive.

When you share a removable drive, you're actually sharing the bay, the empty drive. Once it's shared, the share applies to any disk you place in the bay. This makes it a bit more difficult to decide about access controls. Some disks may have contents that you think everybody can use, and other disks may have contents that you prefer that nobody change.

CD-ROM drives are read-only. However, if you have a CD-R (CD-recordable) drive, never attempt to *burn,* or write to, a CD from a remote machine. It doesn't work properly. Only burn CDs from the machine that holds the CD-R drive.

Trying to set access controls for peripheral drives is foolish because you'd have to spend a lot of time changing the controls, depending on the disk that's inserted at any given time. The solution is to give full access to peripheral drives and then hide any disks in a locked drawer that you don't want other users to access.

# Sharing Folders

If you've decided not to share the hard drives on your network computers, you need to share the folders that hold the files that you and other users need to access when you're working at a remote computer.

But, suppose you've shared the hard drive of your computer, and you understand the parent-child hierarchy, which essentially means that every folder on the shared drive is automatically shared. All a remote user has to do is access the shared drive, expand it to see all the folders, and then find the file she needs. In that case, why bother to share folders?

The reason to create shared folders, even if you've shared a drive, is to make it easier to get to shared folders from the other computers on the network. Remember, when you open Network Neighborhood or My Network Places and double-click a computer icon, all the shares on that computer are displayed. If the only share is the hard drive, it's going to take a lot of mouse clicks to navigate through the drive to get to a specific folder.

In addition, remote users (including you) may want to map a shared folder to a drive letter so that they can open the folder from My Computer or Windows Explorer, instead of opening Network Neighborhood or My Network Places. A folder must be shared to be mapped. Chapter 11 explains drive mapping and the convenience it offers.

You can create as many folder shares on your computer as you please, using the same steps you use to share a drive. However, instead of right-clicking the drive icon in My Computer or Windows Explorer, right-click the icon for the folder you want to share.

In Windows XP, remote users in a peer-to-peer network log on as Guest, so you must make sure the Guest account is enabled.

# Windows XP Security — Sorting Out the Confusion

The problem with protecting or offering shares on a Windows XP computer is that the situation changes depending on your setup. The following combinations are available, and each presents its own set of rules (and steps) for sharing resources:

- Windows XP Home Edition with FAT
- Windows XP Home Edition with NTFS
- Windows XP Professional with FAT
- Windows XP Professional with NTFS

All versions of Windows XP pay as much attention to sharing folders with other users of the same computer as with users who access the computer across a network. The options aren't always clear, nor are they always logical. Depending on your computer's configuration, different steps are required to configure shares. For example, your Windows XP Home Edition computer may not offer security options when you're working normally, but if you boot into Safe Mode, you see the configuration choices for setting security.

Windows XP includes a feature called *simplified file sharing* (sometimes called *simple file sharing*). It's not so darn simple, and it's very rigid. In my opinion, it takes away choices you should be able to make if you want to, but then I always have an "attitude problem" when I'm told "this is for your own good, we know what's best for you, and we don't think you should be able to make your own decisions." You cannot turn off simplified file sharing in Windows XP Home Edition. (You *can* turn it off in Windows XP Professional if you're running NTFS.)

Depending on your combination of Windows XP, you may or may not be able to share your documents if you keep them in the standard My Documents folder. Because all Windows software automatically stores your data in your My Documents folder, this can be a real pain!

Going over all the permutations and combinations would fill several chapters, and you should be able to tell what your options are by the dialog boxes you see on the screen as you set up shared drives and folders. You can get more information on these details by reading *Windows XP For Dummies,* 2nd Edition, by Andy Rathbone (Wiley).

# Using Hidden Shares

You can hide a shared folder from Network Neighborhood or My Network Places. The cool thing about a hidden share is that you can get to it if you know it exists and if you know the trick for accessing it. (I provide the trick in this section.)

A hidden share can be a useful location for documents you don't want other network users to see when you can't easily set security options for the computer that holds those documents.

A hidden share only works if you keep in mind the basic rules about shares:

- Shares are for remote users, and they're irrelevant when somebody is using your computer. The folder you hide isn't hidden from anyone who is using your computer.
- If you want to hide even one folder on a drive, you cannot share the drive, because as soon as you do, every folder in the drive can be seen. Folders are children of drives, and when you share a parent, you share all its children.
- A hidden share must be a parent share, because if it's a child of a share, it's visible in Network Neighborhood and My Network Places as soon as a remote user expands the parent share.

The best way to hide a folder from everyone (users who work at the computer and users who access the computer across the network) is to make it a subfolder of a folder you're not sharing, on a drive you're not sharing.

Create a parent folder for the express purpose of creating a subfolder that you want to hide. Give the parent folder an innocuous name so that nobody who uses your computer would be curious enough to expand the folder in Windows Explorer and find your secret. For example, create a folder on your drive and name it Tools or Maintenance. Then create a subfolder and name it Logfiles or another name that seems equally boring or technical. In Logfiles, you can keep all your naughty and nice lists, and no one will suspect a thing, Machiavelli. Heh, heh, heh.

Another nifty place to put a hidden subfolder is in the Windows folder (`C:\Windows` or `C:\WINNT` in Windows 2000). There's no reason to share the Windows folder because its contents are specific to the local computer. Other people who use the computer are unlikely to scroll through the subfolders in the Windows folders, unless they're suspicious about your ability to be sneaky.

## Creating a hidden share

To hide a folder's share, follow the steps to create a folder share that I describe in the previous section. However, when you give the share a name, make the last character of the share name a dollar sign ($). That's it, the share is hidden. Easy, huh?

## Getting to your hidden share from a remote computer

When you work at a different computer and you want to get to a file that's in your hidden share, follow these steps:

1. **Choose Start⇨Run.**

   The Run dialog box opens.

2. **Type** *ComputerName**ShareName* **in the Open text box, substituting the real names of the computer and the share.**

   For example, if you're trying to get to a hidden share named `Logs$` on a computer named Den, type **\\den\logs$**. A window opens to display the contents of your hidden share.

## Keeping the secret a secret

When you use the Run command, Windows saves the command. The next time you open the Run command, the last command that you typed displays. Just click OK to run the command again. Very convenient, eh? Uh, not if you share the computer with other users.

The way to prevent your command from being visible to another user is to make sure that you log off when you leave the computer you were using. This ensures that nobody else can sit at the computer using your logon name and settings. The Run commands are saved on a user-by-user basis, so when a user named Mom is logged on, only commands issued by Mom are visible in the list.

# Chapter 9

# Setting Up Users

### *In This Chapter*

- Setting up users
- Configuring passwords
- Understanding profile folders

Unless you've bought a computer for every member of the family (rather unlikely), people share computers in your home network. One of the nifty features that you can take advantage of when users share the same computer is to provide each user with his or her own profile.

A *profile* enables each user to personalize the computer environment, and then, every time that user logs on to the computer, the same environment automatically appears. This means you don't have to live with (or constantly correct) the configuration settings that were created by other people who use the computer.

Profiles work differently for each version of Windows, and the big differences are the following:

- Windows 98 and Windows Me don't employ user profiles by default, and even after you enable profiles, the operating system doesn't care whether users log on. As a result, you can't enforce this feature, and you have to depend on the cooperation of all the users in the household to make the feature work properly.
- Windows 2000 and Windows XP insist on user profiles and enforce the rule that users must log on to the computer.

A user profile loads when a user logs on to a computer (using the *logon name* attached to the user account) and enters the password attached to that logon name.

You don't really need a password, because Windows keeps track of your customized settings without one. A password keeps others from logging on to the computer using your name. If another user logs on with your name and makes changes to the configuration, you have to live with those changes (or take the trouble to reset everything). The password is just a way to prevent someone else from pretending that he or she is you.

The technical term for no password is *null password.*

In this chapter, I cover the options that are available for each version of Windows and provide an overview of the tasks you have to perform to manage users.

# Profiles in Windows 98 and Windows Me

Windows 98 and Windows Me don't automatically assume that each person who uses a computer wants to create his or her own individual settings. Before users can customize their settings, you have to make the operating system accept individual profiles.

## Enabling profiles in Windows 98/Me

To create the atmosphere for customized settings, you have to tell the operating system that you want each user to have a personal profile. Follow these steps to turn on the Profiles feature in Windows 98/Me:

1. **Choose Start⇨Settings⇨Control Panel.**

   The Control Panel window opens.

2. **Double-click the Passwords icon.**

   The Passwords Properties dialog box opens.

3. **Click the User Profiles tab.**

   The options for user profiles are presented, as shown in Figure 9-1.

4. **Select the Users Can Customize Their Preferences and Desktop Settings radio button.**

   This option enables individual profiles.

5. **In the bottom half of the dialog box, select either or both profile options.**

   If you choose to include desktop icons and Network Neighborhood contents in user settings, Windows remembers each user's changes to those objects and setup. Select this option to let users design their own desktops.

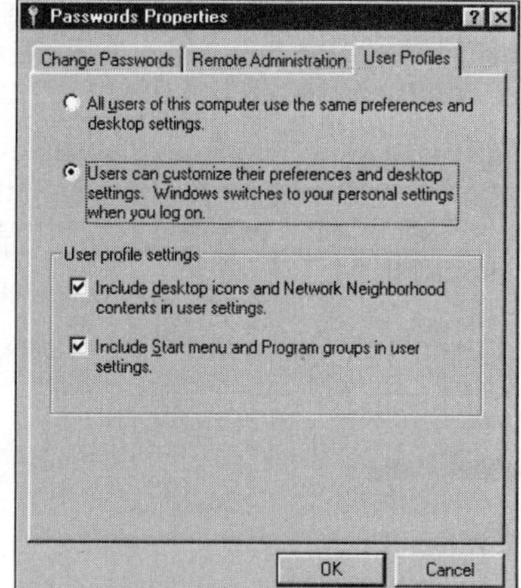


**Figure 9-1:** Configure Windows to save each user's individual preferences.

If you select the option Include Start menu and Program groups in user settings, as each user adds items to the Start menu (usually by installing software), the menu item appears only when that user is logged on. Selecting this option doesn't always work well because other users may occasionally need a program that another user has installed.

6. **Click OK.**

   Now Windows is ready to keep track of all the users who work at this computer. The System Settings Change dialog box opens, prompting you to restart the computer.

7. **Restart your computer.**

If you select the option to include the Start menu and Program groups, don't worry that you won't be able to use software that someone else has installed because your individual Start menu doesn't contain a menu item for that software. You can put the menu item on your menu without installing the software again, but accomplishing this requires some work. See the section, "Tweaking profiles in Windows 98 and Windows Me," later in this chapter.

## Creating users in Windows 98/Me computers

After you tell Windows 98/Me that you want to keep track of each user's settings, you have to start tracking individual users. You have a choice about the way you want to create users:

- You can manually add a user to the computer before that user logs on to the computer for the first time. This option lets you configure the user's default profile, which the user can then customize at will.
- You can wait until the user logs on to have Windows 98/Me automatically add the user to the computer, and create a profile using the system's default profile. This occurs when a user logs on with a name that's not yet set up on the computer.

Windows provides a wizard to add users to a computer. To launch the wizard, follow these steps:

1. **Choose Start⇨Settings⇨Control Panel.**

   The Control Panel window opens.

2. **Double-click the Users icon.**

   The first time you open the Users icon, the Add User Wizard starts automatically. After you create the first user, double-clicking the Users icon opens the User Settings dialog box, and you have to click the New User button to launch the wizard.

3. **Read the information in the first wizard window, and then click Next.**

   The first window is just an introduction to the wizard, so you don't have to provide any information.

4. **In the next wizard window, in the User Name text box, type the name that you want to use when you log on.**

   Most people use just a first name, unless two people in the household have the same first name. If so, you can use Mom and Sis, or Dad and Junior. Nicknames are fine, too, if you're not embarrassed by having a logon box appear that says Dogbreath or Pizzapig.

5. **Click Next.**

   The Enter New Password dialog box opens.

6. **If you want to use a password, type the password in the Password text box of the Enter New Password dialog box, which is shown in Figure 9-2. Type the same password in the Confirm Password text box, and then click Next.**

   If you don't want to enter a password, click the Next button. Either way, the Personalized Items Settings dialog box opens.

   If the entries in the Password text box and the Confirm Password text box don't match, the wizard asks you to type the password again. You can't see the actual characters you're typing, so use a password that's easy to type. For example, if you frequently make mistakes when you type numbers, don't use a number in your password.

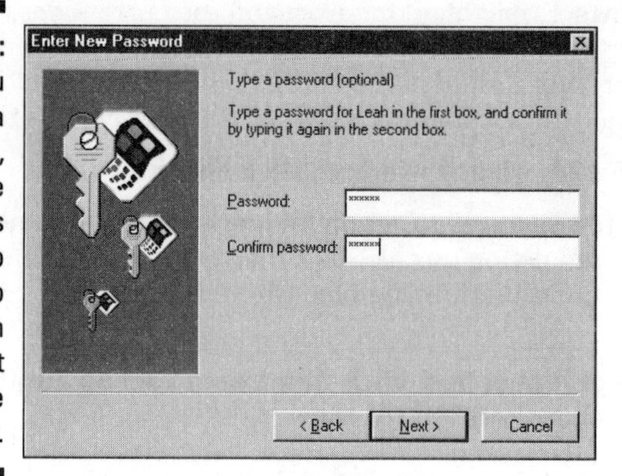


**Figure 9-2:** When you type a password, the characters turn into asterisks so nobody can see what you're typing.

7. **In the Personalized Items Settings dialog box, shown in Figure 9-3, choose the settings that you want to personalize and save in your profile. Also, choose the way that you want to have these items created. Then click Next.**

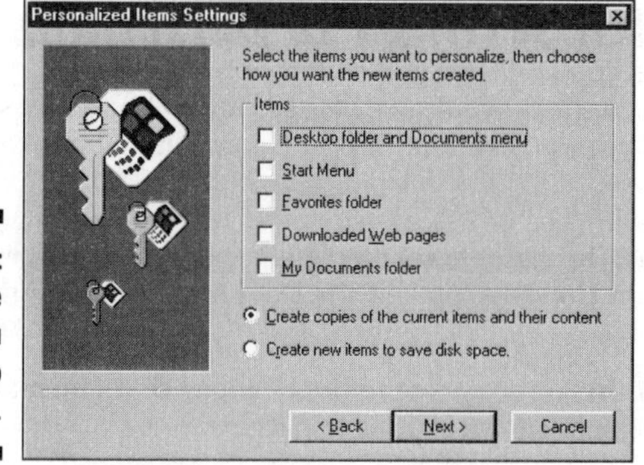


**Figure 9-3:** Choose the items you want to personalize.

You can personalize the Desktop folder and Documents menu, the Start Menu, the Favorites folder, Downloaded Web pages, and the My Documents folder.

The items that you don't select remain unchanged. Even if you make changes while you're working on the computer, those items revert to their current state the next time you log on. See the next section, "Deciding which settings to personalize," for more information on how this works.

If you tell Windows to create copies of the current items, you're asking that the current desktop settings serve as the starting point for your configuration efforts. Everything that exists on the current desktop is automatically copied to your profile, even if you don't really need all the items (and they occupy a lot of disk space). However, if you tell Windows to create new items, the settings are saved as the user creates them.

8. **In the Ready to Finish wizard window, click Finish.**

   Windows takes a few seconds to set up folders and files for a new user. (You see an animated dialog box as this activity proceeds.) Then you are returned to the User Settings dialog box, where the new user name is listed.

9. **In the User Settings dialog box, click New User to set up another user, or click Close if you're finished for now.**

Every time you log on to the computer with this user name, your customization efforts are saved according to the options you set.

Profile folders hold all the information about each user's configuration settings. In Windows 98/Me, you can find each user's profile folders at `C:\Windows\Profiles\`*`UserName`*.

## Deciding which settings to personalize

The Personalized Items Settings window (refer to Figure 9-3) offers several choices for each user's personalization. Here are some guidelines to help you make selections:

- **Desktop folder and Documents menu:** Select this option to save your personal settings for the desktop and the Documents submenu on your Start menu.
- **Start Menu:** Select this option to save the changes that you make to the Start menu, including program groups and items.
- **Favorites folder:** Select this option to save your settings for your Favorites folder, which holds links to your favorite Web sites as well as links to programs and documents that are on your hard drive.
- **Downloaded Web pages:** Select this option to save temporary Internet files and cookies in your own personal folders. (Temporary Internet files are called the *cache. Cookies* are pieces of data that Internet sites place on your hard drive to identify you when you next visit those sites.)
- **My Documents folder:** Select this option to make the My Documents folder on the desktop a private folder for yourself.

## Changing user options

In addition to creating users, the Users icon in Control Panel allows you to manage users. *Managing* means that you can change the options for users, copy an existing user's setup to a new user, or delete any user names you no longer need.

### Copying a user's settings to a new user

Perhaps you have a user who has a really terrific configuration. The good news is that you can use that configuration to set up a new user. Usually, you find the following configuration items: a Programs menu that shows everything that's been installed, lots of handy shortcuts on the desktop, and a beautiful and highly decorative desktop background. Follow these steps to clone a new user from an existing user:

1. **Choose Start⇨Settings⇨Control Panel.**

   The Control Panel window opens.

2. **Double-click the Users icon.**

   The User Settings dialog box opens.

3. **In the Users list box, select the user with the configuration that you want to copy.**

4. **Click Make a Copy to open the Add User Wizard.**

5. **Follow the instructions for adding a new user, clicking Next to move through each of the wizard's windows.**

   The wizard asks for a user name, a user password, and a confirmation of the password. Then you're asked which items you want to personalize. That's all there is to it — the new user has a terrific desktop!

If you clone a user who has been working at this computer for some time, all the documents in that user's personal My Documents folder are cloned. Internet cookies are cloned. Everything that's linked to the user is cloned. To avoid that problem, remove the check mark from Favorites folder, Downloaded Web pages, and My Documents folder when you get to the Personalized Items Settings window.

The best way to use the Make a Copy feature is to create a user, customize the desktop and the Start menu items, and then use that user only for copying the configuration to new users. You may want to name the user *clone* (if you think the person got all his good ideas from you) or *perfect person* (if the person *is* you).

### *Deleting a user*

If your user list contains a name that's no longer used on this computer, get rid of the user name. You not only dump the name but also clear all the folders that are attached to the user, which frees disk space. The only time that you'll probably have to delete a name is if your daughter adds herself to a computer more than once. For example, she may log on as Mary Smith at the beginning of the summer and set herself up as a user. In the fall, she will most certainly return to Harvard (*Hah-vad*), where she's a straight-A student. At Thanksgiving, she may need to use the network to write her rocket science paper and decide that she wants to log on as EngineerLady, or she may even forget that she set up configuration settings as Mary Smith.

Windows doesn't let you delete the user who is currently logged on.

### *Changing a user's password*

You can change passwords in the User Settings dialog box, but you have to know the current password to do so. Windows insists on making sure that you know the old password before you're allowed to enter a new password. This, of course, eliminates the ability to fix things when a user forgets a password (the fix for that problem is covered later in this chapter).

You can also change passwords in the Passwords Properties dialog box in Control Panel. However, the Passwords Properties dialog box works only for the user who is currently logged on; the User Settings dialog box works for any user.

Follow these steps to change your password from the User Settings dialog box:

1. **Choose Start⇨Settings⇨Control Panel.**

   The Control Panel window opens.

2. **Double-click the Users icon.**

   The User Settings dialog box opens, displaying a list of users in the Users list box.

3. **Select the appropriate user name.**

   The name you click is highlighted.

4. **Click the Set Password button.**

   The Change Windows Password dialog box opens, as shown in Figure 9-4.

5. **Type the old password in the Old Password text box.**

   If either the old password or the new password is a null password (no password at all), just make sure that the appropriate box is cleared of any characters.

**Figure 9-4:** Remember to type carefully, because you can't see the characters you're typing.

6. **Type the new password in the New Password text box.**
7. **Type the new password again in the Confirm New Password text box.**

   If you make a mistake, you're asked to try again.
8. **Click OK to return to the User Settings dialog box.**

   A message appears to announce that this user now has a new password.
9. **Click Close to close the User Settings dialog box.**

### *Changing user settings*

You can change the items that a user can personalize by selecting the user's name and choosing Change Settings. When the Personalized Items Settings dialog box opens, as shown in Figure 9-5, you can select or deselect items to indicate what this user can personalize. Most of the time, you make these changes for your own logon name, but if you're acting as the home network administrator, you may have reasons to work with other user names.

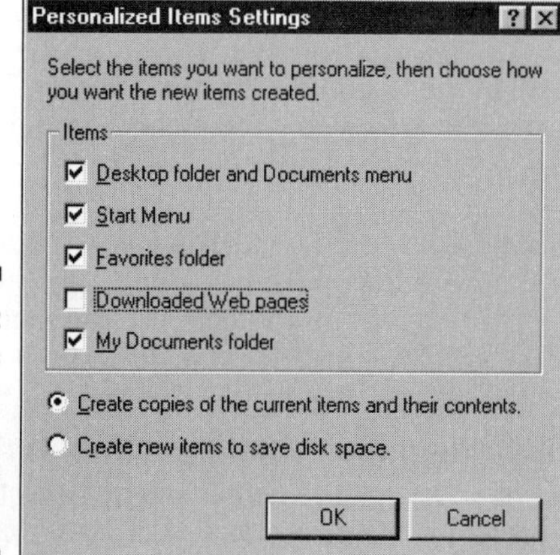


**Figure 9-5:** Some users don't feel the need to personalize every item.

## Sneaking around, resetting passwords, and otherwise foiling Windows 98/Me "security"

People forget their passwords. It's a common, frequent problem. You usually forget your password the next time you try to log on after a password change, but using a password for weeks or months and then suddenly forgetting it is not rare.

Recognizing the symptoms of a user who forgets a password is easy. When the logon dialog box opens, the user stares at it for a moment and then shrieks or moans, "Oh no!" The user is usually frozen in front of the computer for several seconds and then experiences a panic attack. (The symptoms vary according to the way that person handles panic.) However, the problem of a forgotten password is easy to solve, so the user has no reason to panic. The way to solve the problem of a forgotten password is to delete the Windows file that holds the password. That file is checked against your password entry whenever you log on. In fact, sometimes users don't really forget their passwords — the password just doesn't work because a problem has occurred with the user's password file. If a password file becomes corrupted or someone inadvertently deletes the file, the password won't work.

In this section, I go over the steps for the solution, which illustrates why I say that Windows 98 and Windows Me are operating systems devoid of security.

### Get sneaky: Just bypass the logon process

To delete your password file, you must log on to the computer. But how do you log on if you don't have your password? Fortunately (or unfortunately, depending on how you feel about security), logging on to the network and getting around this Catch-22 without a password is as easy as pie. (Don't try this solution on Windows 2000 or Windows XP — it doesn't work.)

To bypass the logon, click Cancel in the Logon dialog box or press Esc to make the Logon dialog box go away. Presto, you're on the computer and you can do whatever you want.

You have a couple of choices about what to do next. You can either choose to continue clicking Cancel every time you log on (thereby negating the usefulness of the scant security you already have) or you can find the faulty password file and zap it into oblivion. To search and destroy, read on.

### Seek and destroy: Finding, removing, and resetting a password file

If you've managed to bypass the "less than heavy-duty" logon security but still have no idea what your password is, you can solve the problem by finding the password file that's associated with your user name and deleting it so that you can reset the password. Follow these steps to find the password file and remove it:

1. **Open Windows Explorer, and select the folder that holds your Windows files (it's usually named Windows).**
2. **Press F3 to open the Find dialog box.**

   You want to find files with the extension `.pwl`, which is the extension that Windows assigns to password files. The Find dialog box should indicate that it is searching your Windows folder, as shown in Figure 9-6.

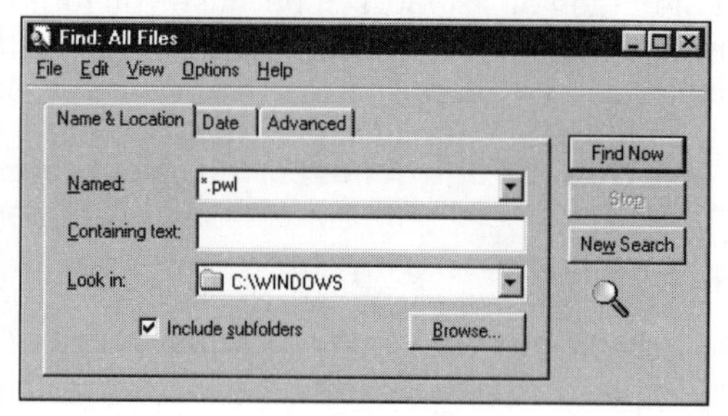


**Figure 9-6:** Search the Windows folder for your password file.

3. **In the Named text box, type** pwl **or** *.pwl, **and click Find Now.**

   The Find dialog box shows a list of all the files that your computer found with the `.pwl` extension.
4. **Select your password file from the list that appears in the Find dialog box.**

   You can recognize your password file because it has the first eight letters of your logon name, followed by the extension `.pwl`. If your logon name has a space in it, the space is ignored in the password filename.
5. **Press Delete to delete the file.**

   Windows asks you to confirm the fact that you want to delete the file.
6. **Click Yes to confirm that you want to delete the file.**

Your computer no longer has any record of your password. You are passwordless, you're nulled.

After you've deleted your password file, your computer has no record of a password for you. This is the same as having a null password. In fact, if you don't want to have a password anymore, you don't have to do anything — just log on without a password. Windows asks you to verify the new password (and if you're opting to skip a password, just press Enter again to verify the null password).

## Back to the drawing board: Creating a new password

If you do want a password, you have two options for resetting your password: You can create a new password immediately after deleting the old one, or you can wait until the next time you log on to create a new password.

### Creating a new password before the next logon

If you want to create a new password before you log on again, you can't use the Passwords icon in Control Panel because it's connected to the current logged-on user, and you didn't log on as yourself because you forgot your password. Use the following steps to create a new password and a new password file at the same time:

1. **Double-click the Users icon in Control Panel, and select your logon name.**
2. **Click Set Password.**
3. **Skip the Old Password text box, and type a new password in the New Password text box.**

   Windows doesn't find an old password because you wiped out the password file.
4. **Type the new password again in the Confirm Password text box.**
5. **Click OK, and then click Close to close the User Settings dialog box.**

   Windows creates a new password file.
6. **Choose Log Off from the Start menu, confirm the logoff procedure, and then log on again as yourself.**

### Creating a new password at the next logon

If you want, you can wait until the next time you log on to create a new password. Just filling out the Password box in the Logon dialog box determines your new password. To log on again right away, click Start and choose Log Off. That Log Off command has no user name, because technically, nobody is logged on, because you bypassed the Logon dialog box. Then click Yes when Windows asks if you're sure you want to log off.

When the Logon dialog box appears again, it contains the name of the last user who had logged on (probably you). You can do one of the following things:

- If you want to keep the null password, type your logon name, skip the Password text box, and click OK. Your password file is re-created with a null password.

- If you want to create a new password, type a new password in the Password text box of the Logon dialog box. When you click OK, you're asked to confirm the password by typing it again. A new password file is created for you, and the password you entered is saved as your new password.
- If you're using Family Logon (covered in the next section), your name appears on the list of users for this computer, but the Password text box is grayed out and inaccessible. Click OK to log on with a null password, because you have no choice. Then use either the Passwords or Users applet in Control Panel to give yourself a new password. (When you're asked to type the old password, remember to leave the box blank because you got rid of the old password.)

If you once again forget the password, find and remove your password file again, but this time, don't create any passwords anywhere. Obviously, you're meant to have a null password.

## Logging on to your Windows 98/Me computer

In Windows 98 and Windows Me, when profiles are enabled, a Logon dialog box appears every time you start Windows. In Windows 2000 and Windows XP, you can't avoid a Logon dialog box, because there's no such thing as enabling profiles — the logon process is for security.

## Switching to another user

Okay, you powered up your computer and logged on. You balanced your checkbook, sent a letter to Mom, and played a game. Now somebody else wants to use the computer. If the new user just sits down in front of the computer, he's looking at your desktop decor and preference settings. In addition, he's using your My Documents folder, which doesn't make either of you very comfortable.

Actually, logging off the computer is a good idea, even if nobody else is standing over your shoulder waiting to use the computer. Logging off saves any changes that you've made to your personal configuration settings. Logging off also puts a Logon dialog box on the screen so that every time a user wants to use the computer, he or she must log on. This prevents anyone from accidentally using your profile and making changes.

Luckily, you don't have to shut down the computer to enable the next user to log on and load his or her personalized desktop. (I say "luckily" because in Windows 98 and Windows Me, the shutdown process is very time-consuming, and the startup process can seem endless.) You can just use the Log Off command by choosing Start⇨Log Off *Yourname*. (Your logon name appears instead of the word *Yourname*.) Click Yes when Windows asks if you're sure you want to log off. The Logon dialog box opens within seconds so that the next user can log on.

When the Logon dialog box returns, the name of the last user who logged on appears in the User Name text box. The new user must remove that name and replace it with his logon name and password (if he has one).

## Getting to know the default desktop

You can bypass the logon process by clicking Cancel in the Logon dialog box or by pressing Esc to make the Logon dialog box go away. The most common reason for users to bypass the logon is because they don't know the password that's required for a successful logon — not always a sign of some sinister intent. Being human, users sometimes just forget their own passwords.

When you bypass the logon, the desktop that appears is the desktop that was in effect when profiles were enabled on the computer. Call it the default desktop. If you turned on the Profiles feature immediately after installing Windows, the default desktop is quite sparse. The only desktop icons are those that appear as a result of installation choices. The Programs menu has only a few items (also the result of installation choices) such as Windows Explorer, the MS-DOS Command Prompt, and the Accessories you installed. You may also find a Startup folder, but it's probably empty. If you have been using the computer for a while — installing software, creating desktop shortcuts, and so on — before you enabled the Profiles feature, the default desktop offers those elements.

Anyone who uses the default desktop can make changes to it. A new default desktop results from saving those changes. The default desktop has two uses:

- It's the desktop for users who skip the logon procedure.
- It's the desktop that's cloned when you create a new user.

You can deliberately skip the logon just for the purpose of making changes to the default desktop. Then, from this desktop, create a new user.

## Using the Family Logon feature

If you think it's hard to believe that users frequently forget their passwords, it probably blows your mind to hear that users also fail to recall their names (okay, not their real names, their logon names). Most of us use nicknames or first names or some cute appellation for a logon name. Most folks don't choose to log on as Bentley T. Backstroke, Jr. The more likely logon choice is Bentley, Bent, or Junior.

Forgetting your logon name is not all that unusual, and I've found that it's a far more common event for people who have strange and esoteric logon names at work. If your company assigns you a logon name of 77645G567 (some companies use names like that) and you decide to use Sammy on your home computer, you can expect a brain fog to settle in when you look at that home-based Logon dialog box. You're sure that you're not supposed to use that weird logon name from work, but you're not really certain what you entered when you set yourself up as a user on your home computer. Was it Sam? Sam Smith? SSmith? Sam S?

You can bypass the logon (see an earlier section, cleverly titled, "Get sneaky: Just bypass the logon process") and use the default desktop to open the Users list in Control Panel, where you can find your name on the list. Write it down, and then log on again.

One way to make sure that nobody forgets his or her logon name is to use a clever logon device called Family Logon. With this feature enabled, the Family Logon dialog box — rather than the traditional Logon dialog box — opens when the operating system starts up. The Family Logon dialog box lists all the users who are registered on this computer, as shown in Figure 9-7. You just have to select your name, type your password (if you have one), click OK, and you're in!

**Figure 9-7:** With Family Logon, you don't have to remember your own name.

Family Logon is available for Windows 98 or Windows Me, not for Windows 2000 or Windows XP. However, Windows XP has a similar feature — the Welcome screen, which displays the names of all users who have accounts on the computer. Just click your own name to begin the logon process.

Installing the Family Logon feature in Windows 98 and Windows Me is easy. Before you begin, however, your Windows files must be available so that the appropriate files can be transferred to your hard drive. Insert the Windows CD in the CD-ROM drive. If the manufacturer preinstalled Windows, the files are probably on the hard drive, and the documentation that came with the computer explains where they are.

Press and hold Shift when you insert a CD to prevent the CD's Setup program from opening automatically.

Follow these steps to install the Family Logon feature:

1. **Choose Start➪Settings➪Control Panel.**

   The Control Panel window opens.

2. **Double-click the Network icon in Control Panel.**

   The Network dialog box opens, with the Configuration tab in the foreground.

3. **Click Add.**

   The Select Network Component Type dialog box opens.

4. **Choose Client, and click Add.**

   The Select Network Client dialog box opens.

5. **In the Select Network Client dialog box, shown in Figure 9-8, choose Microsoft from the Manufacturers pane on the left.**

   Windows Me shows only Microsoft in the left pane.

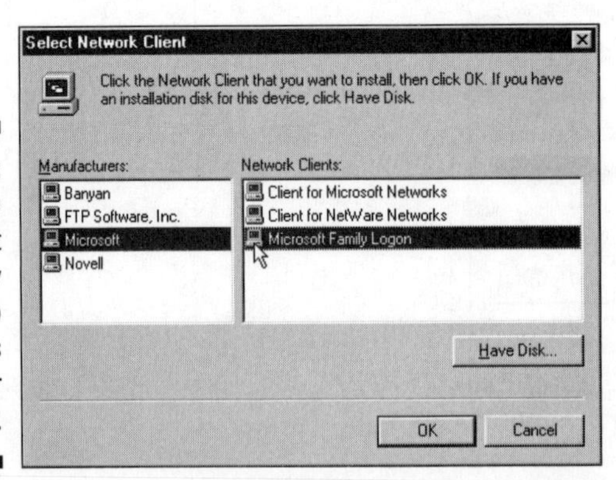


**Figure 9-8:** Choose Microsoft Family Logon to add its files to your computer.

6. **Choose Microsoft Family Logon from the Network Clients pane on the right.**
7. **Click OK.**

   You're returned to the Network dialog box, and the necessary files are copied to your hard drive.
8. **In the Primary Network Logon text box, choose Microsoft Family Logon from the drop-down list.**
9. **Click OK.**

   The Systems Settings Change dialog box opens to tell you that these settings take effect after you restart your operating system.
10. **Click Yes to restart the system.**

    When Windows restarts, the Family Logon dialog box opens so that you can select your user name and type your password.

If your logon name doesn't have an associated password, the password box is grayed out when you select your user name from the Family Logon dialog box.

# Logging Off

After you finish working on the computer — and nobody's standing over your shoulder waiting impatiently to use the machine — play it safe and log off. Otherwise, the next person who sits down in front of the computer may just start working, which can change your configuration. When the computer is up and running, people tend to forget that they need to log off the previous user and log themselves on. Going right to work is just too tempting.

If you don't use a password, you should delete your name from the Select User Name text box in the Logon dialog box that appears after you log off. (Just press Delete enough times to erase the letters.) Removing your name prevents the next user from accidentally clicking OK or pressing Enter, thus getting to your desktop. Such a move happens more often than you may imagine, and the result is two surprised and disappointed users. Your desktop is different the next time you log on, and the user who changed your desktop is annoyed when he logs on properly and the changes he thinks he made to his own profile aren't on his desktop.

When you log off, any open software windows are closed for you. Before the logoff procedure starts, you're given an opportunity to save any data that you've changed in the software since the last time you saved your documents.

If you have an operating system window open, such as Control Panel or My Computer, you can expect to find it open when you log on again. The same is true even if lots of other users log on in the meantime; the window just waits for you to return. Another user can't see the open window on the desktop (unless she left the same window open when she logged off).

## Tweaking profiles in Windows 98 and Windows Me

Your personal profile is a collection of the configuration options you set for yourself. Every time you make changes to the desktop or install software, the results are stored in your profile. When you log on to Windows with your own user name, your own user profile is loaded when Windows starts.

## What's in my profile?

You can see the elements in your profile by looking in the folders that contain your profile information. When you know how to find and identify profile elements, you can take advantage of the tricks and tips that are available for changing your profile easily. To see the elements in your profile, follow these steps:

1. **Choose Start⇨Programs⇨Windows Explorer.**

   The Explorer window opens.

2. **Click the plus sign to the left of the folder in which your Windows software is stored (usually named Windows).**

   In Windows Me, first expand My Computer and then expand the C drive to get to the Windows folder. The subfolders in your Windows folder are displayed in the left Explorer pane.

3. **Click the plus sign to the left of the subfolder named Profiles.**

   Folders for each user on the computer are displayed in the left Explorer pane.

4. **Click the plus sign to the left of the subfolder for your logon name.**

   You can see the subfolders for your own personal profile in the left Explorer pane, as shown in Figure 9-9.

**Figure 9-9:** Your profile folders store all the objects that make up your personal configuration settings.

# Where your desktop really lives

Click the Desktop folder to check out the subfolders and shortcuts it contains. The objects that you see in the folder represent the objects that you find on your desktop when you log on to Windows. You can have both folders and shortcuts on your desktop.

Here are some tidbits of information to note when you view your profile's Desktop folder:

- The default desktop icons aren't represented in your profile Desktop folder. Those icons include My Computer, Network Neighborhood, the Recycle Bin, and the My Documents folder.
- The objects in the profile Desktop folder are linked to your real desktop. If you delete or add an object in either place, the change is made in both places.

# Viewing your Start Menu folder

You can view and manipulate the items that appear on your personal Start menu within your personal profile folders. Click the plus sign next to the Start Menu folder to expand it. Then select the Programs subfolder, and click its plus sign to expand it as well.

The left pane displays the subfolders that are on your Programs menu, and the right pane shows the listings that appear on your Programs menu, as shown in Figure 9-10.

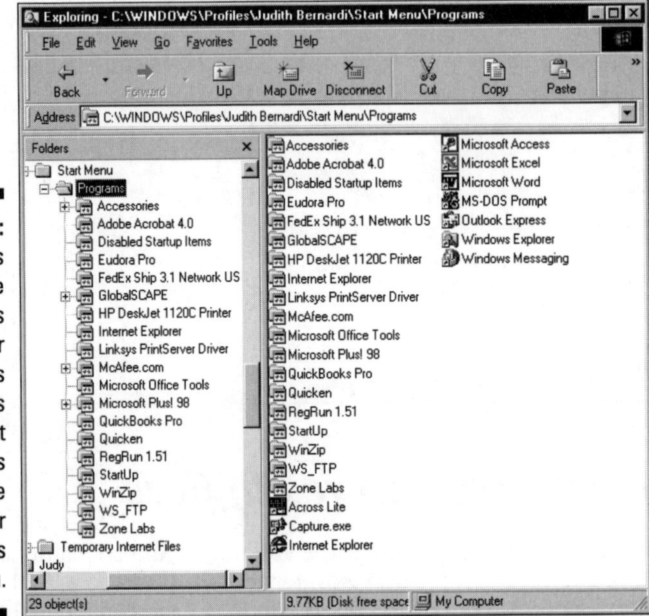


**Figure 9-10:** The objects in the Programs folder and its subfolders represent the listings that are on your Programs menu.

Subfolders in the Programs folder represent program groups that appear on your Programs menu. These are the listings on your Programs menu that have right-facing arrows to indicate a submenu. A folder represents a menu listing, and clicking on the folder in the left pane displays the items that are on the submenu in the right pane.

You can use the objects in these folders to change the way your Programs menu presents items. Common manipulations include the following:

- **Create folders to hold groups of program items.** You can create a new subfolder in the Programs folder and then move related program items into that folder. This action is useful if your Programs menu is very long.
- **Move items from a subfolder to the Programs folder.** This is a handy trick if you use a particular item from the Accessories submenu frequently. Rather than move down another level to open a menu item, you can put it on the main Programs menu.

## Adding software listings to your Programs menu

Adding software to the Programs menu on a computer with profiles enabled creates an interesting problem. If you configured profile settings to include the Start menu, the changes that one user makes to the Programs menu aren't reflected on the Programs menus for the other users.

For example, if your spouse logs on and installs a bookkeeping program, he or she can start the program from the Programs menu. If you want to use that program, however, you can't choose the listing from your own Programs menu because the listing isn't there. You have to put it there yourself! Don't install the software again to accomplish that; use the profile folders.

You can add a listing for any program that's installed on the computer to your Programs menu. The listings in the Programs menu are nothing more than shortcuts that have been placed in the Programs folder in your personal profile. You only have to copy the shortcut to your own Programs folder.

Because many programs install groups of listings, copying the shortcut is the only way to ensure that you have all the choices. Follow these steps to copy a program listing from one user's Programs menu to your own Programs menu:

1. **Click the plus sign to the left of the user profile that has the Programs menu listing that you want to add.**

   All the subfolders for this user's profile are displayed in the left Explorer pane.

2. **Click the plus sign to the left of the Start Menu folder to reveal the Programs folder, and then click the Programs folder.**

   All the folders (groups) and individual items on the Programs menu are displayed in the right Explorer pane.

3. **Right-click the program item that you want to add to your own Programs menu and choose Copy from the shortcut menu that appears.**

4. **Click the plus sign to the left of your own profile folder.**

   All the subfolders for your profile are displayed in the left Explorer pane.

5. **Click the plus sign to the left of your Start Menu folder to reveal your Programs folder.**

6. **Right-click your Programs folder and choose Paste from the shortcut menu that appears.**

   The program listing is copied to your own Programs folder.

# Managing Users and Profiles in Windows 2000

Windows 2000 takes a tough stance about users and logons because it's built for security. You can't dismiss the Logon dialog box the way you can in Windows 98/Me.

User information is maintained in the Security Accounts Manager database, which everyone calls the *SAM* (say the name, not the initials). Users must exist in the SAM to access the computer, and only a user with administrative rights can create a user. Whoever was at the keyboard when Windows 2000 was installed became the administrator.

After setting up Windows 2000, many users continue to log on to the computer with the Administrator account. Microsoft says this isn't recommended and suggests that the administrator create her own account, using her own name or some nickname, and make herself a member of the Administrators group. Then use the new account for day-to-day logging on.

It's beyond the scope of this book to delve deeply into the issues of users, groups, and permissions for Windows 2000 — and the advantages of using the NT file system (NTFS). Don't run the computer on the FAT file system; you lose security features — but you can find out about these things in *Windows 2000 Professional For Dummies,* by Andy Rathbone and Sharon Crawford (Wiley Publishing, Inc.).

## Creating users in Windows 2000

Because of the level of security built into Windows 2000, the system checks every user who accesses resources to make sure that the user account is in the SAM. This means that every user who wants to access the Windows 2000 computer from another computer on the network must be added as a local user. And, of course, you have to create an account for every user who works directly on the Windows 2000 machine. To create a user in Windows 2000, make sure that you're logged on with an account that has administrative rights, and follow these steps:

1. **Open Control Panel and double-click the Users and Passwords icon.**

   The Users and Passwords dialog box opens.

2. **Click the Advanced tab, and in the Advanced User Management section, click the Advanced button.**

   The Local Users and Groups snap-in opens.

3. **Right-click the Users folder in the left pane and choose New User from the shortcut menu.**

   The New User dialog box opens, as shown in Figure 9-11.

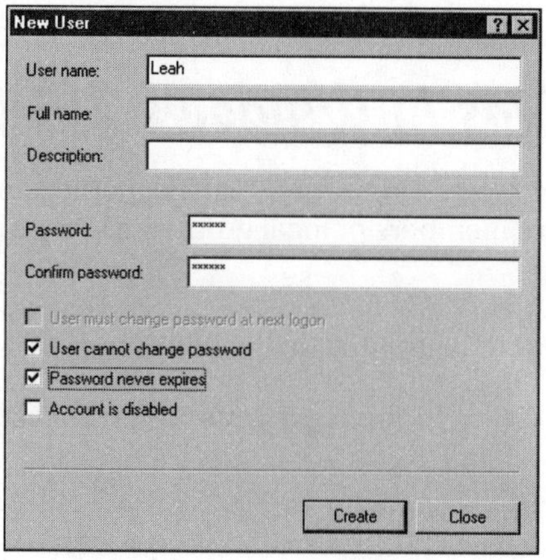

**Figure 9-11:** Set up a new user by entering a logon name and a password.

4. **Type the name for the user you're creating.**

5. **Enter the user's password, and then enter it again in the Confirm password field.**

   If you're creating an account for a user who normally uses another computer, and accesses this computer across the network, you must enter the same password the user enters when logging on to his other computer.

6. **Set the options for passwords.**

   For a home network, it's best to clear the check box labeled User must change password at next logon. Then select the options User cannot change password and Password never expires.

7. **Click Create.**

   This allows you to create another user. When you're finished creating users, click Close.

Windows 2000 doesn't set up a Profiles subfolder in the folder that holds the Windows files. Instead, when a user logs on to the computer for the first time, the system creates a set of subfolders under the Documents and Settings folder on drive C. You can perform the same actions to manipulate your profile as you can in Windows 98/Me; you just do everything from the Documents and Settings parent folder.

If you installed Windows 2000 as an upgrade over a previous version of Windows (usually Windows 98), the system keeps the Profiles folder (and all the user subfolders) in the folder that holds the Windows software. In Windows 2000 Professional, that folder isn't named Windows; it's named WINNT.

## Setting permissions in Windows 2000

You can control the actions of logged-on users by setting permissions. This is accomplished by making users members of local groups (each group has a set of defined permissions).

To make a local user a member of a group, use the following steps:

1. **Double-click the user's listing in the right pane of the Local Users and Groups snap-in.**

   The user's Properties dialog box opens.

2. **Click the Member Of tab.**

   The dialog box displays the Users group, which all local users are members of by default.

3. **Click Add to provide additional group memberships for the user.**

   The Select Groups dialog box appears, as shown in Figure 9-12.

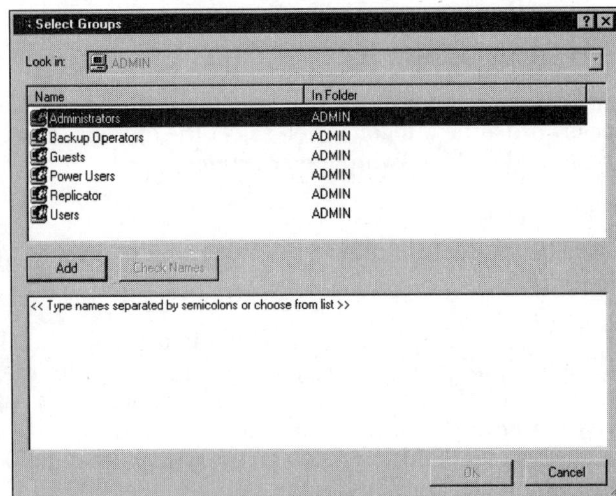


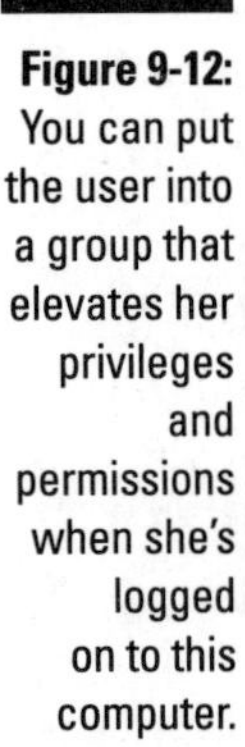

**Figure 9-12:** You can put the user into a group that elevates her privileges and permissions when she's logged on to this computer.

4. **Double-click the listing for the group you want to add this user to.**
5. **Click OK twice.**

   You are returned to the Local Users and Groups snap-in. Close the snap-in window if you're finished working with users.

# Managing Users and Profiles in Windows XP

Like Windows 2000, Windows XP uses logon accounts to control security. During the installation of Windows XP Home Edition, the system creates an Owner account and a Guest account. (Users who access the computer across the network are using the Guest account.) It's a good idea to rename the Owner account so that it becomes your logon account (it automatically carries administrative permissions). Windows XP Pro Edition creates an Administrator account. Also, like Windows 2000, Windows XP stores user profiles in a set of subfolders in the Documents and Settings folder on drive C.

## Creating users in Windows XP

To set up a new user in Windows XP, follow these steps:

1. **Choose Start⇨Control Panel⇨User Accounts.**

   The User Accounts window opens, displaying a list of tasks.
2. **Click Create a new account.**
3. **Enter a name for the account, and click Next.**

   The name you enter is used to log on to the computer; it's a logon name.
4. **Select an account type for this user.**

   The account types are Computer Administrator (with permissions to perform all tasks on the computer) and Limited (with permissions to make changes to the user's own settings only). The first account you create must be a Computer Administrator (and is probably your own account). Then, using this account, you can create and manage users.
5. **Click Create Account.**

   You are returned to the User Accounts window, where the new user is listed.

Completing this process only creates the account; you still have to set up the user's password. To do so, click the new user's listing, and then choose Create a password. Enter the password, and then enter it again to confirm it. You can optionally enter a password hint, which is a word or phrase that reminds the user of the password. This should forestall the problems that arise when a user forgets his password (notice I said *should;* I'm not guaranteeing anything!).

The password hint is visible to anyone who tries to log on as this user. Therefore, don't use a password "123main" with a hint "our address" or a password "spot" with a hint "dog's name." Make the hint something that's a bit obscure to anyone except the user. For example, if the password is "stupidclock," the hint may be "I overslept." That's a memory jog, not a description of the password, and a memory jog is the best type of password hint.

Windows XP is designed to be friendly to computers that have multiple users. Among the features you'll love and rely on are a Welcome window that makes it easier to log on (similar to the Family Logon feature I discuss earlier in this chapter for Windows 98), the ability to switch to a new user without requiring the current user to log off (called *Fast User Switching*), pictures for each user's listing in the Welcome window, and other cool features. It's beyond the scope of this book (which concentrates on networking issues) to provide detailed instructions for enabling these features. Read *Windows XP For Dummies,* 2nd Edition, by Andy Rathbone (Wiley), for more information.

# Part III

# Communicating Across the Network

## In this part . . .

Now for the fun stuff — actually using your network for communicating from computer to computer, printing, exchanging files, and generally getting all the benefits of network computing.

In this part of the book, I walk you through the tasks required for setting up shared printing. You find out how to install and use printers that are attached to your own computer and the other network computers.

You also find out how to get files from any computer on the network, and how to send files from your computer to another computer. And, for real convenience, I'll explain how to open software and work on a file that's on another computer.

# Chapter 10

# Printing Across the Network

### *In This Chapter*

- Setting up printers for sharing
- Installing a network printer
- Tricks and tips for printing
- Troubleshooting network printing

A terrific side effect of installing a computer network in your home is the ability to share a printer. Households without networks face some difficulties when it comes to printing. Network-deficient households (that seems to be a politically correct term, don't you think?) have had to rely on some less-than-perfect solutions.

One solution is to buy a printer every time you buy a computer. I can think of lots of other ways to spend that money, and I bet you can, too.

Another solution is to buy one printer and attach the printer to only one of the computers in your home network. Anyone who uses a computer that doesn't have a printer has to copy files to a floppy disk, go to the computer that has a printer, load the same software that created the files (the same software has to be installed on both computers), open each file from the floppy disk, and print. I guess all this walking comes under the heading of "healthy exercise," especially if the computers are on different floors of the house, but this setup isn't exactly a model of efficiency.

Neither of these scenarios is acceptable after you understand how easy it is to share printers over a network.

## Setting Up Shared Printers

If you want all the computers on your network to be able to access a single printer, you have to set up the Windows printer-sharing feature. Then you have to set up the printer for sharing. You perform these tasks at the computer to which the printer is connected.

The most difficult part of setting up network printing is deciding which computer gets the printer. Here are some common guidelines you can follow:

- **Location.** If you have room for a table at one computer location (and storage space for paper), that's the computer to choose.
- **Usage patterns.** If one computer on the network is used far more often than any other computer, that's the computer to select.

Some households have more than one printer. You may have a black-and-white printer as well as a color printer. When you enable printer sharing, each user can choose a printer every time he or she wants to print.

You can attach two printers to one computer if that's more convenient, as long as the computer has sufficient ports. If one printer uses the printer port, and the other printer connects to the USB port, just plug them in. If both printers use printer ports, you can add a second printer port to the computer for about $25.00. If both printers use USB connections, you probably have a second (or third or fourth) USB port. If you don't have any empty USB ports, you can buy a USB hub (which adds ports) for under $25.00.

## Enabling printer sharing

The first thing you have to do is tell Windows that the printer attached to the computer should be shared with other users on the network. If you didn't set up printer sharing when you originally set up your network, follow these steps to accomplish this simple task:

1. **Open the Properties dialog box for your network connection in Control Panel.**

   In Windows 98 and Windows Me, choose Start⇨Settings⇨Control Panel, and then double-click the Network icon. (Alternatively you can right-click Network Neighborhood, and choose Properties.)

   In Windows 2000, choose Start⇨Settings⇨Network and Dialup Connections. Then right-click the Local Area Connection icon, and choose Properties.

   In Windows XP, choose Start⇨Control Panel and click Network and Internet Connections. Click Network Connections, right-click the Local Area Connection icon, and choose Properties.

   The Local Area Connection Properties dialog box opens.

2. **Enable file and printer sharing.**

   In Windows 98 and Windows Me, click the File and Print Sharing button and click the I Want to Be Able to Allow Others to Print to My Printer(s) check box to put a check mark in the check box. Then click OK twice. You must restart the computer to put the new settings into effect.

In Windows 2000 and Windows XP, click the File and Printer Sharing for Microsoft Networks check box to put a check mark in the check box. Then click OK. You do not have to restart the computer.

## Installing a printer

You have to *install* a printer, which means setting up the files Windows needs to communicate with the printer. Those files are called *printer drivers*. Well, of course, *installing* also means the physical installation of the printer, but that's quite simple, and the documentation that comes with your printer explains all the steps.

Then you must tell Windows that this printer is going to be shared with other users on the network. When you have a printer on a computer, and you share that printer, your computer becomes a *print server*.

If you already installed a printer (and its drivers) on this computer, you can skip this task and move ahead to the section "Sharing a printer," later in this chapter.

### Using Windows files to install a printer

You may need your Windows CD to install a printer, if the printer driver files weren't transferred to your computer when you installed Windows. If your printer came with its own CD or floppy disk, read the section "Using manufacturer disks to install a printer," later in this chapter.

Put the Windows CD in the CD-ROM drive. Press and hold Shift so that the CD doesn't open automatically and offer to install Windows. If it does open, just close it. Then follow these steps to install your printer:

1. **Open the Printer folder.**

   In Windows 98, Windows Me, and Windows 2000, choose Start⇨Settings⇨Printers.

   In Windows XP, choose Start⇨Printers and Faxes.

   The Printers folder opens. If this is the first printer you're installing on this computer, the only icon in the folder is the one named Add Printer. In Windows XP, no icon exists, but an Add a Printer command is in the left pane. (If you installed faxing services, you have an icon for Microsoft Fax.)

2. **Double-click the Add Printer icon.**

   In Windows XP, click the Add a Printer command in the left pane.

   The Add Printer Wizard window opens. The first window explains that the wizard helps you install a printer. Click Next.

3. **Select Local Printer, and then click Next.**

   The wizard wants to know whether this printer is a *local printer* (attached to the computer) or a *network printer* (attached to another computer). You can find information on installing a network printer in the section "Installing a Network Printer," later in this chapter.

4. **In Windows 98 and Windows Me, select the manufacturer and model for the printer.**

   Scroll through the Manufacturers list in the left pane (see Figure 10-1) to find the company that made your printer. When you select it, the Printers pane on the right displays all the printers from that manufacturer. Scroll through the list to find the right printer model. Then click Next.

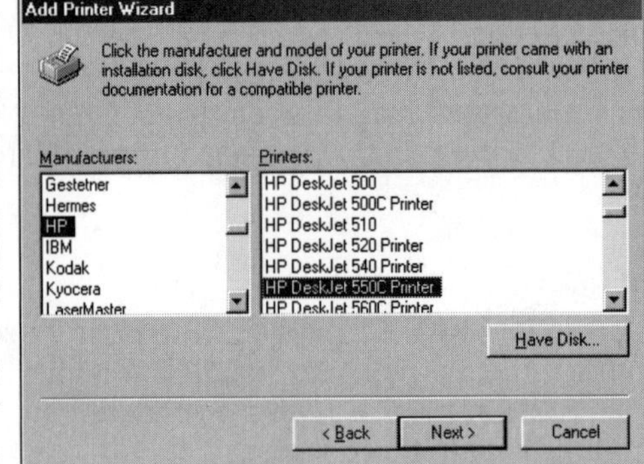


**Figure 10-1:** The wizard lists a slew of manufacturers and models, so you shouldn't have a problem finding your printer.

If you can't find the exact printer model, read the documentation that came with your printer. Look for the section on printer emulation to find out which model most closely matches your printer.

5. **In Windows 2000 and Windows XP, select the option Automatically detect and install my Plug and Play printer.**

   If the documentation for your printer instructs you to use drivers from the manufacturer, don't select the option to detect the printer.

   If Plug and Play finds the printer, the wizard moves on automatically. If your printer isn't found, continue to walk through the wizard.

6. **Select the port to which you've attached your printer.**

   The port is probably LPT1, but if this printer is the second printer you're attaching to this computer and you've installed another printer port, choose LPT2. Click Next after you select the port.

7. **In Windows 2000 and Windows XP, select the manufacturer and model of your printer.**

   This window only appears if Plug and Play couldn't find your printer.

8. **Name the printer, and specify whether it is the default printer.**

   Type a name for this printer in the Printer Name text box. By default, the wizard inserts the model name for the printer, which is usually perfectly acceptable as a name.

   You also have to tell Windows whether this printer is the default printer for Windows software. Select Yes if you expect to use this printer when you print from your software programs. Of course, if this is the first printer you're installing, it has to be the default printer.

   The default printer is the printer that is automatically selected when you print from software. If you have other printers, you can use the software Print dialog box to change to another printer. More importantly, for those occasions when you don't have a choice of printers, the default printer delivers your print job. Examples of not having a choice include printing by clicking the Print icon on a toolbar, printing from Notepad, and printing from many DOS programs.

   Click Next to move on.

9. **Select Yes to print a test page.**

   The wizard gives you a choice, but it's foolish not to test the printer.

   Click Finish because you've reached the last wizard window, although you're not quite done.

   The files that Windows needs are transferred from the CD to your hard drive. Then the test page is sent to the printer. Look at the test page. (It congratulates you on setting up the printer successfully and prints all sorts of technical information about the printer drivers that were installed.)

10. **Tell Windows whether the test page printed correctly.**

    If the test page printed successfully, you're finished. If not, Windows opens a Print Troubleshooter. (See Figure 10-2.)

    Select the appropriate choices, and the troubleshooter makes suggestions. Keep going until you solve the problem. If the problem isn't solved by the time the troubleshooter runs out of suggestions, call the printer manufacturer for more help.

### Using manufacturer disks to install a printer

Windows supports most printers, which means that the printer drivers are on your Windows CD. However, Windows doesn't support some printers, in which case you must use the drivers that are supplied by the printer manufacturer. Those drivers probably came with the printer (on a CD or floppy disk), but if not, you can call the company or visit its Web site to get the files.

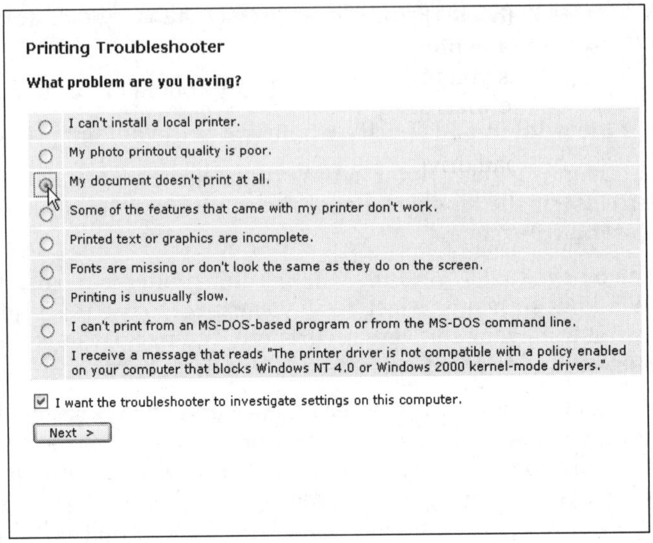

Printing Troubleshooter

**What problem are you having?**

- I can't install a local printer.
- My photo printout quality is poor.
- My document doesn't print at all.
- Some of the features that came with my printer don't work.
- Printed text or graphics are incomplete.
- Fonts are missing or don't look the same as they do on the screen.
- Printing is unusually slow.
- I can't print from an MS-DOS-based program or from the MS-DOS command line.
- I receive a message that reads "The printer driver is not compatible with a policy enabled on your computer that blocks Windows NT 4.0 or Windows 2000 kernel-mode drivers."

I want the troubleshooter to investigate settings on this computer.

Next >

**Figure 10-2:** This Print Trouble-shooter is from Windows XP. The Print Trouble-shooters in other versions of Windows offer slightly different choices.

In addition, some printers come with software that works with the manufacturer's drivers to enhance your ability to control and manipulate the printer's features.

If you are using the manufacturer's disks, read the directions to find out which of the following two methods you should use:

- Use a setup program on the disk to install software.
- Use the Printer Wizard, and choose Have Disk when the wizard presents a window that lists printer manufacturers and models.

If you're instructed to use a setup program, the software can usually be launched automatically by placing the CD in the CD-ROM drive. If the CD-ROM doesn't start, follow these steps to begin setup manually:

1. **Double-click the My Computer icon.**

   In Windows XP, choose Start⇨My Computer.

   The My Computer window opens, displaying the computer's drives.

2. **Double-click the CD-ROM drive icon.**

   The opening window of the CD-ROM drive varies, depending on the manufacturer. Usually a menu appears, sometimes in icon form. Choose the installation item. If the installation procedure isn't evident on the opening screen, read the documentation that came with the printer to find out how to install the software.

If you're instructed to use the Windows Printer Wizard, follow the steps that were enumerated in the previous section to install a printer. When you get to the window that asks you to select the manufacturer and model, click Have Disk. Then follow the wizard's prompts to install the drivers.

You can also download drivers from the manufacturer's Web site. Follow the instructions for installing the downloaded files, and then select the folder you saved the files in (instead of a CD or floppy disk) when Windows asks you for the location of the drivers.

## Sharing a printer

After your printer is installed, you can begin using it on your computer. But the household members who are using the other computer(s) on your network want to print, too. You have to share this printer with them. If you don't, they'll just keep bothering you to insert a floppy disk, load software, and print the documents they've created. To save yourself all that aggravation, follow these steps to share the printer with others on the network:

1. **Open the Printers folder.**

   An icon for the printer you installed on this computer is in the folder window.

2. **Right-click the icon for the printer you want to share, and choose Sharing from the shortcut menu that appears.**

   The printer's Properties dialog box opens, and the Sharing tab appears in the foreground.

3. **Select the option to share the printer.**

   The wording of this option differs, depending on the version of Windows.

4. **Type a name for the printer in the Share Name text box.**

   You can accept the name that Windows automatically enters, which is usually a shortened form of the printer model name. Or, you can use a name of your own choice.

5. **In Windows 98 and Windows Me, optionally type a description in the Comment text box.**

   Large companies with large networks and lots of printers use the Comments text box to help users identify the printers. For example, "Laser printer next to the cafeteria" may be a good identifier for a corporate printer, while "Den printer" or "Color printer" may work well for home use. Users only see the comment text if they select the Details view in Network Neighborhood or My Network Places when they double-click the icon for the computer that is directly connected to the printer.

6. **In Windows 98 and Windows Me, optionally enter a password for the printer.**

   If you choose to require a password, users who don't have the password won't be able to use the printer. On a home network, you rarely need to use this option. Companies with printers that hold checks use passwords for those printers. If you do type a password, you're asked to confirm the password by typing it again. You won't see the actual password as you're typing because Windows substitutes asterisks for your characters. Security in Windows 2000 and Windows XP is applied through standard security and user settings that are built into the operating systems. Use the Security tab of the printer's Properties dialog box to set permissions, but usually the default permissions are fine — everyone can use the printer and manage their print jobs.

7. **Click OK.**

   You are returned to the Printers folder, and your printer icon has a hand under it, indicating that this printer is a shared resource. This computer is now a print server.

# Installing a Network Printer

Put on your running shoes! After you configure a printer for sharing, it's time to run to the other computers on the network and install that same printer.

Of course, you're not going to perform a physical installation; the printer is staying right where it is. Installing a printer on a computer that has no physically attached printer means that you're installing a *network printer.*

## Choosing an installation method

Two approaches are available to you for installing a network printer:

- **Use Network Neighborhood or My Network Places.** Double-click the icon for the computer that has the printer. All the shared resources (folders and printers) for that computer are displayed. Right-click the printer icon, and choose Install from the shortcut menu that appears.
- **Use the Printers Folder.** Choose Start⇨Settings⇨Printers to open the Printers folder, and then double-click the Add Printer icon. Walk through the wizard's step to install the printer.

Both methods require the installation of software drivers for the printer, so you may need your Windows CD or disks from the printer manufacturer available.

## Running the installation procedure

For this example, I use the option to select the printer from Network Neighborhood or My Network Places, because it's faster and more efficient. If you want to use the Add Printer function in the Printers folder and follow the wizard's prompts.

Be sure that your Windows CD, or the printer's software CD or floppy disk, is in the appropriate drive, and then follow these steps:

1. **Open Network Neighborhood or My Network Places.**
2. **Double-click the computer that has the printer you want to use.**

   All the shared resources on that computer (printers and folders) are displayed.
3. **Right-click the icon for the printer, and choose Install or Connect.**

   In Windows 98 and Windows Me, the Install command is on the shortcut menu; in Windows 2000 and Windows XP, the Connect command is on the shortcut menu.
4. **Follow the wizard's prompts to install the printer.**

   Similar to the installation of a printer attached to the computer (described earlier in this chapter), the wizard copies Windows drivers from the Windows CD or the manufacturer's drivers from a source that you specify.

   Windows XP copies many printer drivers to the hard disk when you install the operating system. Most of the time, installing a printer requires no other steps after you select the Connect command (Step 3).

The printer files are copied to your hard drive, and a test page is sent to the printer. Of course, because the printer is on a remote computer, you have to walk to the printer to see the document — or yell to whoever is in the room where the printer is located and ask that person to check the printout. If the test page prints correctly, select Yes in the dialog box that asks about the success of the test. If the test page does not print properly or doesn't print at all, select No. Then use the printer troubleshooter to try to resolve the problem. See the section "Installing a Network Printer," earlier in this chapter, for information about the Print Troubleshooter.

An icon for the printer appears in your Printers folder. Whenever you print, the print job is sent to this remote printer.

For convenience, you can keep the driver files (especially if you downloaded them from the manufacturer's Web site) on a network share that is easily accessible. Also, it may be easier if the drivers are on a CD (either Windows CD or manufacturer CD) to share the CD-ROM drive on a single PC, and then simply access that drive over the network as well. After all, that's why you have a network.

## Renaming network printers

After you install a remote printer (a printer that's not connected to the computer you're working on), you can change its name to something that reminds you where it is or what it does. Doing so changes the printer name only on your computer; it doesn't change anything on the computer to which the printer is attached. Follow these steps to give the network printer a personalized name:

1. **Open the Printers folder.**
2. **Right-click the icon for the network printer, and choose Rename from the shortcut menu that appears (or select the icon and press F2).**

   The icon title is selected (highlighted), which means you're in edit mode.
3. **Type a new name, and press Enter.**

   Choose a name that describes the printer for you. For example, HP-Den is a good descriptive name and is easier to remember than Printer Numero Uno or Clive.

## Using both local and network printers

If you have two printers in the house, you can attach them to separate computers. Just follow the steps that were explained earlier in this chapter for installing local printers, and then follow the steps to install each printer as a remote printer.

You can switch between printers when you want to print by using the Print feature of your Windows software. All Windows software works in the same fashion, so you can count on being able to use the following steps to switch printers:

1. **Choose File⇨Print from the menu bar of your software program.**

   The Print dialog box opens. The appearance of this dialog box differs depending on the particular software you're using, but the essential features are the same.
2. **Click the arrow to the right of the printer Name text box.**

   A list of installed printers (both local and network) appears in the drop-down list, as shown in Figure 10-3.

If you click the Print button on the toolbar of your Windows software or you print from Notepad, the currently selected printer receives the print job. No dialog box opens to afford you the chance to choose a different printer.

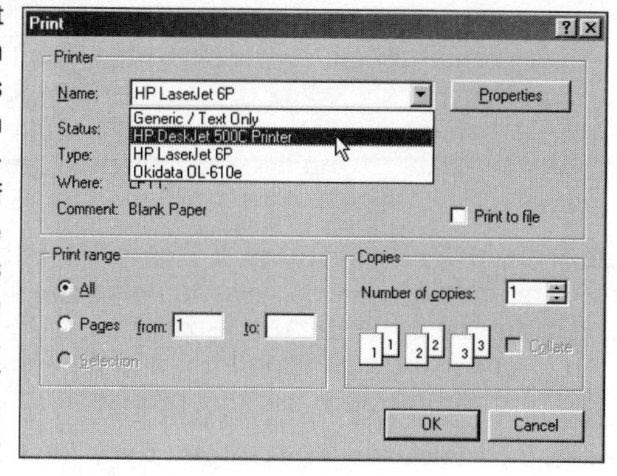


**Figure 10-3:** The Print dialog box in a Windows program has a drop-down list of all the printers you've installed, whether they are local or network.

## Using password-protected printers

Windows 98 and Windows Me offer a way to password-protect printers. It's highly unusual to password-protect printers in a home network environment, but you may have a reason to do so. For example, if you've loaded special paper in the printer (for example, checks or photographic paper), you may want to password-protect the printer and not let anyone know the password. When you put the regular paper back into the printer tray, remove the password. Anyone who tries to use a remote printer that's password-protected is asked to supply the password (which you haven't shared, in this case).

## Devising schemes for using multiple printers

You can design all sorts of arrangements to take advantage of having multiple printers on your network, with each printer attached to a different computer. When you devise a method to manage your printers, your decisions should be based on the types of printers you own. Consider the following suggestions:

- **Make the local printer the default printer.** This option works well if all the printers are the same type, or at least similar — for example, if they're all monochrome ink jet printers (which print in black and shades of gray), laser printers, or color ink jet printers.

With this scheme, you don't need the network printer unless something happens to the local printer. If the local printer stops working or the cartridge goes dry and you don't have a spare one handy (or you're in a hurry and decide to worry about replacing the cartridge later), you can switch to the network printer quickly. Using the local printer for most print jobs saves you the annoyance of getting up and walking to the network printer every time you print. (If you need the exercise, you can always reverse the scheme.)

- **Configure the printers for different features.** If your printers have the capability of holding different paper sizes, you can make one of them the letter-size printer and make the other the legal-size printer. Or, you can put inexpensive paper in one printer and good bond in the other. Then just use the appropriate printer for each printing project.
- **Use each printer for its best feature.** For example, if you have a dot-matrix printer and an ink jet or laser printer, use the ink jet or laser printer for stuff that has to look good (for example, your resume or a letter to your senator). Use the dot-matrix printer for everything else. Or, if one printer is an ink jet and one is a laser printer, use the laser for multiple-page print jobs (lasers usually print faster) or for print jobs with a lot of graphics (most laser printers have more memory than most ink jet printers).

Some of these printer setup schemes are important for more than convenience; they lower the cost of using printers. The business term for getting the most out of your printers (or any other piece of machinery) is *TCO* (total cost of ownership), and it's a significant consideration when you buy and use any type of equipment.

After you design your scheme, you have to do two things to make sure that the plan is implemented successfully:

- **Rename the printers with names that reflect their intended uses.** Follow the instructions in the section "Renaming network printers," earlier in this chapter, to find out about renaming networked printers.

  Renaming the local shared printer can be complicated. If you rename the icon, Windows doesn't change the name of the shared resource. In fact, if you rename the icon, the printer is no longer shared. Windows considers the printer to be a new and different printer after a name change. Be sure to follow the steps that show you how to create a shared printer in "Renaming network printers" (again) if you rename a local shared printer.
- **Explain the plan to all the members of the household.** This part works best if you use a threatening tone or some other means of making everyone take you seriously. Try tapping the flat of your left hand with a rolling pin and sneering.

# Managing Network Printing

Keeping the printing process on an error-free, even keel is slightly more complicated with network printing than it is for a one-computer, one-printer environment. However, it's not overly complex, and printer problems aren't all that common.

## Understanding the spooler

When you send a file to a printer, Windows does some work on the file with the help of those files (drivers) you copied to your hard drive when you installed the printer. Windows checks the file to make sure that everything is sent to the printer in a format that the printer understands. The work that Windows performs is saved in a file, and that file is called a *spool file.* This process is called *spooling,* and it happens, unbeknownst to you, in the background. In addition to the spool file, Windows creates a second file, called a *shadow file,* which contains the name of the user who sent the job to the printer, the data format type of the print job, and other technical information.

The two files sit in the spooler, waiting for their turn at the printer. Documents are sent to the printer in a first-come, first-served order (unless you interrupt that order using a process that I discuss in the next section, "Manipulating print jobs"). This lineup of documents waiting to go to the printer is called the *queue.* After the print job is done, the spool file is deleted automatically. The shadow file hangs out until the next time you restart the computer, even though it's of no use to you. Of course, the shadow file doesn't do any harm — unless you print a lot of documents and you don't reboot your computer every day, because you end up with a lot of shadow files that take up disk space.

## Manipulating print jobs

You can control individual print jobs that are sent to the printer, but you have to move fast, because everything happens very rapidly.

Printing controls are available in the printer's dialog box, which you can open with the following steps:

1. **Open the Printers folder.**
2. **Double-click the icon for the printer.**

   The printer's dialog box opens, displaying any print jobs that are currently in the queue.

You can pause, delete, and move the print jobs that are in the queue, but which print jobs you see depend on the following factors:

- If you open the dialog box for a remote printer, you see the jobs that you sent to that printer.
- If you open the dialog box for a local printer, you see all the jobs that the local and remote users have sent to that printer. (See Figure 10-4.)

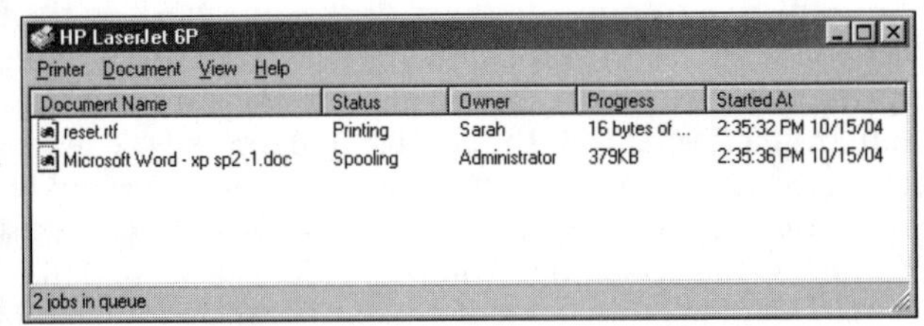


**Figure 10-4:** The printer that's attached to this computer has jobs from remote users waiting in the queue.

You can manipulate each job, or the printer itself, with the commands that are available in this dialog box. You can change the way that documents print in the following ways:

- **Pause a print job.** Right-click the listing for the print job, and choose Pause Printing from the shortcut menu that appears.

  A check mark appears next to the Pause Printing command to indicate that the job status has changed to Paused. The print job is temporarily stopped, and the next job in line starts printing.

  Pausing a print job is a quick way to let an important print job jump ahead of the job that's in front of it.

- **Resume a print job.** Right-click a paused print job, and choose Pause Printing again from the shortcut menu that appears to remove the check mark.

  The job status changes to Printing.

- **Pause the printer.** Choose Printer➪Pause Printing from the menu bar in the Printer dialog box.

  All the print jobs are paused. Most of the time, you use this command to clear a paper jam in the printer or to change paper. To use this command on a Windows 2000/XP printer, you must have administrative rights (controlling the printer, rather than the print job, is an administrative task).

- **Cancel a print job.** Right-click a print job listing, and choose Cancel Printing from the shortcut menu that appears.

  The document does not print.
- **Cancel all the print jobs.** Choose Printer⇨Purge Print Documents from the menu bar of the printer's dialog box. Because this is a command to the printer, not the print job, this requires administrative rights.

When you pause or cancel a print job, the printer usually keeps printing. It does so because any data that has been sent to the printer is in the printer's memory and continues to print.

You can also drag print jobs around to change the order of printing (for Windows 2000/XP you must have administrative rights). Select the job you want to move, and drag it up in the queue if it's important or down in the queue if it's less important. However, dragging print jobs has two restrictions:

- You can't move any print job ahead of the job that is currently printing.
- You can't move the job that is currently printing — it's too late.

# Printing Tricks and Tips

The printing processes in Windows run smoothly and automatically most of the time, even across a network. However, knowing a few tricks makes network printing easier for all the users on your network. This section covers those tips.

## Using a printer shortcut on the desktop

Most of the time, you print from a software program. You create a document, and then you print it. But sometimes you just need a printed copy of an existing document, and you don't want to open the software, open the document, and use the commands that are required to print the document.

If you put a shortcut to the printer on your desktop, you can drag documents to the shortcut icon to print them effortlessly. Follow these steps to create a printer shortcut on your desktop:

1. **Choose Start⇨Settings⇨Printers.**

   The Printers folder opens.
2. **Right-drag the printer icon to the desktop.**

   When you release the right mouse button, a shortcut menu appears.

3. **Choose Create Shortcut(s) Here from the shortcut menu.**

   A printer shortcut appears on your desktop.

A good place to put the printer shortcut is on the Quick Launch toolbar. That way, an open window can't hide it.

Using the printer shortcut is easy and timesaving. You can use it whenever you have any folder or window open (such as Windows Explorer, My Computer, or My Documents) that contains document files. Just drag a document file to the printer shortcut on the desktop. That's all you have to do — Windows does the rest. You can leave the room or sit and watch as the following events take place:

1. **The software that was used to create the file opens.**
2. **The file opens in the software window.**
3. **The software sends the file to the printer.**
4. **The software closes.**

   Cool!

If you right-click a document file instead of dragging it to a desktop shortcut, you can choose Print from the shortcut menu that appears. The same automatic printing events occur.

## Using separator pages to identify users

If everyone in your household uses the printers, you are likely to experience a lot of printer traffic. Not everyone's going to run immediately to the printer to pick up his or her print jobs. What you have after a day or so is a nice jumbled pile of papers — and no one willing to claim them. Or worse, one user may wander over to the printer to pick up his print jobs and notice that several other print jobs are in the tray. This user may pick up the first piece of paper and read it — it isn't his print job, so he tosses it aside (invariably, it lands on the floor instead of on a tabletop). The user will probably continue to shuffle through the papers, taking his own documents and tossing the others helter-skelter.

It's less messy if each job comes out of the printer with a form that displays the name of the owner. Luckily, such a form exists in Windows, and it's called a separator page. A *separator page* (sometimes called a *banner*) automatically prints ahead of the first page of each document.

The downside of separator pages is that they can be a huge waste of paper. They work best if most of your print jobs are made up of multiple pages. You may end up spending the money you save on ink purchasing ream after ream of paper. Also, if your household is filled with people who don't believe that "neatness counts," you'll just have one extra piece of paper per print job to get shuffled around in a big ugly pile.

### *Adding separator pages in Windows 95, 98, and Me*

For a Windows 95, Windows 98, or Windows Me print server, go to the computer that has the printer attached to turn on separator pages using these steps:

1. **Choose Start⇨Settings⇨Printers.**

   The Printers folder opens.

2. **Right-click the appropriate printer icon, and choose Properties from the shortcut menu that appears.**

   The printer Properties dialog box opens, with the General tab in the foreground.

3. **Click the arrow to the right of the Separator page list box, and choose a Separator page type.**

   The Separator page choices are None, Full, and Simple. Both the Full and Simple separator pages contain the document name, the user name, and the date and time that the document was printed. The Full option uses large, bold type, while Simple uses the Courier typeface that's built into the printer.

4. **Click OK.**

### *Adding separator pages in Windows 2000 and Windows XP*

If you have a Windows 2000 Professional print server, follow Steps 1 and 2 in the previous section "Adding separator pages in Windows 95, 98, and Me," and then follow these steps:

1. **Click the Advanced tab.**
2. **Click the Separator Page button.**

   The Separator Page dialog box appears.

3. **Click Browse to select a separator file.**

   Separator files have the `.sep` extension. Choose Sysprint.sep for PostScript printers or Pcl.sep for non-PostScript printers.

4. **Click OK twice to close the dialog box.**

## Using a Hardware Print Server

Most manufacturers of network equipment offer a hardware device called a *print server.* A print server is a standalone hardware device that holds the network printers you're sharing (instead of using computers as the hosts for printers). A print server can provide some practical benefits, such as the following:

- **A convenient location.** You can put your printers where they're convenient for all users on the network. If your network computers aren't physically near each other, printing becomes more work for any user who is printing to a remote printer. Well, printing is still easy — it's walking to the printer to pick up the printed document that's tiring.
- **Full-time availability.** The print server is always on, while computers that hold printers are sometimes shut down.
- **Faster printing.** Most print servers have components designed to deliver the data to the printer faster.

Print servers range in price from about $50 to slightly over $100, depending on features (especially the number of printer ports).

## Attaching a print server

The print server has two types of connectors: one type connects to your printer(s), and the other type connects to your network. When you buy a print server, you must choose a model that matches your printer(s) and your network connections.

You can buy a print server with USB ports, regular printer ports, or both. The range of models includes single-port devices for one printer, or multi-port devices for multiple printers (up to four). To connect to your network, print servers are available as Ethernet devices or wireless devices.

The print server plugs into the network the same way a computer does, either by connecting it to a hub, switch, or router with Ethernet cable, or by sending wireless signals (if it's a wireless print server). It's just a network node, like a computer is a network node, so all the computers on the network can access it.

## Installing a print server

To a computer, a print server is like a printer. Each computer has to install drivers for the print server, in addition to installing the drivers for the printers attached to the print server.

Each manufacturer supplies a CD that has the drivers. Of course, you can share one computer's CD drive and have each user install the drivers for each computer, instead of walking the CD around the house to each computer. Aren't networks nifty?

The CD that comes with the print server also has setup and maintenance software for the print server. You can use the utilities on the software to check the status of the print server, and the status of the printers. You access the print server's utilities through your browser, using the print server's IP address. Each manufacturer provides clear, easy to follow, documentation.

# Troubleshooting Network Printing

Sometimes when you're printing to a remote printer, you see an error message indicating that there was a problem printing to the port. (The *port* is the path to the remote computer that has the printer attached.) Before you panic, thinking that something awful has happened to your network printing services, check the condition of all the hardware.

## Check the print server

Computers that have printers attached (called *print servers*) have to be turned on if you want to print from a remote computer. If the computer is turned off, turn it on.

It doesn't matter whether you know the logon password for the user name that appears during the logon process because you don't have to complete the logon process. Nobody has to be logged on to a computer to use its shared printer. The Windows operating system on that computer simply must be started. That's a really nifty way to design network printing!

## Check the printer

If the computer is turned on and you still get error messages when you try to print, check the printer. Make sure that it's turned on. Check any buttons, indicator lights, or message windows that may be trying to tell you that something is amiss.

Most printers have a "ready" light, a button that lights up to say that everything is cool and the printer is ready to do its work. If the ready light isn't on, follow the instructions in the printer manual to investigate the problem. The most common problems are that the printer is out of paper, a paper jam has occurred, or the cartridge is out of toner (or ink).

## Check the network cable

If the computer is on and the printer is fine, check the network cable. A cable that isn't connected properly can't send data.

## Check the Windows XP SP2 Firewall

If a shared printer is on a computer running Windows XP SP2, make sure the firewall is configured to allow access to the printer by remote computers. Use the following steps to view or change the firewall's settings:

1. **Open the Properties dialog box for the network adapter.**
2. **Click the Advanced tab.**
3. **Click the Settings button.**
4. **Click the Exceptions tab.**
5. **Be sure a check mark exists in the File and Printer Sharing option.**

# Chapter 11

# Getting Around the Neighborhood

### In This Chapter

- Visiting the network's neighborhood
- Opening shares to see what's in them
- Using shortcuts to move to folders on other computers

To get resources from another computer, you have to access that computer across the network. Windows offers several ways to communicate with a remote computer from where you're sitting (the computer you're sitting in front of, and using, is called the *local computer*). In this chapter, I show you all the ways to get to remote computers so that you can access the resources on each computer.

In addition, you also find out about shortcuts that are available for working in a network environment. You can use these tricks to make accessing remote computers on your network easier and faster.

## Traveling on the Network

The computers on your network are displayed as icons in a single Windows window, which makes it easier to find them. In Windows 98, the computers hang out in a place called Network Neighborhood. In Windows Me, Windows 2000, and Windows XP, the hangout is named My Network Places. Except for Windows XP, an icon for the gathering place is automatically placed on your desktop.

### Visiting Network Neighborhood (Windows 98)

When you double-click the Network Neighborhood icon, you see all the computers on your network. Figure 11-1 shows a home network with two computers.

### The Entire Network icon

The Network Neighborhood window includes an icon for the entire network. If you double-click that icon, you see an icon for the *work-group* (the group that the computers on your network belong to). If you double-click the workgroup icon, you see the individual computers in your workgroup, which are the same computers you saw in the original Network Neighborhood window. You're back where you started. The Entire Network icon is really for larger networks that may have multiple workgroups, but that's not the way home networks are configured. So, unless you don't see your network computers in the Network Neighborhood window, don't bother with the Entire Network icon.

**Figure 11-1:** Network Neighborhood displays icons for the computers on the network, including the one you're using.

You can see the shared resources (called *shares*) on a remote computer by double-clicking that computer's icon in Network Neighborhood. (A *share* is a folder, drive, or peripheral hardware device that's been "shared" so that other computers on the network can access it.) A new window opens to display a list of all the shares on the computer. When you double-click a share, yet another window opens to show you the contents of the share.

# Calling on My Network Places (Windows Me, 2000, and XP)

The My Network Places window works just a bit differently from the Network Neighborhood window. In addition, its contents are different depending on whether you're using Windows Me, Windows 2000, or Windows XP.

- Windows Me has three icons in the window: Add Network Place, Home Networking Wizard, and Entire Network.
- Windows 2000 has two icons in the window: Add Network Place and Entire Network.
- Windows XP has no icons in the window but has links in the left pane (see Figure 11-2).

For Windows XP users, this section assumes that you've retained the Windows XP interface. If you've switched your Windows XP computer to Classic Start Menu, follow the instructions for Windows 2000.

To enter the neighborhood in Windows 2000, and Windows Me — that is, to see all the computers on the network the way they're displayed in a Network Neighborhood window — double-click the Entire Network icon. That action opens a window in which you see an icon for your workgroup. Double-click that icon to open a window that displays all the computers on the network — finally! Double-click any computer to see its shared resources.

In Windows XP, select the link View Workgroup Computers to display the computers in your workgroup. Double-click any computer to see its shared resources.

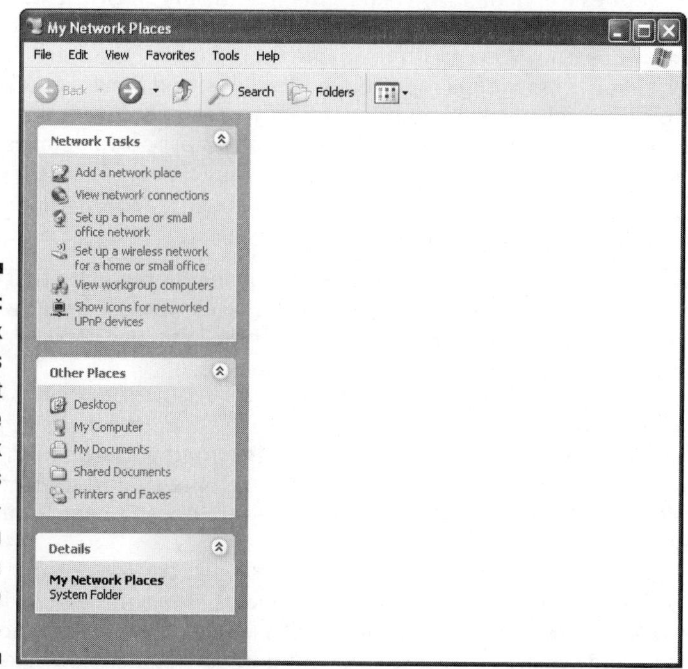


**Figure 11-2:** My Network Places doesn't display the network computers automatically — you have to do a little work to see them.

Windows XP doesn't have a desktop icon for My Network Places; instead you click icons on the Start menu for My Computer and My Network Places. Alas, by default My Network Places is not listed on the Start menu. If you click My Computer, you see a link to My Network Places in the left pane.

You can configure Windows XP to add an icon for My Network Places to the Start menu by taking the following steps:

1. **Right-click a blank spot on the taskbar, and choose Properties.**

   The Taskbar and Start Menu Properties dialog box appears.

2. **Click the Start Menu tab.**
3. **In the Start Menu section, click the Customize button.**

   The Customize Start Menu dialog box appears.

4. **Click the Advanced tab.**
5. **Scroll through the list of Start menu items to find My Network Places, and click the check box to place a check mark in it.**
6. **Click OK twice to close all the dialog boxes.**

   An icon for My Network Neighborhood is now on your Start menu.

If you prefer desktop icons, you can right-click the My Network Places icon you created on the Start menu and choose Show on Desktop to place a shortcut on your desktop. You can do the same thing for My Computer. Remember, however, that desktop icons require double-clicks, and Start menu items require only a single click. In addition, when you have software windows open, you can't see the desktop, but clicking the Start button makes everything on the Start menu available.

### Adding a network place

To avoid all that mouse clicking, you can put a shared resource that's on a remote computer into the main My Network Places window with the Add Network Place Wizard (you do almost everything in recent versions of Windows with a wizard).

A shared resource is indicated with the format `\\ComputerName\ShareName`. For example, if you have a computer named Den, and you shared the folder named FamilyBudget using a share name Budget, the shared resource is `\\Den\Budget`. Notice that the name of the share doesn't have to match the name of the folder.

Windows 98 computers can't see a share name that has more than 12 characters, so if you're going to share a folder with a long name, make sure the share name is 12 characters or less. Chapter 8 has detailed information about all this stuff.

You can even put a Web site into My Network Places and double-click its icon to travel to that site.

To add an icon for a network place, follow these steps in the My Network Places window:

1. **Double-click the Add Network Place icon.**

   In Windows Me and Windows 2000, the first Add Network Place Wizard window has a place for you to enter the address.

   In Windows XP, click the Add a Network Place link in the left pane, and then follow the wizard's prompt to indicate whether you want to add an Internet address or a network address.

2. **Enter the address of the place you want to add, and skip to Step 5. If you don't know the address, click the Browse button to locate the place.**

   If you know the address, use the format `\\ComputerName\ShareName` for a network share. For a Web site, use the Web address of the Web page you want to visit.

   If you click the Browse button, the computers on your network are displayed in the Browse for Folder window.

   The format of a Web page address is called a *URL,* which stands for Uniform Resource Locator. The format of a network share is called a *UNC,* which stands for Universal Naming Convention.

3. **Click the plus sign next to the computer that has the shared folder you want to get to.**

   All the shared resources (called *shares*) on the selected computer are displayed in the window.

4. **Select the share you want to use, and click OK.**

   If the share has a plus sign next to its icon, this means it contains folders (shared drives always fit this description). Even though those folders aren't set up as shares, you can select one and click OK. (See the discussion on parent-child relationships for shares in Chapter 8.)

   After you click OK, you are returned to the wizard window, where the UNC for the network share you selected is in the text box.

5. **Click Next.**

6. **Enter a name for this network place.**

   This is the name that appears in the main My Network Places window. Windows automatically enters the share name, along with the name of the computer on which it resides, which is usually just fine. If you selected a subfolder of a share, Windows uses its folder name. However, you can enter a different name if you prefer to.

**7. Click Finish.**

A window for the shared folder you selected opens, and you can choose the file you want to work with. If you're merely setting up the share as an icon in your My Network Places window, close the window for the shared folder. You are returned to the My Network Places window, where an icon for this share now appears.

### *Managing the icons in the My Network Places window*

Windows also adds places to the My Network Places window. Every time you open a share and access a file, an icon for that share appears in your My Network Places window. After a while, the window can become incredibly crowded, as shown in Figure 11-3.

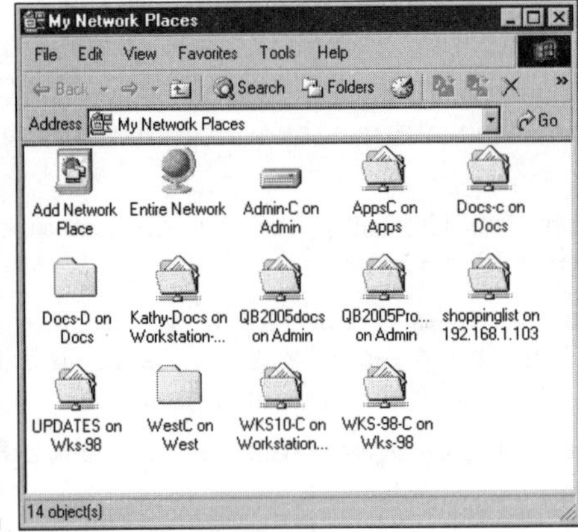


**Figure 11-3:** When the My Network Places window is this crowded, it's hard to find the share you need.

I don't know about you, but I get both annoyed and lazy when I see a window that's this crowded. As a result, when I need to get to a share on another computer, I just double-click the Entire Network icon and find the share. Although doing that defeats the whole purpose of these handy-dandy icons, I just find it easier and less confusing.

Consider the following additional points about the icons in the My Network Places window:

- Every icon of a share that's in this window is a shortcut — just like the desktop shortcuts you create for frequently used programs. You can, therefore, delete the icons without affecting the real share.
- Every once in a while, delete all the icons except for the few that you use often. Press and hold Ctrl, and click each superfluous icon. Then press Delete.

- Even better, delete all the icons whenever you open the My Network Places window and use mapped drives for the shares you access often. See the section "Mapping Drives," later in this chapter, to find out how to use that feature.

## Viewing information about the neighborhood residents

By default, the computers in Network Neighborhood and My Network Places are displayed as icons. The name of the computer is displayed along with the icon.

When you double-click a computer's icon, the window that opens to display its shares also uses icons as the default view. The name you assigned when you created the share is also displayed.

When you create a share, you have the opportunity to enter not only a name for the share but also a comment (description). If you want to see the description fields that you or other users have entered, you must change the way Network Neighborhood and My Network Places display computers and shares. The descriptions don't show in the default view (which is the Large Icons View).

To see the descriptive information about all the components on your network, change the view by choosing View➪Details from the menu bar of the window.

Descriptions are rather important for shares. Most of the time, the share name makes sense to the person who created the share, because he knows what's in the folder or what the printer does (for example, it prints color, has a certain type of paper in the tray, and so on). However, other household members may not understand those share names, and giving others more information is an act of kindness. Figure 11-4 shows the window that appears after double-clicking a computer to see its shares, with the Details View selected. The descriptions for the shared folders and printers are quite useful.

You don't have to use the View menu to change to Details view every time you open a window. Windows remembers the view you select for a window and presents the same view every time you open that window.

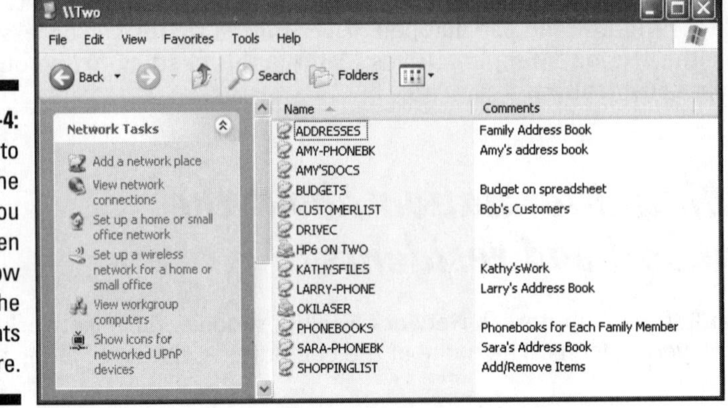


**Figure 11-4:** It's easier to locate the share you need when you know what the contents are.

## Exploring the neighborhood in Windows Explorer

You can view Network Neighborhood or My Network Places in Windows Explorer. You can also scroll down the left pane to find the listing for Network Neighborhood or My Network Places, depending on your operating system. Select the listing to see all the computers in the right pane, or click the plus sign to expand the listing to display the computers in the left pane.

To see the shares, expand a computer's listing by clicking the plus sign. Select a share in the left pane to see its contents in the right pane.

# Psst — What's the Password?

If the person who created a shared resource on a Windows 98 or Windows Me computer wants to limit access to the resource, he or she can create a password (see Chapter 8 for information about creating passwords for shared resources). If that person doesn't tell you the password, you're outta luck. Only the favored few who receive the password can open the shared resource.

## Opening a password-protected share

You can't tell whether a share is password-protected until you try to access it. To access a password-protected share, follow these steps:

1. **Open the share in Windows Explorer, Network Neighborhood, or My Network Places.**

   The Enter Network Password dialog box appears, as shown in Figure 11-5.

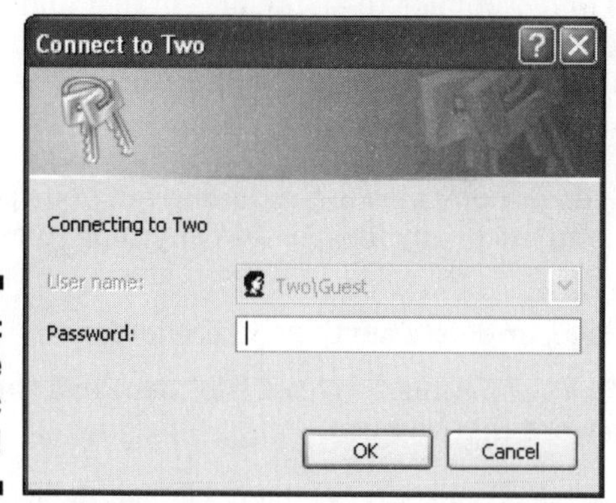


**Figure 11-5:** Enter the magic word!

2. **Enter the password for the share in the Password text box, and click OK.**

   When you enter the password, you don't see the characters that you type because they appear as bullets. This is a security measure to prevent anyone who may be hanging around from seeing the password.

   You also have the option to select the Save This Password in Your Password List check box. If you select this check box, the local computer stores the password. Then, the next time you want to open this shared resource when you're working at this computer, the computer fetches the password from your password file and enters it automatically. You don't even see the Enter Network Password dialog box, unless the person who created the shared resource changes the password. This information is saved in your own user profile, so if any other user logs on to the same computer, the password isn't available to that person.

If the password that you enter isn't correct, or you saved the password and the user who created the shared resource changed the password, Windows displays an error message. If you think that you may have mistyped the password, click OK and try again. If that doesn't work, click Cancel in the Enter Network Password dialog box. Then find the person who created the shared resource and either get the password or find out why you can't have it.

If you need one particular file from a password-protected folder, ask the owner of the folder to move that file to a different folder if he or she doesn't want to compromise the security of the folder.

### Creating permission-level passwords

In Windows 98 and Windows Me, you can additionally configure passwords to determine what users can do with the contents of a share. The *permission level* that's set for a shared folder applies to all the files in that folder (see Chapter 8 for more information about setting up passwords and permissions on shares). The person who created the shared resource decides what type of permissions to grant, as follows:

- **Read-Only:** You can open or copy files in this folder, but you can't delete any files, change the contents of any files, or add anything (files or subfolders) to the folder.
- **Full:** You can add, change, or delete anything in the folder.
- **Depends on Password:** Your permission level is either Read-Only or Full, depending on the password that you use.

Unfortunately, you receive no message that indicates your permission level for the folder that you use. After you enter the correct password, the only way to find out whether you have Read-Only permission is to do something that requires Full permission (such as saving a file to the folder or changing the name of a file) and see whether you get an error message. It's like driving in a state you're not familiar with, where you don't know whether the state permits right turns on red until you see the first sign that says "No Turn on Red."

## Say UNC-le: Understanding UNCs

When you access remote resources, you're using a convention called the *universal naming convention* (UNC). The format for displaying the UNC works like this: `\\computername\resourcename`.

### Naming your computers and shared resources

Computers on Windows networks have names. Naming a computer is part of the configuration process when you set up the network features on your Windows computer. You can name your computers whatever you want. Some people use descriptive names (Den, Kitchen, Laptop, and so on); some people use names that reflect the owner or primary user of the computer (Dad, Sis, and so on); and others just give computers names that don't necessarily have any meaning. I have a colleague who named the computers on his home network Zeke and Fred because "when I brought them home and set them up, they looked like a Zeke and a Fred." Hey, whatever works.

In addition to the computer name, you have to consider other names when you work on your network — the share names. Each shared resource has a name, because providing a name is part of setting up the share.

Share names are usually a bit more descriptive than computer names because people tend to use the name of the drive or folder that's being shared. For example, if you have a folder on your computer named Addresses, you probably named the share Addresses when you configured the folder for sharing.

## Understanding the UNC format

When you understand that a computer has a name and a shared resource has a name, using a formatted style to refer to a particular shared resource on a particular computer makes sense. Once upon a time, a computer nerd said, "Hey, let's call that the UNC." And everybody who needed to access shared resources in this way said, "Okey-dokey."

So, if you're working on your network and you open a folder named Budgets on a remote computer named Bob, you're working at a UNC named \\Bob\Budgets.

Now this format may look familiar because it's very similar to the way you enter paths when working in MS-DOS. For example, your Windows files are located in C:\Windows, which means that they're on drive C in a folder named Windows. Some important operating system files are in a subfolder named System. The path to that subfolder is C:\Windows\System.

In a path, the letter (for example, *C*) followed by a colon (:) indicates the drive. In the same way, in a UNC statement, a double backslash (\\) followed by a name indicates a remote computer.

Your own computer has a name, too, because it's on a network. If your computer's name is Bigdaddy, your system files are in \\Bigdaddy\Windows\System. Anyone working at another computer on the network uses that UNC to get to that folder. You don't use the UNC to get there on the computer that you're using; you use an MS-DOS path statement, which tells your computer that the target folder is on the local computer instead of a remote computer.

## Displaying UNCs

You can see the path or UNC for any object on any computer when you're working in Windows Explorer and Network Neighborhood/My Network Places, if you configure those windows to display this information (they don't display the UNC by default). Use the following steps to display path and UNC details in Windows Explorer:

1. **Open Windows Explorer, Network Neighborhood, or My Network Places.**
2. **In Windows 95 or 98, choose View⇨Folder Options. In Windows Me, 2000, or XP, choose Tools⇨Folder Options.**

   The Folder Options dialog box opens.
3. **Click the View tab of the Folder Options dialog box.**

   The View options appear, as shown in Figure 11-6.

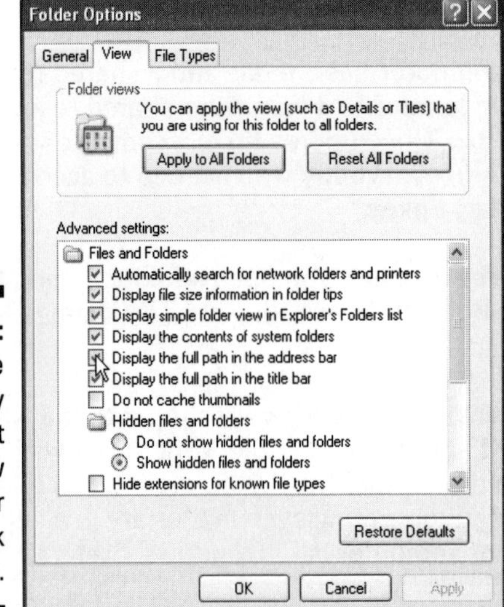


**Figure 11-6:** Configure the way you want to view computer and network objects.

4. **Select the check box that indicates Display the full path in the address bar.**
5. **Click OK.**

Now when you select drives or folders on your own computer or on remote computers, you see the full path or UNC statement in the window.

## Opening a share by typing the UNC

If you get tired of double-clicking your way through Network Neighborhood or My Network Places, you can open a share on another computer by typing the UNC, as follows:

- **In the Run dialog box:** Choose Start⇨Run, and type the UNC in the Run dialog box. After you click OK, a window opens, displaying the contents of the share.

What's nifty is that after you do this once, the UNC is saved in the Run dialog box command list. The next time you want to run a UNC, click the arrow to the right of the Open text box and select the UNC from the drop-down list.

- **In a Web browser:** You can use your browser to open a share and display its contents in the browser window, as shown in Figure 11-7. Just enter the UNC in the Address bar of your browser window, and press Enter. As with your favorite Web sites, you can add UNCs to your Favorites list (or bookmarks, if you're using Netscape).

**Figure 11-7:** Use your browser to access shares, and add oft-used UNCs to your Favorites list.

## Creating UNC shortcuts

If you access a particular UNC frequently, you can create a shortcut to the share on your desktop or your Quick Launch bar. A shortcut saves you all those mouse clicks you need to navigate through Network Neighborhood or My Network Places. Follow these steps to create a shortcut:

1. **Open Network Neighborhood or My Network Places.**

   Don't open the window in full-screen mode — you want to be able to get to the desktop.

2. **In Network Neighborhood, double-click the computer that has the share you're after. In My Network Places, double-click the Entire Network icon, double-click the workgroup, and then double-click the computer that has the share you want to open.**

   In My Network Places, don't use any of the shortcuts to shares that appear in the window (they're shortcuts, not icons).

3. **Right-drag the share to the desktop or to the Quick Launch bar.**
4. **Release the mouse button, and choose Create Shortcut(s) Here from the menu that appears.**

# Mapping Drives

You can use a feature called *mapping* to more easily access a shared resource on another computer. Mapping means assigning a drive letter, such as *E* or *F,* to a shared resource on another computer.

The drive letter you use becomes part of the local computer's set of drive letters, and these letters show up in the My Computer and Windows Explorer windows as if they were part of the local computer. The drives you create are called *network drives.*

## Understanding drive letters

The computer you use already has at least two drive letters. The floppy drive is A, and the hard drive is C. If you have a second floppy drive, it's B. If you have a CD-ROM drive, it also has a drive letter (probably D). If you have a Zip, Jaz, or other peripheral drive attached to your computer, a drive letter is assigned to that device, too.

To see the drive letters that your computer is already using, open My Computer. All the devices on your computer that have drive letters are displayed in alphabetical order.

For example, say that a computer named Eve, located in the kitchen of a house that has a home network, has the following three drive letters that belong to local resources:

- Drive A is a floppy drive.
- Drive C is a hard drive.
- Drive D is a CD-ROM drive.

Drive C is configured as a shared resource named EveDriveC. The hard drive has many folders, of course, and some of them have been configured as shared resources that can be accessed by users on other computers. Eve's shares include the following folders:

- AddressBook, which has the share name Addresses
- FamilyBudget, which has the share name Budget

The other computer on the network is in the upstairs hallway (in a handy little nook that was just perfect for a computer console). That computer is named Adam, and it has the following resources with drive letters:

- Drive A is a floppy drive.
- Drive C is a hard drive.

The hard drive on Adam is a shared resource named AdamDriveC. It has lots of folders, too, and the following folders have been configured as shares:

- LegalPapers, which has the share name Legal
- Letters, which has the share name Letters

Of course, when Adam looks at Eve, or Eve looks at Adam, those shares are UNC statements. If Adam wants to get to a file named MyFile on Eve's hard drive, entering `C:\MyFile` would not work, because even though Eve's drive is named C, that drive letter designation is connected to (mapped to) Adam's local computer.

# Mapping a UNC

Even if you have two floppy drives, two hard drives, a CD-ROM drive, and a Zip drive, most of the letters of the alphabet are unused. So put the alphabet to work! Turn a UNC into a drive letter. When you assign a drive letter to (in other words, map) a UNC, your life gets easier. (Well, your life as a computer user gets easier; the rest of your life is your problem, not mine.) Here are some of the benefits of mapping:

- Every object on your computer that has a drive letter is displayed in Windows Explorer in a logical list, so you don't have to expand Network Neighborhood or My Network Places in Windows Explorer to find a mapped share.
- Every object on your computer that has a drive letter is displayed in My Computer. You can double-click the My Computer icon and then open a local drive or a remote share with equal ease.
- You can use an MS-DOS command session and MS-DOS commands to work with any remote storage object (drive or folder) that has a drive letter. For example, to copy documents from a remote folder that you've mapped to drive G to your documents folder, you can type the following at the DOS prompt:

  ```
  copy g:*.doc c:\documents
  ```

When you access the hard drive of a remote computer, you can use any folder on that drive. However, if a folder isn't configured specifically as a shared resource, you can't map it. Ask the person who uses that computer to create a shared resource for that folder. Or, go to the computer and do it yourself.

The easiest and fastest way to do anything with the remote computers on your network is with Network Neighborhood or My Network Places, because they're dedicated to displaying network resources. Follow these steps to map a network drive to a UNC:

1. **Open Network Neighborhood or My Network Places.**

   Double-click as needed to display the computers that are on the network.

2. **Double-click the icon for the remote computer that you want to use.**

   All the shared resources on the remote computer appear in the window (see Figure 11-8).

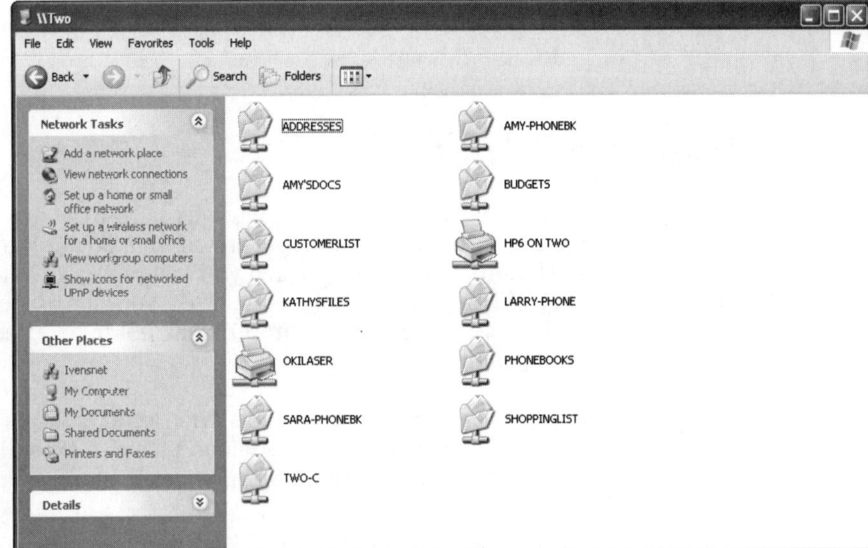


**Figure 11-8:** This computer has shares for the hard drive and some folders.

3. **Right-click the share you want to map as a network drive.**

   The shortcut menu for the share appears.

4. **Choose Map Network Drive from the shortcut menu.**

   The Map Network Drive dialog box opens, as shown in Figure 11-9. By default, all versions of Windows except Windows XP show you the next available drive letter. Windows XP starts at Z and works backward.

5. **Select the Reconnect at logon check box if you want to map this drive automatically every time you start this computer.**

   This feature can become a bit complicated; see the section "Reconnecting mapped drives," later in this chapter, for more information.

6. **Click Finish.**

The folder for the UNC you just mapped opens in a window, displaying its contents. You can open a file and go to work, or map another network drive by repeating these steps.

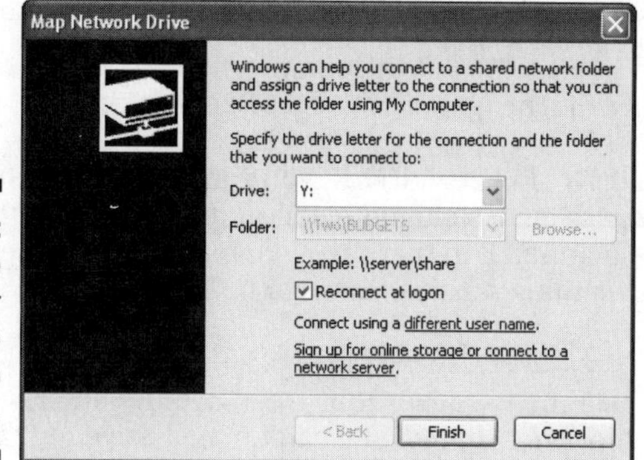


**Figure 11-9:** Choose the drive letter you want to assign to this share.

If you don't want to see the contents of the share you just mapped, hold the Shift key while you click Finish.

You can also map a network drive in Windows Explorer. Just click the Network Neighborhood icon in the left pane, click the icon for the appropriate computer in the right pane, right-click on the share you want to map, and choose Map Network Drive.

## Viewing and using mapped drives

After you map a UNC as a drive, you can move easily to its share by using one of these techniques:

- **Open My Computer.** All the drives on your computer, including network drives (UNCs that are mapped to a drive letter), appear in the My Computer window. Just open the drive and go to work.
- **Open Windows Explorer.** All the drives on your computer appear in the left pane, including every remote share (UNC) that is mapped to a drive letter. Click the minus sign next to drive C to get rid of the folder display so that you can see all your network drives more easily. Open any drive to use it.

Using the example of Eve and Adam (if you haven't yet met Eve and Adam, see the section "Understanding drive letters," earlier in the chapter), you can see how this works.

Adam has a computer named Adam. On the C drive of that computer is a folder named LegalPapers. He shared that folder and gave the share the name *Legal*. Eve uses files in that folder constantly, and to make life easier, she mapped drive E to the share. Here's how easy it is for Adam and Eve to access their mapped drives:

- When Eve wants a file, she opens drive E, which is a network drive that is mapped to the UNC `\\Adam\Legal`.
- When Adam wants a file, he opens `C:\LegalPapers`.

Once you've mapped a drive, like real drives, you can get to everything on that drive. For example, Adam also shared his hard drive, giving it the share name AdamDriveC. Eve mapped F to that drive share, and when she opens drive F, she sees the same thing Adam sees when he expands drive C in Windows Explorer.

If Eve finds that she constantly uses files that are in a folder on drive F (drive C to Adam), but that folder isn't shared, she can't map a drive to that folder. Mapping works only for shared resources. She can ask Adam to share that folder, too, so she can map it. Or, she can continue to expand drive F and move to that folder in the same way she moves through folders for real drives on her computer, using Windows Explorer.

## Reconnecting mapped drives

When you're mapping a UNC to a drive letter, you can select the Reconnect at logon option. This means that every time you log on, Windows verifies the network drive — in other words, it peers down the network cable to make sure that the shared resource that's mapped to the drive is there. This verification slows the logon process, but you probably won't notice a big difference.

Incidentally, the reason that the option is Reconnect at logon instead of Reconnect at startup is that the mapped drives you create are part of your personalized profile. If multiple users share a computer, the mapped drives that appear are those that were created by the user who is logged on. If a user named Sandy logs on to the computer that Eve uses, Eve's mapped drives don't exist. Sandy has to create her own mapped drives (which may very well duplicate the mappings created by Eve).

The jargon for mapped drives that are configured to reconnect at logon is *persistent connections.*

### Remapping when reconnection fails

You can easily imagine that a problem may arise if you have two computers on your network and both have mapped network drives that are configured for reconnection at logon. The computer that runs the logon procedure first loses, and the computer that logs on second wins!

When the first computer looks for the mapped drive during logon, the second computer isn't yet up and running. The UNC isn't available, so the mapping function fails. Windows displays a message telling you that the mapped drive isn't connected and asking if you want to reconnect the next time you log on. Say Yes. If your computer can't reconnect to a mapped drive at logon, it's no big deal. The logon process works, and everything's fine.

### Configuring reconnection options

You can configure Windows 95 and Windows 98 to wait until you need to use the drive before the network resource is checked. If the computer that contains the shared resource isn't ready, you won't suffer any delay during the logon process (Windows keeps searching for several seconds before giving up). On the other hand, when you use the network drive, Windows checks this drive's availability first, delaying access to the network share for a few seconds.

The following configuration choices are available:

- **Quick logon:** The network drives that you mapped are listed in Windows Explorer and My Computer, but during the logon process, Windows doesn't check to see if they're really available.

  Your computer doesn't try to connect until you actually try to use the drive, which is when Windows checks to make sure that the remote share is available. This speeds the logon process, but it delays the connection process by a few seconds.

- **Logon and restore network connections:** Your computer connects to the remote resources for the mapped drives during the logon process. This delays the logon process, but you know immediately if a problem exists with any of your mapped drives.

Follow these steps on a Windows 98 computer to configure the way you want mapped drive reconnections to work:

1. **Choose Start⇨Settings⇨Control Panel.**

   The Control Panel window opens.

2. **Double-click the Network icon.**

   The Network dialog box opens with the Configuration tab in the foreground.

3. **Select the component named Client for Microsoft Networks to highlight it.**

4. **Click the Properties button.**

   The Client for Microsoft Networks Properties dialog box opens, as shown in Figure 11-10.

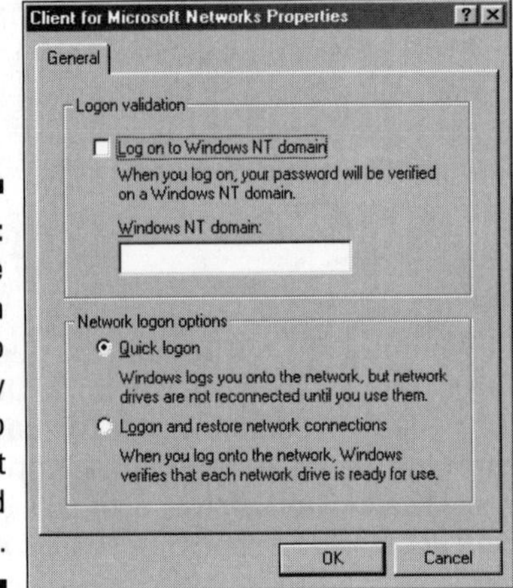


**Figure 11-10:** Change the logon options to suit the way you want to reconnect to mapped drives.

5. **Select either Quick logon or Logon and restore network connections.**
6. **Click OK twice.**

Windows displays a message that tells you to restart the computer to put this change into effect. In fact, the message dialog box offers to restart Windows for you. Because you don't particularly need to make the change right now, and it's only important the next time you log on, you can just click No and restart later.

## Working with mapped drives in Windows Explorer

When you map drives for all the network resources you use often, the first thing you notice is that you save a whole lot of time in Windows Explorer. If you want to copy or move a file, everything you need is right in front of you in the Explorer window. The mapped drive is listed in the left pane of the Explorer window, along with all the folders on your local hard drive and all the other drives on your computer. You don't have to expand Network Neighborhood; expand the computer that has the share that you want to use, and then click the share.

If you have a long list of folders on your hard drive and you have to scroll through them to see the other drives on your computer (including mapped drives), save yourself the trouble. Enter the letter of the drive that you want to access in the Windows Explorer Address bar.

Both the Address bar and the Go To dialog box also accept UNC statements. You can enter the UNC for a remote share to display its contents in Windows Explorer. This feature is handy if you haven't mapped a drive for a remote resource.

## Working with mapped drives at the command line

If you're comfortable working with MS-DOS commands, you can use those commands on a mapped drive just as if you were working on a local drive.

In a couple of situations, I find that using the command line is faster and easier than using Windows Explorer. For example, if I need to rename a group of files that have similar filenames (all the files start with abc), I can accomplish that in one command, as follows:

```
ren abc*.* xyz*.*
```

In Windows Explorer, I'd have to rename each file separately.

Follow these steps to use a mapped drive in a command prompt window:

1. **Open the command prompt window, as follows:**
   - In Windows 95 or 98, choose Start➪Programs➪MS-DOS Prompt.
   - In Windows Me, choose Start➪Programs➪Accessories➪MS-DOS Prompt.
   - In Windows 2000, choose Start➪Programs➪Accessories➪Command Prompt.
   - In Windows XP, choose Start➪All Programs➪Accessories➪Command Prompt.
2. **Enter the drive letter for the mapped drive, followed by a colon (for example, E:).**

   You're now working on the remote computer, and you can perform any command-line tasks.

You can even map a drive with a command prompt. Windows has a command named Net Use. The syntax for creating a mapped drive with the Net Use command is: `net use x: UNC`, where *x* is the drive letter that you want to use and *UNC* is the UNC statement for the shared resource. To disconnect the mapped drive, enter **net use *x*: /delete**.

For example, to map G to the shared resource named Letters on the computer named Adam, enter **net use g: \\adam\letters** and wait for the response "The command completed successfully." Now drive G is mapped, and it shows up in Windows Explorer and My Computer.

I use the Net Use command as part of an MS-DOS command file (called a *batch file*) to back up files. I copy bunches of files from different folders across the network, and I do it twice: once to a shared folder on another computer and once to a shared Zip drive on another computer. If I tried to back up ten different folders to a remote share, I'd have to select each folder in Windows Explorer or My Computer and use the Copy and Paste commands to complete the task. Because the files were backed up yesterday, I'd see messages from Windows indicating that the files already exist, and I'd have to notify Windows that it's okay to copy them anyway. When all the copying is finished, I would have to go through the same routines again to make the second backup to the Zip drive. Using the command line allows the whole process to be unattended: I can map the drive, control error messages, and disconnect the drive when the process finishes. I do all that work without being near the computer because the commands are on autopilot — I'm in the dining room enjoying dinner.

# Chapter 12

# Using Files from Other Computers

### *In This Chapter*

- Copying files
- Relocating files
- Deleting files
- Opening files in software across the network
- Exchanging files with a Macintosh

One nifty advantage to a network is that you can work on any file, anywhere, at any time. Other users are creating files on other computers all the time. Occasionally, you may want to see one of those files. In fact, you may want to work on one of those files. Perhaps you want your very own copy of a file that currently resides on another computer.

If you find yourself working on different computers at different times, you probably have files of your own on all of them. That can be nerve-wracking. Imagine that you're sitting in front of the computer that you use most of the time, looking for that letter to Uncle Harry. You know you started it yesterday, and today you want to finish and mail it. But where is it? You look through all your document subfolders; you even use the Windows Find command to search for it. It's nowhere to be found. Think back — could you have begun the letter on the computer in the den? And now you're working at the computer in the kitchen?

You don't have to get up and walk to a remote computer to use a file that's on it, whether you or another household member created the file. Let the network cable do the work by transferring the file from the other computer to the one you're using now.

# Working with Remote Files

When you open remote folders to access the files within them, you can do almost anything with those files that you could do if they were on your own computer. The only hindrance that you may face is when a remote folder is configured for limited actions (see Chapter 8 to find out about setting permissions for file manipulation). For this discussion, however, I assume that you have full permission to manipulate the files in the remote folder.

## Copying files between computers

You can copy a file from a remote computer to your own computer by either dragging it or using the shortcut menu.

You can use the same techniques to copy files in the other direction, from your computer to the remote computer. Just reverse the processes that I describe here.

### Copying by dragging files

If you drag a file from a remote computer to your own computer, you copy it, which means the original file is still on the remote computer, and a copy of that file is on your computer. This process is different from dragging a file from one folder to another on the same drive on your own computer, which *moves* the file instead of copying it. That's because Windows assumes that you don't want to deprive the other computer's user of the file. It's a good assumption.

To make dragging files from a remote computer to your own computer easier, use Windows Explorer, because you can see both the remote computer and your own computer in a single window. Follow these steps to copy a file by dragging it in Windows Explorer:

1. **Open Windows Explorer.**

   In Windows 98, choose Start⇨Programs⇨Windows Explorer.

   In Windows Me and Windows 2000, choose Start⇨Programs⇨Accessories⇨Windows Explorer.

   In Windows XP, choose Start⇨All Programs⇨Accessories⇨Windows Explorer.

   The Explorer window appears on your desktop.

2. **Expand the network listing by clicking the plus sign.**

   In Windows 95 and 98, the listing is named Network Neighborhood.

   In Windows Me, 2000, and XP, the listing is named My Network Places.

   All the computers in your network are displayed in the left pane.

3. **Click the plus sign next to the remote computer that has the file you need.**

   All the shared drives and folders on that remote computer are displayed in the left pane.

4. **Click the remote folder that holds the file you want.**

   The files in the remote folder appear in the right Explorer pane. If necessary, scroll through the right pane so that the file you want is visible.

5. **In the left Explorer pane, expand the drive and folder of your own computer to get to the correct folder.**

   The correct folder is the folder into which you want to copy the file. Don't select (click) the folder; just use the plus sign to expand drives and folders until you can see the target folder in the left pane. You want the files from the remote computer to remain in the right pane.

6. **Use the scroll bar on the left pane to position the target folder near the file you want to copy.**

   This maneuver just makes it easier to drag the file — the distance is shorter.

7. **Drag the file to the local folder in the left pane.**

   When your mouse pointer is on the correct folder (as shown in Figure 12-1), release the mouse button.

Only folders that have been configured for sharing are displayed when you look at a remote computer in Windows Explorer. If the folder that holds the file you want isn't a shared folder, click the plus sign next to that folder's parent folder, which reveals all the child folders in the left pane. Then select the folder you need.

### Dragging between separate windows

Some people find it a bit difficult to drag files within the Windows Explorer window because the objects are small, so your movements have to be rather precise. If you agree, you can drag files from one computer to another over separate windows. In fact, you have several ways to accomplish this, as follows:

1. **Double-click the Network Neighborhood or My Network Places icon on the desktop.**

2. **Double-click the computer and then the shares on the remote computer to get to the window that has the file you want.**

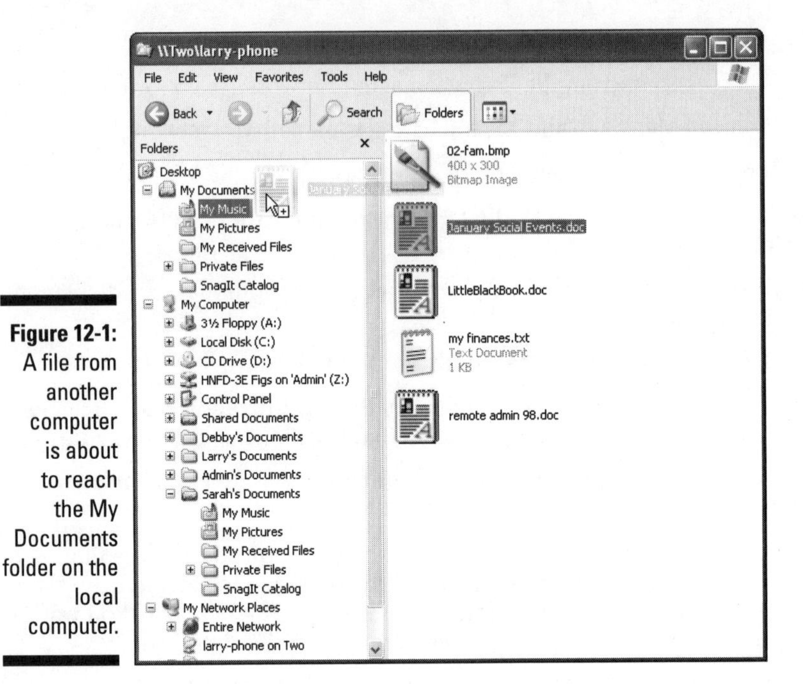


**Figure 12-1:** A file from another computer is about to reach the My Documents folder on the local computer.

3. **Open My Documents and any subfolders to open the window that has the contents of the target folder. If you're not putting the file in My Documents, open My Computer instead and double-click the drive and folder(s) necessary to open the target window.**
4. **Position the windows near each other.**

   It's okay if they overlap or if they're separated — you just need to be able to get to each window.
5. **Drag the file from one window to the other.**

If you want to copy multiple files, press and hold Ctrl and select all the files that you need. Then drag one file to the target folder; all the other files come along for the ride.

### Copying by right-dragging files

Perhaps you're not very adventurous and you're afraid that you may move the file instead of copying it. Or perhaps you can't remember whether dragging moves or copies files when you're working with multiple computers.

To play it safe, drag with the right mouse button (called *right-dragging*). When you release the mouse button, a menu appears. Choose Copy Here from the menu.

### Copying with the shortcut menu

You can use the shortcut menu that appears when you right-click an item to copy a file. This method eliminates the need for a second window. Follow these steps to copy files from a remote computer to your own computer:

1. **Open Windows Explorer.**
2. **Expand the Network Neighborhood (or My Network Places) listing, and then expand the remote computer to select the folder that holds the file you need.**

   The files in the selected folder appear in the right Explorer pane.
3. **Right-click the file that you want to copy.**

   The shortcut menu appears. If you want to copy multiple files, press and hold Ctrl as you click each file. Then right-click any file to see the shortcut menu.
4. **Choose Copy from the shortcut menu.**

   The file (or group of files) is placed on the Windows Clipboard.
5. **In the left Explorer pane, right-click the folder on your local computer into which you want to copy the file.**
6. **Choose Paste from the shortcut menu that appears.**

   The file is copied to your local folder.

## Relocating (moving) files

Sometimes you may want to move a file, removing it from the remote computer and placing it on your local computer (or the other way around). Moving files is less common than copying files, but if you used to work on the computer in the den and have decided that you prefer the computer in the kitchen, you may want to move your files to your new computer.

### Moving by right-dragging files

You can drag files from the remote computer to your own computer with the right mouse button (called *right-dragging*). If you drag with the left mouse button, you copy the files instead of moving them.

Use the steps that I discuss in the section "Copying by dragging files," earlier in this chapter. You can use either Windows Explorer or two windows, depending on your comfort level. Then right-drag the file or files you need from one computer to the other. When you release the right mouse button, a menu appears. Choose Move Here from the menu. The files move from the original location to the new location.

#### *Using the shortcut menu to move files*

If you don't want to open separate windows to drag files, you can use the file shortcut menu to cut and paste files.

Follow the steps in the section "Copying with the shortcut menu," earlier in this chapter, to select the file(s) you want to move. Instead of choosing Copy from the shortcut menu, choose Cut. Then choose Paste to move the files to the folder of your choice on your own computer. The files move from the original location to the new location.

### Deleting files from remote computers

You can delete a file from a remote computer as easily as you can delete files from your own computer. Just select the file and press Delete. The same thing is true of folders. However, deleting a file from a remote computer is much more dangerous than deleting files on your own computer. The problem is that the Recycle Bin doesn't work across the network. A deleted file is really deleted, so you can't recover it from the Recycle Bin right after you say "oops."

Okay, now I hear you talking to this page. You're saying that when you look at the contents of a hard drive on a remote computer, you can see the Recycle Bin, so I must be wrong. Well, double-click that Recycle Bin to open it. Now, double-click the Recycle Bin on your own desktop. Notice anything strange? The files in the two Recycle Bins are identical.

This is a cute trick that Windows plays on network users. When you open the Recycle Bin on a remote computer, instead of flashing a message that says "Access Denied" or "No Way, Go Away" and refusing to open the folder, the system acts as if you're opening a real Recycle Bin. But you're really opening a copy of your own, local Recycle Bin.

## Opening Remote Files in Software Windows

You don't have to take the trouble to copy or move files to your own computer when you want to work with them in a software program. You can open and save files on remote computers right from the software. In fact, software that's written for Windows is designed to do this.

Both computers need to be running the same software. In other words, if you want to open a Microsoft Excel document that you see on a remote computer, you must have Microsoft Excel installed on your own computer.

This feature is handy if you don't always work at the same computer. Of course, if you have enough clout to tell whoever is working on your favorite computer to move to another machine, you don't have to worry about this eventuality. And, you should be writing books on effective family dynamics. Most of us with more users than computers in the household have to use whatever computer is available.

## Opening distant files

If you work in a Windows software program and you want to work on a file that's located on a remote computer, you can accomplish that right from the software. Follow these steps to use a remote file in your software:

1. **Click the Open button on the software toolbar, or choose File➪Open from the menu bar.**

   The Open dialog box appears. The contents of the default document folder are displayed (usually the My Documents folder on your own computer).

2. **Click the arrow to the right of the Look In box, and select the network listing from the list of locations (see Figure 12-2).**

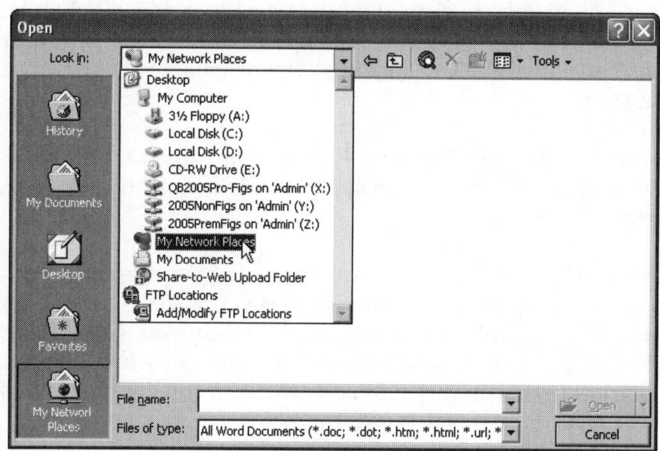


**Figure 12-2:** The Open dialog box in any Windows software can take you to any resource on your computer or on the network.

   In Windows 98, select Network Neighborhood; in Windows Me, Windows 2000, and Windows XP, select My Network Places and then select Entire Network.

   The Open dialog box displays the computers that are on your network.

3. **Double-click the icon of the remote computer that you want to access.**

   Icons for the shared drives and folders on the remote computer appear in the Open dialog box.

4. **Double-click the folder that holds the file you want to use.**

   The files located in that folder are displayed in the Open dialog box.

5. **Select the file, and click Open.**

   The file loads in your software window, so get to work!

If the file that you need is located in a subfolder of a shared resource, it doesn't appear when you double-click the computer's icon (only the folders that are configured for sharing show up in the display). You must open the shared parent folder, and then open the subfolder to get to the file.

This is one of the scenarios in which mapped drives are handy. If you've mapped a drive to a folder on the remote computer, you can get to its contents by using its drive letter (which is listed as one of the drives on your local computer). See Chapter 11 to find out about mapped drives.

## Saving remote files

If you open a file from a remote computer, saving it doesn't change its original location. Every time you click the Save button on the toolbar, press Ctrl+S, or choose File⇨Save, you save the file in its original location on the remote computer.

The same thing is true for files that you open in software that resides on your local drive — they're saved to the same location every time you click the Save button.

Suppose that you open a file that's on a remote computer and work on it in a software program, and then you decide that you want to have a copy of it on your own computer. Well, doing that is easier than you may think, because you don't have to close the software and use the Copy function that I describe earlier in this chapter. You can work on the document and copy it in one fell swoop, using the features in the software program.

The same shortcut action is available for documents that you create on your local computer, if you decide that you want to share the file with a user on another computer.

### Saving a remote file to the local computer

You've opened a software program and loaded a document from another computer on the network, using the steps discussed in the section "Opening distant files," earlier in this chapter. You work on the document, making creative changes and adding brilliant new text. Then your brain comes up with a thought that matches one of the following ideas:

- The user who created the document likes it just the way it is. If you prefer the changed document, you should keep it on your own computer.
- The original document is meant to be used as a template, and you'd prefer to have your own copy of it.
- You haven't finished working on the document, and reloading it is faster if the file is in your local My Documents folder.
- You know that you want to continue working on the document, and just in case the other computer isn't running the next time you need it, you don't want to climb the stairs to the den.
- You just want your own copy because you just want your own copy.

For any of those common reasons (or for some reason I didn't think of), you can save the file to your own local computer. To accomplish this, follow these steps:

1. **Choose File⇨Save As from the menu bar of your software window.**

   When the Save As dialog box opens, the saving location is the same remote folder that you opened to fetch the file.

2. **Click the arrow to the right of the Save In text box.**
3. **Choose the folder that you normally use for saving files on your local computer.**
4. **Click Save.**

   You can change the name of the file before you click the Save button if you don't want both files to have the same name.

You now have a copy of the file on your local computer, and the original file remains on the remote computer.

### Saving a local file to a remote computer

When you work in a software program and you create an absolutely terrific work of art, a fantastic poem, or a mathematically brilliant budget that helps your family save 20 percent of your income without any deprivation, you should show it off — er, share it. If you just created the document, you should save it to your local documents folder first, because having your own copy of a document is a good idea.

Or, in another scenario, perhaps you're working on the computer in the kitchen because somebody else is working on your favorite computer (in the den). You're sure the next time you want to use a computer, you'll be able to get to the machine in the den. Therefore, it makes sense to save the file on the den computer, where it will be handy when you want to continue working on it.

Follow these steps to save the document on another computer:

1. **Choose File⇨Save As from the software menu bar.**

   The Save As dialog box appears.

2. **Click the arrow to the right of the Save In text box, and select the network from the list of locations.**

   In Windows 98, select Network Neighborhood; in Windows Me, 2000, and XP, select My Network Places and then select Entire Network.

   Icons for the computers that are on your network appear in the Save As dialog box.

3. **Double-click the icon for the remote computer on which you want to store a copy of your document.**

   The shared folders on the selected computer appear in the dialog box.

4. **Double-click the folder into which you want to save the document.**

   If the folder you want to use is a subfolder of a shared folder, open the shared folder first and then open the subfolder.

   If the only shared resource is the hard drive, open the hard drive and then open the appropriate folder.

5. **Choose Save to copy the document to the remote location.**

   If you want, you can also change the name of the document before you save it to the remote computer.

## Uh oh, two documents with the same name

If you have a document with the same name on two different computers, your life could get a bit complicated (well, at least your life as it relates to this document). Your real-life complications are probably unrelated to computer networks.

The two files most certainly have different content — you opened the file from one computer, made changes, and saved it on another computer. Here's the problem: If you open the copy on your local computer and use the Save As command to save it in the My Documents folder on the remote computer, you replace the file that was on the remote computer. In fact, Windows displays a message that asks you if you really want to replace that file. The same thing occurs if you do it the other way around (open the remote file and use the Save As command to save it on your local computer).

If you've been working on both files, you don't want to replace one file with the other — you'll lose your changes. The solution is to change the name, sort of. Make it a rule that every time you use the Save As command on a document that's shared between computers, you append text to the filename. The best text to append is a number. For example, if the original file had the name Budget, the first time you save it on another computer, change the filename to Budget2. Each time you use the Save As command to change the location of the file to another computer, increase the number.

When you're working locally, just keep saving the file under the same name — you don't need to use the Save As command until you want to change the computer on which you're saving the file.

Eventually, if the document is one that you've worked on numerous times, you'll probably end up with several copies of the file on each computer. Perhaps the computer in the den has files named Budget2 and Budget4, while the kitchen computer has files named Budget and Budget3.

At some point, open all the copies of the file on one computer, at the same time (all Windows software lets you open multiple files at the same time). Cut, copy, and paste parts of the document into one document to create one masterpiece that contains every change you want to keep. Then delete the other copies.

The same danger occurs if you copy or relocate files instead of opening them in software. Be careful not to replace one file with another if the file that's going to disappear contains data you want to keep.

## Understanding documents in use

If you try to open a document that's already open on another computer, the software displays a message telling you that the document is being used. The document may be one that lives on the local computer (the one you're working on) and has been opened remotely by a user on another computer. Or, the document may live on another computer, and a user on that computer is working with it.

Software that is properly written for Windows displays a message telling you that the file is in use, and offers to load a copy and then notify you when the person who is using the document closes it (see Figure 12-3).

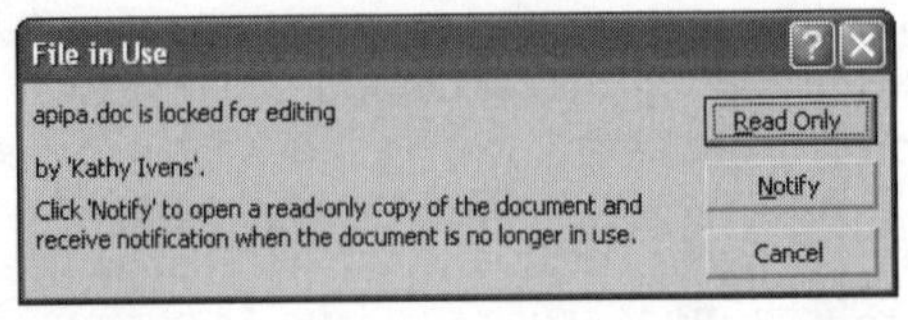


**Figure 12-3:** Somebody is using this document, but you can have a copy of it.

Click Read Only to have a copy of the document placed in your own software window. The file is in *read-only* mode, which means that you can't save it on its originating computer using the same name. Actually, read-only means you cannot use the Save command; only Save As works.

Click Notify if you want to be notified when the other user closes the file. In the meantime, the software loads a read-only copy of the file in your software window.

It's important to realize that the copy that's loaded in your software window is from the hard drive of the remote computer, not the software window of the remote user. This means that you get a copy of the file the way it looked the last time the remote user saved it, which may have been three minutes ago, yesterday, or last week. That user is obviously still working on the file, but any changes or additions since the last time she saved aren't copied to your software window.

So, now you have a copy of the file in your software window. You can make all the changes and additions that you care to, just as if the file weren't in use.

### Saving a document that's in use

Eventually, you're going to want to save the file. If you don't remember to use the Save As command on the File menu, an error message appears to remind you the file is read-only. Click OK, and a Save As dialog box appears so that you can save the file under a different name or in a different location. You have the following options:

- **Use a different filename, and save the file in the original location on the remote computer.** For example, add your initials to the end of the existing filename.
- **Save the file to your local computer.** Click the arrow to the right of the Save In text box, and select your local hard drive or the My Documents folder.

  The problem with the second option is that you now have two files with the same name, but different content, on the network (albeit on two separate computers). If you think that you and the original user may want to compare and combine the two documents, save the file under a different name when you save it to your local computer.

If you save the file to your computer, using the same filename, and then later copy the file back to the original computer, a message appears asking you if you want to overwrite the existing file. If you click Yes, you replace the file that the first user saved. Now leave home because your life is in danger. This is a dirty trick, because you end up overwriting all the work that was saved by the first user.

If you selected the option to be notified when the first user closes the file, a message appears to tell you the file is unlocked, and asking if you want to remove the read-only lock (see Figure 12-4).

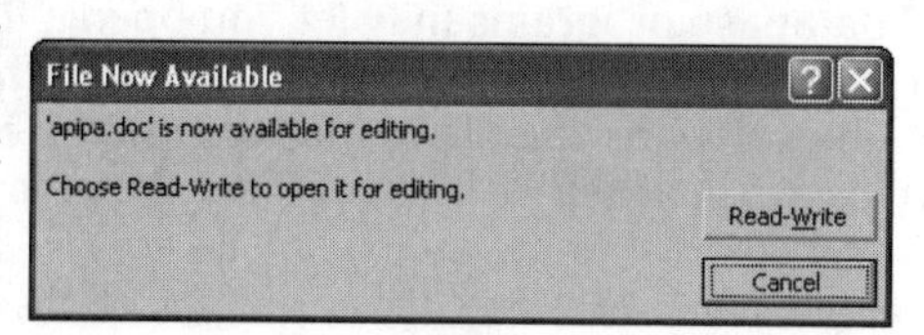


**Figure 12-4:** Making this file read-write instead of read-only means you can save it normally, under its original name — which may not be a good idea.

If you click Read-Write, the file is reloaded into your software window and all the changes the first user made are added to the file (you have a copy of that person's final saved file). Because you had to open that file as a read-only file, you didn't make any changes to the original file.

If you've saved the file under a different name (with the Save As command), because you wanted to save the changes you made, you can open that file and paste your changes into the original file. However, your contributions to the file will come as a surprise (and not necessarily a welcome one) to the original user.

Play it safe — close the original file and continue to use the file you saved with the Save As command. Later, you and the other user can discuss the differences and decide whether it's okay to combine the contents of the two files.

## Files that should never be opened across a network

Don't open files from software programs that automatically save data as quickly as you enter it. This is usually true of database programs that aren't designed for multiple users or for which you don't own a multiuser copy. No Save or Save As command is available — as soon as you enter data and move on to the next record, the data is saved automatically. If somebody else is working on the same record, you end up with conflicting data.

Most database programs have safeguards against this behavior — they're built for shared access by multiple simultaneous users. For example, you may be using accounting software that is specially designed for multiuser activities. (One example of this type of software is QuickBooks, but you must purchase the multiuser version.)

However, some single-user database programs may let you open a file that's in use and manipulate it. Then, when you finish entering data and the automatic save process begins, the software, unable to manage multiuser procedures, goes crazy. The software may crash or freeze, or the data may become corrupted.

Play it safe — don't share database files unless you've purchased database software that's built for multiuser access.

## Licenses and other complications

Most software that's designed to let multiple users access the files in a peer-to-peer network requires you to install the software on every computer. The data file is stored on one computer, so the data can be shared.

When you buy software that works in this manner, you're actually buying a license to use the software; you're not buying the software program itself. That license has terms, and you agree to the terms when you install the software. It is almost always illegal to purchase one copy of a single-user software program and then install it on multiple computers on your network. You must buy a separate copy for each computer.

Breaking the license agreement is illegal. It's also immoral. It's no different from buying a can of vegetables at the grocery store, hiding another can in your coat pocket, and paying for only one can at the checkout counter. Just as shoplifting is illegal, so is installing software for which you didn't buy a license. When you set up a home network, your actions are visible to your children. Stealing is not the kind of example you want to set.

# How About Including My Macintosh?

This is the part of the chapter in which I'm supposed to tell you how to include a Macintosh computer into the file-trading circle you've established for your PC-based network.

Here's the deal: If you're running OS X on your Mac, it can join your network easily. Otherwise, the only way I could move files between a Macintosh and the PCs was by launching a browser and using the FTP feature to download and upload files.

FTP, which stands for File Transfer Protocol, is commonly used to transfer files between Web sites and your computer. FTP uses the Internet's Transmission Control Protocol/Internet Protocol (TCP/IP) to move files. The Web site acts as a server, and your computer acts as a client. If you have the right permissions, you can also upload files from your computer to the Web site. When you're on the Internet, you don't normally have such permissions, except on your own Web site, where you use a password to upload the files required for your Web pages.

When you set up a Macintosh, you make sure that the Mac, which is acting as a server, is configured to give you uploading rights. Otherwise, you would only get files from your Mac; you wouldn't send the Mac any files from your PCs.

FTP is just one of the protocols that are part of the TCP/IP protocol. Among the other TCP/IP protocols you use are http (Hypertext Transfer Protocol) for viewing Web pages and SMTP (Simple Mail Transfer Protocol), which moves your e-mail between your computer and the Internet.

To make it worse, after I figured out how to transfer files between a Mac and my PCs, I found out that the configuration settings, and the ability to use the Mac as a server, differ among different Mac models, and among different versions of the Mac operating system.

After I returned to my chair from my "walk to the wall and bang your head against it" episode, I started contacting Mac network experts, some of whom are well-known authors of books about Macintosh computers.

"I want to network a Mac," I'd say. "Sure, easy," each replied. "Install File and Print services for Macintosh on your Windows 2000 or Windows NT 4 domain and on all the servers in your network that will be responsible for Mac client/server processes."

"No, no," I would say. "This isn't in a business network; it's a peer-to-peer home network."

"Sure, easy," came the replies, as long as you're running Mac OS X. When I asked about earlier versions of Mac operating systems, some of them laughed. One person said, "You can't get there from here." But a few experts said that I could buy software to accomplish this. You can buy software for the PCs or software for the Macintosh. You don't need both.

Check with magazines and books that are devoted to Macintosh users to find out about software for incorporating your older Macintosh into your network. Or, check out the programs that I cover next, which were recommended by some Macintosh experts whom I talked to.

## Mac, meet Dave

For the Macintosh, buy Dave. Yep, that's the name of the software. It's from Thursby software, which you can reach at `www.thursby.com/default.html`.

This software uses TCP/IP on the Mac, so your PCs can recognize and interact with the Mac. In effect, it makes the Macintosh look like a PC to the other PCs that are on the network. Macintosh purists (sometimes regarded as a cultlike group) may not love that description. It even lets the Mac user log on to the network the way PC users do.

You must be using a Mac with a 68030 or higher processor, and you must have at least 16 MB of RAM. The software supports Mac OS 8.6 and higher. You can download a free trial, which is a limited version of the software, before deciding to purchase it (the purchase price is about $150.00 for a single-user version).

The company also has a product called MacSOHO that has fewer features, but it does support file sharing between Macs and PCs. You may want to investigate it.

## From a PC LAN to a PC MACLAN

Miramar Systems, at `www.miramar.com`, offers a product called PC MACLAN, which is installed on PCs that need to interact with Macintosh computers (the software adds the AppleTalk protocol to the PC).

PC MACLAN comes in two versions: one for Windows 95/98/Me and another for Windows NT/2000/XP.

# Part IV
# Network Security and Maintenance

## In this part . . .

*Securing the network* is the technical terminology for keeping the bad stuff — including viruses and Internet invaders — away from all the computers on the network. You probably know what a virus is (even if you've never encountered one on your computer), but you may not know what Internet invaders are. These are malicious people who try to break in to your computer while you're connected to the Internet, a feat that's amazingly easy to do if you don't take the proper precautions. In this part, you find out what steps you can take to keep the bad stuff out of your network.

*Maintenance* is the technical term for, well, maintenance — I guess there's no better word. Your computers and your network need maintenance to stay healthy — just like your car or your teeth. In this part, you discover techniques and tools you can use to keep things humming along.

# Chapter 13

# Making Your Network Secure

***In This Chapter***

- Combating computer viruses
- Keeping Internet spies out of your computers
- Fending off evil-doers

As users, we make mistakes. We inadvertently delete important files (including software files) and perform other accidental actions that can totally mess up a computer.

However, some people deliberately work at the task of destroying computers, and they perform their dirty deeds by installing viruses on your computer. Other nasty folks invade your computer while you're on the Internet, and they get private information from your files (or leave viruses on your computer).

This chapter discusses methods you can use to make sure that the computers on your network have as much protection as possible against the misery these actions can cause. However, the most important ingredient in your scheme to protect your network is a healthy dose of paranoia. Be suspicious. Be very afraid.

## All About Viruses

A *virus* is programming code that is designed to cause damage and is disguised to appear to be a normal program. Most viruses are also designed to clone themselves if they find a network environment so that they can move on to the other computers.

Almost all virus infections occur over the Internet, either attached to e-mail or to a file that you download. Three major classes of viruses exist, and each class has a number of subclasses, as rogue programmers devise innovative ways to ply their nefarious trade.

A virus is a program, although it's frequently disguised as something else (for example, it may pretend to be a screen saver). The code in the program is designed to cause harm. In addition, code exists to make sure that the virus is replicated to other drives on your computer, to other computers on a network, or to other computers on the Internet.

The severity of the damage a virus leaves behind depends on the viciousness of the programmer. Viruses can erase data, replace program files, and change system files. Some viruses cause enough damage to the operating system files to make it impossible to boot the computer, rendering the machine useless. Some viruses go to work as soon as you inadvertently start them, but other viruses are programmed to wait until certain circumstances cause their code to be executed (usually a certain date).

Viruses arrive in many categories, and within each category of viruses, many subcategories exist. Covering all of these variants would fill a thick book. As a result, I'll briefly go over some of the basic virus types so you can learn how to spot (or be suspicious about) problems that may be caused by the most frequently encountered virus types.

## File-infecting viruses

File infectors are the oldest virus type, and they've been around as long as personal computers have been around. These viruses attach themselves to program files, which are usually files with the filename extension `.com` or `.exe`. However, some file-infecting viruses don't need the main executable file to infect your system. They can attach themselves to another file type, one that is loaded by the main executable file. Among the file types that programs load (and viruses can use) are filenames with the extensions `.sys`, `.ovl`, `.prg`, and `.mnu`.

When the program is loaded, the virus is loaded as well, and it does its work independent of the program that runs when you open the program file. The program file is just the mode of transportation — the way the virus gets itself loaded into memory.

Some viruses can also be programs at the same time. The filename is innocuous, and the filename extension is `.exe`. Opening the file unleashes the virus. This virus type is frequently transmitted to its victims as an e-mail attachment.

## How to avoid being fooled by Windows

People who know that file-infecting virus types are connected to executable files are frequently surprised when their computers become infected. They're always careful about examining the file names of e-mail attachments and downloaded files, looking for a file extension that indicates an executable file. When they see an attachment with the file extension `.txt`, they stop worrying and then go crazy trying to figure out how a virus slipped past their guard.

These people have been fooled by Windows. Unfortunately (okay, I'd rather say "stupidly"), Windows doesn't display file extensions by default, so a file that seems to be named readme.txt could really be named readme.txt.exe. I've never understood the logic (or lack of it) that went into Microsoft's decision to hide file extensions when you're viewing files. To avoid this Windows "gotcha," the first thing to do when you set up a computer is to change the default setting for viewing files so that file extensions are visible. To do this, follow these steps:

1. Open My Computer or another system folder, such as Windows Explorer or Control Panel.
2. Choose Tools⇨Folder Options (or View⇨Folder Options in Windows 98).
3. Select the View tab.
4. Scroll through the Advanced settings list to locate the item Hide file extensions for known file types, and click the check box to remove the check mark.
5. Click OK.

### System and boot infectors

System and boot infectors infect the code that's placed in certain system areas on a drive. On a floppy disk, they attach themselves to the DOS boot sector. On hard drives, they attach themselves to the Master Boot Record (MBR).

This virus type doesn't launch itself into memory and go to work until the next time you boot your computer. If you boot to a floppy disk — using the infected disk — the virus is activated. If you start your computer normally, the virus loads itself into system memory when the boot files on the MBR load.

Once it's loaded into your system memory, the virus can control basic computer operations, and it can replicate itself to other drives on the computer or to other computers on the network. Some boot sector viruses are designed to destroy the computer's ability to boot; others permit startup and then perform damaging processes all over the computer (and any computers that are attached through a network).

## Macro viruses

Probably the most common viruses today, macro viruses are usually programmed to do the same damage as file-infecting viruses, but they use a different vehicle to arrive at your computer. They don't attach themselves to an executable file, nor do they arrive as a self-contained executable file. Instead, they attach themselves to a document and launch themselves when the document file is opened. Then they carry out their damaging agenda and replicate themselves into other documents.

Macro viruses should really be called VB viruses, because they attach themselves to Visual Basic (VB) code, which some software programs use to create or run macros. (Macros are automated procedures that you can use to perform tasks in software.) VB files have the extension `.vbs`.

All the software applications that are included in Microsoft Office use VB code for macros. In fact, almost all the software that you can buy from Microsoft uses VB code for a variety of tasks.

A neat trick is available for avoiding VB viruses, but if you use VB yourself, you can't use it. Personally, I think avoiding these common viruses is important enough to stop using VB. The essence of this trick is to make your computer think that VB code is text, and because text files can't execute program code, the VB virus code never executes. The way to implement this trick is to change the association of files with the extension `.vbs` from Visual Basic to Notepad (the Windows text editor). Here's how to make this change:

1. **Open My Computer or another system folder, such as Windows Explorer or Control Panel.**
2. **Choose Tools⇨Folder Options (or View⇨Folder Options in Windows 98).**
3. **Select the File Types tab.**
4. **Scroll through the list of registered file types, and select VBS.**

   The file association information about the `.vbs` file extension is displayed, as shown in Figure 13-1.
5. **Click the Change button.**

   The Opens With dialog box appears (see Figure 13-2).
6. **Select Notepad, and click OK.**
7. **Click Close.**

VBS viruses now lack an executable association, which means they can't run. Of course, neither can you run VBS macros, but because most users aren't macro programmers, that's probably just fine.

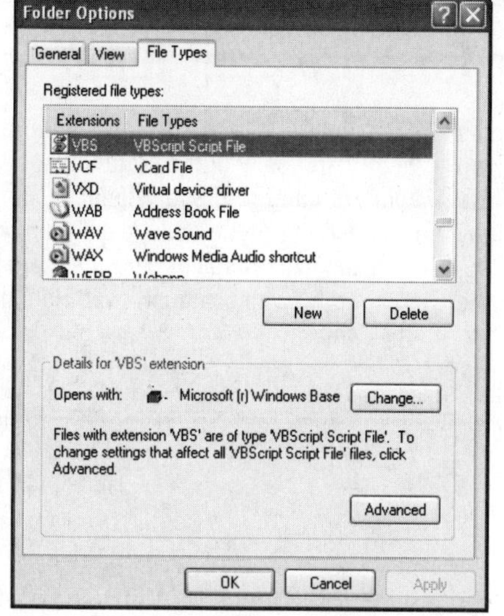


**Figure 13-1:** VBS files are associated with VBScript, which is an executable program.

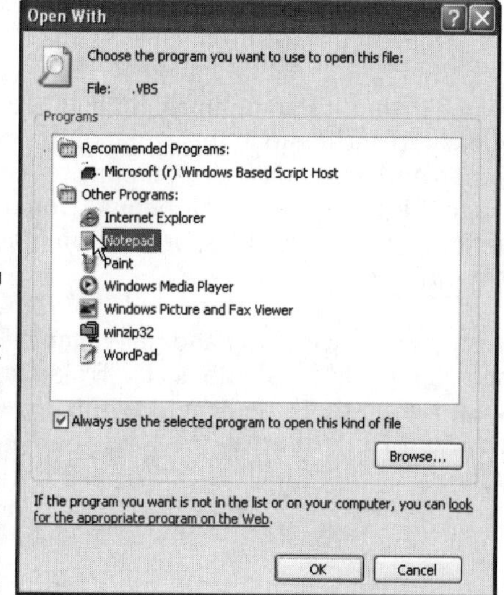


**Figure 13-2:** Select Notepad to create an innocuous association for VBS files.

Some software programs that provide the power of macros use their own proprietary code that doesn't run separately from the program. It's much more difficult for a virus to insert itself within macro code that doesn't use VB. WordPerfect is an example of a software program that provides powerful macro abilities (more powerful than Word, in fact) without using VB.

## A strange name for a program, huh?

The name *Trojan horse* comes from Homer's *Iliad,* which tells the story of the Greeks faking out the Trojans during a long, bitter war. The Greeks pretended to give up, and then they offered a giant wooden statue of a horse to the Trojans, calling it a peace offering. What the Trojans didn't know was that the statue was hollowed out and within it were armed soldiers. That night, while the Trojans celebrated their victory, the belly of the statue opened, and the soldiers emerged, overwhelming the Trojans. Because the rogue code in a Trojan horse program disguises itself as a normal, safe program, somebody (who obviously read Homer) applied this name.

## Trojan horses

A *Trojan horse* performs the same malicious deeds that viruses perform, but a Trojan horse doesn't qualify as a true virus because it doesn't fit the technical definition of a virus in terms of replication. Trojan horses don't replicate themselves. Of course, if you've been victimized by a Trojan horse, those definitions are piddling.

One problem with a Trojan horse is that it's sometimes difficult to remove the damage it does, even after you catch and remove the Trojan horse file. You almost always have to contact an antivirus software company to get instructions for eliminating the damage the Trojan horse left behind. You may have to undo changes to the registry, replace system files, or perform other manual tasks to rid your system of the damage

Most antivirus programs can successfully identify and delete most Trojan horses, but if you find yourself facing continual attacks by Trojan horses, you may want to install a software program that's dedicated to this type of virus. Experts give high recommendations to PestPatrol (`www.safersite.com`) and Tauscan (`www.agnitum.com`).

## Worms

A *worm* is always a self-contained program, so it never has to attach itself to any other program to launch itself. A worm must be opened manually, at which point it does its damage and replicates itself (often by mailing itself to recipients in an Outlook or Outlook Express address book).

One characteristic of a worm is its ability to propagate itself across drives and computers that are connected via a network. Because they don't need to attach themselves to other programs, worms propagate easily and rapidly. They don't need to find a host file, so they can just plop themselves down anywhere they want and then clone themselves all over your drives (including drives of connected computers). Sometimes each clone that's created carries a different assignment, so when all these copies leap into action, they can do the maximum amount of damage. Worms almost always arrive as e-mail attachments.

If you use Outlook or Outlook Express for e-mail, it's urgent that you pay attention to Microsoft's security alerts, fixes, and upgrades. Unfortunately, this can be a frequent chore (those of us who gave up Outlook/Outlook Express in favor of Eudora tend to get a bit smug about this).

# Antivirus Programs: For Prevention and Cure

An important defense against viruses is an antivirus program. Good antivirus software performs the following tasks:

- Scans your drive, looking for viruses
- Checks every executable file as you open it to make sure that no virus is piggybacked onto it
- Checks your e-mail to find viruses as messages that are brought into your inbox
- Removes any virus code it finds (or deletes the file if it cannot remove the virus)

A number of antivirus software programs are available, and the following are the two most popular:

- Norton AntiVirus (`www.symantec.com`)
- McAfee VirusScan (`www.mcafee.com`)

I'm sure that other existing programs are just as good as these, but I've used both of these and can personally endorse them.

Antivirus software has two main components:

- The engine, or the program itself
- The virus information data files, which have information about known viruses, making it possible for the software to spot virus files

New viruses are invented every minute (reliable sources put the number of new viruses at 400 per month). Usually, the cures are found quickly. The cures are put into the virus information data files, and you can download those files from your antivirus software vendor (which is not the same as downloading a complete update to the software). Configure your antivirus software to check for updates to the virus information data files on a regular basis (every few hours), or manually check for updates every day.

The antivirus software engine/program has the following parts:

- The on-access component, which runs all the time and automatically checks files as they're received or opened
- The scanning component, which checks all the files on your computer when you initiate a scan

Antivirus software works by intercepting computer operations, such as reading files or receiving e-mail messages, so that it can scan the files before allowing the operating system to continue with the operation. The scanning process involves the following steps:

- Matching the contents of the file against the information that's in the virus data information files. The software looks for a known signature, called a *marker,* which is a string of characters or bytes that's found in every instance of a specific virus.
- Looking for unusual file attributes, such as unexpected changes in the size of existing executable files.
- Looking for suspicious behavior by using heuristic scanning to sniff out suspicious code (see the sidebar "Heuristic scanning," later in this chapter, for more information).

When the software finds a file that's infected, it flashes a message. Usually, the message asks you to decide how to handle the file. The choices vary depending on the software, but you're usually offered one of the following choices:

- **Clean the file:** This choice works when a virus has infected an existing file. The software tries to clean the virus out of the file, reverting the file to its original condition. If the software can't clean the file, you're notified of that fact, and you must delete the file. (Use the Delete option in the antivirus software window; don't open Windows Explorer to delete the file.) If the file that you delete is required by the operating system or an application, you'll have to replace it with the original.

## Heuristic scanning

*Heuristic scanning* is a way to analyze the behavior of an executable file to try to determine whether the file offers a potential threat. Antivirus software companies use this technique to try to catch viruses that are new and therefore have not yet been added to their virus information data files. Each antivirus software company has its own method for determining a potential threat and for defining "suspicious behavior" during heuristic scans. Heuristic scanning is really a guessing game, but it uses educated guesses.

Heuristic scanning has some side effects, but none of them are serious enough to turn off the feature (most antivirus software lets you turn off the heuristic scanning option). It makes scanning slower, it can sometimes produce false alarms when a good program has code that seems to resemble the code in a virus, and it can miss a new virus that doesn't behave in typical virus fashion. Personally, I think it's best to maintain an attitude of paranoia, so even though the technology for heuristic scanning is not as advanced as it probably will be one day, you're better off letting your antivirus software use this feature.

- **Delete the file:** When you delete the file through the antivirus software window, the file is not sent to the Recycle Bin; it is permanently deleted.
- **Isolate the file:** Some antivirus software programs offer a method for isolating infected files, usually in a folder that the software creates, and isolates, by locking the folder to prevent any file in the folder from damaging the computer. Later, you can delete the contents of the folder, or you can send the files to the software company (if you're participating in a program that asks you to do this).

The software always identifies the name of the virus it found, and you should note the name and go to the antivirus software company's Web site to find out more about the virus. You may have to do more than just delete the infected file to clean up your computer, and the company has instructions for any other steps you should take. This is especially true of Trojan horse viruses.

# Common Sense: Part of Your Arsenal

If you develop an enhanced sense of suspicion, even paranoia, you're less likely to suffer a virus attack. Therefore, changing your normal friendly, naive personality into that of a suspicious curmudgeon makes sense.

## Develop e-mail paranoia

The most common delivery method for viruses is e-mail. That's because rogue programmers have figured out that if they can invade e-mail software, they can automatically send their destructive code to lots of additional victims — they use your address book and send the virus to every e-mail address they find. This practice is why many people end up with virus infections. The virus came from somebody they know (even though that person didn't know he or she was sending the virus).

Therefore, follow these precautions when reading e-mail:

- Don't open any files attached to an e-mail message from somebody you know, unless you know in advance that those files are coming to you.
- Don't open any files that are attached to an e-mail message from somebody you don't know.
- Don't open any files attached to an e-mail message if the subject line is strange. In fact, don't even open the e-mail message if the subject line seems weird — some viruses are capable of launching themselves when the message is opened. Just delete the message without reading it.

## Develop Internet download paranoia

Be careful about downloading files from the Internet. Here are specific precautions to take:

- If you're not sure of the source, avoid downloading the file.
- Make sure that your antivirus program is configured to check the files on the download Web site. If your antivirus software can't do that, and you're reasonably certain that the site is safe, take the precaution of having your antivirus software scan the folder you used to save the file before you install the software.
- If your kids are downloading multimedia files (music and video), do whatever you need to do to make them paranoid and suspicious. Kids download many of the viruses that attack family computers.

## Virus hoaxes

The threat of viruses is real enough to those of us who are nervous about safe computing, but dealing with virus hoaxes makes it worse. People who fall for these stupid hoaxes often end up damaging their systems by following the advice they receive. (I've seen messages that tell me to look for a certain file and delete it immediately, and it's almost always a valid Windows system file.)

People fall for this stuff because they don't have enough technical knowledge to recognize that most of the information doesn't make sense, so I'll give you some helpful hints for identifying virus hoaxes.

### Never take technical advice from a chain letter

Anyone who forwards a chain letter without checking the facts first is, de facto, not computer literate. So why would you take advice from this person?

Some virus hoax messages aren't warnings; they're advisories on avoiding the spread of viruses. The most famous example is the "Add !0000 to your address book" chain letter that's been traveling the Internet for a long time. The e-mail message includes a tip for adding the recipient !0000 to your address book (newer versions of this hoax use the recipient AAAAA), explaining that when a virus tries to send itself out to everyone in your address book, the e-mail software will fail on the bogus address, stopping any mass e-mail attempt. The hoax message includes the information that this recipient always appears first in your address book because of the way computers alphabetize lists. It's true that computers alphabetize starting with numbers and move on to letters, but that's the only true fact in the message.

### Check with antivirus experts

Lots of virus hoax messages are circulating all the time. If you get one, do everyone in your address book a favor — don't click the Forward button in your e-mail software window. Check the facts first by going to the Web site of your antivirus software vendor, which has information on virus hoaxes.

### How to identify a virus hoax

Virus hoax messages have some things in common, so in this section I present some guidelines for identifying them.

Look for a plot that reminds you of a soap opera. It's a long, drawn-out story about somebody's cousin who has a brother-in-law who works at a widget manufacturer, which had a customer who was a cosmetic surgeon, who went to some Internet site, and . . . it just goes on and on.

At least one person in the cast of characters of the soap opera is some sort of computer expert; he works at Microsoft or IBM, or is the IT director of a major technical company. This is the old "credibility" trick; don't fall for it.

Often a sentence appears that says "I personally got this virus and it wiped out my machine." You're supposed to assume that "I" is the person who sent you this message (whom you probably know, or else why would your e-mail address be in the sender's address book?). Because this message has probably been traveling around the Internet for a long time, using the Forward buttons of a thousand e-mail software installations, the "I" probably refers to somebody who has either been informed of the facts by one of his recipients and now regrets clicking that Forward button, or has died of old age.

The chain letter instructions include an urgent plea to distribute this information immediately to the whole world. This part of the message is usually in capital letters to promote a sense of urgency: SEND THIS MESSAGE TO EVERYBODY IN YOUR ADDRESS BOOK. Or, SEND THIS TO EVERYBODY YOU KNOW, HAVE EVER MET, OR MIGHT MEET IN THE FUTURE.

# Firewalls: Defense for Internet Attacks

Some of the people who use the Internet are annoying, or even dangerous, jerks. They're like the kids who destroy property just for the fun of it, or break into homes and steal personal items. Mostly, these jerks are kids — at least emotionally. They're the kind of kids we called "punks" in my salad days. Today, some people call these punks *hackers,* but the real root of that word isn't negative — it used to mean people who hacked away at programming code, out of curiosity. Frequently, these people improved the code. However, I'll use the current jargon and refer to this danger as *Internet hacking.*

Fortunately, you can protect your network from Internet hackers by purchasing and installing a firewall. A *firewall* is a program that protects computers from users on other networks (remember, the Internet is another network). In fact, a firewall can protect computers from other computers, but if you have a network, you don't want to isolate your computer from the other computers on your network.

Windows XP comes with a built-in firewall, but if you have a home network (and I assume you do or you wouldn't have bought this book), you can't use the Windows XP firewall. See the section "Windows XP firewalls," later in this chapter, for more information.

## Why do you need a firewall?

While you're on the Internet, you're vulnerable to any malicious act that a hacker wants to perpetrate. This is especially true if you're using an always-on connection to the Internet, via a cable modem or a DSL device.

When you're on the Internet, your computer has an Internet Protocol (IP) address. That address is needed for communication between you and other computers on the Internet, and data flows in both directions. A malicious hacker can access your computer through that IP address.

Internet hackers select an IP address and then try to connect to that IP address. Most of the time, they have no particular victim in mind. They use software that selects an IP address at random, and then their software tries to access the computer that's linked to that address.

If the access attempt fails, the software picks another IP address. If the attempt succeeds, the intruders have access to your computer and its contents. You won't know that anything is going on, even if you're working at the computer, because everything happens in the background, and the attack doesn't interfere with anything you're doing. Here are some of the common actions performed by intruders:

- Sending executable files that contain viruses to your computer
- Renaming or deleting the files that run at startup and are needed to run software
- Copying your documents to their own systems, where they hope to find personal and sensitive information that they can use
- Sending enormous files or a massive number of small files, just for the "fun" of filling your hard drive

That's not a complete list, but it should be enough to scare you (which is my intention). Defend yourself by blocking your computer with a firewall.

## What a firewall does

A firewall works by watching everything that happens on your computer that has anything to do with activity outside your computer. Unless you say that it's okay, no action can occur between your computer and another computer. That other computer could be on the Internet or on your network.

Because the firewall stops any computer from accessing your computer, you must configure the firewall software to accept communications between your computer and the other computers on your network. Doing so frees the firewall to concentrate on communications between your computer and a computer on the Internet.

The firewall blocks communication in both directions — to and from the Internet. The software you use to access the Internet, such as your browser and e-mail program, must be given permission to do its job.

Any computer that tries to access your computer is either stopped dead in its tracks or is stopped temporarily until you tell the firewall whether to let the computer gain access (depending on the way you configure the firewall's behavior).

When an intruder attempts to reach your IP address, it's really your communication ports that are being examined. Computers send and receive data via ports. You already know about ports, because you've connected a printer to a parallel port, attached a modem to a serial port, or attached some device to a Universal Serial Bus (USB) port. Besides these ports, which you can see, your computer contains thousands of virtual ports. You can't see a virtual port, because it's a software service rather than a physical connector. However, just like a physical port, a virtual port accepts and sends data.

Almost every type of computer communication is programmed to use a specific port. Ports are numbered from 0 to 65536, and the ports between 0 and 1024 are reserved by certain services. For instance, http (the protocol you use when you're visiting a Web page) uses port 80. Ports work by "listening" for data, and when data arrives, the ports automatically open to accept it, if the data announces that it's the right data type for the port.

Internet hackers use ports to move data between their computers and your computer. They have access to software that lets them test whether a port on a remote computer is listening, which means that it's vulnerable to attack. Some of the software tests only certain ports (by pretending to be sending data of a type supported by that port). This technique is called *port scanning,* and it's the most popular method of testing computer vulnerability. The hacking software uses that information to attack, masquerading the data to resemble the appropriate type of data for the listening port. A port that is *listening* is, in effect, an open port that is willing to accept data. If it weren't willing to accept data, it wouldn't be listening.

Firewalls examine the ports to see whether the type of data is appropriate for the port that's being used. This process is called *stateful inspection,* and it involves checking the data that is passing through the port. As a result, stateful inspection can catch data that identified itself as being appropriate for the port, but when the actual data stream is examined, the firewall discovers a false data type, because the data doesn't match the type that it pretends to be.

## Examining a firewall's log file

After you install a firewall program on your network, open your firewall's *log file* (a list of all the attempts made to access your computer) and look at the information (a command exists on the menu bar of the firewall software to accomplish this). All the computers that have tried to get into your computer are listed by their IP addresses. Go to one of the Web sites that provides reverse lookups; these sites allow you to enter an IP address, and they return the name of the offending computer. (I use `www.eons.com/iplookup.htm`.)

Sometimes the IP address belongs to an Internet service provider (ISP), and it's part of a range of addresses that are assigned to that ISP. This means that a customer of that ISP, who has been assigned that IP address for his Internet session, is trying to get into your computer. You probably won't be able to determine the identity of the customer. However, you can notify the ISP that at a certain time on a certain date, this particular IP address was trying to break in to your computer, and the ISP can determine to whom the address was assigned at that moment. Ask the ISP to let you know what it does to resolve the problem.

## My experience with ZoneAlarm

I've tried several firewall software programs, and the one I eventually chose is ZoneAlarm, from Zone Labs (`www.zonelabs.com`). I think it's the best firewall available for a home network. By the time you read this, other software companies may have made firewalls available, and you should check computer magazines and experts to get other recommendations.

Within moments of installing ZoneAlarm, a message popped up telling me that another computer was trying to access my computer over the Internet. ZoneAlarm asked if I wanted to let this computer in — it gave me the IP address of the unknown computer. I clicked No, and a few minutes later another pop-up message appeared. These messages kept appearing. I was amazed and a little frightened about all the time I had operated without a firewall.

Finally, I got tired of saying no every few minutes, and I configured ZoneAlarm to stop asking and just say no. I also chose to keep a log file of all the attempts. Every once in a while, I open the log file, and I'm always amazed at the number of times that outside computers are trying to invade my computer. The log file gets very large, very fast.

Sometimes the IP address is identified as belonging to a particular company. I've found a lot of marketing companies snooping around my computer. They're trying to see which Web sites I visit, and then they can sell my e-mail address to spammers who want to sell me stuff that's related to my interests. I usually go to the companies' Web sites and send e-mail to the highest-ranking contact I can find listed. The messages say "gotcha, cut it out."

You can't tell whether a snooper was trying to do some damage, either by leaving behind a virus or stealing personal information. You can only tell that the snooper has tried to hack into your computer.

## Testing the security of your system

You should test each computer if you haven't installed a firewall, but also test it after your firewall is running. Use the following steps to test your system:

1. **Enter** www.grc.com **in your browser's Address bar.**

   This is the Web site of Gibson Research, which has been around for many years. The techies at Gibson are absolute geniuses when it comes to computers.

2. **Click the ShieldsUP! logo.**

   The ShieldsUP page appears.

3. **Scroll to the ShieldsUP logo, and click it.**

The ShieldsUP program determines how vulnerable your computer is to spying, prying, and destructive hacks. Click Yes when the message about going to a secure site appears.

4. **On the next Web page, follow the prompts to test your computer's ports.**

   The probe begins. The process takes a while, perhaps a full minute or so.

5. **Read the report.**

   The report tells you the following information, depending on whether you have a firewall:

   - **If you're not running a firewall:** The first thing you see is `Hello <your name>`. The test software peeked into your computer and found the file that holds your logon name. Then the real scary stuff begins, as shown in Figure 13-3.

     The stuff you see in Figure 13-3 is just the beginning. As I scrolled down to read the rest of the report, I found that the test software was able to get into all my shared folders. It knew stuff about the technical side of my Internet connection that added up to an invitation to invade.

   - **If you're running a firewall:** You should get a report similar to the one shown in Figure 13-4.

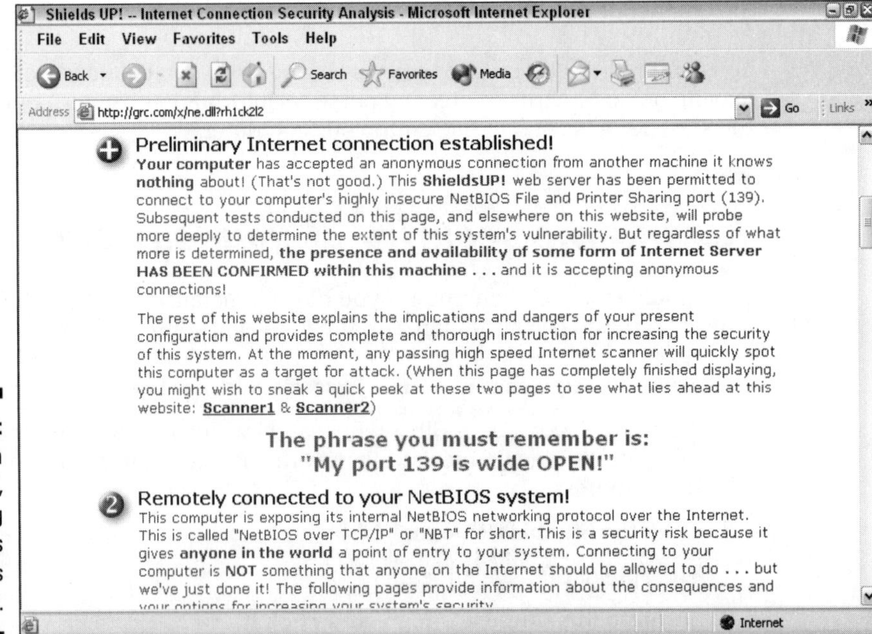


**Figure 13-3:** Without a firewall, nothing in this computer is a secret.

**Unsolicited Packets:** PASSED — No Internet packets of any sort were received from your system as a side-effect of our attempts to elicit some response from any of the ports listed above. Some questionable personal security systems expose their users by attempting to "counter-probe the prober", thus revealing themselves. But your system remained wisely silent. (Except for the fact that not all of its ports are completely stealthed as shown below.)

**Ping Echo:** PASSED — Your system ignored and refused to reply to repeated Pings (ICMP Echo Requests) from our server.

| Port | Service | Status | Security Implications |
|---|---|---|---|
| 0 | <nil> | Stealth | There is NO EVIDENCE WHATSOEVER that a port (or even any computer) exists at this IP address! |
| 21 | FTP | Stealth | There is NO EVIDENCE WHATSOEVER that a port (or even any computer) exists at this IP address! |
| 22 | SSH | Stealth | There is NO EVIDENCE WHATSOEVER that a port (or even any computer) exists at this IP address! |
| 23 | Telnet | Stealth | There is NO EVIDENCE WHATSOEVER that a port (or even any computer) exists at this IP address! |
| 25 | SMTP | Stealth | There is NO EVIDENCE WHATSOEVER that a port (or even any computer) exists at this IP address! |
| 79 | Finger | Stealth | There is NO EVIDENCE WHATSOEVER that a port (or even any computer) exists at this IP address! |
| 80 | HTTP | Stealth | There is NO EVIDENCE WHATSOEVER that a port (or even any computer) exists at this IP address! |
| 110 | POP3 | Stealth | There is NO EVIDENCE WHATSOEVER that a port (or even any computer) exists at this IP address! |

**Figure 13-4:** Thank goodness for a good firewall.

While you're on the `grc.com` site, travel through its pages to find out more about the kind of spying, prying, and destructive actions that outside computers can wreak on your computers.

## Windows XP firewalls

Windows XP has a built-in firewall, which is intended to save you the trouble or expense of installing and configuring a software firewall. In the following sections I'll discuss the firewalls for Windows XP, and for SP2 of Windows XP.

### Original (not SP2) Windows XP firewall

The firewall built into Windows XP before the release of SP2 is called Internet Connection Firewall (ICF). This program is primitive and lacks desirable features. One flaw in ICF is the fact that it only checks incoming data packets. While this eliminates the majority of damage from Internet-based evildoers, it doesn't prevent your computer from sending out packets of data. Some viruses send data from your computer to the virus originator, and ICF doesn't prevent that. However, if you have antivirus protection on your computer (discussed earlier in this chapter), the danger is reduced.

More important to you, as the network administrator for your home network, is the fact that ICF can't be configured to permit data traffic from safe sources while blocking data traffic from other sources. This means that you can't tell the firewall to permit the flow of data from the computers on your network while blocking Internet data.

The ICF-protected Windows XP computer can communicate with other computers on the network (except any that are running Windows XP and have ICF enabled) because ICF doesn't care about outgoing traffic.

The other computers on the network can see the ICF-protected Windows XP computer in Network Neighborhood or My Network Places. However, any attempt to access the computer produces an error message that says the computer can't be found.

If you haven't installed Service Pack 2 (SP2) for Windows XP, turn off ICF and either install a software firewall program, or use a router with a firewall feature (discussed later in this chapter). To turn off ICF, follow these steps:

1. **Choose Start➪Control Panel➪Network and Internet Connections➪Network Connections.**

   The Network Connections folder opens, displaying an icon or listing for your Internet connection(s).

2. **Right-click the Local Area Network Connection, and choose Properties.**

   The Properties dialog box for your connection opens.

3. **Click the Advanced tab, and deselect the option to use ICF.**

### Windows XP SP2 Firewall

With the release of Service Pack 2 for Windows XP, Microsoft updated and improved the built-in firewall. In fact, they renamed it Windows Firewall, replacing the original appellation, Internet Connection Firewall.

The new Windows firewall can be configured, so you can use it with a network, protecting the computer from Internet attacks while permitting network communications.

Most of the time, as you set up features in Windows XP, the operating system automatically enables the appropriate firewall settings. For example, when you enable file and printer sharing, Windows automatically configures the firewall for network communications among the computers on the LAN. Other features you enable may require additional changes in the firewall's configuration.

You can view or change the firewall configuration settings by opening its Properties dialog box with one of the following actions:

- Choose Start➪Control Panel➪Network and Internet Connections➪Windows Firewall.
- Click the Local Area Connection icon on your taskbar, and then click Properties. Click the Advanced tab, and then click Settings.

In this section, I'll offer some guidelines for configuring Windows Firewall in Windows XP SP2 (if you're not running SP2 you should upgrade as soon as possible).

### Firewall General Tab

The General tab (see Figure 13-5) contains the basic configuration options that enable or disable the firewall.

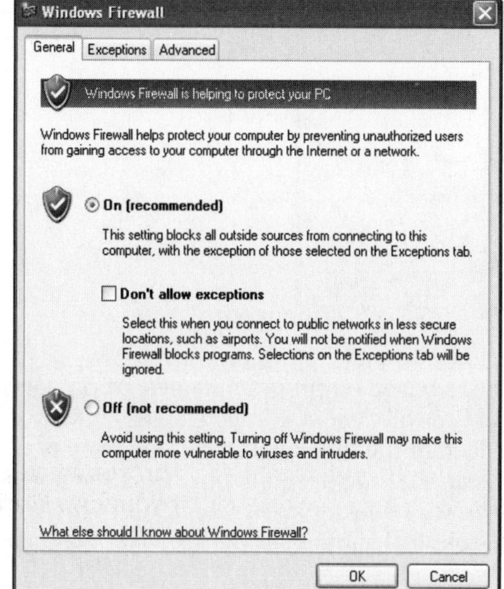


**Figure 13-5:** Use the General tab to enable or disable basic firewall features.

By default, the firewall is enabled (on), and permits exceptions. These are the normal settings for a computer running in a network environment, because the exceptions (covered next) permit the exchange of data between this computer and the other computers on the network.

### Firewall Exceptions Tab

The Exceptions tab is where you open data streams that would otherwise be blocked by the firewall. You can create exceptions for programs and for ports. To save you the trouble (and the attendant research) of determining which programs and ports need to be opened for common communications, Windows lists some pre-defined exceptions that you can enable (see Figure 13-6).

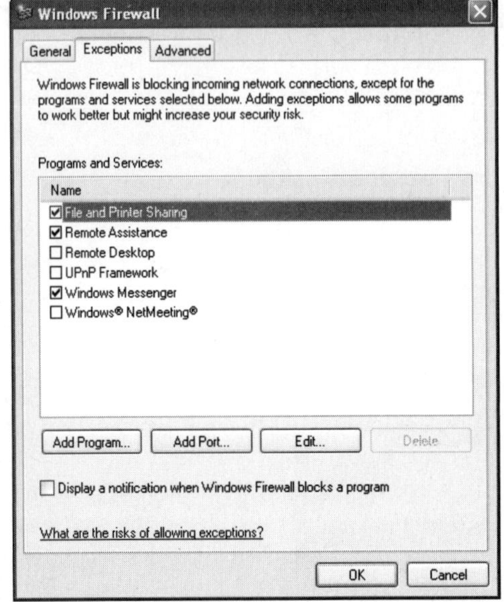


**Figure 13-6:** Use the Exceptions tab to open the firewall for specific programs and ports.

You can configure exceptions based on program names, or on ports. If you select program names, the firewall almost always knows which ports to open, so that's the easiest approach. If the firewall doesn't open any ports for a program you specify, it can mean that the program only uses the ports that are already open, or that the firewall doesn't know which ports the software uses. If in doubt, contact technical support at the software company.

To create an exception for a program, click Add Program. The Add a Program dialog box appears with a list of programs (mostly games you can play over the network and the Internet). If the program you want to add to the exception list isn't there, click Browse to locate the program on your hard drive.

To open a port manually, click Add Port. In the Add a Port dialog box, specify whether the port is a TCP or UDP port. Then, enter the name of the service or program that will use this port, as well as the port number. To get the information you need, you have to check the technical specifications of the service or program that needs the port.

You can edit any exception by selecting its listing and clicking Edit. The Edit a Service dialog box opens, displaying the ports used by the selected exception. Editing involves changing the *scope* of a port (or multiple ports), which means defining the network, or part of a network, from which the excepted data stream can originate. To change the scope, select the applicable port and click Change Scope. In the Change Scope dialog box (see Figure 13-7), select one of the available options, described next.

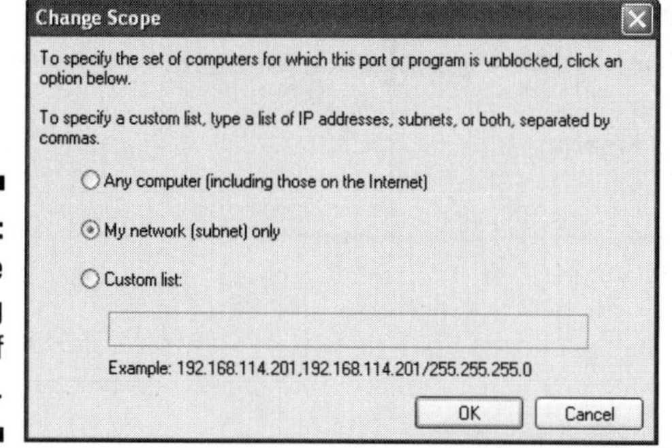


**Figure 13-7:** Change the originating source of data traffic.

**Any computer (including those on the Internet).** Selecting this option means you want to allow data into your computer through this port from any computer, anywhere in the world. Needless to say, this is rather dangerous. The only reason to opt for this level of traffic is to maintain a Web site (which you wouldn't be doing from a computer running Windows XP). Any computer with a firewall that's been opened this wide should be configured for all sorts of security.

**My network (subnet) only.** If the computer is a part of a network, this is the default setting, and it means that traffic is allowed only from IP addresses that match the local network segment (subnet). For example, if the network connection has an IP address of 192.168.0.03 and a subnet mask of 255.255.0.0, excepted traffic is only allowed from IP addresses in the range 192.168.0.1 to 192.168.255.254. If you're sharing an Internet connection, that range matches the range of IP addresses assigned to computers on the network.

**Custom list.** Use this option to specify allowed traffic from one or more IP addresses, separated by commas, or IP address ranges separated by commas. For example, if the computers on your network have fixed IP addresses, you can determine which computers can, or cannot, send data to this computer. Fixed IP addresses are usually found in networks with business-class (expensive) DSL services. Your network computers probably don't have fixed IP addresses; instead, the network connection is configured to obtain an IP address automatically. Don't use this option if your network computers obtain IP addresses automatically, even if you know the current IP address of a computer you want to include or exclude. That current IP address changes often, because it's leased from the DHCP service for a finite period of time (by default, 24 hours). When the lease is renewed, the IP address often changes.

### Firewall Advanced Tab

The Advanced tab (see Figure 13-8) contains the following sections:

- Network Connection Settings
- Security Logging
- ICMP
- Default Settings

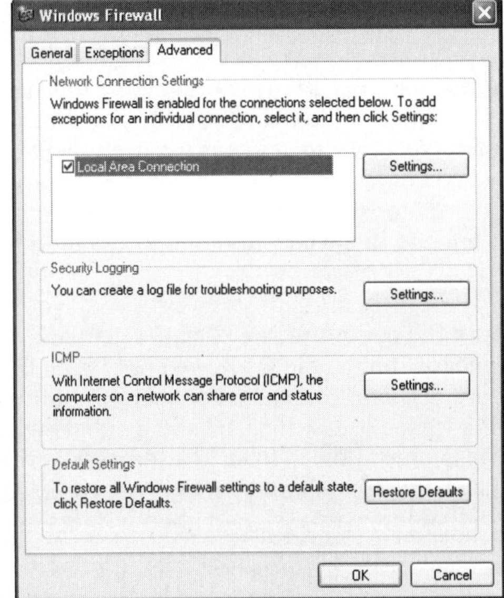


**Figure 13-8:** You can tweak the firewall's settings in the Advanced tab.

Except for Default Settings, each section has a button labeled Settings, which opens additional configuration dialog boxes. The Default Settings section has a button labeled Restore Defaults, which is your life saver if you've messed around with the firewall's configuration, and ended up with network communication problems.

The Network Connection Settings dialog box offers advanced options for permitting traffic from the Internet. Because it's unlikely you're running a Web server on your Windows XP computer, you shouldn't change the settings. If you have some reason to make changes, you need a great deal of knowledge about port data types.

The Security Logging feature lets you create a log of the data stream coming into this computer. You can track successful or unsuccessful connections, and save the data in a log file. It's not common to need this information, so don't enable logging unless you've been having a network communications problem and a support technician asks you to keep a log.

The ICMP (which stands for Internet Control Message Protocol) settings let you determine the circumstances under which a remote computer receives a message from this computer, after the remote computer attempts to communicate. These settings are usually changed to enhance troubleshooting efforts, and shouldn't be accessed unless you're working with a support technician.

# Troubleshooting Windows XP SP2 Firewall

You may find that you can't configure the Windows XP SP2 firewall to match your needs, or the firewall may interrupt network communications. In this section, I'll give you some troubleshooting tips for the problems commonly encountered in home networks.

## Configuration Options Aren't Available

If the options on the General, Exceptions, and Advanced tabs aren't available (they're grayed out), it means you are not logged on to the computer with a user account that has administrative permissions. A user with administrative permissions must log on to the computer to change the firewall options, or to change your user account to an administrative account. (See Chapter 9 for more information about setting up user accounts.)

## Firewall Service May Not Be Running

If you're having trouble communicating with the other computers on the network, or the other computers are having a problem accessing this computer, check the configuration options of the firewall. If file and printer sharing is enabled, and you can't find any reason for the firewall's apparent blocking of communications, make sure the firewall service is running properly on the computer. Use the following steps to check the service:

1. **Choose Start⇨Control Panel⇨Performance and Maintenance⇨ Administrative Tools. Then, double-click Services.**

   The Services console appears (see Figure 13-9).

2. **In the right pane, scroll through the list to find the listing for the Windows Firewall (WF)/Internet Connection Sharing (ICS) service.**

3. **Double-click the listing to open its Properties dialog box (see Figure 13-10).**

   The Startup type must be set to Automatic. If it's not, select Automatic from the Startup drop-down list.

   The Service status must be "Started". If it's not, click Start. After a few seconds, if the service doesn't start, you have a more serious problem. Write down the text of any error messages that appear, and call an expert to help you figure out what's wrong with your Windows setup.

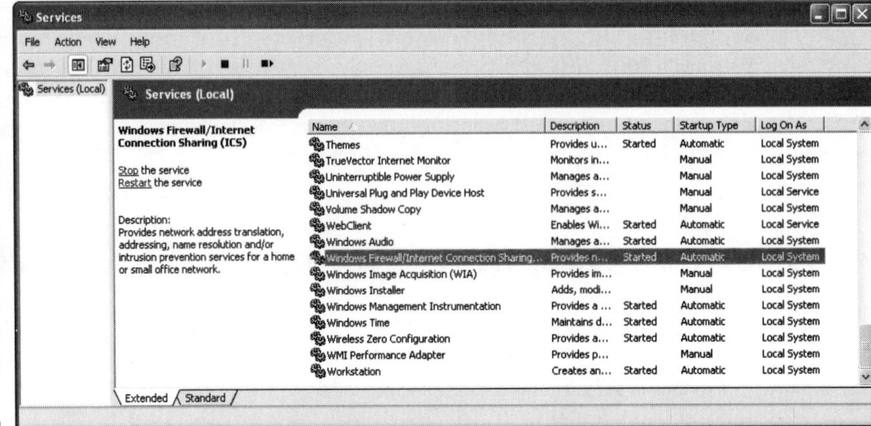


**Figure 13-9:** The Windows XP firewall is actually an operating system service, and it can be checked in the Services console.

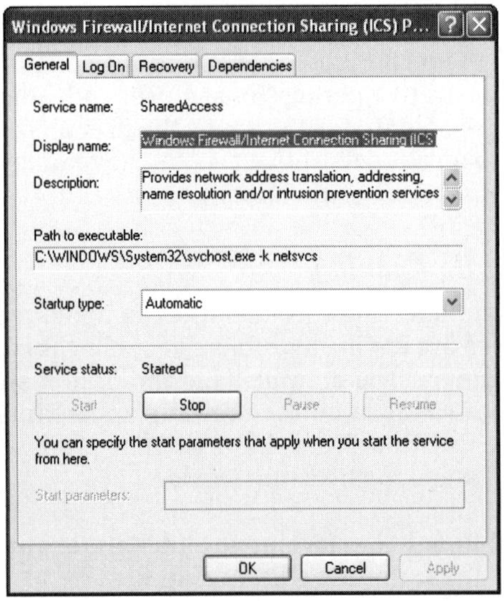

Windows Firewall/Internet Connection Sharing (ICS) P...

General | Log On | Recovery | Dependencies

Service name: SharedAccess

Display name: Windows Firewall/Internet Connection Sharing (ICS

Description: Provides network address translation, addressing, name resolution and/or intrusion prevention services

Path to executable:
C:\WINDOWS\System32\svchost.exe -k netsvcs

Startup type: Automatic

Service status: Started

Start | Stop | Pause | Resume

You can specify the start parameters that apply when you start the service from here.

Start parameters:

OK | Cancel | Apply

**Figure 13-10:** Make sure the firewall service is running, and is configured properly.

## Avoid Firewall Clashes

If you're running a software firewall, or you have a firewall-enabled router (covered next), turn the Windows XP firewall off. Running multiple firewalls doesn't double your protection; instead, the firewalls usually conflict with each other, which could make your computer vulnerable.

## Hardware firewalls in routers

If you're sharing an Internet connection, and you're using a cable or DSL modem, the easiest, most efficient, and most powerful way to share the connection is to install a router. In fact, in Chapter 7, I go over everything you need to know to share an Internet connection with a router.

You can buy routers that have built-in firewalls. The firewall-enabled router sits between your modem and the rest of your network, separating the Internet and your network into two independent unconnected networks (or, into two armed camps, which is the way I see it when I'm setting up a firewall). The only device that's seen from the Internet is the router, which has a firewall. All the computers on the network are invisible to the Internet.

Several router manufacturers offer routers with firewall protection, and the equipment is available with a wide variety of options. Here are some of the manufacturers who offer hardware firewall devices:

- Linksys (www.linksys.com)
- D-Link (www.dlink.com)
- Belkin (www.belkin.com)
- NetGear (www.netgear.com)

If you've installed a software firewall, or you're using the Windows XP SP2 firewall, disable the router's firewall. This is one case where "the more the merrier" doesn't work.

## Troubleshooting router firewalls

Believe it or not, if your router firewall isn't configured correctly, the symptoms usually appear when you try to access other computers on the network — not when you try to get to the Internet. The firewall in the router is usually automatically set up to let every computer on the network access the Internet, because a hardware firewall only looks at incoming data streams, not outgoing communications (which is why I prefer software firewalls, which do both). If your firewall is blocking incoming ports, your router blocks those ports for all computers on the network. To communicate within your network, you need to make sure the firewall knows it's okay to let data from within the network travel through those ports.

Each manufacturer has a unique configuration tool, along with documentation and instructions for configuring your network. To enter the configuration tool, you must open your browser and enter the router's IP address in the address bar. Here are the IP addresses of the popular routers:

- Belkin 192.168.2.1
- D-Link 192.168.0.1
- Linksys 192.168.1.1
- Netgear 192.168.0.1

All router configuration tools are configured to make you enter a user name, or a password, or both. If you haven't changed the default user name and password, use the entries provided in Table 13-1. Then, secure the router's configuration tool by creating your own login name and password.

**Table 13-1 Login Names and Passwords for Popular Routers**

| *Manufacturer* | *Login Name* | *Password* |
|---|---|---|
| Belkin | (Field does not exist) | (Do not fill in) |
| D-Link | admin (lower case) | (Do not fill in) |
| Linksys | (Do not fill in) | admin (lower case) |
| Netgear | admin (lower case) | password (lower case) |

Read the instructions from the router's manufacturer, and from your ISP, to configure the router. You can set basic LAN configuration options, or, if necessary, more exotic (and complicated) options (see Figure 13-11).

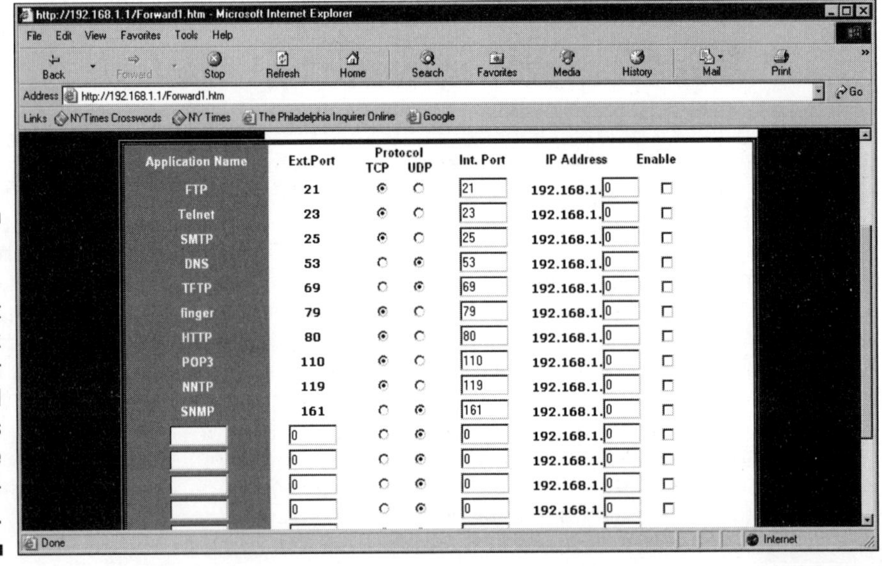


**Figure 13-11:** You can troubleshoot and tweak router firewall settings in the configuration tool.

Don't mess with advanced settings unless you do so under the guidance of a trained professional.

# Spyware

Spyware is a software program that installs itself (without your knowledge) on your computer. Once installed, the software collects information about you, and when you're online it sends the information to the spyware program's owner. Most spyware fits into either of two categories:

- Surveillance spyware
- Advertising spyware

Surveillance spyware scans documents on your computer, and can capture your keystrokes as you type. This could be forms you're filling out on a Web site (such as your login password or your credit card number), and the text you enter in a chat window. Government and detective agencies have been known to use this type of software, as have jealous spouses.

Advertising spyware is software that is installed when you're installing other software (usually software you download from the Internet), or is installed in the background while you're visiting a Web site. It's common for advertising spyware to be included (without telling you), when you install software that's advertised as "free, if you don't mind seeing advertisements when you use it". One of the most pervasive distributors of spyware is software you download to take advantage of "peer to peer" file exchanges (for music and video). Advertising spyware logs information about your computer, and also about you. The information includes passwords, your Web browsing habits, your online buying habits, and so on.

Both types of spyware can also install viruses and worms on your computer. Many of them change your browser settings (such as your home page), and your efforts to correct the changes are temporary — the spyware changes them again.

One of the annoying features of spyware is its connection to popup ads. Using the information it has collected about you, the spyware initiates popup ads whenever you connect to a Web site. The spyware software producer receives income whenever you respond to one of these popup ads, so the theory is "the more the better". After a while, using the Internet becomes almost impossible because of the barrage of popups. Regardless of your Internet Explorer controls for your children, the popups often contain pornography.

The only way to remove spyware from your computer is to use software designed for that purpose. The following two programs are well regarded by computer professionals (and I use both of them because I tend to operate in "overkill mode" when it comes to security and privacy):

- Ad-aware from Lavasoft (`http://www.lavasoft.de/ms/index.htm`)
- Spybot S&D (for Search & Destroy) (`http://www.safer-networking.org/en/download/`)

# Windows XP SP2 Security Center

Service Pack 2 for Windows XP introduced a new section in Control Panel — the Security Center. When you click the Security Center link, you see the Windows Security Center, which is chock-full of utilities and information (see Figure 13-12).

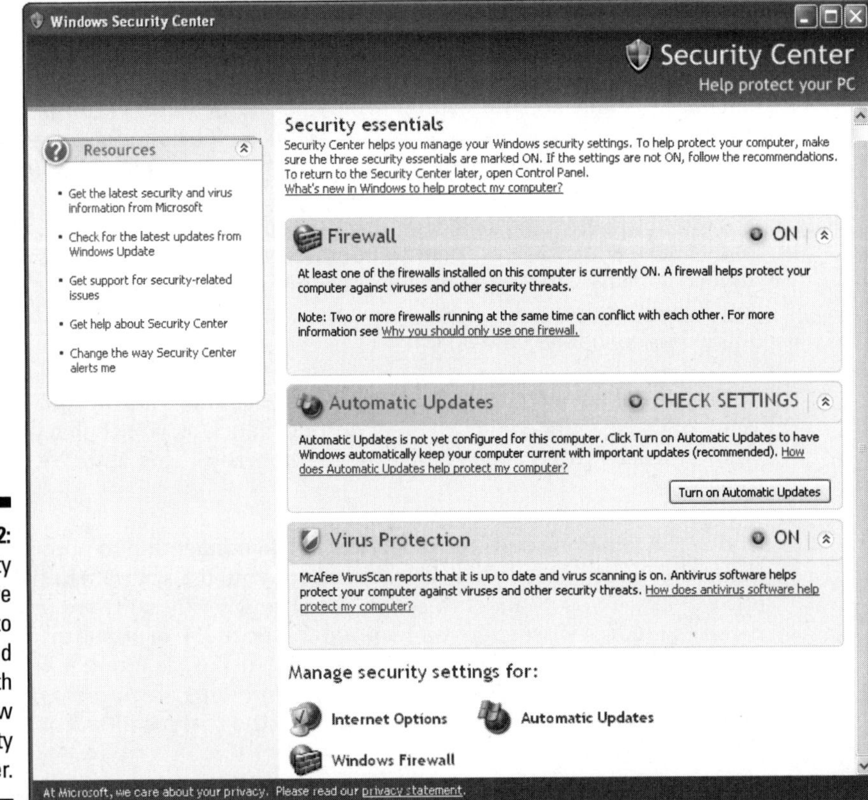


**Figure 13-12:** Security issues are easier to track and apply with the new Security Center.

The Security Center is your one-stop headquarters for keeping your computer safe, and if you update all your computers to Windows XP with SP2, your entire network is easier to secure.

When you open the Security Center, it checks the status of your computer for the three following essential security components: Firewall, automatic updates of the operating system, and virus protection.

## Checking for a firewall

The Security Center checks your computer to make sure a firewall is running. It doesn't have to be the Windows XP firewall, the Security Center is happy if it finds a software firewall running instead of the built-in firewall. However, the Security Center cannot detect a hardware firewall, such as a firewall that operates within a router.

If no firewall appears to be operating, the Security Center can issue an alert (see "Security Center alerts," later in this section).

## Checking for automatic updates

The Security Center checks to see whether you've enabled and configured automatic updates for Windows. Microsoft issues operating system updates whenever a problem needs fixing, and most of the time, these updates fix security holes.

To enable (or disable) automatic updates, click Automatic Updates in the Manage Security Settings section at the bottom of the Security Center window. In the Automatic Updates dialog box (see Figure 13-13), choose the option you prefer for updating Windows XP. The safest course is to check for updates on a daily basis. Pick a time when the update procedure won't interfere with your work. If you choose the middle of the night, don't shut down your computer before you go to bed.

If you don't want to put your computer on auto-pilot for downloading and installing updates, you can choose one of the other options for updating the operating system. For example, if you select the option to download updates, but install them manually, you can perform a custom installation that lets you see what the update affects, and decide whether you want it (see Figure 13-14).

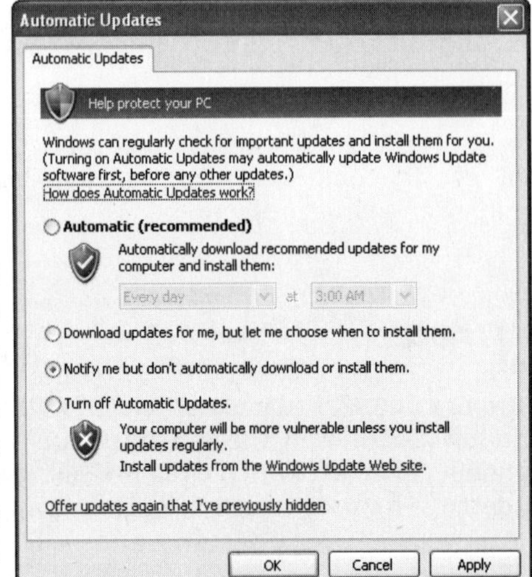


**Figure 13-13:** Choose the way you want to handle updates for Windows XP.

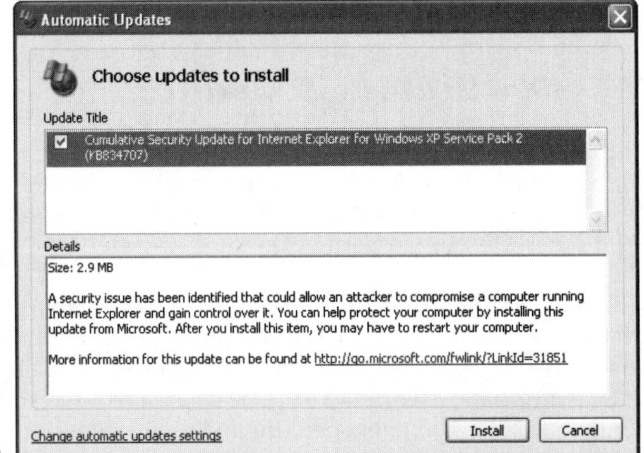


**Figure 13-14:** You can control the installation of updates.

If you select the option to turn off automatic updates, you must periodically check the Microsoft Windows XP Update Web site for updates that keep your computer running properly and safely. You can perform this task right from the Automatic Updates dialog box, by clicking the Windows Update Web site link.

If you have an always-on Internet connection, there's no reason to turn off automatic updates. Choose automatic installation, or automatic download with manual installation.

## Checking virus protection software

The Security Center checks your computer to make sure you're running antivirus software, and also makes sure virus identification files are up to date. Some antivirus software isn't detected by the Security Center, and some antivirus software is detected, but offers no way for the Security Center to ascertain its status (whether it's up to date).

If the Security Center cannot confirm the fact that you're running antivirus software, or can't ascertain whether it's up to date, the Virus Protection section of the window says Off or Unknown. In addition, a Recommendations button appears. Click the button and select the option labeled I have antivirus software that I'll monitor myself. Then click OK to stop the Security Center from issuing alerts about the lack of virus protection.

## Security Center alerts

When your computer is vulnerable, the Security Center issues an alert in the form of an icon on the right side of your taskbar. Hover your mouse over the icon to see the alert message. For example, a Windows Update alert has an icon that looks like a shield, and a message that tells you that updates are available on the Microsoft Web site, or updates have been downloaded and need to be installed (depending on your settings for updates).

To configure the alerts, in the Resources section on the left side of the Security Center window, select the link labeled Change the way Security Center alerts me. In the Alert Settings dialog box (see Figure 13-15), select the alerts you want to see.

**Figure 13-15:** Make sure you get an alert when your computer is vulnerable.

## Security Centers don't play well with others

The job of the Security Center is to observe, analyze, and generally babysit your security features. As the chief honcho for safety, the Security Center is the quarterback of your offensive team. Like any football team, you can only send one quarterback on the field, or the whistle blows and you get a penalty for an illegal formation.

Some antivirus software applications (such as McAfee antivirus software) also run Security Centers. To avoid the penalty (which is a vulnerable system), you need to choose your quarterback. When you open the Windows XP SP2 Security Center for the first time, and select options, it automatically names itself your quarterback. At some point (usually the next time you start the computer), your antivirus Security Center may ask you to decide who's calling the plays for this team.

You can make either Security Center the default quarterback. If your antivirus software also provides firewall services, it probably doesn't matter which Security Center you select. If your antivirus software program doesn't include a firewall, it may not check (or even acknowledge) your firewall, so use the Windows XP SP2 Security Center.

# Chapter 14

# Disaster Planning and Recovery

### *In This Chapter*

- Avoiding electrical catastrophes
- Doing preventive maintenance on your hardware
- Devising a backup plan
- Restoring after a disaster

Sometimes, things go wrong with the computer itself — the physical parts of a computer. You can avoid many problems with a little preventive maintenance.

The important consideration, now that you're a network administrator, is that you're protecting your network in addition to protecting each individual computer.

Network computers are connected — they talk to each other, and they interact with each other. Each computer on the network has a physical relationship with the other computers on the network. The computers can pass problems around the network neighborhood in the same way that they can pass files around.

In this chapter, I tell you how to care for your hardware to avoid an epidemic of sick computers. I also tell you how to prepare for the day that your preventive measures don't work — in the end, all hard drives die.

## Avoiding Zapped Computers

You know that electricity is dangerous, so you probably avoid sticking your fingers into live light-bulb sockets and electrical outlets. Your computers may not have fingers, but they're sensitive to electricity, too, and it's up to you to protect them from a variety of electrical dangers.

## Protecting against electrical surges

An *electrical surge* is a sudden spate of very high voltage that travels from the electric lines to your house and ultimately to your computer. Computers are particularly sensitive to surges, and a real surge can fry your computer. The chips burn up, and your computer becomes a doorstop.

Most of the time, surges occur as a result of a lightning strike, but the danger of a surge also exists if there's a brief blackout followed by a return of electricity. During the return of power, the voltage can spike. (See the section "Protecting against lightning hits," later in this chapter.)

You can safeguard against spikes by plugging your computer into a *surge protector*. The surge protectors that are commonly used look like electrical power strips, usually with four or five outlets. Read the specifications before you buy a surge protector to make sure that it's rated for real surge protection. (Voltage can rise by 10 volts or hundreds of volts, so make sure the surge protector you buy can handle these extreme surges.)

Surge protectors work by committing suicide to protect your computer. They absorb the surge so it doesn't travel to your equipment. (Some surge protectors have reset buttons that bring the strip back to life.)

If a power surge hits any piece of equipment that is attached to your computer by cable, the surge can travel to your computer. Therefore, plugging the computer into the surge protector isn't quite enough; you also have to use the surge protector to power the accessories that are connected to your computer.

Because any surge received by a single computer can travel over the network cable to the other computers on your network, make sure that all the following equipment for each of your computers is plugged into surge protectors:

- Monitors
- External modems
- External removable drives
- Speakers

Notice that I didn't list a printer. Never plug a printer into the same surge protector that your computer is already plugged into. (In fact, if you have a laser printer, you should *never* plug it into the same circuit as your computer.) See the section "Protecting Printers," later in this chapter, for more information.

## Protecting against telephone line surges

I've seen several large networks destroyed during a lightning storm, and in each case, the surge came through the telephone lines, not the electrical lines. This is what happens: Lightning hits the telephone line; the surge comes through the telephone jack in the wall; it travels along the telephone cable from the wall to the modem; it travels from the modem to the computer's motherboard; it travels from the motherboard to the rest of the computer parts, including the network interface card (NIC); the NIC sends the surge out to the network cable; the cable sends the surge back to every NIC on the network; and each NIC sends the surge to its computer's motherboard. Every computer on the network is fried.

In most communities, the power company installs lightning arresters, which help diffuse the effects of a direct lightning hit on the electric lines. However, I know of no telephone company that protects its phone lines against lightning. When a lightning storm is close, unplug your modem telephone cable at the wall jack and then unplug the computers.

If your telephone company has fiber optic lines (rather unlikely), you don't have to worry as much about lightning hits because those lines don't conduct electricity. Ask your telephone company what types of lines are connected to your home.

## Protecting against lightning hits

If lightning hits your power lines or your house, your surge protector may not be able to protect your equipment against the resulting surge. Thousands or tens of thousands of volts — sometimes more — result from a lightning strike. A surge protector can provide only so much protection, and a direct lightning hit exceeds that limit.

The only protection against lightning strikes is to unplug your computers and all your computer equipment. Stop working. Then walk around the house and unplug other equipment with chips that could fry during a lightning storm (like your microwave oven, VCR, and so on).

## Protecting against power loss

When you're running Windows, you *can't* just turn off your computer when you don't want to use it anymore. You must initiate a shutdown procedure using the Shut Down command on the Start menu. Otherwise, you may have a problem restarting your computer, or you may run into mysterious problems when you try to use software and Windows features after a power failure.

The electric company doesn't know and doesn't care about the need for an orderly shutdown, and if the folks there did know or care, they couldn't do much to warn you about a power failure, giving you time to use the Shut Down command.

You can keep your computers running long enough to complete an orderly shutdown of all your software and the operating system if you have an *uninterruptible power supply* (UPS). A UPS is a mega-battery that you plug into the wall, and you then use the UPS outlets to connect your computer and monitor. If your power fails, your computer draws power from the battery, giving you enough time to shut down everything.

UPS units come in a variety of power configurations (measured in watts). Some have line conditioning (see the next section "Understanding and fixing low-voltage problems") in addition to the battery feature. Some have software that performs the orderly shutdown for you. (The UPS unit connects to your computer through a serial port to communicate.) This is a nice feature if your power dies while you're away from the computer. The cost ranges from about $75 to several hundred dollars, depending on the wattage and the features you want. The best-known (and, in my opinion, most reliable) UPS units are made by APC. They're available anywhere computer peripherals are sold.

## Understanding and fixing low-voltage problems

Sometimes, when everyone in town is using electrical gadgets at the same time, an area's all-around voltage drops. This is called a *brownout.* Computers — especially their hard drives and motherboards — are extremely sensitive to brownouts.

Well before you see the lights flicker, your hard drive can react to a brownout. Most of the time, that reaction destroys the part of the drive that's being accessed, and the result is that your drive develops bad spots — parts of the drive that can't be written to or read from. You can mark the bad spots to prevent the operating system from using those spots to hold data, but if the spots that go bad already have data on them, that data goes bad, too. (See Chapter 15 for a discussion of the Windows tools that can help you find and mark bad spots on your hard drive.)

You can prevent most of the problems associated with bad spots caused by brownouts, and you can overcome those problems that you can't prevent by purchasing a *voltage regulator.* This clever device constantly measures the voltage coming out of the wall and brings it up to an acceptable minimum; the device sells for about $50 to $100 (depending on how many devices you want to plug into it). Several companies make voltage regulators (try TrippLite, `www.tripplite.com`), and some UPS units have built-in voltage regulation.

If you purchase a voltage regulator in addition to a UPS unit, plug the voltage regulator into the wall. If you're also using a surge protector, the surge protector is always plugged into the wall, with any other devices plugged into the surge protector.

Here are some of the causes of low voltage, along with possible fixes:

- **Too many appliances are plugged into the same circuit as your computer.** This is something you can fix. Move stuff around, buy some very long heavy-duty extension cords to get to an outlet on another circuit, or call an electrician and get more outlets connected to empty breakers.
- **An appliance that's a voltage pig (for example, air conditioning and electric heating systems) kicks on, disrupting voltage throughout the house.** Plug your computer into a voltage regulator.
- **Your laser printer (or powerful ink jet color printer) is plugged into the same circuit as your computer.** See the section "Protecting Printers," later in this chapter. You shouldn't plug these printers into the same circuit as your computer. If you have no choice, plug the computer into a voltage regulator. Do not plug the printer into the voltage regulator.
- **The electric company is sending low voltage into your home.** Sometimes, the electric company just can't keep up with demand, and it delivers lower-than-normal voltage to your home. When the voltage really drops, the electric company calls it a brownout. This frequently occurs during very hot weather, when air conditioners in your area are running constantly and working hard. The problem also occurs around 9:00 in the morning, on weekdays, as businesses all over town are turning on copy machines and laser printers, and elevators are constantly going up and down.

  The solution? Plug your computer into a voltage regulator.

## Preventing static electricity damage

Static electricity is responsible for more damaged computers than most people realize. One day, when some hardware component mysteriously dies, you may not realize that you zapped it yourself.

Static electricity charges that zap your computer come from you. You pick up static electricity, carry it with you, and pass it along when you touch any part of the computer. Usually, the keyboard receives your first touch, and even though it's connected to your computer, it doesn't always pass the electricity along to the computer.

However, if you touch the monitor or the computer box, you can pass a serious or fatal amount of electricity to the motherboard (fatal to the computer, not to you) or to any component in your computer (including chips).

You must discharge the electricity from your body before you touch the computer. Touch anything metal (except an electric appliance such as a computer or a lamp). A filing cabinet is good if one is handy. If nothing metal is within reach, attach a metal bar to the desk or table that your computer sits on.

Computers and carpeting create the ideal atmosphere for zapping. New carpeting is really dangerous, followed by carpeting with a thick pile. If you can't pull up the carpeting, go to an office supply store and buy one of those big plastic mats that goes under the desk and your chair. If you don't, each time you move your feet, you'll collect static electricity and eventually pass it to the computer.

# Caring for Network Hardware

If you receive an error message while trying to move files between computers or when you open the Network Neighborhood window, it's time to check your network hardware.

The network hardware, connectors, cable, and NICs may require some maintenance. In the following sections, I list the hardware components in the order in which they usually cause problems. Connector problems are the most common, then cable problems, and finally defective NICs.

## Checking connectors

Cable connectors are the weakest link in the network hardware chain. Because of this, you should check the connectors first when your computers can't communicate.

If you wired your network with Cat-5 (twisted-pair) cable, you should check the following:

- See if the connectors are properly inserted in the NICs.
- Make sure that the connectors are properly inserted in the concentrator (hub, switch, or router).
- Be sure that the concentrator is plugged in. (A concentrator usually doesn't have an on/off switch — if it's plugged in, it should be working.)

Here's what to check if you're using your household telephone line for your network:

- Make sure that the connectors are firmly seated in both the NICs and the wall jack.
- If you're using a splitter (also called a *modular duplex jack*) to plug in both a telephone and the network cable, make sure that the splitter is firmly positioned in the jack.

  Splitters weigh more than the fraction of an ounce that the connector on the end of a phone cord weighs, and sometimes this extra weight pulls the splitter out of the jack just a bit. Frequently, you don't notice this problem when you look at the connection, but if you push on the connector, you do notice that it isn't all the way in the phone jack. The splitter may have come out of the jack for the following reasons:

  - The cable between the splitter and whatever the other end of the cable plugs into (either the telephone jack or the NIC) is taut.
  - The telephone has moved, because it's either placed somewhere else or because a person who is using the telephone walks around while chatting.

Check the following things if you're using your household electric lines for your network:

- Check the connector at the computer end to make sure that it's firmly inserted in the port.
- Check the connector in the wall plug to make sure that it's firmly inserted.
- Make sure that the connector at the line end is plugged into the wall and not into a surge protector (unless you purchased a special surge protector designed for this purpose).

Here's what to check if you're running a wireless network:

- Make sure that all the antennas are unblocked — check to make sure that a computer hasn't been pushed under a metal desk, or close to metal such as a file cabinet.
- If you recently moved a computer, move it back — you may have exceeded the antenna's power.
- Be sure that you haven't introduced interference into your system. Did you put a cordless radio frequency (RF) device near a computer (such as a cordless phone)?

## Checking cables

Make sure that the cables aren't pinched or bent to the point that they can't handle data. Have you ever sharply bent a water hose? The water stops flowing. The same thing can happen to cable.

If you have excess cable, don't twist it into a knot to avoid having it spill on the floor. Gently roll the cable into a circle and use a twist tie to keep it together. (Don't tie it tightly.)

I pounded thin nails into the backs of the tables that hold my computers, and I hang coils of excess cable on those nails to keep the cable off the floor.

## Checking NICs

It's unusual for a NIC to give up, roll over, and die (unless you had a power surge or did something dumb like stick a bobby pin in the connector).

However, sometimes NICs — like all hardware — just stop working. If your NIC has a light on the back panel near the connector, it should glow green. If no light is glowing and you've checked the connectors and the cable, the only way to check the NIC is to replace it. If the new NIC works, the old NIC was bad. If the new NIC doesn't work, recheck your connectors and cable. Take the new NIC back to the store and get a credit (or, now that you have a spare NIC, get another computer and enlarge your network).

If your NIC has two little light bulbs and the red one is glowing, your NIC is working but isn't receiving or sending data. You can be fairly sure that you have a connector or cable problem. Check the documentation that came with your NICs to see the color schemes for the lights — your bulbs may be different colors.

# Monitoring Monitors

Monitors require some special attention, and too many people maul and mishandle them. By no coincidence, those are the same people who have to buy new monitors more frequently than necessary.

A monitor's screen attracts and collects dust — I believe it actually sucks it out of the air. You can't avoid monitor dust, but you can remove it by wiping the screen with a soft, dry cloth. It's best to turn off the monitor before cleaning it. (Static electricity, which is responsible for attracting the dust, can build up to explosive levels when you rub the screen.)

If you're a person who points to the screen when you show somebody a beautiful sentence you just composed or a mind-blowing graphic you just created, you probably have fingerprints on your monitor. Fingerprints are oily and don't always disappear with a dry cloth. Office supply stores sell premoistened towelettes for cleaning monitors. You just pull one out and wipe the screen. (Remember to close the container's lid to keep the remaining towelettes moist. They're like the towelettes that you use on infants when you change diapers, although I assume that the moistening agent is different and isn't so gentle on a baby's bottom.)

If you want to use the bottle of window cleaner that you keep around the house, spray it on a cloth, not on the monitor; the monitor isn't sealed properly to avoid leaks. Then wipe the moistened cloth across the screen.

You can also use a cloth that's moistened with window cleaner on the keyboard and mouse (the other collection points for fingerprints and dust).

# Protecting Printers

You should regularly perform a few maintenance chores to make sure that your printed documents look terrific and that your printers perform without errors:

- Don't overfill paper trays — doing so results in printer jams.
- If you have to clean up a printer jam, unplug the printer. Never yank on the jammed paper. Pull it steadily and gently.
- Always clean a laser printer when you change toner cartridges, following the directions that came with the cartridge.
- Dust is the printer's biggest enemy. Keep printers covered when they aren't in use.
- Don't put label sheets back into the printer for a second pass. If you only used a couple of labels on the sheet, throw away the sheet. The chemicals on the sheet can damage the internal mechanisms of the printer.
- Use paper that's compatible with your printer. (Check the documentation that came with your printer.)
- When you use heavy paper stock, labels, transparencies, or envelopes in a laser printer, open the back door to let the paper go through the printer in a straight path. That way, the stock doesn't have to bend around the rollers.
- Use the features in the software that came with your color ink jet printer to check the alignment of the color cartridge. (No alignment maintenance is required for monochrome cartridges — you simply replace the cartridges when they run out of ink or dry up.)

Besides protecting your printer, you also need to protect your computer from your printer, especially if you use a laser printer or a powerful color ink jet printer. These printers use a lot of power, and if they're on the same circuit as your computer, you're probably causing minor brownouts for the computer, which can harm your hard drive and your data.

### Learning to love canned air

Office supply stores sell cans of air. It's not just air; it's air that comes out of the can with enough pressure to push dust out of places that it shouldn't be in. The cans come with little straw-like tubes that you can attach to the sprayer so that you can get inside your removable drives, between the keys of your keyboard, and in the paper pathway in your printer.

Spray every opening, pore, and vent in your computer frequently. Built-up dust can interfere with the operation of your computer. CD-ROM drives and floppy drives that stop reading files usually have nothing wrong with them except they are dusty. (Don't tilt the can when you're spraying air — if the can isn't upright, you won't get the power blast that you need, and you may release some unwanted vapors.)

I use canned air everywhere. It's the handiest cleaning tool I have in my house. I spray all the openings on my CD player, television set, radio, and cable box. It works great on the ridges that hold my storm windows and screens, too.

# Establishing a Plan for Backing Up Data

If you take the time to establish a plan of attack, you can fight back when disaster strikes. For computers, the best plan of attack is a well-designed plan for backing up your data. Your plan must provide protection for important files and must be so easy to implement that you won't be tempted to skip doing it.

You should back up files on all the hard drives in your home network every day. But you won't. People don't back up regularly until they have a disaster and they realize how long it's been since they did a backup. That's an awful situation, and it provides the impetus for backing up religiously (at least for a while, until the memory fades).

## Back up often

Computers die. Sometimes only one part of a computer dies, but it's usually one of the important parts, like the hard drive. You have to approach the use of computers with the attitude that one of the machines on your network could go to la-la land, or that a hard drive could go to hard-drive heaven, tomorrow.

If you don't plan for a sudden demise of your equipment, the computer fairies figure it out — they notice that you're complacent (they call it smug), and they break something. Computer fairies must be the culprits — nothing else explains the fact that most computers bite the dust the day after the user has finished writing the greatest novel in the history of literature or an important report for the boss that's sure to mean a promotion, and no backup files exist.

Making a backup doesn't prevent the death of a computer. And there's no proof that skipping a backup invites a serious problem — it just seems to happen that way. But just in case, backing up important files every day is imperative.

You need to back up your data files religiously. If you have a tape backup system or a large removable disk, such as a Jaz drive or a CD-ROM burner, you can back up everything on each computer in the network, but it's really only important to back up essential data.

## Configure computers for efficient backups

If something bad happens to one of your network computers and you haven't backed up, you can reinstall the operating system and all your software, but you can kiss that letter to grandma and that promotion-earning PowerPoint presentation goodbye. Say "so long" to that fat inheritance check and that office with a view.

The easier it is to back up data files, the more likely it is that you'll perform the task every day. Think about it: If you keep the vacuum cleaner in the hall closet, your house will stay cleaner than it would if you kept the vacuum cleaner in the attic. Convenience is an invaluable assistant.

Store all data files in the `My Documents` folder, and make sure that all the people who use the network do the same. If you like to organize files by type, either by software application or by some other scheme (perhaps separating letters from other documents), create subfolders for each type of file. When you copy the `My Documents` folder, you copy all of its subfolders.

Some software applications (for example, Quicken) have a backup routine that's built into the software. If the software backs up your data files to a floppy disk, that's best. If, however, the software backs up your data files to a separate backup directory on your hard drive, redirect that backup to a subfolder under your `My Documents` folder. Otherwise, you have to take the time to back up that separate folder in addition to your `My Documents` folder.

## Safeguard software CDs and disks

If a hard drive on the network dies, you have to install Windows on the replacement drive. Then, if you have a total backup of your entire drive, including the registry, you can restore that backup and put everything back the way it was before the demise of your equipment. You usually have to do a bit of tweaking, but essentially, the move to the new drive goes pretty smoothly.

If you don't have a total backup of your drive, all isn't lost. As long as you backed up the data files, you can reinstall the operating system, reinstall your software, and then restore the data files that you backed up.

This plan works only if your original software CD or disks are available. Storing the original disks for Windows and the software that you purchased in a safe place is important. I recommend that you use one of those fireproof boxes that you can buy in office-supply stores.

If you have software that you downloaded from the Internet, copy it to a subfolder in the `My Documents` folder so that it's backed up when you back up your documents. If you have a large removable disk drive on your system, dedicate one cartridge to downloaded software programs (most downloaded programs don't fit on a floppy disk).

## Safeguard backup media

Whatever backup media you choose — whether it is floppy disks, Zip cartridges, backup tapes, or CDs — make sure that you have more than one disk, cartridge, or tape on hand. Don't back up on the same disk, cartridge, or tape that holds your last backup — if something goes wrong during the backup, not only do you not get a good backup this time, but you also destroy your previous backup.

The ideal situation is to have a disk, cartridge, or tape for each day of the week. If that seems too difficult or too expensive (in the case of cartridges and tapes), create one set of disks, cartridges, or tapes marked *Odd* (for odd days) and another set marked *Even* (for even days).

If a fire, flood, or other catastrophe strikes, then after you clean up the mess, you can replace the computers. You can replace and reinstall software, but you have no way to restore all those important documents, accounting information, and other data that you created on your computer unless you have a backup that's stored out of harm's way.

That's why, once a week, you should take your backup media out of the house and leave it with a neighbor, at work, or at your vacation home. Don't forget to bring the backups back the following week so that you can put a current backup on the media and take it away again. You'll probably be able to find a neighbor with a computer and backup media who wants to do the same thing, so the two of you can trade disks or tapes.

# Using Microsoft Backup

Microsoft provides backup software with Windows, and because it's free, many people use it. In this section, I walk you through using Microsoft Backup to ensure a safe computing environment.

## Installing Microsoft Backup

If you're using Windows 2000 or Windows XP Professional Edition, the backup software is installed automatically. Microsoft Backup is not installed during a typical installation of Windows 98, Windows Me, and Windows XP Home Edition.

### Installing Windows XP Home Edition backup software

Here's how to install Microsoft Backup in Windows XP Home Edition:

1. **Insert the Windows XP Home Edition CD-ROM in the CD-ROM drive.**

   Press and hold the Shift to prevent the installation program from starting automatically.

2. **In My Computer or Microsoft Explorer, right-click the icon for the CD-ROM drive, and choose Explore.**
3. **Navigate to the subfolder \Valueadd\Msft\Ntbackup.**
4. **Double-click the file named Ntbackup.msi.**

   The backup installation wizard opens.

5. **Follow the wizard's prompts to install the backup software.**

When installation is complete, the backup tool is on your menu system. When you want to run the program, simply choose Start➪All Programs➪Accessories➪System Tools➪Backup.

### Installing Windows 98 backup software

Here's how to install Microsoft Backup in Windows 98:

1. **With your Windows CD in the CD-ROM drive, choose Start⇨Settings⇨Control Panel.**

   The Control Panel window opens.

2. **Double-click the Add/Remove Programs icon.**

   The Add/Remove Programs Properties dialog box appears.

3. **Click the Windows Setup tab.**
4. **Click the System Tools listing (not the check box), and then click the Details button.**
5. **Select Backup from the list of components, and then click OK.**

   The necessary files are transferred to your hard drive. A message appears to tell you that you must restart your computer to finish the installation process.

6. **Click Yes to restart the computer and finish the installation.**

After the restart, the backup tool is on your menu system. When you want to run the program, simply choose Start⇨Programs⇨Accessories⇨System Tools⇨Backup.

### Installing Windows Me backup software

To install the backup program for Windows Me, use the following steps:

1. **With your Windows CD in the CD-ROM drive, double-click the My Computer icon on your desktop.**
2. **Right-click the icon for your CD-ROM drive, and choose Explore from the shortcut menu that appears.**

   An Explorer-like window opens to display the contents of the CD.

3. **Click the plus sign next to the Add-ons folder to expand it.**

   The subfolders appear in the left pane.

4. **Select the `MSBackup` subfolder.**

   The files in the subfolder are displayed in the right pane.

5. **Double-click the `msbexp.exe` file.**

   Installation of the backup program begins. The necessary files are transferred to your hard drive, and the system displays a message announcing that it's finished.

6. **Click OK.**

   A message appears to tell you that you must restart your computer to finish the installation process.

7. **Click Yes to restart the computer.**

After the restart, the backup tool is on your menu system. When you want to run the program, simply choose Start➪Programs➪Accessories➪System Tools➪Backup.

If you upgraded to Windows Me from Windows 98 or Windows 95, and you had installed the backup program in that previous operating system, you don't have to install the Windows Me backup software (the programs are almost identical, and either backup software works fine in Windows Me). Instead, use the backup software that you installed while you were running Windows 98 or Windows 95. Here's how to activate that software:

1. **Choose Start➪Programs➪Accessories➪Windows Explorer.**

2. **Click the plus sign next to My Computer, and then click the plus sign next to drive C.**

   The folders on drive C are displayed in the left pane.

3. **Click the plus sign next to Program Files to expand it.**

   The subfolders in the `Program Files` folder are displayed in the left pane.

4. **If you upgraded from Windows 98, click the plus sign next to Accessories to expand it, and then select the `Backup` subfolder. If you upgraded from Windows 95, select the `Accessories` folder.**

   You can see the backup software file in the right pane: `msbackup.exe` (for Windows 98 upgraders) or `backup.exe` (for Windows 95 upgraders).

5. **Right-click the file, and choose Send To➪Desktop (Create Shortcut) from the menu that appears.**

   The shortcut to the backup software appears on the desktop.

For easier access to the program, drag the desktop shortcut to either or both of the following locations:

- **The Start button:** The program is added to the top of your Start menu.
- **The Quick Launch bar:** You have one-click access to the backup software.

## Full backup is the only way to go

One of the configuration options for Windows Backup is to back up only those files that changed since the last backup; this is called an *incremental backup.* The theory behind an incremental backup is that any files that haven't changed are already in a previous backup file, so there's no need to back them up again.

This is a rather inefficient theory. When your drive dies and you need to put your data back on the new drive, you must go back to your first backup file and restore each backup file in chronological order. This could take hours or days. It also means that you have to save every backup file you ever make.

The purpose of backing up is *not* to make backing up quick and easy — the purpose is to make restoring your data quick and easy so that you can get right back to work after a drive crash or after you purchase a new computer. Incremental backups are not easy to restore.

# Configuring Microsoft Backup

When you use Microsoft Backup for the first time, you need to create a backup job (a set of instructions to tell Microsoft Backup which files to back up and when they should be backed up). You have the following configuration options in a backup job:

- The folders and files that you want to back up
- Whether you want to back up all the files you've selected or only those that have changed since the last backup
- The target media — the location to which you want to save your backup files

After you configure the backup options, you can give the backup job a name. For example, if you select a full backup, you could name it *full,* whereas you could name a backup of your `My Documents` folder *docs.* Thereafter, when you start the backup software, you can select an existing job or create another job with a different configuration.

Backups are not like copies. You can't retrieve the individual files from the target media, because the entire backup is one big file. The backup software makes a catalog that it displays if you need to restore any files. You must select the individual files from the catalog — you won't see the filenames on the media.

You can, if you want, back up individual files, which is much more convenient if you only have to restore a single file.

For full explanations of backing up and restoring your computer, read *Windows 98 For Dummies, Windows 2000 Professional For Dummies, Microsoft Windows Me For Dummies,* or *Windows XP For Dummies,* all published by Wiley Publishing.

# Backing Up Data on Floppy Disks

You can back up your data files to floppy disks. You have the following methods to choose from to get your files to the disks:

- **Using Microsoft Backup:** You can configure the backup software that's available with Windows 98 and Windows Me to back up to floppy disks. Just select your floppy drive as the backup target when you're configuring your backup.
- **Using Send To:** You can copy files to a floppy disk to create a backup. Select all the files that you want to back up and right-click any file. Choose Send To from the shortcut menu that appears, and then choose the floppy drive.

  When the disk is filled to capacity, an error message appears to tell you that the disk has no more room on it. Put another formatted, blank floppy disk in the drive, and then click Retry. Keep doing this until all your document files have been copied to floppy disks.

Send To doesn't really *send* the file; it copies it. The original file stays where it was.

# Backing Up Data to Removable Drive Cartridges

Removable drives are terrific backup targets. You can use them with Microsoft Backup or with the Send To command (or by clicking your way through the files and folders in Windows Explorer if you like to do things the long way).

You can use a removable drive for backing up, and it doesn't have to be attached to your computer. Remote drives (drives that are attached to another computer on your network) also work just fine.

### One disk drive, so many users

When you share a removable drive so that everyone on the network can use it for backups, you're sharing the drive, not a disk that goes into the drive. You must have a separate disk for each user who backs up to the drive; otherwise, each user's backup process may overwrite the last user's backup.

Put a paper label on each disk to identify the user. You should also have at least two disks for each user. Label one *odd days* and label the other one *even days*. That way, if something goes wrong with the backup, you have not destroyed the previous, good backup. The ideal is to have seven disks for each user, one for each day, but that's expensive.

## Using Microsoft Backup with removable drives

Microsoft Backup works beautifully with removable cartridges. If you're using a Jaz drive or another large-capacity drive, you can probably back up everything on your computer. If you're using a Zip drive, you probably have to be more selective about the files you're backing up because you have less space. Make sure that you back up all your data files, and if any room is left after that, you can back up some of your software folders. This is especially useful for software you've configured, tweaked, and manipulated until it's just perfect.

You can do a full backup on a cartridge that's smaller than the amount of hard drive space that you're using as long as you have extra cartridges. The backup software tells you when it's time to put another cartridge in the drive.

## Using Send To with removable drives

You can use the Send To command that appears when you right-click a folder or file to copy that folder or file to a removable drive. Oops, you just looked at the Send To choices, and you don't see a removable drive as one of the options. Okay, you're right; it's not on the Send To submenu. Wouldn't it be handy if it were? Well, go ahead and put it there! It's not hard to add a removable drive to the Send To submenu. Just follow these steps:

1. **If the removable drive is on your computer, double-click the My Computer icon. If the drive is on a remote computer, double-click the Network Neighborhood (or My Network Places) icon and then double-click the icon for the computer that holds the drive.**

   The icon for the removable drive appears.

2. **Right-drag the removable drive's icon to the desktop.**

   A menu appears when you release the right mouse button.

3. **Choose Create Shortcut(s) Here from the menu.**

   The shortcut appears on the desktop.

4. **Drag the shortcut to one side of the desktop.**

   This step is important, because you need to see the shortcut after you open the `Send To` folder window.

5. **Choose Start⇨Run, and then type** sendto **in the Open text box.**

6. **Click OK.**

   The `Send To` folder appears on your screen.

7. **Drag the shortcut from the desktop to the `Send To` folder.**

   That's it! The removable drive is on your Send To command list. Cool!

Now you can select folders or groups of files and use the Send To command to copy them (back them up) to the removable drive.

## Backing up data on CDs

If your computer can burn CDs, you can back up data to CD, directly (if you're using Windows XP) or indirectly, by using backup software that writes a file to your hard drive and then copying the file to a CD.

## Backing up data on tapes

Zip drives may be all the rage right now, but the capacity of tapes is usually much larger than any removable drive cartridge. Tape systems vary widely in price, starting at several hundred dollars and increasing to thousands of dollars for business systems.

You can also use Microsoft Backup to back up to a tape drive if your tape drive is supported by Microsoft Backup. Check the documentation that came with your tape drive.

One disadvantage of using tapes is that they wear out. The edges fray, the tension disappears, and an assortment of other problems can show up. Tapes are not as durable as the cartridges for removable drives. So protect your tapes by keeping them in sealed boxes, away from moisture and direct sunlight.

If you purchase a backup tape system, software comes with it. Not all backup programs perform in the same way, so I can't tell you exactly how to configure and use your particular software. But use the following basic guidelines for getting the most out of your tape backup system:

- **Pay attention to the configuration options available in your backup software.** Remember that you're likely to need the tape to restore files if your hard drive dies. Therefore, if the software presents an option to put a copy of the catalog on the tape, select that option. (The *catalog* is the list of folders and files that you backed up.) The catalog on the hard drive dies with the drive. Although the software will re-create the catalog by reading the contents of the tape, this process takes a long time, so a preloaded catalog on the tape saves time.

- **Always configure the backup software to include the registry in your backup files**. That way, if you have to restore everything, you also restore the registry. The *registry* is a database that keeps track of the configuration options, software, hardware, and other important elements of your Windows system. In Windows XP, this backup option is named System State.
- **Verify the backup.** Select the option to verify the backup, which means that the software makes sure that the copy of the file on the tape matches the file that's on your hard drive.
- **Clean out the catalogs.** Many backup software programs keep copies of every catalog. These copies take up a lot of hard-drive space, so do some hard-drive housekeeping and get rid of the catalogs that you no longer need. When you record over a previous catalog, you can get rid of the original one.

# Backing Up to Remote Computers

One easy way to back up your data files is to use another computer on the network. If your network has two computers, each computer uses the other as the place to store backups. If your network has more than two computers, you can pick one of the other computers. In fact, you can back up your data to every remote computer in a frenzy of cautiousness.

This technique works if you operate on the theory that it is highly unlikely that all the computers on the network could die at the same time. The fact is that a fire, flood, or power surge from lightning could very well destroy every computer that's on your network. If you use remote computers for backing up, you should also back up on some sort of media, whether it is floppy disks, removable-drive cartridges, or tapes, on a weekly or monthly basis. Or, sign up for a backup service with your Internet service provider (ISP). This works by uploading your backup files to the ISP's servers.

Start by creating a folder for yourself on the remote computer. Make it a shared resource, and call it *Fred* (unless your name isn't Fred). To find out about creating shared resources, refer to Chapter 7.

After you create a backup folder, perform the following steps every day to use Windows Explorer to back up data to a remote computer:

1. **Open Windows Explorer on your own computer.**
2. **Right-click your** `My Documents` **folder, and choose Copy from the shortcut menu that appears.**
3. **Click the plus sign to expand the Network Neighborhood listing in Windows Explorer, and also expand the computer that has your backup folder.**
4. **Right-click your personal folder, and choose Paste from the shortcut menu that appears.**

If you're making another backup on another remote computer for safety's sake (who, me, cautious?), repeat the preceding steps.

# Restoring a System after a Disaster

If you've replaced a drive or computer, you can restore all your data because you were wise enough to back it up. Here are the tasks you need to perform (in the order in which you perform them):

- **Install Windows.**
- **Install the tape drive or removable media drive you used to make your backup.**
- **If you backed up to another computer on a network, install and configure the NIC so that you can get to the remote computer on the network.**

- **Install the backup software you used to create your backup.**

  For most people, this is Microsoft Backup, but you may have installed a third-party application. It doesn't matter, because the process is the same.

- **Open the backup software, and select the option to restore backed up files.**

  A restore wizard opens to walk you through the process of restoring your files.

- **Choose the files you want to restore.**

  Choose the location of your backup files, and then choose the backup file you want to restore, which is usually the last backup file you made. Microsoft Backup displays the date and time that each backup file was made, so it's easy to select the right file.

If you've accumulated a lot of backup files, more than a couple of weeks' worth, you can delete the older files.

# Using System Restore

Windows XP and Windows Me offer a component called System Restore. If you have a serious problem with your computer (actually, with the operating system), you can restore your operating system to a previous state. Your data remains intact.

System Restore monitors the operating system files and program files you install, and periodically writes a copy of the system's setup and configuration to a set of files. That set of files is called a *restore point.* If something goes amiss, you can tell Windows to go back to a previous restore point.

It's beyond the scope of this book to provide detailed information about configuring and using System Restore, but you can learn more about it in other books from Wiley Publishing, including *Windows XP For Dummies* and *Windows Me For Dummies.*

# Chapter 15

# Using Windows Maintenance Tools

### In This Chapter

- Checking the condition of your hard drives
- Managing hardware
- Automating maintenance tasks

Windows has a virtual toolbox built into the operating system. This toolbox is filled with a bunch of handy programs that you can use to perform maintenance checkups and even repair some of the problems that may crop up with the computers in your network.

## Checking Your Hard Drive for Damage with ScanDisk

ScanDisk is a program that checks the condition of your hard drive, looking for the following specific problems:

- Damaged sections of the drive
- Pieces of files that don't seem to belong anywhere (or the operating system can't figure out where they belong)

If a damaged section is identified, ScanDisk takes files off the damaged section (if possible) and moves them to a good spot on the drive. Then the program marks the damaged section as bad so that the operating system doesn't use it to store files again.

If pieces of files are found and ScanDisk can't figure out where they belong, the software puts the pieces into files that you can look at to see whether you can identify them. However, you usually can't do anything with these files except delete them. Those files are placed in the root of the hard drive (not in any folder), and they're named `FILE0000.CHK`, `FILE0001.CHK`, and so on. You could try to read them, but even if they're readable (most of the time they're not text, so you can't decipher them), you can't do anything with them. Just delete them.

## Why hard drives develop problems

I bet you're wondering how you get pieces of files floating on your drive. As I explain in the section "Defragging Your Hard Drive," later in this chapter, Windows keeps track of the location of a file on the hard drive every time that you save it. The information about file locations is kept in an index in the File Allocation Table (FAT) if you're running Windows 98 or Windows Me. If you're running Windows 2000 or Windows XP, you have a choice of file systems: FAT or NTFS. If you're running NTFS, the index is in the Master File Table (MFT). (See the sidebar "NTFS — a file system with muscle.")

Windows provides two versions of the FAT file system: FAT and FAT32. FAT32 is better than FAT because FAT32 supports technologies that FAT doesn't, primarily support for large hard drives. For information about the differences, read *Alan Simpson's Windows XP Bible* from Wiley Publishing.

If your computer unexpectedly shuts down while files are open, the operating system has no opportunity to tell the FAT where all the files or parts of files that are currently in memory came from — their locations on the hard drive. The data is on the drive, but the FAT doesn't contain any reference for it. This means you may lose parts of any open files, both data and software, because Windows doesn't know how to send them home.

Unexpected shutdowns aren't limited to sudden power failures. If you shut off your computer without going through the Shut Down dialog box, that counts as an unexpected shutdown and can do just as much damage to your file system as a power failure. In fact, after an unexpected shutdown, ScanDisk runs automatically in Windows 98 and Windows Me the next time you start your computer.

If you enabled power-management features for your monitor and your screen goes dark while ScanDisk is running, do not press the spacebar or Enter to bring the display back. Pressing either of those keys stops ScanDisk (the safe keys to press are Ctrl or Alt). If you want to watch the ScanDisk progress and your monitor goes dark after the specified amount of time of inactivity, use any key except the spacebar or Enter to bring the monitor back.

## NTFS — a file system with muscle

Instead of a File Allocation Table, which only tracks file locations and has a finite size, NTFS tracks all sorts of information about files and folders in a special file called the Master File Table (MFT). The size of the MFT is dynamic, which means that it's automatically extended when necessary. The MFT is like a robust database, able to store plenty of information about files and folders in your system.

One important piece of information the MFT stores is the permissions that individual users possess to manipulate a file or folder. This means that NTFS can control users, letting some users create or change files, allowing other users to read files but not change or add files, and even preventing users from looking at files. If you're running NTFS on your Windows 2000 or Windows XP computer, when you right-click a file or folder, you see a tab named Security. You can use that tab to specify permissions for specific users who access that file or folder.

For more information on NTFS, see *Windows XP All-in-One Desk Reference For Dummies* by Woody Leonard and *Windows 2000 Server For Dummies* by Ed Tittel, both from Wiley Publishing.

# Running ScanDisk in Windows 98/Me

In Windows 98 and Windows Me, the ScanDisk tool is on the menu system. In Windows 2000 and Windows XP, it's not (see the following section for details). Here's how to run ScanDisk in Windows 98 and Windows Me:

1. **Open My Computer.**

   The My Computer window opens, displaying the drives on your computer.

2. **Right-click the icon for the drive you want to check, and choose Properties from the shortcut menu that appears.**
3. **Click the Tools tab of the Properties dialog box.**
4. **Click the Check Now button in the Error-Checking section of the dialog box.**

   The ScanDisk dialog box opens, displaying options for checking the drive (see Figure 15-1).

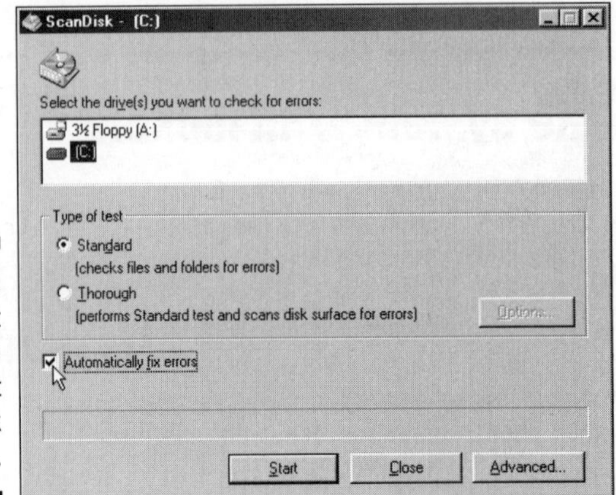


**Figure 15-1:** Select the drive you want to check up on.

5. **Choose one of the following types of tests to run:**

   - **Standard:** This test checks the files and folders that are on your hard drive.

     Most of the time, the Standard test is sufficient, because the files and folders are where most system errors are found.

   - **Thorough:** This test examines the surface of your drive, looking for physical errors (bad spots).

     This test takes much longer. It isn't necessary to select a Thorough test unless you've seen some peculiar behavior, such as messages about an error trying to read or write from the drive.

6. **Select the Automatically fix errors check box.**

   After all, there's no point in running a test if you don't fix any problems that are found. If you don't select this check box, the errors are reported to you, and then you have to run ScanDisk again to fix them. Why do twice the work?

   If want to, you can click the Advanced button to see the Surface Scan Options dialog box, shown in Figure 15-2, where you can specify the test procedures more precisely.

7. **Click Start.**

   ScanDisk runs, and if your drive is large and has a lot of folders and files, ScanDisk may run for quite some time. When the program finishes, it issues a report of the results (see Figure 15-3).

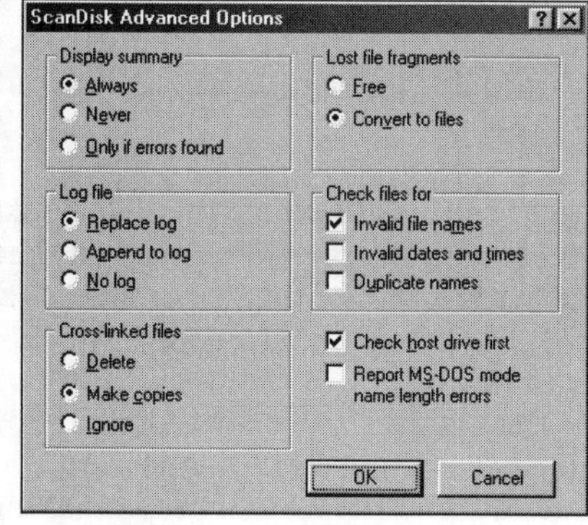


**Figure 15-2:** You can decide what you want ScanDisk to check, but the system defaults are usually the best choices.

ScanDisk Results - (C:)

ScanDisk did not find any errors on this drive.

2,107,695,104 bytes total disk space
0 bytes in bad sectors
1,765,376 bytes in 393 folders
23,490,560 bytes in 163 hidden files
595,267,584 bytes in 5,331 user files
1,487,171,584 bytes available on disk
4,096 bytes in each allocation unit
514,574 total allocation units on disk
363,079 available allocation units

Close

**Figure 15-3:** ScanDisk reports on its findings.

8. **Click Close to close the report, and then click Close again to close the ScanDisk window.**

# Running ScanDisk in Windows 2000 and Windows XP

Windows 2000 and Windows XP are more powerful and protective operating systems, and running ScanDisk isn't the one-two-three-done procedure that it is in Windows 98 and Windows Me. To fix file system errors, ScanDisk locks the drive. But because the drive is in use, it can't be locked. Catch-22!

To get around the problem, if you want to fix errors, ScanDisk offers to run the next time you start your computer. If you've been seeing errors when you attempt to open or save files, you should run ScanDisk in its fix-stuff mode the next time you reboot.

On the other hand, if you just want ScanDisk to check the disk, looking for bad sectors (and marking them as bad so that files aren't saved there in the future), you can perform that task without rebooting. Of course, the program doesn't perform the important work of fixing any problems it finds.

You should be aware that this process is much more thorough than it is in Windows 98 or Windows Me, and it takes quite a bit of time. You may want to start the process at the end of the day. The report will be waiting for you when you go back to the computer.

To run ScanDisk in Windows 2000 and Windows XP, follow these steps:

1. **Open My Computer.**

   The My Computer window opens, displaying the drives on your computer.

2. **Right-click the icon for the drive you want to check, and choose Properties from the shortcut menu that appears.**
3. **Click the Tools tab of the Properties dialog box.**
4. **Click the Check Now button in the Error-Checking section of the dialog box.**

   The Check Disk dialog box opens, displaying options for checking the drive.

5. **Select the Scan for and attempt recovery of bad sectors option or the Automatically fix file system errors option, or both (depending on what you think is necessary).**

   Selecting the option to fix errors means that you must reboot the computer to start the process.

6. **Click Start.**

   If you selected only the option to check the bad sectors, ScanDisk begins checking the disk. Now would be a good time to have lunch, clean the bathroom, or take a nap. The process takes many minutes. The larger your drive, the longer it takes. On my system, a 30GB drive that's half filled took about 40 minutes to check.

   If you selected the option to fix file system errors, ScanDisk displays an error message telling you that it cannot fix errors because the drive is in use. The program then offers to run ScanDisk the next time the system boots. Click OK. If you want, you can shut down your computer immediately to get the task moving.

# Defragging Your Hard Drive

Disk Defragmenter is a program that takes fragments of files and puts them together so that every file on your drive has its entire contents in the same place. This makes opening files a faster process.

Before I discuss the Disk Defragmenter tool, it's important to understand a piece of jargon. Nobody who is hip (well, as hip as a computer geek can be) uses the term *Disk Defragmenter.* In fact, nobody uses the terms *fragmented* or *defragmented.* Instead, when your disk is *fragged,* you "run the *defragger* to *defrag*" it. If you're not already a tech geek, at least now you can talk like one.

Files get fragmented (oops, I meant fragged) as a matter of course; the fragging (there — I've redeemed myself) isn't caused by anything you do or any problem with your computer. The more a drive fills with files, the more likely it is to become fragged.

## Why hard drives get fragged

After you've used your computer for a while, your hard drive starts to get full. One day, you launch your word processor and open a document that's on your hard drive. That document is 50,000 bytes in size. You add more text to the document, and when you save the document, it's 75,000 bytes. The particular section of the drive where the file was originally stored has room for 50,000 bytes, so the operating system puts 50,000 bytes of your new version back where it was and finds another spot on the drive to lay down the remaining 25,000 bytes.

The sequence of events that takes place goes something like this:

1. Windows makes a note about that file, and the note says something like, "I stuck the first 50K here and put the next 25K there." The note isn't a note, though; it's an entry in the *File Allocation Table,* or the *Master File Table.*
2. The operating system fetches all those fragments, in the right order, after checking the FAT or MFT to see where the pieces of the file are.
3. Because you're never satisfied, you feel compelled to add even more information to the file. When you're finally satisfied (at least for the moment), you resave the file.
4. The operating system puts the first two sections back where they were and then finds another spot for the additional bytes that are needed for your additions and changes.

5. The next time you open the file to add to it or make other changes, more sections of the disk are used to hold the pieces of the file (when will you ever be finished?), and the various file fragments must be fetched from more separate locations.

   This process continues for as long as you keep making changes (which goes on forever if you're trying to write a novel). In fact, this is the standard process that occurs with files that you create and save in all your other software programs.

So, you're saying to yourself, "Big deal. As long as my computer knows where to get all these fragments so I can obsessively re-edit and add to my documents, why do I care how the process works?" Well, after a while, your system slows as a result of all this searching and piecing file fragments together. You may notice that loading and saving documents takes a lot longer. That's because your operating system must do all this legwork to fetch and lay down the file parts.

Eventually, you need to tell the operating system to pick up all the parts and put them together, putting all the parts of every file in the same location on the drive, making the file contents *contiguous* (all the bytes together in one place). This is what the Disk Defragmenter does. Read on to find out how to use this tool.

If you're using NTFS, your drive doesn't frag as quickly as it would with FAT, because NTFS is a much more efficient file system. However, you still need to run the defragger occasionally.

## How to defrag your drive

The Disk Defragmenter juggles file parts, holding some in memory while it finds room for them and then laying the parts on the drive in a place that has room for the stuff. Although the process may seem tedious (how would you like to search out and find every piece of data that creates a whole document?), the process is pretty pain-free. Follow these steps to defrag your drive:

1. **Open My Computer.**

   The My Computer window opens, displaying the drives on your computer.

2. **Right-click the icon for the drive you want to check, and choose Properties from the shortcut menu that appears.**

3. **Click the Tools tab of the Properties dialog box.**

4. **In the Defragmentation section of the dialog box, click Defragment Now.**

   In Windows 98 and Windows Me, the program begins defragging the drive immediately. In Windows 2000 and Windows XP, the program window offers a button named Analyze, which you can click to display a report on the level of fragmentation to help you decide whether to defrag the drive (see Figure 15-4).

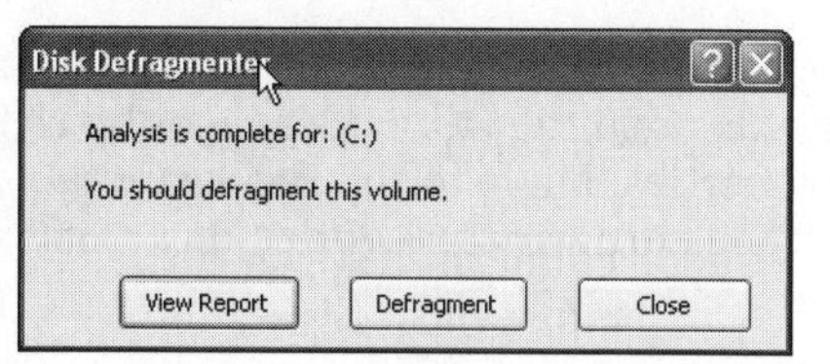


**Figure 15-4:** The defragger reports on its analysis.

   During the defragging process, the program displays a progress report so that you can see how much work remains to be done.

5. **Click the Show Details button to see a full-color representation of your hard drive and its fragmented files.**

   You can watch the pieces of files being put together as the defragging proceeds.

   Here are a few points about the defragging process:

   - Technically, you can do work on your computer during the defragging operations, but things go very slowly (because the computer and the hard drive are very busy), and the defragmenter program itself is slowed by your actions. Go grab a bowl of cereal and watch a few commercials instead of trying to work while defragging is underway.

   - If you must perform some task at the computer during this procedure, click the Pause button in the Disk Defragmenter dialog box. After you finish your work, click Resume. You can also click Stop to end the process.

   - If you pause or stop the Disk Defragmenter, the response isn't immediate. The program finishes the file that it's currently working on and updates the FAT or MFT information. Then it responds to your selection.

A message lets you know when the defragging is complete. After the defragging, you should notice a much peppier response when you load or save files. Of course, you're going to continue to open and save files, so the fragging starts all over again; eventually your system will slow, and you'll have to defrag again.

# Managing Devices with the Device Manager

The Windows Device Manager is a powerful tool. You can use it to view all sorts of information about the hardware that's in your computer. You can also use it to make changes to the way hardware is configured or the way it behaves.

In Windows 2000 and Windows XP, open the Device Manager by right-clicking My Computer and choosing Properties. Move to the Hardware tab, and click the Device Manager button. All the hardware categories that exist in your computer are displayed, as shown in Figure 15-5.

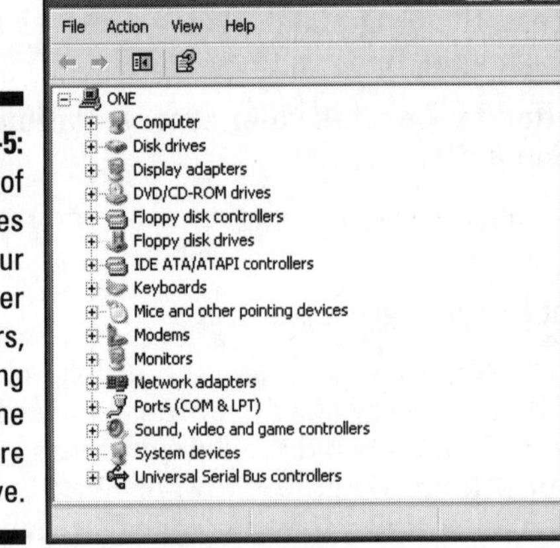


**Figure 15-5:** The list of devices for your computer differs, depending on the hardware you have.

To use the Device Manager in Windows 98 and Windows Me, right-click the My Computer icon and choose Properties from the shortcut menu that appears. When the System Properties dialog box opens, click the Device Manager tab.

The following sections describe what you can do with the information in the device listings.

## Viewing a specific device

The first list that appears when you open the Device Manger window is a list of hardware types, not the actual hardware that's installed in your computer. Click the plus sign to the left of a device type to see the hardware that's installed on your system. You usually see an exact description, sometimes including a brand name and model.

Select the specific device, and click Properties to see information about the device and the way it's configured. The information in the Properties dialog box differs according to the type of device you're examining.

You can change the configuration for some devices right in the Properties dialog box. Just select the setting that needs to be changed, and enter a new setting.

## Managing device problems

If any device is experiencing a problem, the specific device listing appears when you first open the Device Manager window, because Windows expands the device type listing to show you the problematic device. An icon appears in the listing, indicating the type of problem. The icon may be a red *X,* which means that the device has been disabled, or a yellow exclamation point, which means that Windows can't find the device or is having a problem communicating with it (see Figure 15-6).

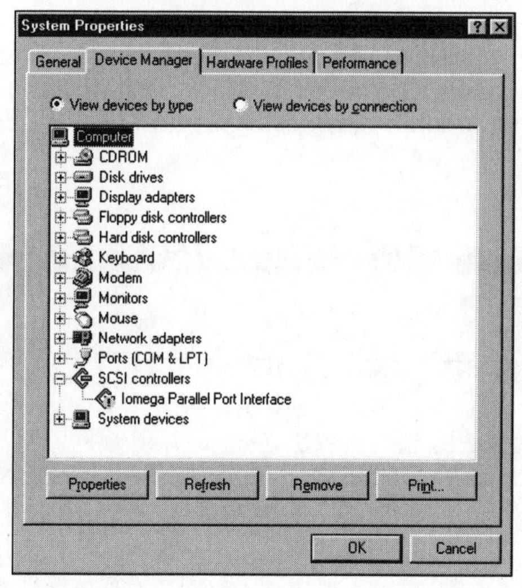


**Figure 15-6:** Windows is confused because it can't find one of the devices — I removed it without telling Windows to disable it.

Select the device, and choose Properties to see a message explaining the problem. Sometimes, the problem isn't so serious, and the device continues to operate. Other times, you may have to reinstall or reconfigure the device. The Properties dialog box usually provides enough information to guide you to a resolution.

## Printing a report about devices

It's a good idea to have a list of all the devices in your system and the resources they use. I've found that such a list is handy in the following situations:

- If you have to reinstall everything when you replace a hard drive, all the configuration information for each device is available in your list.
- If you want to install additional devices, you know which resources on your computer are available by viewing your list.

To print a report on all the devices in your system, click the Print button in the Device Manager dialog box. Select the option to print a summary, unless you want to use a whole ream of paper.

# Determining Who's on Your Computer

In Windows 98 and Windows Me, you can use Net Watcher to keep an eye on visitors — that is, those users who are working on other computers on the network who are accessing your computer. Net Watcher gives you all kinds of who, what, and where information.

To open Net Watcher, choose Start➪Programs➪Accessories➪System Tools➪Net Watcher. The window that opens displays a list of visitors, if any other users are accessing your computer (see Figure 15-7).

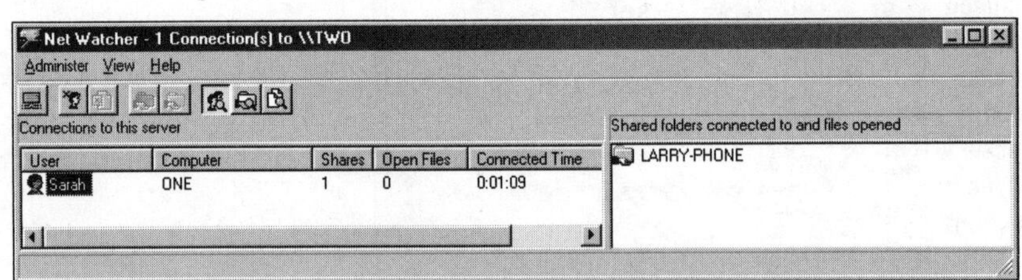


**Figure 15-7:** Keep an eye on users who access files and folders on your computer.

By default, the window displays a User view, which provides the following information about each visitor:

- The user name
- The name of the remote computer

- The number of shares in use
- The number of open files
- The length of time that the visitor has been connected to your computer

You can select a specific user and see which shared folder that user is accessing (the information appears in the right pane of the Net Watcher window).

The Shared Folders view (choose View⇨Shared Folders) displays all the shared folders on your computer. You can double-click any folder to see the name of the user who is accessing the folder. This view is not named correctly because it not only displays shared folders, but it also lists all the shared resources on your computer (printers, removable drives, and so on).

The Show Files view (choose View⇨By Open Files) lists all the open files in use by visitors. Incidentally, only software program files are tracked, not data files. In addition to the name of each open file, the name of its shared folder is listed, as are the name of the remote user and the type of access (Read-only or Full).

In addition to viewing all this information, you can perform a number of tasks in the Net Watcher window, including the following:

- Close a file that somebody's using
- Add a new shared folder to your computer
- Stop sharing a folder that's currently shared
- Change the properties of a shared folder (such as passwords and access options)
- Disconnect a user

Some of these options sound like dirty tricks — I mean, after all, disconnecting a user? But if you think of Net Watcher as a security measure, you'll understand why this tool can be important. Suppose that your son and his friend are using a computer and decide to open the family budget or personal letters. If you use Net Watcher, and as a result, discover that remote users are accessing files and folders you'd prefer to keep private, you can adjust the way you configured the privacy level for your shared resources.

In Windows 2000 and Windows XP, you can view the same information, and perform the same tasks, by taking the following steps:

1. **Right-click My Computer, and choose Manage from the shortcut menu.**

   The Computer Management (Local) snap-in opens.

2. **Expand the Shared Folders icon in the left pane.**

3. **Click the Sessions folder in the left pane to see who's visiting this computer (see Figure 15-8).**

   To disconnect a user, right-click the listing in the right pane and choose Close Session from the shortcut menu.

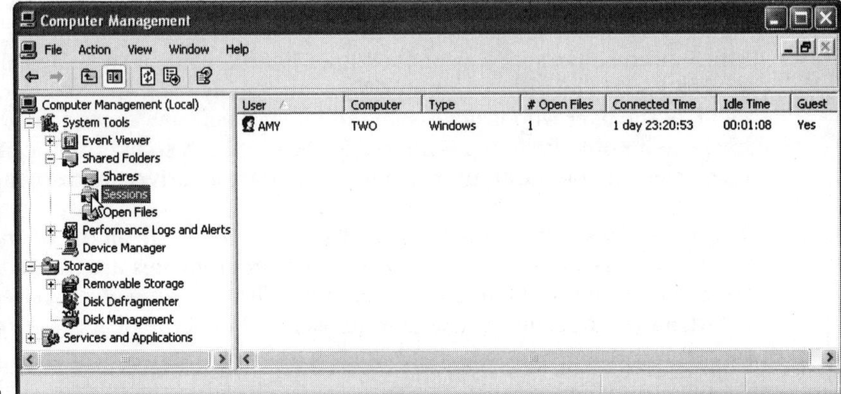


**Figure 15-8:** Keep an eye on the people who are using your computer.

4. **Click the `Open Files` folder in the left pane to see which files your visitors are using.**

   To close a file, right-click the listing in the right pane and choose Close File from the shortcut menu.

5. **To add a share, or modify an existing share, click the `Shares` folder in the left pane.**

   Then you can use the commands on the shortcut menu that you see when you right-click the folder, or right-click any of the shares displayed in the right pane.

# Cleaning Up Files with Disk Cleanup

Using the Disk Cleanup tool is like bringing in a housekeeper to clean up all that junk you never use — the stuff that's been lying around taking up space.

In your house, that stuff could be old magazines, newspapers, or clothing that you haven't been able to fit into for years. On your computer, that stuff is files you don't use and probably don't even realize are stored on your drive. Those are the files that Disk Cleanup looks for and offers to sweep out.

Follow these steps to run the Disk Cleanup program:

1. **Choose Start➪Programs➪Accessories➪System Tools➪Disk Cleanup.**

   The Disk Cleanup tool takes a few seconds to examine your computer and then opens the Disk Cleanup dialog box, as shown in Figure 15-9. File types that are candidates for safe removal are already selected.

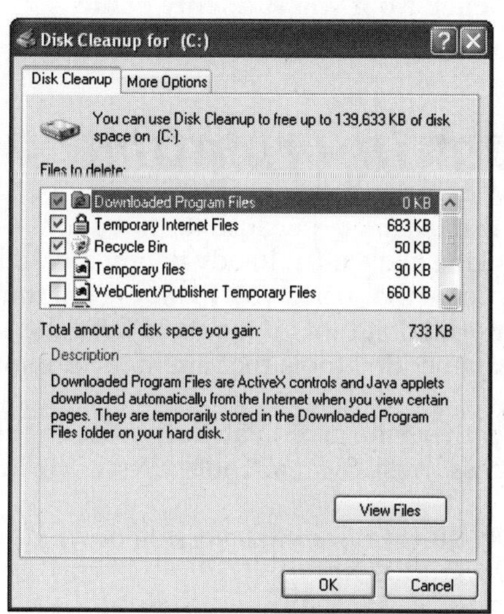


**Figure 15-9:** Files that seem safe to remove are preselected, and you can select additional file types if you want to clean more aggressively.

2. **Scroll through the list of file types in the Files to delete list box, and select any additional file types you want to remove. (Click each file-type listing to see more information in the Description box.)**

   If the listing includes Old ScanDisk Files in the Root Folder, select that file type for removal. These are the files I discuss in the section "Checking Your Hard Drive for Damage with ScanDisk," earlier in this chapter. These files contain lost data, but you can't do anything with them.

   In Windows 98 and Windows Me, the last item in the Files to Delete list box is Non-Critical files. If you select this file type, the cleanup is not automatic. Instead, the files are displayed so that you can decide which of them you want to delete. Plan on doing nothing else for the rest of the day!

   In Windows 2000 and Windows XP systems that are running NTFS, a listing named Compress Old Files exists. Selecting this option tells Windows to compress the old files to save disk space, instead of deleting them. The files are still available; they're just not taking up as much space.

If you compress files in your NTFS system, be sure to select the option to display compressed files in a different color when you're viewing files in My Computer or Windows Explorer. The option is on the View menu of the dialog box that appears when you select Tools➪Folder Options.

3. **When you're ready to clean out all this stuff, click OK.**

   Disk Cleanup asks if you're sure you want to delete these files.

4. **Click Yes to proceed, or click No if you suddenly panic.**

# Working with System Information

The System Information tool is misnamed, because it's not a tool — it's an entire toolbox. It starts off looking like a nifty, handy-dandy tool, but then you discover a menu item named Tools that leads you to more cool tools. In this section, I cover the System Information tool (*SI* for short) and then follow up with sections for some of the embedded tools that are in its toolbox.

The primary focus of SI is to gather information and diagnose problems. Just choose Start➪Programs➪Accessories➪System Tools➪System Information.

The SI dialog box looks slightly different for each version of Windows. Figure 15-10 shows the SI window in Windows XP.

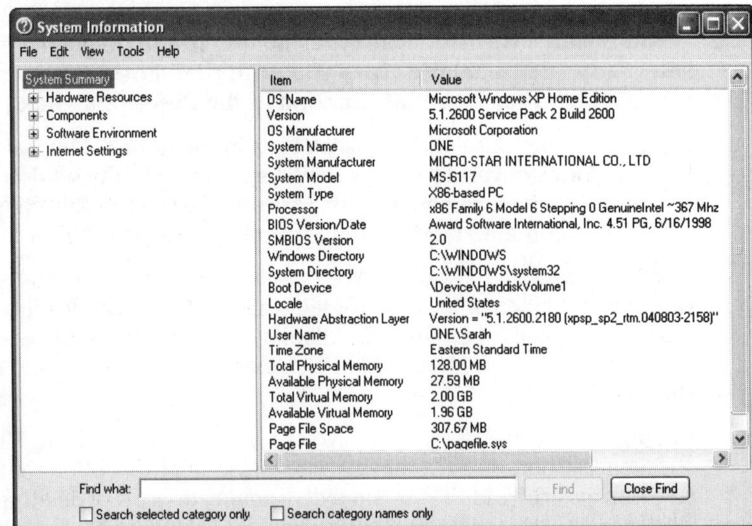


**Figure 15-10:** Windows XP System Information.

The differences between the versions aren't terribly important in the ultimate scheme of things. (This is a fancy way of saying that the job gets done regardless of the graphical look of the dialog box.)

The Windows Me version of SI runs as part of the Help system. That means that after you select System Information from the menu, you have time to brew a pot of coffee, mow the lawn, or take a short nap. If they ever award a prize called "the most annoyingly slow to load component in the history of computers," the Windows Me Help system will win, hands down!

# General System Information

Selecting the System Information category in the left pane displays general information about your computer in the right pane. You can't do anything with this information — it's purely informative.

# Hardware Resources

Click the plus sign to the left of the Hardware Resources category, and select a subcategory to view information in the right pane. (Not every subcategory appears in every version of Windows.) The following subcategories are available for Hardware Resources:

- **Conflicts/Sharing:** This subcategory lists any resource conflicts. It also identifies resources that are being shared by Peripheral Component Interconnect (PCI) devices. This information can be helpful when you're trying to discover whether a hardware conflict is to blame for a device problem.
- **DMA:** This subcategory displays the status of devices that are using Direct Memory Access (DMA). DMA lets some attached devices (such as a disk drive or a printer) send data directly to the computer's memory. This frees up the processor.
- **Forced Hardware:** Select this subcategory to see a list of devices that have user-specified resources instead of resources that are assigned by the system. Sometimes this information is helpful when you're having trouble installing a Plug and Play device that should have been easy to install.
- **I/O:** Selecting this subcategory produces a list of all the I/O addresses (parts of memory assigned to a device) that are currently in use. The devices that occupy each address range are also displayed. You can use this information to avoid the occupied addresses when you're configuring a new device.

- **IRQs:** Select this subcategory to see a display of the interrupt requests (IRQs) that are in use, along with the devices that are using each IRQ. (An IRQ is a channel of communication that a device occupies.) This subcategory also contains a list of unused IRQs, which is handy when you're configuring a new device.
- **Memory:** This subcategory displays a list of memory address ranges that are being used by devices. Most of the time this information is used when you're troubleshooting a device, especially if you call the manufacturer's customer support line. Support technicians often ask for this information.

## Components

The Components category contains all sorts of information about your computer's configuration, including information about the status of device drivers as well as a history of all the drivers you've installed. (It's not unusual to upgrade drivers when they become available from manufacturers or from Microsoft.) Information about components in your system is available, including all sorts of highly technical data about memory addresses. Most of the time the data is incomprehensible, but if you're on the telephone with a support person, this technical mumbo jumbo may be significant. This category also contains a summary of devices that the System Information tool suspects are not working properly.

Table 15-1 lists descriptions of the subcategories in the Components list. Not all categories appear in every version of Windows.

**Table 15-1 Components Category Descriptions**

| *Subcategory* | *Information Provided* |
|---|---|
| Multimedia | In Windows 98/Me/2000, lists installed sound cards and joysticks. Other subcategories provide specific information about audio, video, and CD-ROM configuration. In Windows XP, contains only information about settings; other information is in a separate component listing named CD-ROM. |
| CD-ROM | In Windows XP only, contains information about the CD-ROMs on the system. |
| Sound Device | In Windows XP only, contains information about the sound controller on the system. |
| Display | Informs you about your video card and monitor. |

| Subcategory | Information Provided |
|---|---|
| Infrared | Provides information about infrared devices you've installed. |
| Input | Tells you about your keyboard and mouse. |
| Modem | Only in Windows 2000/XP, contains information about attached telephone modems. |
| Miscellaneous | Only in Windows 98/Me, gives information about printers you've installed (both local and network), as well as about a potpourri of other devices. |
| Network | Offers information about network adapters and client services and protocols you've installed. |
| Ports | Gives you information about serial and parallel ports in your computer. |
| Storage | Tells you all about your hard drive(s), floppy drive(s), and removable media. |
| Printing | Tells you which printers and printer drivers (including drivers for printers on other computers) are installed on the computer. |
| Problem devices | Gives you the status of devices that have problems. |
| USB | Tells you about the Universal Serial Bus (USB) (also known as Plug and Play) controllers installed. |
| History | Only in Windows 98/Me, gives you the history of all the drivers that have been installed on the computer, including updates and changes. Use this subcategory to see all the changes you've made to the system if something goes wrong. |
| System | Only in Windows 98/Me, tells you all about the Basic Input/Output System (also called the BIOS), the motherboard, and other key built-in devices. |

# Software Environment

The Software Environment category covers information about the software that's loaded in your computer's memory. Included are drivers, software programs, tasks that are currently running, and all sorts of technical data that's hard to understand. However, the information can be useful to support desk personnel if you're calling for help.

## Internet Explorer

The Internet Explorer category (called Internet Settings in Windows XP) displays information about the Internet Explorer version, the temporary files, and security settings.

## Saving system information to a file

You can save all the information that the SI tool provides in a file and then use that file as a reference when you configure new devices or call a support desk. To send the data to a file, choose File➪Export from the System Information menu bar. A Save As dialog box opens so you can name the file and select the folder in which to save it. The file is a text file, so you can open it and print it in a word processor.

## Checking Windows 98 system files

Windows 98 provides a tool called the System File Checker that you can use to, well, check your system files. System files are the files that Windows 98 installs to make the operating system run. All the files for all the Windows components you install are transferred to your hard drive during the installation process. Most of the files end up in the Windows folder or one of the subfolders in the Windows folder.

Sometimes a system file gets corrupted or disappears. The System File Checker verifies the files on your hard drive, and if any of them is corrupt or missing, they're replaced from the original Windows 98 CD.

If a system file disappears, you can bet that it wasn't an accident, and somebody probably deleted it. It's very dangerous to open Windows Explorer and delete files from the Windows folder or one of its subfolders.

Newer versions of Windows do a better job of protecting system files, and if one of those files is corrupt or missing, the operating system has an automated process for replacing it.

Follow these steps to run the System File Checker from the SI window in Windows 98:

1. **Choose Tools➪System File Checker from the SI menu bar.**

   When the System File Checker dialog box opens, the Scan for Altered Files option is already selected, as shown in Figure 15-11.

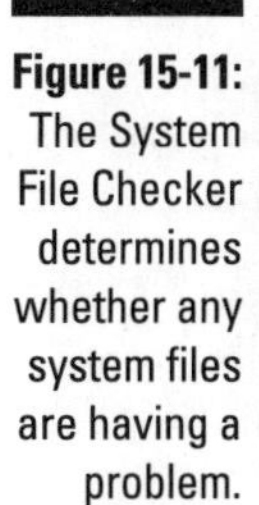

**Figure 15-11:** The System File Checker determines whether any system files are having a problem.

2. **Click Start to have the System File Checker go through your hard drive(s) and check all the Windows system files.**

   The process takes a couple of minutes.

   If any files have been altered, you're prompted to restore the original file from the Windows CD (or the Windows 98 files folder if your computer came with the operating system preinstalled).

   If you're a control freak, you may want to click the Settings button so that you can configure the way the System File Checker works. The available options are self-explanatory, and if you're not sure about an option, you can right-click it and get information from the What's This dialog box that opens.

If you're very comfortable with computers and operating systems, you can click the Tools menu item in the SI window and run any of the tools listed in the drop-down menu. Some of these tools are complicated, dangerous, or both.

# Automating Maintenance Tasks

You don't have to do any work to run maintenance tasks regularly, if you take advantage of the automation that's available in Windows. The automated tools differ among versions of Windows, and I cover all these nifty tools in this section.

## Maintenance Wizard in Windows 98 and Windows Me

Available only in Windows 98 and Windows Me, the Maintenance Wizard is a nifty way to make sure that important maintenance tasks are performed regularly and automatically. In addition, you can schedule these chores so that they take place at times that don't interfere with your work.

To open the Maintenance Wizard, choose Start➪Programs➪Accessories➪System Tools➪Maintenance Wizard. Each wizard window presents a question to answer or an option to select. Click Next to move through the wizard's windows.

If your computer is running the FAT file system instead of the FAT32 file system, every time you open this program, you're asked if you'd like to convert to FAT32. You probably should — it's a more efficient file system than FAT16. Basic operating system configuration is beyond the scope of this book, but you can find out more about file systems in *Windows 98 For Dummies, Microsoft Windows Me Millennium Edition For Dummies,* and *Windows XP For Dummies,* all written by Andy Rathbone and published by Wiley Publishing.

The opening window of the Maintenance Wizard offers the following two configuration options:

- **Express:** Automatically configures the wizard for the most common maintenance settings.
- **Custom:** Allows you to select your own settings.

The common maintenance settings differ according to the software and Windows features you've installed in your system. However, the following programs usually run:

- ScanDisk
- Disk Cleanup
- Disk Defragmenter

The following sections explain the Express and Custom setup options in more detail.

## Doing an Express setup

With the Express setup option, you schedule the three maintenance programs listed in the preceding list. You also choose the time at which the Maintenance Wizard performs its tasks. The Maintenance Wizard usually takes about three hours to complete its tasks, and the computer must be running. The schedule options are as follows:

- **Nights — midnight to 3:00 a.m.:** This is convenient, because it probably won't interfere with your work.
- **Days — noon to 3:00 p.m.:** This is handy for households with folks who work or go to school during the day.
- **Evenings — 8:00 p.m. to 11:00 p.m.:** This may be convenient if the members of your household don't work at the computers after dinner.

Click Next to see a summary of the wizard's plans (see Figure 15-12). If you want, you can instruct the wizard to run all the tasks now and then follow your schedule in the future. (Only run the tasks now if you know you don't want to use the computer for a few hours, and nobody else on the network needs the computer.)

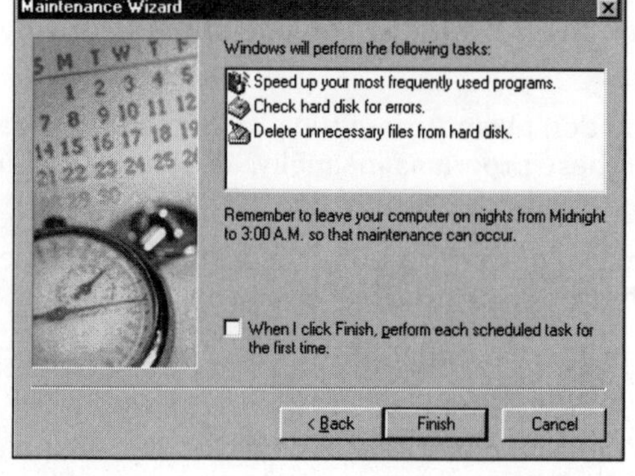


**Figure 15-12:** The wizard presents the results of your configuration.

## Doing a Custom setup

With the Custom option, you can specify a day and time for each task, rather than running all of them back to back.

After you select the Custom option in the first window of the Maintenance Wizard, follow these steps:

1. **In the Select a Maintenance Schedule Wizard window, select a schedule option and then click Next.**

   Select the Custom option if you're planning to create a schedule that differs from the available schedules.

   The wizard shows you a list of programs that run every time you start Windows.

2. **Deselect any program that you want to remove from the startup list.**

   Removing a program makes booting your computer a faster process.

   If you run Quicken, you'll probably see Billminder in this list. Quicken doesn't put Billminder in the Startup folder of the Programs menu, where you could easily remove it. Instead, the Quicken programmers use a hidden (okay, I call it *sneaky*) method to start Billminder every time you start your computer. Most Quicken users don't care if the Billminder feature isn't operating and wouldn't notice if it disappeared. The Billminder program takes up memory, and it does not have to be running all the time — Quicken does everything you need it to do without wasting precious memory and computer resources on this feature. Take this opportunity to kill it.

3. **In the following windows, the wizard presents each of the maintenance programs individually so you can decide if and when you want to run the program. In each window, do one of the following and then click Next:**

   - Click No if you don't want to run the program automatically (you can run all of these programs manually, as described earlier in this chapter).
   - Click Yes if you want to run a program, and then click the Reschedule button to create your own schedule for it.

     Each schedule interval (monthly, weekly, and so on) has its own options for fine-tuning the schedule.

     You can also develop multiple schedules for any maintenance tool. For example, you may want to schedule a program to run monthly every three months at 3:00 a.m. and then also run it at 1:00 a.m. every week on Friday. Actually, I've never found a good reason to develop multiple schedules for any of these utilities, but the option exists, so I'm mentioning it.

     When you're finished scheduling tasks, a window appears, summarizing the tasks that you've scheduled.

4. **Click Finish to complete the wizard.**

The Maintenance Wizard is a good way to make sure that health checkups are performed regularly. Being able to run these programs in the middle of the night is a definite advantage. After all, even if you aren't planning to use your computer for a couple of hours to run maintenance programs, you're running a network — which means that other users on other computers may need to get into your computer.

# Task Scheduler

The Windows Task Scheduler is available in all versions of Windows. In fact, you can use it to schedule maintenance tasks in Windows 98 and Windows Me, but because those versions of Windows offer the Maintenance Wizard for automating maintenance tasks, it's easer to use that tool.

To open the Task Scheduler, choose Start➪Programs➪Accessories➪System Tools➪Scheduled Tasks. If you have any existing scheduled tasks, you see an icon for each one (many antivirus software programs add a task to check the software company's Web site for software updates on a regular basis).

## Adding a new scheduled task

The window contains an Add Scheduled Task icon, which you use to create a new scheduled task, using the following steps:

1. **Double-click the Add Scheduled Task icon.**

   The Scheduled Task Wizard appears to walk you through the process of establishing a new scheduled item. Click Next to begin creating the new task.

2. **Select a program from the list the wizard displays, or click Browse to find the program if it isn't listed.**

   Many utility programs aren't listed by the wizard, so you must browse your system to find them. Open the appropriate folder, and select the program. Then click Next.

3. **Name the scheduled task, select the frequency for performing the task, and click Next.**

   The wizard automatically uses the program name for the task, but you can change the name if you want.

4. **Follow the wizard's prompts to schedule the task.**

   The options the wizard presents vary, depending on the frequency you choose. For example, if you choose Monthly, you must tell the wizard which day of the month in addition to setting a time.

   If you're running NTFS on Windows 2000 or Windows XP, the wizard also prompts you for the name and password of a user who has sufficient permissions to perform the task (any user with Administrative rights).

5. **Click Finish to schedule this task.**

   You can also click the option Open advanced properties for this task when I click Finish to fine-tune the schedule.

### Working with existing scheduled tasks

In the Scheduled Tasks window, you can delete or modify any tasks you've created, and you can check their status. (Did they run or did they have problems?) Here are your choices for working with existing scheduled tasks:

- **Delete a scheduled task.**

  If you change your mind and decide you no longer want a scheduled task to run, right-click its listing and choose Delete. Windows asks you to confirm your decision.

- **Change the schedule for a task.**

  Right-click a task listing, and choose Properties from the shortcut menu. Click the Schedule tab of the Properties dialog box to change the schedule for a task. You have all the options that were available when you originally set up the task.

- **Configure behavior for a scheduled task.**

  You can tweak automated tasks to make sure they run, or don't run, under certain conditions. This is a good way to make sure the program that's launched automatically can't cause problems. To manipulate the settings for a task, click the Settings tab of its dialog box, as shown in Figure 15-13.

  The fields in this dialog box are self-explanatory, but some of the default settings are a bit ridiculous. For example, it's probably a good idea to stop a task if it runs for more than 4 or 5 hours, instead of 72 hours. In fact, except for defragging, most scheduled tasks should take less than an hour. The bottom section of the dialog box applies to laptop computers.

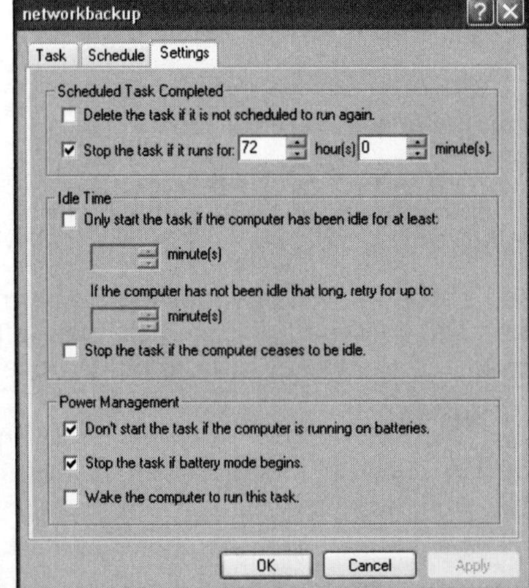


**Figure 15-13:** You can fine-tune the settings for a scheduled task.

- **Start a task immediately.**

  To run a program right now, right-click its listing and choose Run from the shortcut menu. This action has no effect on the schedule; the task will run at its next scheduled time.

- **Check the scheduled tasks log.**

  If the information in a task's listing looks suspicious (the task didn't run or something you don't understand is displayed in the Status column), you can check the log. The Task Scheduler keeps an error log, which you can see by choosing Advanced⇨View Log.

  Depending on the information in the log, you may want to change settings for a task, as described earlier in this section. For example, if a task is terminated because a computer stopped being idle, you may want to change its setting so it doesn't only run while the computer is idle.

# Troubleshooting Disk Errors

If a physical problem exists with your hard drive, you'll probably see one of the following messages (substitute the letter of your hard drive for *X*):

- Serious Disk Error Writing Drive *X*
- Data Error Reading Drive *X*
- Error Reading Drive *X*
- I/O Error
- Seek Error — Sector not found

If you get any of these error messages, your hard drive may have a serious health problem that could even be fatal.

Perform a backup immediately, as explained in Chapter 14 (although some files from the drive may not be readable and won't be backed up). If the backup doesn't work without producing error messages, manually back up as many important data files as you can. Then, take your computer to a computer store to buy a new drive.

# Part V
# The Part of Tens

## In this part . . .

The Part of Tens is a tradition in the *For Dummies* series. In this book, it's also a breath of fresh air and a release from the other chapters, which put you through technical twists and turns, forcing you to concentrate on minutiae and geeky details. In this part, you discover ten fun things that you can do on your network, as well as find out ways to protect your children from the dangerous parts of the Internet.

# Chapter 16

# Ten Fun Things to Do on Your Network

### In This Chapter

- Playing a game across the network
- Setting up message centers, bulletin boards, and other "communications-central" features
- Creating central locations for data that everyone uses

Believe it or not, a networked computer system isn't just about connections, cables, and user profiles. After all that setup stuff is finished, there are a zillion handy reasons for having a home network. Well, perhaps "zillion" is an exaggeration, but it isn't hard to think of ten things, and here they are.

## Play Hearts

In my house, we play Hearts across the network for lots of excellent reasons:

- We don't have to search the house for a deck of cards.
- We don't have to clean off the kitchen table to make room for playing cards.
- We don't argue about whose turn it is to keep score.
- We don't have to search for a pencil and paper to keep score.
- We don't argue about the score because computers don't make math errors.
- We don't have to argue about who should put the cards away.

People who stop by while we're playing get a kick of out us — you can hear the "gotcha" yells from different rooms in the house. This ritual seems strange to visitors, but we think of it as normal.

Hearts is built into Windows (except Windows 2000, but I have a workaround for that — read on). In Windows 98/Me you can play it alone or with other players on the network. In fact, the game is built for network use. Its proper name is The Microsoft Hearts Network (check the title bar of the game's window). Up to four people can play Hearts across the network. If fewer than four human, breathing players are available on the network, the computer provides the missing participants. Windows XP only lets you play alone, against computer-generated players.

Even if you play the game alone (with the computer representing all the other players), the first time you open Hearts after a reboot, there's a delay before the game appears while the program searches the network to see if anyone else is currently playing the game.

Windows 2000 Professional doesn't come with Hearts (after all, it's built from the ground up for business users), and although you can install a copy on a Windows 2000 computer, it's a single-player game — it won't find other players on a network. If you're running a Windows 2000 Professional computer on your network and you want to play Hearts by yourself, you need to copy two files from a computer that's running Windows 98 or Me: `Mshearts.exe` and `Cards.dll`. Make sure that you put both files in the same folder.

You can open Hearts by choosing Start⇨Programs⇨Accessories⇨Games⇨Hearts. But that's far too many steps for my taste, so I suggest creating a shortcut to it. To do so, position your mouse pointer on the Hearts listing and right-drag the listing to the desktop. Then choose Create Shortcut(s) Here from the menu that appears. For even quicker access, you can drag the shortcut to the Quick Launch bar rather than the desktop.

Follow these steps to play Hearts across the network:

1. **Open Hearts and enter your name (or accept the name that's automatically filled in).**

   If you're the first player to open Hearts (or you're playing alone), select the I want to be dealer option.

   Along the bottom of the Hearts window, you can see a message that Hearts is waiting for others to join the game.

2. **If you're playing against the computer because nobody else is on the network or nobody else on the network wants to play, press F2 to begin playing alone.**

3. **If someone else wants to play the game, have that person choose the I want to connect to another game option and click OK.**

4. **If you're joining a game, enter the name of the computer that the dealer is using in the Locate Dealer dialog box. Then click OK.**

   The Hearts window opens, displaying a message at the bottom that everyone is waiting for the dealer to start the game — if that's you, press F2!

If you don't like the names the computer chooses for the nonhuman players (or if a computer name duplicates a human player's name), you can change them. Choose Game⇨Options, and enter names you like better.

# Set Up a Message Center

A computer-based household message center is a place to leave notes for other members of the family. This type of message center is much more efficient than the old system of hand-scrawled notes left on the blackboard in the kitchen, or the less-organized system of dashing off incomplete words and phone numbers on the back of an envelope with your youngest child's crayon. With a message center, you're less likely to run out of room when you take a message for your family members (especially from your teenage daughter's friend Mindy, who just, like, got back from the mall and can't wait to talk about her, like, new shoes), and even more importantly, no one has to try to decipher your chicken-scratch handwriting.

## Creating a shared folder for the message center

Choose one computer to serve as the message center, and then follow these steps to set up a shared folder for messages on it:

1. **Open My Computer.**

2. **Double-click the drive where you want to locate the folder.**

   Unless you have multiple drives in the computer, you'll only have drive C.

3. **Choose File⇨New⇨Folder.**

   A new folder icon appears and the name *New Folder* is highlighted, which means the name is in edit mode. As soon as you press any key, the characters you type replace the name.

4. **Name the folder.**

   Naming the folder *Messages* seems like a good idea.

5. **Right-click the new folder, and choose Sharing from the shortcut menu that appears.**

   In Windows XP, the command may be Sharing and Security, instead of Sharing (depending on whether you're running NTFS).

   The Sharing tab of the Message Properties dialog box appears.

6. **Select the option to share the folder.**

7. **Set permissions for network users.**

   In Windows 98 and Windows Me, select Full in the Access Type section, and don't set any passwords.

   In Windows 2000, all network users are automatically given full permissions on a folder when it's shared.

   In Windows XP, select the option to share the folder on the network. Then select the option to let network users change the files (see Figure 16-1).

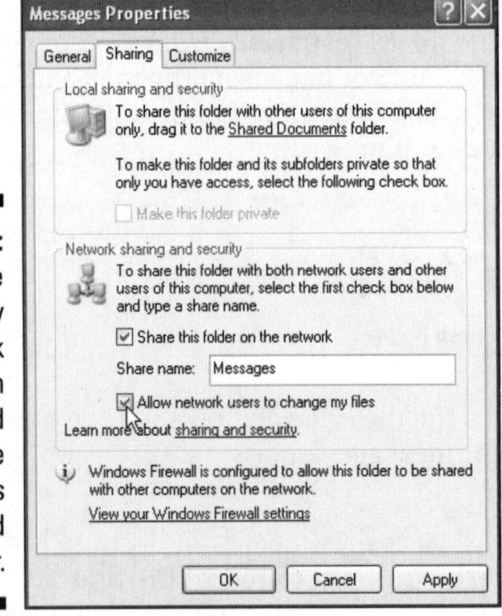


**Figure 16-1:** Make sure every network user can both read and write data to this shared folder.

8. **Click OK.**

   A hand appears under the folder's icon to indicate it's a shared resource.

Now the share is visible when network users open Network Neighborhood (or My Network Places) and double-click the computer you used to create the message center.

## Creating individual message boards

After you create the Messages folder, you're ready to create the individual message-board files for every member of your family. The best way to create a message-center file is to take advantage of a nifty feature that's available in Notepad. Notepad can create a date and time stamp on every entry that's put into a file. Here's how to set up this electronic wizardry:

1. **On the message-center computer, choose Start⇨Programs⇨ Accessories⇨Notepad.**

   The Notepad window opens.

2. **Type** .LOG, **and press Enter.**

   Make sure that the period is the first character on the line and that you use capital letters for the word LOG (and no spaces please).

3. **Choose File⇨Save.**

   The Save As dialog box appears.

4. **Save the file in the Messages folder, using your name as the filename.**

   Use the arrow to the right of the Save In box (at the top of the dialog box) to navigate to the Messages folder. In the File Name box, enter your first name or nickname — Windows automatically adds the extension .txt to the filename. Then click Save.

   The title bar of the Notepad window shows the filename, which is *Yourname*.txt (of course, your *real* name is on the title bar, not *Yourname*).

5. **Choose File⇨Save As, and then save the file under another user name.**

   Use the name of another user. You're creating the same file for another user in your household. Repeat this step for every household member.

6. **When you're finished creating files, exit Notepad.**

Now the message center (the Messages folder on the message-center computer) contains an electronic message board for every user on your network. Everyone on the network can open other users' files to leave messages. And every time you open one of those messages, a time stamp appears.

## Testing the message boards

The files you created in the preceding section are designed to work as message centers, noting the date and time of each entry. Make sure that the time-stamp feature is working by opening one of the files. Here's how:

1. **On the message-center computer, open Windows Explorer and select the `Messages` folder in the left pane.**
2. **In the right pane, double-click a message-board file.**

   The file opens in the Notepad window. The current date and time are pre-entered, and your cursor is waiting for input on the next line, as shown in Figure 16-2.

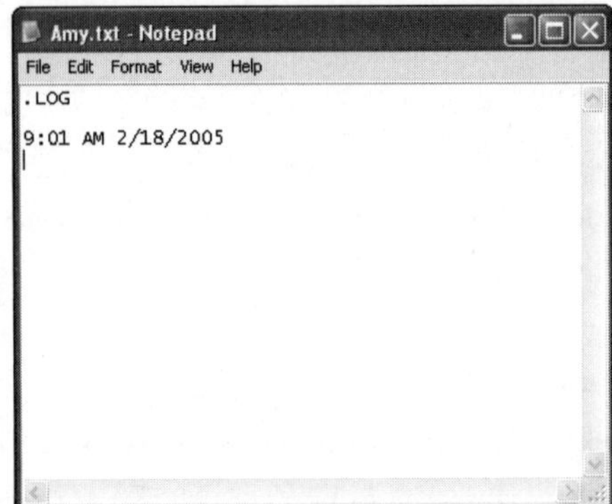


**Figure 16-2:** Is this time-stamp feature cool, or what?

If you don't see a time stamp, you made an error when you entered the original text. Make sure that no characters, not even a space, appear in front of or after the text .LOG. Also make sure you entered a period, not a comma (a common error). Make corrections, save the file, and open it again to test it.

## Tricks and tips for using the message center

After you have the message center in place, here are some tips for getting the most out of it:

- **Leave a blank line at the end of messages.** After you type a message in a user's file, be sure to press Enter to force a blank line to appear before the next automatic time stamp. The blank line makes it easier to separate the individual notes in the file.
- **If you don't want to save a message, close Notepad and click No when prompted to save the changes.** If you open another user's file and change your mind about leaving a message (perhaps you opened the wrong file, or maybe you just changed your mind), close Notepad and

click No when Windows asks if you want to save the changes you made to the file. If you click Yes, the time stamp remains in the file with no message below it. This will drive the user nuts.

- **Use the file to write notes to yourself.** Most of the time, you'll open your message board file just to read the text, not to add text. You can, of course, use the file to write notes to yourself, perhaps entering reminders about tasks or appointments. However, don't enter any information you don't want others to see.
- **Clean out old messages to keep message files as small as possible.** You can delete each message as you read it, save some messages for future reference and delete others, or save all the messages forever. However, if the file grows too large for Notepad, when you double-click your file, Windows offers to open it in WordPad instead. WordPad doesn't support the time-stamp feature. ***Note:*** The Windows 2000 and Windows XP versions of Notepad have no size limit.
- **Delete the time stamp that was automatically added when you opened the file.** Before you save and close your message file, after you've deleted the messages you don't need to keep, remember to delete the time stamp that was automatically inserted when you opened the file.

## Hold all my calls! Gaining easy access to the message center

I'm sure everyone in your family gets a lot of phone calls, and I'm sure everyone agrees that the easiest way to do something is the best. That's why you should create a shortcut to the message center for each user on the network. That way, when the phone rings, you don't have to go through the whole folder hierarchy just to find the message center folder.

To create a shortcut, follow these steps:

1. **Locate the message-center folder and right-click it.**
2. **Choose Create Shortcut from the menu that appears.**

   Windows opens a message box that says you cannot create a shortcut here and offers to create the shortcut on your desktop.
3. **Click Yes to create a shortcut on your desktop.**

For even quicker access to the message center (when you're working in software, you can't always see the desktop), drag the shortcut to the Quick Launch bar or drag it to the Start button to put the shortcut at the top of your Start menu.

If multiple users share a computer, each user must log on to the computer and create the shortcut. Desktop shortcuts are linked to the profile of the user who created them. See Chapter 9 for information about user profiles.

# Keep a Family Shopping List

Many families keep a shopping list on a blackboard, usually in the kitchen, and everybody in the family adds items to the list. Personally, I don't see the point. Does the person who is heading for the store take the blackboard down and carry it to the store? If not, then the person who's heading for the store has to get a pen and paper and write down everything that's on the blackboard. Hello? Sorry, I'm too lazy for this scheme (and I'm usually the person heading for the store).

The next-best plan is to keep a pad and pen (or pencil, if you have one — I haven't seen a pencil in my house since my kids got out of elementary school) in a central location, like the kitchen. Everybody can add items to the shopping list, and the person (Dad?) who next heads for the store just takes the list with him. Much better, wouldn't you say? Except, in my house, people "borrow" the pad, which always involves moving it to another room. Even more frequently, people take the pen. In fact, putting a cluster of pens next to the pad doesn't work; it's only a matter of a few days before those pens are all in pocketbooks, pockets, and other rooms.

The best place for a family shopping list is in a document on a computer. This list is easy to use and easy to print. Nobody can put the computer in his pocket (or in her pocketbook) and walk away with it, so the list is always available.

## Creating the shopping list

To create a shopping list, follow these steps:

1. **Choose a computer to hold the shopping list.**
2. **Create a folder on that computer to hold the shopping list file, and then share that folder.**

   Use the steps outlined in the "Creating a shared folder for the message center" section, earlier in this chapter, to create and share the folder.

   If you also set up a family message center, as described earlier in the chapter, you can use that same folder for your shopping list. (It's not necessary to create a time-stamp document for a shopping list.)

3. **Have all the users create shortcuts to the folder on their own desktops.**

   Refer to the section "Creating a shared folder for the message center," earlier in this chapter, for information on how to create shortcuts.

4. **Use the computer that holds the shared folder to create the shopping list file: Open the software, enter the first item on the list, and save the file in the shared folder. You can name the file *Shopping List* or choose something more clever or creative.**

   You can create the file in any software that is available to everyone on the network. Notepad and WordPad come installed on every Windows computer, so either one of those programs will do. If everybody uses the same word processor, you can also use that software.

## Using the shopping list

Any person in the household who wants to add an item to the shopping list can open the shortcut to the shared folder, double-click the file to open it, and add athlete's-foot cream, zit zapper, prune juice, or another desperately needed item. Be sure that everyone knows to save the file. Easy, huh?

Always press Enter before you add an item to the list so the item is on its own line. This extra space makes the list much easier to read when the designated shopper prints it.

Managing the list's efficiency and workability is important, or else the concept dies. Then you may have to go back to copying lists from a blackboard. Yuck! When removing items, be sure to remove items from the list; *do not* delete the file. You can either remove all the items on the list and "clean the slate," so to speak, or manually remove only the items you found at the store — and leave "12 pounds of caviar" on the list for next time. I'll leave that up to you to decide.

### Deletion tips for the designated shopper

Pass on these simple tips to the person who does the shopping for your family, and make sure that if Dad's doing the shopping, he also maintains the list:

- To remove everything in the file, press Ctrl+A (which selects all the text in the file), press Delete, and then save the now-empty file.
- To remove an individual item, place your pointer at the beginning of the item. Press and hold Ctrl and Shift, and press ↓; this selects the entire paragraph. Then press Delete. Repeat this sequence for other individual items, and save the file.
- For multiple items that are listed contiguously, follow the instructions in the preceding bullet but continue to press ↓ to add those items to the selected text. Then press Delete, and save the file.

If you're using Notepad for your shopping file, press and hold Shift while you press ↓, instead of pressing and holding Ctrl and Shift.

Here's some other organizational advice regarding shopping lists:

- **You can create separate shopping lists for different types of stores.** Your shopping list probably contains food items, paper goods, cleaning supplies, and other items that are available in your local supermarket. Create a file named `hardware` if you tend to purchase nails, tools, propane cylinders, and other hardware-store items frequently. Do the same for other types of stores.

  You could create a file for clothing, but the thought of a single household member shopping for clothing for teenagers makes me laugh. Come to think of it, the thought of sending another household member out with a list of clothing items for me makes me nervous.

- **You can create shopping lists for special items for each person in the household.** Be careful about naming the files if you're using message files — don't overwrite the time-stamp file for any user. Instead, choose a filename that indicates the contents are a shopping list, for example, `Fred-Shopping` (a dash is an acceptable character in a filename).

  Individual shopping-list files for household members are also great wish lists. Consult another user's shopping file before his birthday.

# Collaborate on Documents

If everybody on the network is using the same word-processing software, two of you (or all of you) can collaborate on documents. Common collaborative documents include the annual holiday letter to friends and relatives, a note to a family member who's away at school, or a family wish list for vacations, household repairs, and so on. All modern word processors provide a mechanism for handling multiple-user input. In fact, you can collaborate on documents in several ways, but I discuss only the easiest and most straightforward method here. I'm using Microsoft Word for this discussion because it's the most popular word processor. If you use another product, you shouldn't have trouble figuring out which commands to use to accomplish these tasks — just consult the program's Help system.

The trick to managing a document that has input from multiple users is to configure the document to show each person's input. In Microsoft Word, that feature is called Track Changes (people who use this feature a lot call it *show revisions* or *revisions on*). Follow these steps to use this feature to track changes that are made to a document (I'm using Microsoft Word 2000 in this example — later versions of Word use slightly different commands):

1. **Open the document that you want to edit.**
2. **Choose Tools⇨Track Changes⇨Highlight Changes.**

   The Highlight Changes dialog box appears, as shown in Figure 16-3.

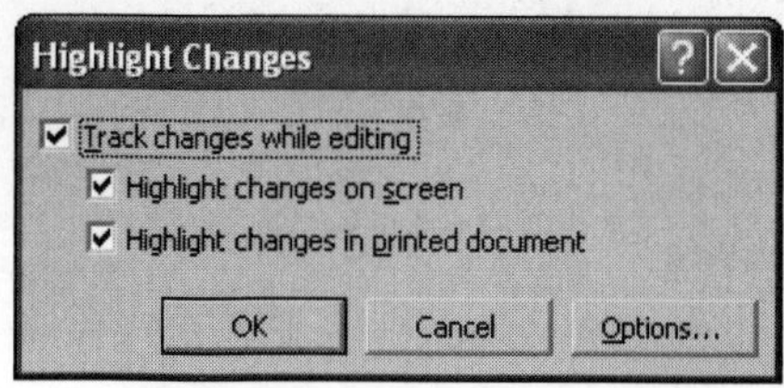


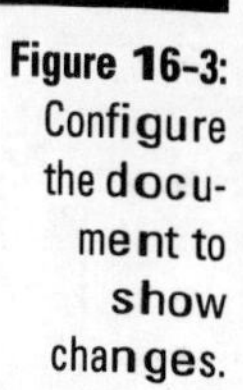
**Figure 16-3:** Configure the document to show changes.

3. **Select the Track changes while editing and Highlight changes on screen check boxes.**

   These options enable you to see what changes you're making to the document:

   - All your edits appear in a specific color. If more than one user edits the document, each user is assigned a different color automatically. Everything red came from one user, everything blue came from the second user, and so on.
   - Deleted text isn't really deleted; it has a line through it (called strikethrough).
   - Additional text is underlined.

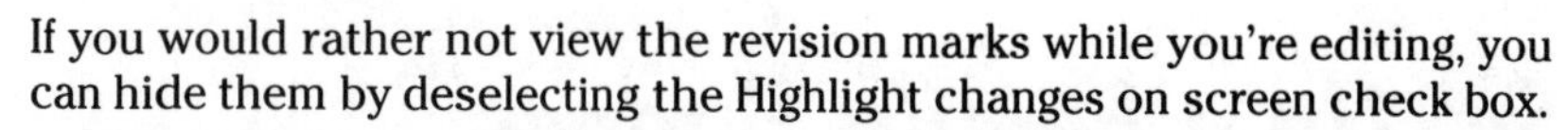
   If you would rather not view the revision marks while you're editing, you can hide them by deselecting the Highlight changes on screen check box.

4. **Edit the document by adding and deleting text, as appropriate, and then save the document.**

   Make sure that you save the document with the same filename and in the same folder on the original computer.

5. **If additional people want to edit the document, have them repeat these steps.**

If more than one person has edited a document, you can see the name of the person who made a change by positioning your pointer over any changed text (see Figure 16-4). You can also figure out which color is assigned to each user.

You can accept some changes and reject others, or you can accept or reject all the changes at once. When you accept or reject a change, the text reverts to regular formatting so it looks as if you wrote it. Check the Help files in your word processor to see how to perform these actions. (In Word 2000, choose Tools➪Track Changes➪Accept or Reject Changes, and use the dialog box that appears.)

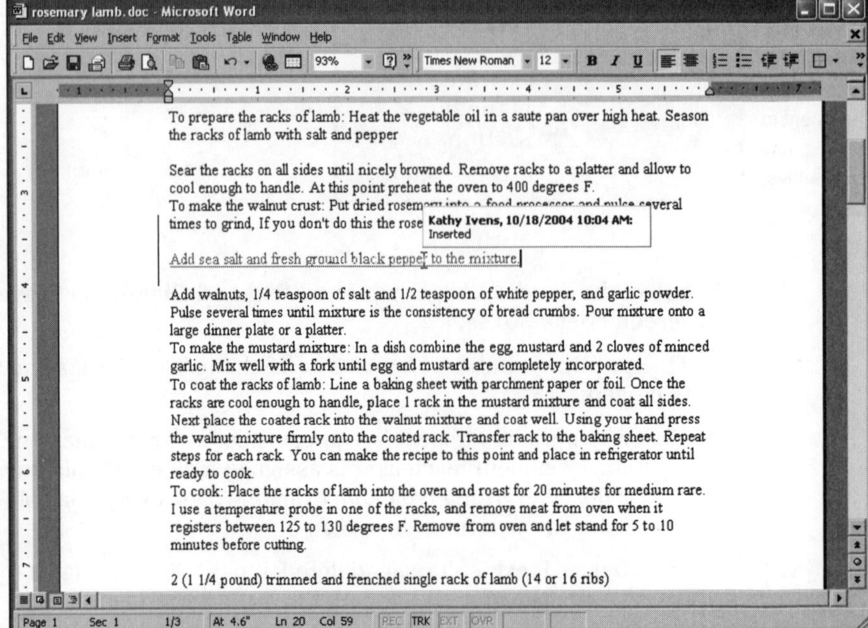


**Figure 16-4:** You can't see the colors here, but you can see that the document is changed and that it's easy to see the changes.

# Set Up a Family Budget

Setting up a budget center on a home network is a clever idea, especially for finance-conscious families. A budget center not only gives you a way to see the latest and greatest version of the household budget, but it can also help kids learn how to manage their own money.

## Selecting a software program for your budget

You don't necessarily have to spend money on a bookkeeping program like Quicken. You can prepare your budget using several types of software. Most word processors have a Tables feature that you can use to create lists and columns of numbers, and the software adds up those numbers for you. Spreadsheet programs are designed for budget-type documents.

If you are using a bookkeeping program, you may not be able to separate the budget file from the other data files, but you can usually discover a way to export the budget to a format that you can use in a word processor or in spreadsheet software.

### Setting up and using the budget center

After you select a software program, set up a shared folder on one computer so that everybody in the household can access the budget files. (Follow the instructions in the section "Creating a shared folder for the message center," earlier in this chapter.) Then save any budgets that you want to share in the budget center folder.

The real budget — the one that you use to run the household — must have a column in which you can enter the actual numbers. But you can also create other specialized budgets, such as a savings plan for a vacation, a new car, or college tuition. Budget regular contributions, and then update the document each time you make a deposit.

If you want to play "what if" games with your budget, copy the budget and save it with a different filename. Then you can change figures in the budget to see how it affects the results. What if you put $100 a month into a mutual fund and reduce other budget categories to make up for that expenditure? You figure out quickly whether the trade-off is worthwhile.

The budget center is also the place to track your investments. And, if you track investments online, you can save financial updates that you download from the Internet in your budget-center folder.

You may want to have one budget-center share for everyone in the household and then create a second share for the "real" budget. Password-protect the second share and give the password to your spouse if you don't want to share it with the kids.

## Set Up a Family Document Library

Lots of documents that family members create are of interest to everyone in the family, so it makes sense to create a library where anyone can find these documents.

Follow the instructions in the section "Creating a shared folder for the message center," earlier in this chapter, to set up a shared folder on one computer so everybody in the household can access the documents. If you want to keep the documents you create on your own computer, you can just copy them to the share you're using as the document library.

# Set Up a Download Center

If family members download files from the Internet, it's a good idea to maintain a download center on the network. Here are a few reasons why:

- **You can run your anti-virus software using the download folder as the target.** Running anti-virus software on downloaded Internet files is important because many viruses enter computers this way. However, most people don't run virus scans on their computers as often as they should because it takes so much time. Running anti-virus software on one particular folder is quick and easy.
- **A download center avoids duplicates that waste disk space.** If several members of the family want to download a game or a music file, checking the download center first avoids parallel downloading.

Choose the computer with the most disk space for this shared folder. And, clean out the folder frequently to get rid of files that are no longer needed.

When you download a file, a Save dialog box opens because you're actually saving the file on your local drive. That dialog box usually has default selections for the folder that accepts the downloaded file, as well as the filename. Use the tools in the Save dialog box to change the destination folder to the network download center. (Don't change the filename.)

# Have a Family Meeting

All versions of Windows except Windows XP come with a nifty program called NetMeeting. Windows XP comes with Windows Messenger, which provides the functions available in NetMeeting. This software lets you run a meeting across the network — it's sort of like bringing everybody into a chat room. Here's how to open the software:

- In Windows 98, choose Start⇨Programs⇨Accessories⇨Internet Tools⇨NetMeeting.
- In Windows Me and Windows 2000, choose Start⇨Programs⇨Accessories⇨Communications⇨NetMeeting.
- In Windows XP, choose Start⇨Run, and in the Open dialog box, enter **conf**.

The first time you open NetMeeting, a wizard walks you through the setup. Answer the questions and supply information as prompted. While you're configuring NetMeeting, make sure you indicate that it's for a local-area network (LAN) instead of for over the Internet.

It's beyond the scope of this book to go over the instructions for using NetMeeting, but the Help files should get you rolling quickly.

While you're all together in the meeting, you can share documents, open a whiteboard (a blank graphic screen in which every participant can enter comments, text, or whatever), or participate in a chat with all or selected participants (see Figure 16-5).

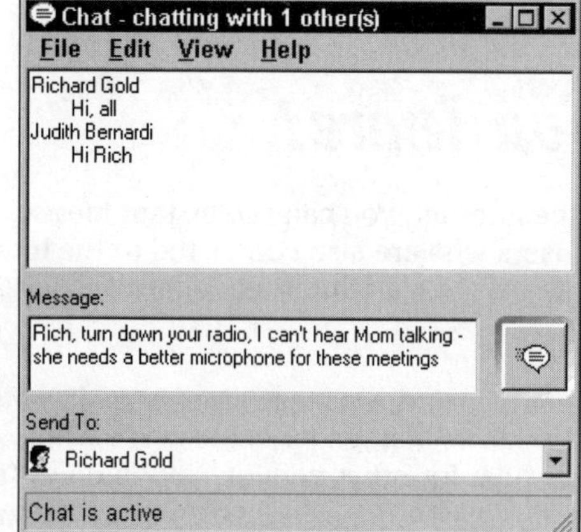


**Figure 16-5:** A private chat on the side.

# Family Blogging

Do you ask your kids "How was school?", "How was your day?", or "How was the party?". Do you ever get a real answer? Probably not, unless you count "Fine" or "OK" as a reasonable response. I learned to stop asking, which salvaged my nerve ends.

I have a workaround to suggest — encourage your kids to blog, and create your own blogs to stimulate their participation. Blogs are the hottest things on the Internet. In fact, lots of people have figured out how to use blogs for both fun and profit.

Blogs are journals (diaries), and the Web-based blogs are kept up-to-date using special software. But you can maintain local blogs by setting up a blog folder for each family member. Each blogger can decide whether to share the blog with other family members. Even if your kids don't share their blogs, the exercise of writing a journal provides a great educational advantage — teachers agree that the more students write, the more they read, and the more literate they become.

If the kids are reluctant to expose their thoughts and activities so blatantly, think about maintaining one family blog. Share the folder that holds the blog document file and encourage everyone to participate anonymously. People can offer thoughts and suggestions about family activities or family problems, and respond to other blog postings.

The best blogs have the latest entry at the top, so you have to remember to press the Enter key at the top of the document to insert a line at the top. Then start typing.

# I'm IMming, Are You There?

When you're connected to the Internet, you can use Instant Messages (IMs) to chat with other network users who are also connected to the Internet. Of course, this is much easier if your network Internet connection is an always-on service (DSL or cable).

Microsoft offers two IM programs: Windows Messenger, and MSN Messenger (which has more features). Windows Messenger comes with Windows XP, and you can download MSN Messenger for other versions of Windows (and for Windows XP, too).

## Getting an IM account

To use IMs, you must sign in to the IM service with a Microsoft Passport account. You can sign up for a free Microsoft Passport account from the Messenger window, using your e-mail address. Each user on your network must have his or her own unique account, and each account is only permitted one sign-on. If you're signed in to Messenger and another user on another computer signs in with the same name, you're automatically disconnected.

## Windows XP SP2 settings for IMs

If you're using Windows XP SP2, you must configure the firewall to permit IMs. When you first launch Messenger, Windows asks if you want to make a firewall exception for the program. If you didn't see such as message, set the fireware manually, as follows:

1. Open the Properties dialog box for the network adapter.
2. Click the Advanced tab.
3. Click the Settings button.
4. Click the Exceptions tab.
5. Select Windows Messenger to put a check mark in the check box.

# Meet George Jetson: Automate Everything That Isn't Stapled Down

Is anyone besides me old enough to remember that show about space-age families? Well, today that cartoon is a reality, and you can automate almost anything in your home from your computer.

Here's what you can do:

- Control the on/off state of any electric appliance.
- Operate your front-door lock — let people in from your computer instead of walking to the front door.
- Operate a camera security system (which can be useful before you perform the tasks in the preceding item).
- Preprogram lights, stereo systems, and so on to go on and off at specific times.

Here's how you do it:

- You install remote-control software in every computer on the network.
- You buy special plugs for the electrical outlets into which you plug the electric appliances that you want to control.
- Your computer software sends signals to the special plugs.

For example, you can plug a special module into the outlet that controls one of the lights in your living room. (You plug the light into the module.) Then you can sit at one of the computers on your network (perhaps the one in the den) and turn the light off and on. Or, you can move the doohickey into the kitchen and turn on the coffeepot from the computer in the bedroom, which could be a real timesaver in the morning.

# Chapter 17

# Ten Ways to Make the Internet Safe for Children

***In This Chapter***

- Helping children understand what's dangerous about the Internet
- Using filters to prevent children from visiting undesirable Internet sites
- Setting guidelines for games and violence-oriented Web sites

Parents worry about the kind of stuff kids can run into on the Internet, and they're not being paranoid — Internet safety is a real issue. Fortunately, you can do some things to help make the Internet safer for your children, which is good, because you probably can't keep them away from the Net.

Kids love the Internet. In fact, in most households, the kids can find an Internet site faster than the parents. While parents wade through vague searches, due to vague search criteria, kids seem to guess right instinctively. They're at the site they need, reading or downloading, while their parents are still trying to figure out which site holds the stuff they're looking for.

Because you're sharing the Internet across your network, if you're working at a computer while your kids are on other computers, you can't see what your kids are doing.

In this chapter, I discuss some solutions for controlling Internet access. Don't rely on them, because you can only impose them in your own house. Your kids are almost certainly going to access the Internet from friends' houses, or from public computers. In the end, there is no substitute for good parenting — discussing the issues openly.

# Talk to Your Children about the Internet

Like any other danger, the Internet is less threatening if you have an open and frank discussion with your children about the perils they can encounter online. Approach this subject head on; you can't pussyfoot around it. You didn't mince words when you warned your kids not to get into a stranger's car — use the same approach to warn your kids about the Internet.

Be aware that just because you have a definition in your own mind about terms like pornography, hate crimes, child molesters, bomb making, violent games, and so on (sorry, but those are some of the dangers on the Internet), your kids may not have a clearly defined notion of their meanings. Depending on the kids' ages, you have to decide what explanations and terminology are appropriate for them. But the bottom line is, you must discuss these issues.

# Place Your Computers in the Right Locations

The best way to keep your kids away from the Web sites you don't want them to visit is to provide a deterrent. The best deterrent is sort of a psychological deterrent — one that implies that they could get caught if they don't follow the rules.

My best advice is: Don't put a computer in a child's room. It's a bad idea on several levels, according to many educators and child psychologists who point out that part of a healthy childhood is interaction with other children. Kids who have computers in their rooms tend to spend much more time alone, using the computer (mostly on the Internet), than kids who use computers that are in less-private locations.

Put computers in rooms where it's normal and natural for other household members (especially parents) to walk through those rooms.

# Set Controls on Content

Internet Explorer lets you block Web sites that have content you don't want your children to see. The sites are qualified by rating services, and you can take advantage of these services with a configuration change in Internet Explorer. Open Internet Explorer and follow these steps:

1. **Choose Tools⇨Internet Options.**

   The Internet Options dialog box appears.

2. **Click the Content tab, and in the Content Advisor section, click Enable.**

   The Content Advisor dialog box appears (see Figure 17-1).

3. **Use the slider on the Ratings tab to set limits on the level of the types of content listed in the dialog box.**

   The more you slide to the right, the more liberal your controls become (the opposite of the way political blocs work).

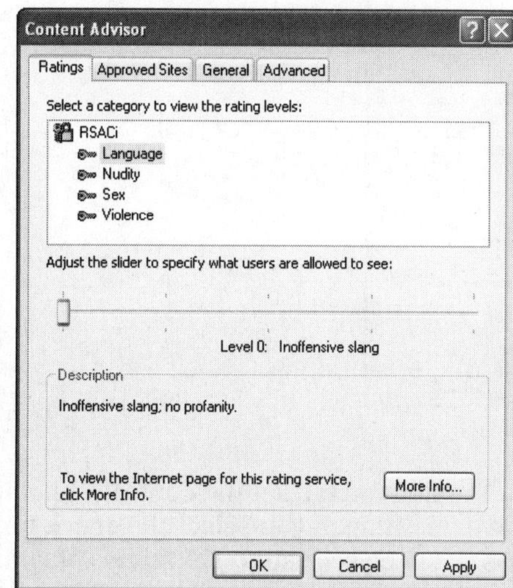


**Figure 17-1:** Use the Content Advisor to control access to Web sites.

The Ratings tab displays RSAC as the rating service. This service is the Recreational Software Advisory Council, which no longer exists. It's been merged into the Internet Content Rating Association (ICRA). ICRA is an international organization that's dedicated to making the Internet safer for children, while respecting the rights of content providers.

## Password-protect your settings

Even very young children can figure out how to access the Ratings dialog box, and move that slider to the right. Therefore, you must lock your settings by requiring a password to override the configuration changes you make.

The lock is on for all users, even the parents. Give the password to the adults in the house, but not to the children. Make sure adults who write down the password hide the piece of paper that holds the password.

To set a password that protects your configuration settings, move to the General tab (see Figure 17-2).

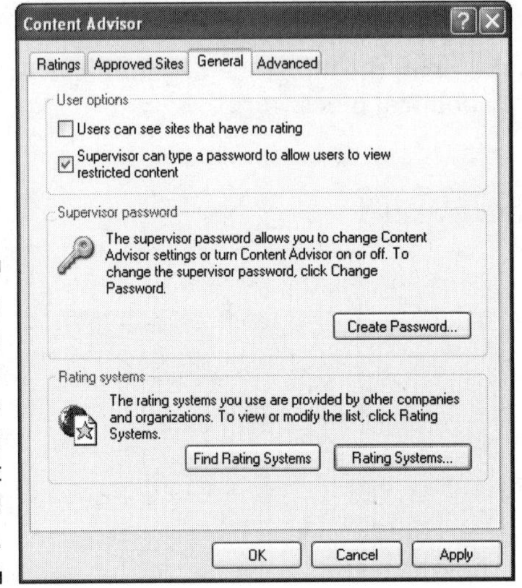


**Figure 17-2:** The General tab has options for locking your content control settings.

The two options at the top of the General tab set the controls. The first option is Users can see sites that have no rating. If you select the check box, users can view any Web site that has not been self-rated. This almost guarantees that users will see objectionable material, because not all Web sites subscribe to ratings. If the check box is clear, users cannot view any unrated Web page, no matter how benign the content may be.

The second option, which is selected by default, is Supervisor can type a password to allow users to view restricted content. This means that the adults in your house can use the password you create to view any site on the Internet. If you clear the check box, even you won't be able to view Web sites that don't pass your content configuration controls.

To use a password, click Create Password to open the Create Supervisor Password dialog box seen in Figure 17-3.

Enter a password, and then enter it again to confirm it. Enter a hint to help you remember the password if you forget it. When you're finished, click OK.

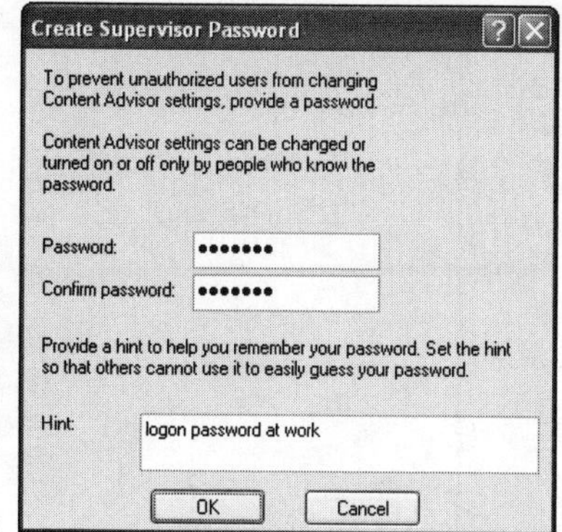


**Figure 17-3:** Create a password the kids can't guess.

To use rating services in Netscape Navigator, use the Netwatch function (consult the Help files for instructions for your version of Netscape).

# Create Your Own Site Filters

In Internet Explorer, you can create your own Web site filters, which are useful in the following circumstances:

- You don't want to use a rating service.
- The rating service you use permits access to a site you don't like.
- The rating service you use blocks access to sites you feel are appropriate for your children.

Use these steps to create a list of sites that you want to filter for:

1. **Choose Tools⇨Internet Options.**

   The Internet Options dialog box appears.

2. **Click the Content tab, and in the Content Advisor section, click the Settings button.**

   If you haven't previously used this feature, the Settings button is grayed out. If this is the case, click the Enable button to open the Content Advisor dialog box and then skip ahead to Step 4.

3. **Enter your password.**

   The Content Advisor dialog box opens.

4. **Click the Approved Sites tab (shown in Figure 17-4).**

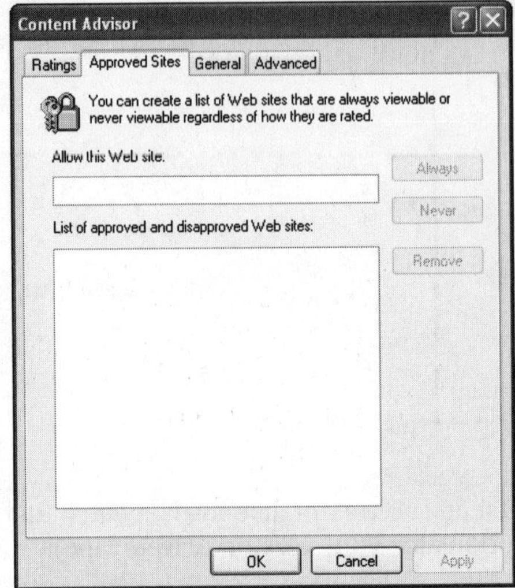


**Figure 17-4:** You can create your own list of allowed or forbidden sites.

5. **Enter the URL for a Web site you want to filter for, and then click the Always or Never button. Repeat this step as many times as you want.**

   If you click the Always button after entering a URL, that site is always accessible, even if you're using a rating service that disallows it. Furthermore, sites designated as Always never require your password. Sites designated as Never require a password.

6. **When you're finished, click OK to close the dialog box and save your changes.**

   If this is your first time using this feature, you're prompted to create a password.

# Use Software to Filter Sites

A number of software programs are available that control and/or monitor Internet activities. Here is a list of several programs that have received reasonably good reviews, along with their URLs:

- Net Nanny at `www.netnanny.com`
- Cyber Patrol at `www.cyberpatrol.com`
- Cyber Sentinel at `www.securitysoft.com`

These programs work similarly to the rating services: They filter access to Web sites. The advantage you gain by using software is the ability to configure the software to create the filters. Your children's ages, interests, and your own general attitude about censorship can be reflected in your configuration choices.

For a comprehensive list of filter software, go to

```
www.safetysurf.com
```

# Use ISP Restrictions

Several ISPs offer built-in control features for children. In this section I'll provide an overview of the restrictions available in popular ISPs.

## AOL Parental Controls

If you use AOL, filtering doesn't take place via the AOL browser; filtering is built into the user's screen name. When you create a user name for your child, you can designate an age group. Your choices are Kids Only, Young Teen, Mature Teen, and Unrestricted Access (intended for the parents). These categories determine to what extent AOL filters Web content and activities. Although some of the settings can be customized, the following describes the default limitations:

- The Kids Only category (usually considered to cover up to age 12) blocks IMs.
- The Young Teen category (ages 13 to 15 or 16) provides IM access, but blocks the ability to exchange files.
- The Mature Teen category limits chat features and Web surfing, but permits all IM features.

You can use the Parental Controls feature to restrict e-mail so that kids can only send or receive e-mail from a selected group. You can also control the time periods your child can log in to AOL, and for how long. This is a good way to manage teenagers who seem to spend too much time online.

Limits imposed by the parental controls for AOL only apply to features built into the AOL software. Most children figure out that they can launch the "real" browser instead of the browser built into AOL, so even if you use AOL, you should follow the recommendations earlier in this chapter for limiting your browser. Kids also figure out how to sign up for IMs outside of AOL (such as Microsoft Messenger). To resolve these problems, you can turn on AOL's Internet Access Controls, which prevents the use of non-AOL software.

## MSN Parental Controls

At MSN, the parental control categories are the following:

- Teen (described as ages 13 to 17), which provides access to IMs and most of the Web
- Preteen (ages 9 to 12), which has some restrictions on Web access, as well as limits on e-mail and IMs
- Young child (under age 9)

Within each age category, parents can adjust IM settings as follows:

- No Access, which blocks all use of Microsoft Messenger
- Restricted Access, which allows IMs from people on the child's contact list (parents can approve the child's contact list)
- Full Access, which has no restrictions

MSN also has a parental control that lets you block file downloads. In addition, MSN will e-mail reports to parents about their children's activities. The reports don't include the text of the child's conversations, but they will tell you which Web sites were visited and the online identity of everyone the child communicated with using MSN Messenger and MSN e-mail.

You can enable the recording of online IM conversations. Sign into your child's account and choose Tools⇨Options, and then select the Messages tab. Select Automatically keep a history of my conversations. Because this setting is within the child's account, not a parental control, your child can disable it if he or she realizes it's enabled.

The parental control settings apply to MSN software. MSN lets you control the use of other browsers, but it does not let you top your child from using non-Microsoft IM programs.

## Comcast Parental Controls

For cable broadband subscribers using Comcast, a wide set of parental controls is available. (Incidentally, since Comcast has been buying other broadband services, such as AT&T, you may be a Comcast customer soon.) Comcast's parental controls including the following features:

- Web site content filtering, with customized exceptions.
- E-mail messages that report visited Web sites.
- Specific restrictions for each child account.
- Limits on time of day, and length of online sessions.

Other ISPs, such as Earthlink, provide parental controls. Call the customer support or sales department to learn about your ISP's offerings.

# ISP E-mail Filtering Features

Most ISPs now offer e-mail restrictions designed to protect your children's mailboxes from offensive e-mail. The restrictions are implemented by filtering the mail that arrives. The filters are automatic, based on criteria set up by the ISP. You can get more information about the filtering process from your ISP's Web site.

Most ISPs also offer filtering for spam, and because a great deal of offensive mail arrives as spam, enabling the spam filters for your family's mailboxes usually works to avoid offensive content in your kids' mailboxes.

# Be Wary of Chat Rooms

Kids love chat rooms. They make virtual friends. They get a chance to create a persona and become the person they'd like to be. Reality and truthfulness are in short supply in chat rooms.

Chat rooms abound on the Internet, although many parents aren't aware that they exist outside of AOL. Many chat rooms are dedicated to special interests and topics, but most kids hang out in generic chat rooms, some of which are organized by age group.

One concern for parents is that the language used in chat rooms can be offensive, violent, and (to many parents) disgusting. But most of the time language, per se, isn't dangerous. The inherent problem with chat rooms is that you don't really know whom you're chatting with. Neither you nor your children have any way of verifying that a person is indeed who he says he is. Your son may think he's chatting with a 12-year-old boy when in fact he's chatting with an adult who's posing as a young boy. Predatory adults — mostly child molesters — often hang out in chat rooms and try to befriend young children. The organizations devoted to finding missing children point out that some missing children were lured from their homes to meet chat-room friends.

The best advice is to "pick your battles," and when you're weighing the subjects, the people in the chat room pose a larger threat than the language in the chat room. Make sure that your children follow these safety tips:

- Use a generic, asexual screen name that doesn't indicate your age or location. Often, online handles reflect some physical or other characteristic, but for children, that's a no-no. If you're an esoteric parent, you can have a lot of fun picking strange names. (How about *Orange, Wallpaper,* or *Lantern* for screen names?)
- Never reveal your real name, address, or telephone number to any chat-room acquaintance. Don't even reveal the region you're from, the name of your school, or the name of your Little League team. With enough personal information, nefarious types can piece together more than you realize.
- *Never* accept an invitation to meet a chat-room acquaintance.

## Find Acceptable Sites for Your Children

One way to control what sites your children visit is to steer them toward sites that you've picked out and approved. The Internet contains tons of great sites geared for kids — not just homework helpers (oh, Mom, borrrring), but for games, puzzles, books, and other interests. Here are some recommendations from some young acquaintances of mine:

- Girls who read books by Judy Blume recommend `www.judyblume.com`.
- Every kid I spoke to reports visiting `http://harrypotter.warnerbros.com/`. One of my granddaughters tells me she loves the games on this site.
- Kids (mostly girls) whose mothers introduced them to their own favorites report enjoying the Nancy Drew site at `www.mysterynet.com/nancydrew/kids/`.

For parents who are overwhelmed at the thought of trying to ferret out new sites for their kids, here are a couple of places to look for ideas:

- **Parent News (**`www.parent.net`**):** This site covers lots of topics of interest to parents, including Web safety, good Web sites, and parenting hints unrelated to computers.
- **FamiliesConnect (**`www.ala.org/ICONN/familiesconnect.html`**):** This site provides great info for parents about Internet issues.

# Set Guidelines for the Level of Violence in Computer Games

Almost every time the headlines announce a tragic shooting by a teenager, usually at a school, the background information on the accused includes the fact that the child was devoted to violent computer games — some of which are available for children to play interactively on the Internet.

No research exists that shows that a perfectly normal kid can be turned into a mass murderer as a result of a violent game. But the experts are polarized and locked into extreme positions, and parents have a hard time knowing who to believe. Violent games are fascinating and popular, especially among boys (according to research), so knowing where you stand as a parent is essential. Here's what you need to do:

- Talk to your children about violence in *all* media, such as movies, music, television, and computer games. Make sure that the boundaries you set are clear to your children, and listen to their opinions.
- If you decide to let your kids play video games, develop guidelines for your children. These guidelines should explain your own value systems and your own definitions of, and reaction to, violence. For example, some parents object to anything that's connected to guns, whereas other parents explain that hurting another person isn't amusing. By setting guidelines, you can send your kids off to gameland with some moral and emotional equipment, which can help them put their activities into perspective — this is a game, not life.
- If you decide that some of the games are indeed extremely violent, you have every right as a parent to forbid your kids to buy or play them. Get familiar with all the games that are popular with kids so you're credible in the eyes of your kids.

One of the best ways to stay on top of computer games is to search the Internet for reviews of games. For reviews, visit these sites:

- Microsoft Computing Central (`http://computingcentral.msn.com/games`)
- The American Library Association (`www.ala.org/parentspage/greatsites`)

Many of these sites offer links to additional sites, and most of those sites offer newsletters that you can subscribe to in order to keep up with the latest games.

# Index

## • Symbols and Numerics •



## • A •



## • B •



## • C •

## • G •



## • H •



## • I •

## • M •



## • N •

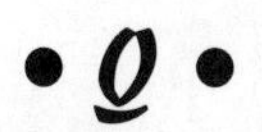



• R •

## • T •

## • U •



## • V •



## • W •

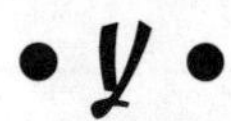



• Z •

# Notes

## SPORTS, FITNESS, PARENTING, RELIGION & SPIRITUALITY

0-7645-5146-9

0-7645-5418-2

**Also available:**

- Adoption For Dummies 0-7645-5488-3
- Basketball For Dummies 0-7645-5248-1
- The Bible For Dummies 0-7645-5296-1
- Buddhism For Dummies 0-7645-5359-3
- Catholicism For Dummies 0-7645-5391-7
- Hockey For Dummies 0-7645-5228-7
- Judaism For Dummies 0-7645-5299-6
- Martial Arts For Dummies 0-7645-5358-5
- Pilates For Dummies 0-7645-5397-6
- Religion For Dummies 0-7645-5264-3
- Teaching Kids to Read For Dummies 0-7645-4043-2
- Weight Training For Dummies 0-7645-5168-X
- Yoga For Dummies 0-7645-5117-5

## TRAVEL

0-7645-5438-7

0-7645-5453-0

**Also available:**

- Alaska For Dummies 0-7645-1761-9
- Arizona For Dummies 0-7645-6938-4
- Cancún and the Yucatán For Dummies 0-7645-2437-2
- Cruise Vacations For Dummies 0-7645-6941-4
- Europe For Dummies 0-7645-5456-5
- Ireland For Dummies 0-7645-5455-7
- Las Vegas For Dummies 0-7645-5448-4
- London For Dummies 0-7645-4277-X
- New York City For Dummies 0-7645-6945-7
- Paris For Dummies 0-7645-5494-8
- RV Vacations For Dummies 0-7645-5443-3
- Walt Disney World & Orlando For Dummies 0-7645-6943-0

## GRAPHICS, DESIGN & WEB DEVELOPMENT

0-7645-4345-8

0-7645-5589-8

**Also available:**

- Adobe Acrobat 6 PDF For Dummies 0-7645-3760-1
- Building a Web Site For Dummies 0-7645-7144-3
- Dreamweaver MX 2004 For Dummies 0-7645-4342-3
- FrontPage 2003 For Dummies 0-7645-3882-9
- HTML 4 For Dummies 0-7645-1995-6
- Illustrator CS For Dummies 0-7645-4084-X
- Macromedia Flash MX 2004 For Dummies 0-7645-4358-X
- Photoshop 7 All-in-One Desk Reference For Dummies 0-7645-1667-1
- Photoshop CS Timesaving Techniques For Dummies 0-7645-6782-9
- PHP 5 For Dummies 0-7645-4166-8
- PowerPoint 2003 For Dummies 0-7645-3908-6
- QuarkXPress 6 For Dummies 0-7645-2593-X

## NETWORKING, SECURITY, PROGRAMMING & DATABASES

0-7645-6852-3

0-7645-5784-X

**Also available:**

- A+ Certification For Dummies 0-7645-4187-0
- Access 2003 All-in-One Desk Reference For Dummies 0-7645-3988-4
- Beginning Programming For Dummies 0-7645-4997-9
- C For Dummies 0-7645-7068-4
- Firewalls For Dummies 0-7645-4048-3
- Home Networking For Dummies 0-7645-42796
- Network Security For Dummies 0-7645-1679-5
- Networking For Dummies 0-7645-1677-9
- TCP/IP For Dummies 0-7645-1760-0
- VBA For Dummies 0-7645-3989-2
- Wireless All In-One Desk Reference For Dummies 0-7645-7496-5
- Wireless Home Networking For Dummies 0-7645-3910-8

## HEALTH & SELF-HELP

0-7645-6820-5 *†

0-7645-2566-2

**Also available:**

- Alzheimer's For Dummies 0-7645-3899-3
- Asthma For Dummies 0-7645-4233-8
- Controlling Cholesterol For Dummies 0-7645-5440-9
- Depression For Dummies 0-7645-3900-0
- Dieting For Dummies 0-7645-4149-8
- Fertility For Dummies 0-7645-2549-2
- Fibromyalgia For Dummies 0-7645-5441-7
- Improving Your Memory For Dummies 0-7645-5435-2
- Pregnancy For Dummies † 0-7645-4483-7
- Quitting Smoking For Dummies 0-7645-2629-4
- Relationships For Dummies 0-7645-5384-4
- Thyroid For Dummies 0-7645-5385-2

## EDUCATION, HISTORY, REFERENCE & TEST PREPARATION

0-7645-5194-9

0-7645-4186-2

**Also available:**

- Algebra For Dummies 0-7645-5325-9
- British History For Dummies 0-7645-7021-8
- Calculus For Dummies 0-7645-2498-4
- English Grammar For Dummies 0-7645-5322-4
- Forensics For Dummies 0-7645-5580-4
- The GMAT For Dummies 0-7645-5251-1
- Inglés Para Dummies 0-7645-5427-1
- Italian For Dummies 0-7645-5196-5
- Latin For Dummies 0-7645-5431-X
- Lewis & Clark For Dummies 0-7645-2545-X
- Research Papers For Dummies 0-7645-5426-3
- The SAT I For Dummies 0-7645-7193-1
- Science Fair Projects For Dummies 0-7645-5460-3
- U.S. History For Dummies 0-7645-5249-X

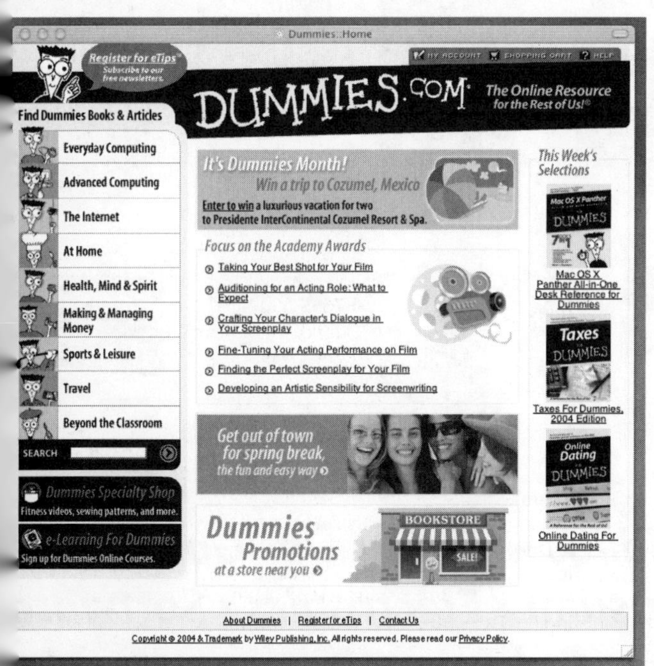


# Get smart @ dummies.com®

- **Find a full list of Dummies titles**
- **Look into loads of FREE on-site articles**
- **Sign up for FREE eTips e-mailed to you weekly**
- **See what other products carry the Dummies name**
- **Shop directly from the Dummies bookstore**
- **Enter to win new prizes every month!**

*** Separate Canadian edition also available**
**† Separate U.K. edition also available**

Available wherever books are sold. For more information or to order direct: U.S. customers visit www.dummies.com or call 1-877-762-2974. U.K. customers visit www.wileyeurope.com or call 0800 243407. Canadian customers visit www.wiley.ca or call 1-800-567-4797.